Recognition and revelation often attend Big Ideas. Nowhere is this truer than in Sandra Easter's epic exploration of ancestry, *Jung and the Ancestors*. Her depth psychological study confirms a number of connections: that history is not separate from myth; that the dead are alive in the living; and that memory is delighted to be in cahoots with the future. Reading her insights into the loam of ancestry, we are now able to relinquish so many outmoded beliefs about the separation of the past from the present. Sandra's thesis insists repeatedly how, in the words of the novelist William Faulkner, "the past is never dead; it is not even past."

—Dennis Patrick Slattery, author of *Creases in Culture: Essays Toward a Poetics of Depth* and *Our Daily Breach: Exploring Your Personal Myth Through Herman Melville's* Moby-Dick.

Dr. Easter's important book invites us to consider our ancestry as a psychic force that influences us unconsciously until we explore it. Who were our ancestors? Where did they come from? What legacies did they leave us that now confront us whether or not we realize it? Beyond posing these and other crucial questions, *Jung and the Ancestors* offers us a set of tools for engaging emotionally and imaginally with the lingering presence of those who came before. This engagement is in service not only to our own individuation, but perhaps that of the ancestors as well. The book also fills a gap in Jungian studies by showing us how Jung dealt with these presences in his own life and work. Craig Chalquist author of *Storied Lives: Discovering and Deepening Your Personal Myth* and, *Rebearths: Conversations with a World Ensouled.*

Jung and the Ancestors

Jung and the Ancestors

Beyond Biography, Mending the Ancestral Web

Sandra Easter

First published by Muswell Hill Press, London, 2016.
This edition published by Aeon Books Ltd, Lewes, 2020.

© 2016 Sandra Easter

www.aeonbooks.co.uk

British Library CIP Data available

ISBN: 978-1-913274-33-7

I dedicate this book to my daughters, Margaret and Melissa. And to the children of their children's children, the ancestors yet to be born. My work and life is in service to theirs. I hope this book makes the ancestors smile.

Contents

Foreword

Several years ago my wife and I and a few friends were in Johannesburg, South Africa. While we were there we visited what has come to be known as the "Cradle of Humanity," the location where it is believed that *Homo sapiens,* the human race, had their beginning some 3.2 million years ago. It is a place set apart with a visitor's center and includes a descent to an underground excavation site that is still going. Here is the place of Mrs. Ples, the 3.2-million-year-old skull of our female ancestor that is only matched by the famous remains of what is now referred to as Lucy.

When we arrived, we gathered around our South African guide who greeted us all with the words "welcome home." Needless to say, those were words not easily forgotten. I remember walking the landscape near the center considering that probably not much had changed since that time so many eons ago. Here was ground upon which they had walked. Here were the sunsets and sunrises and phases of the same moon we see today. It was as though there was no time between then and that moment in which I found myself. This experience pushes the Mosaic law of honoring your father and mother back to where it makes the most sense, to our beginnings, to all those who have preceded us and made possible the emergence of our individual and collective life today. It is what Sandra Easter has so artistically and respectfully reminded us to honor in that one word, ancestor.

Yet, here is a word that has had its limitation in the minds of most people of the Western world, which has been dominantly influenced by hands on, empirically validated, and logically grounded conclusions. As valuable as such approaches are, they leave out possibilities that push the edges of logical constructs and take us to the world of quantum leaps, acausal synchronicities, spontaneous visions, the timeless/spaceless world of dreams and intuitive insights. In this regard, remember, for example, what Albert Einstein is quoted as saying: "I never made one of my decisions through the process of rational thinking." And with that shaky intuitive ground under him, just think what doors opened to him that took him beyond the logic of his time.

I confess, when I read Sandra Easter's book, I initially felt some skepticism regarding the extent to which she "opened the doors" to the influence of our ancestors. Even though I experience myself as a very open-minded thinker, this skepticism is understandable given the way we all have been trained to think in this corner of the world. It did not take long, however, to move from skepticism to fascination with the possibilities of how far back we dare to go and can go in seeing how the ancestors influence us today. This is far beyond the influence of parents, grandparents, great-grandparents, or great-great-grandparents who for most of us would be as far back as we go. Though it certainly includes them, the ancestral impact probably extends as far back as the Cradle of Humanity. In that sense our personal story is part of a greater story that stretches throughout human history and is built into the evolution of the human species. But then I thought, why is it just the human species, why not all of life? In fact, is it not also the earth upon which we live and which nourished us into existence at the beginning of life on this planet? I am glad that Sandra Easter made reference to the indigenous ground we all share because the word indigenous itself means to be "born within." And though it has been used by anthropologists in specific ways, we all have not only an indigenous past through our ancestors, we are all indigenous today in that we are all "born within" the context of the earth itself. The soil of the earth is the soil that constitutes our body. The word human comes from the Latin *humus,* which means soil. And *being* comes from the Latin *esse* meaning "to be." We are of the soil that evolved our body and soul. So, who really are our ancestors? The furthest limit of that answer may be the stars themselves. To our indigenous ancestors and to the ancestral depths of our collective unconscious, this is more than a poetic or romantic idea. It constituted a basic belief of all of our ancestors at one time long ago, along with existing indigenous groups today. It is based on the deep spiritual belief that all of life in whatever form is our relative. I am convinced that this belief is deeply lodged in the unconscious of every one today.

Though this book gives more than adequate respect for such a truth, its main focus is on the ancestral connections we have of our own species. Just recently, I visited the graves of my parents' side by side with my father's parents and great-grandparents. It had been some time since I had been there. It awakened in me an ever-deepening inquiry as to whom these people really were. What was passed down to my sister and me? What was the world view of their times that shaped them, that gave them their dreams, their sense of limits, their prejudices, their hopes and aspirations? These questions have a reflective quality to them that can provide a widening of one's personal understanding of one's psychological inheritance beyond personal characteristics. Such a widening of our view of ancestral inheritance can give us a sense of freedom and make forgiveness of past violations more possible. What I am saying is that the more we understand what was passed down, who these people were, and what forces shaped them, the freer we are from personally identifying with the accumulation of ancestral shadow. With that, the possibility of forgiving any violations of that history is made possible.

So often in my practice as an analytical psychologist and pastoral counselor, I suggested to people that the darkness they were experiencing was not of their own making but was the accumulation of family shadow, perhaps going back many generations, that was now manifesting in their life. It is one thing to have to manage one's personal shadow; it is another thing to have to handle collective shadow. The latter, as it manifests in psychological and physical symptoms, is almost always overwhelming. The individual's task now was to bring closure to what never had been finished in their family history. A good Jungian Hindu colleague of mine, Ashok Bedi, refers to this dynamic as "clan karma."

What I experienced at that grave site, however, was just the beginning. Sandra Easter challenges the reader to stretch far back into history. In her own case, she went back eleven generations to her relative, Roger Williams, and the burning of Providence, Rhode Island. Her research into the events surrounding Williams and the struggles he endured were parallel to the issues in her own life. Here the reader will be challenged with the unspoken response of "really?" The parallel question would be "why not?" If all things are connected, as modern physics testifies, and if Einstein's theory of the relativity of time holds true, then why is it not possible to think of past, present, and future being a continuum that circulates through one's personal and our collective history. We speak of past history but is history ever past?

Years ago, I had the opportunity to attend a conference on Native American spirituality in Washington State. It was conducted by Natives for non-natives to help those not of their tradition better understand their culture. I will never forget one native woman who shared why an occasional gathering of her people would take place. She said every once in a while her people would gather in the local gymnasium to listen to one of their elders tell their stories in their native language. Most of her people, she said, only knew a little of the language though they knew the stories to which he was referring. The people would sit there for two or three hours while young children would fall asleep in their parent's arms. She said they did that because that elder was the keeper of their stories and if they lost their stories they would cease to be a people.

Stories carry our history. To lose a sense of history that carries what has gone before us and paves the way for our emergence on the present stage of life leaves us without psycho-spiritual roots. A great danger today in North America is that so few people even know American history let alone European or world history. Then, take it back further into the middle ages or ancient history or even prehistory. The further back we go, the dimmer the light of consciousness of where we came from and the underlying evolutionary force of life without which we would not even exist. It is not possible to know all that preceded us, but it is possible to raise a consciousness of respect for the ancestral foundation that supports us today.

Sandra Easter challenges the reader to imagine what the ancestors are saying to us today. What business do they want us to finish or what violations do they want us to repair and redeem? In this regard, she quotes from *The Red Book* in which Carl Jung describes an imaginary conversation with Ezechiel who says to him, "I see behind you, behind the mirror of your eyes, the crush of dangerous shadows, the dead, who look greedily through the empty sockets of your eyes, who moan and hope to gather up through you all the loose ends of the ages, which sigh in them." In those words is the summary of her entire book. She quotes many case examples from people with whom she worked to give further credence to the reaches of how literal or metaphorical we allow ourselves to experience the voices of the ancestors. Do the ancestors want to and do they speak to us literally? Such a question does push the limits of how we logically think in our world today. Or, is it all metaphoric, projections of voices deep inside us? In the end, it does not matter. The reader is encouraged to hold his or her judgment because, in the end, we really cannot prove either possibility. What does matter is to imagine and respect what the ancestors might say to us if they were to knock on our psychological door. Would we welcome and invite them in? In conclusion, would the cradle of humanity now find a new home in the conscious life we share with one another?

Fred Gustafson

Acknowledgments

I thank all of the elders and ancestors on whose scholarship this work rests. Some of their names appear on the pages in this book. Some I have known in person. Others I know only through their writing. Of special note are C. G. Jung, James Hillman, Malidoma Some, and Vine Deloria, Jr. Their words and presence accompanied and supported me on this journey of discovery and transformation. Their dedication to and passion for ever-evolving understanding based in experience and an amazing breadth and depth of scholarship are inspiration itself.

I thank Dennis Slattery who supported me in standing in the truth of what I know and finding ways to express it that were both scholarly and poetic. And Pat Katsky whose intuitive understanding often opened my eyes to the work before I could see it myself. And Jerome Bernstein whose work and understanding of Borderland consciousness helped me embrace and get grounded in the ways that I know and in what I know. The depth of his listening and his insightful comments and questions were transformative and brought more consciousness to this work. And Stephen Aizenstat who opened the door to a practice and way of being in a world where psyche and world are one, where action in the world is always informed by the figures of soul. I offer my wholehearted gratitude to Barbara Ford, my 12th-grade English teacher, who recognized and supported the expression of gifts that have taken a lifetime to develop. I thank all of my other teachers and mentors. Expressing my appreciation for and acknowledgment of them would require an entire book. Without their work and their belief in me and in this work, this book would never have been imagined or written.

I thank Keiron Le Grice for making the publishing of this book possible. He saw value in this work and recommended me to the publisher. Even more importantly, he's been my editor. He made me think, really think, which for someone who's an intuitive feeling type, as I am, can be torturous. His comments, critiques, challenges, and suggestions have strengthened the scholarship that underlies this work. This story began when an Englishman, my ancestor, left his homeland to come to America over three centuries ago. It seems fitting that an Englishman helped bring our story into the world.

I thank the four women whose stories are shared in this book—Diane, Janis, Kathryn, and Tracy—for saying "yes" and for allowing me to share their stories. Their integrity, courage, honesty, compassion, and love is evident. Their capacity to listen and support themselves, each other, and me opened my heart.

I especially want to acknowledge and thank JoEllen Koerner and her daughter Kristi, whose story is also shared in this book. JoEllen generously and enthusiastically gave me permission to use her story. In response to my request she wrote, "I visited with Kristi, and of course, we would both be totally delighted if ANYONE can learn anything from our own story." My hope is that their story touches you as much as it has touched me.

I wholeheartedly thank my friends, especially Pam Bjork, Craig Chalquist, Tracy Johansson, Linda Schultz, Jennifer Selig, and Debra Sorensen. They have been there from the moment this work was born into consciousness, have been there throughout its evolution, and continue to offer their unwavering support personally and professionally.

I offer my deepest gratitude to Hendrika de Vries, who held me *and* the depth and breadth of this work through all of our transformations. Her love was and is unfailing.

I thank my ex-husband, Clark Easter, for his ongoing support of this work and his belief in me, and for suggesting that first trip across the country on our ten-year wedding anniversary to attend the Introduction to Dream Tending.

And my mother Shirley, who taught me so much about love in the most unexpected and unimaginable ways. And my father Bruce whose presence is always just a breath away.

I am so deeply grateful to my daughters Melissa and Margaret. This work is inspired by my love for them and is and always will be in service to their lives.

Sandra.
Santa Barbara, September 2015

Preface

The idea that our ancestors have any kind of existence beyond this earthly one, much less that they have a desire to be in relationship with us, is unusual for many of us in modern Western culture. An experience I had fifteen years ago, which I share later in this book, compelled me to understand my relationship with the ancestors and theirs with us. However, the story of my relationship with the ancestors began the day of my birth. Many years later, I came to realize that my life was inextricably connected to the past in anticipation of and hope for the future. I came to understand that the ancestors were "speaking" to me through dreams, synchronicities, and psychological and physical symptoms.

This book is based on the work that evolved out of my need to understand these experiences. My story and the stories of seven other women are shared in this book. Each serves as an illustration of the way the ancestors are present in our lives in the present. True to its roots in depth psychology, this work originates in story, moves to theory for understanding, and returns to story. Theory and story are woven together creating an ever-evolving spiral of understanding between lived experience and theory.

In his autobiography Jung writes that he can only "tell stories . . . Whether or not the stories are 'true' is not the problem. The only question is whether what I tell is *my* fable, *my* truth."[1] Stories and myths are the language of soul. According to D. Stephenson Bond, a Jungian analyst and author of *Living Myth: Personal Meaning as a Way of Life,* "myths are not only the universal stories told around ancient fires, but just as well the haze of subjective contexts we walk through day by day."[2] Each personal story, while subjective and uniquely individual, also reflects universal patterns. Seeing the way our life is part of an unfolding story that is informed by the stories of our ancestors and foreshadowed and anticipated by our descendants informs our understanding of our personal myth. The intention and purpose of our individual life begins to reveal itself in new ways within this larger context. When we see our story this way, meaning, as Jung suggests, "glows below the surface of the simple acts of daily living."[3]

Like holographic pieces that contain and represent the whole while also being parts of that whole within the larger web of being, each of our stories is integral to and representative of our collective story. Bond suggests that in the collective psyche at this moment in time, the new collective myths and stories will come to consciousness through the experiences, dreams, and stories of individuals. The individual stories shared in this book, as parts of the story of life on this planet, may contain and elucidate the unfolding collective narrative.

Telling stories, or as one of my teachers often says, "talking story," has great power. "Talking story" opens an exploration into what has been buried, lost to consciousness, waiting to be remembered. Storytelling, by nature, is an interactive, collaborative, and reciprocal process that is created within the relationship between storyteller and listener. It is a way of knowing ourselves, each other, and our world. Listening to or reading the story of another—imagining the story from one's personal perspective, measuring it against one's experiences and beliefs, feeling its truth—the possibility exists that our understanding of ourselves, our personal narrative, and even our conception of reality will be engaged. In this dialogue between teller and listener "reality" is constantly being created and recreated.

As storyteller, I will serve as a guide through the landscape of the phenomenon of the lived experience of the presence of the ancestors in the here and now. I invite each reader to be open to and be aware of the ways in which you may be touched, moved, disturbed, challenged, and provoked, when you feel resonance and dissonance with what you are reading. I invite you to allow the stories shared in this book to set your own inner life in motion, to reveal what may be waiting to be discovered in your own story.

After finishing the book, I realized that every story, except for Jung's, was a woman's story. It was not intentional. My clients and the individuals who participate in the workshops I offer have all been women. It would only be speculation to try and explain or understand why this is so. I believe that our experiences and the dynamics that come to light in our stories are not gender specific. It is my hope that this book also speaks to men and their relationship with the ancestors.

I invite you to engage with and question the ideas and experiences that are shared in this book—to think critically and measure them against your own experience.

CHAPTER 1

Introduction to the Work

What the ancients did for their dead! You seem to believe that you can absolve yourself from the care of the dead, and from the work that they so greatly demand, since what is dead is past. . . . Do you think that the dead do not exist because you have devised the impossibility of immortality? . . . The dead produce effects, that is sufficient.[1]

— Ezechiel to C. G. Jung in *The Red Book*

Whatever one believes about what happens after our hearts stop beating, our ancestors have both a physical and psychical reality. Their bones and flesh lie in the ground on which we walk everyday of our waking lives, in the ground on which we build our homes and cities, in which our food grows, and in which our bodies will also come to rest. Their stories feed our memories and define how we see ourselves in relationship to our personal and collective history and to the land. Their DNA inclines us to particular diseases and links us through time to the origins of life on this planet.

How do we know them? How are they known to us? They speak to us through the stories that endure each generation's telling. Our conscious memories of them live in these stories, in their letters and diaries, in particular fixed moments of their lives captured in photographs, in family heirlooms, recipes, and rituals. Over time memories can change or be forgotten, details and emphases altered as they are subjected to each person's, each family's, and each culture's editing. These absences, this forgetting, result in breaks in the continuity of the far reaching historical story of which our life is one small but integral and significant part. Our connection to the deepest roots of our being is tenuous as a result of these discontinuous threads. The loss of stories from our personal lineage and the absence or omission of significant parts of our shared collective history as it was experienced and enacted by our ancestors, I would suggest, leave us standing in relationship with ourselves, our families, our ancestors, and the land

and all beings on shaky ground. Although lost to consciousness, the stories of our ancestors live in the reality of the unconscious psyche.

Every memory, every story, has both conscious and unconscious aspects within it. From a Jungian perspective, every narrative has its shadow.[2] This shadow contains memories that are too painful or traumatic to remember and aspects of ourselves that are contrary to our ideas of who we are individually, as a family, and collectively. Some family memories are taken to the grave to linger in these shadows. What is absent in these stories is as important as what is present. Although forgotten, intentionally or unintentionally, excluded parts of our ancestral story, like any repressed memory, continue to haunt us in the present. As Ezechiel tells Jung, the dead produce effects. The shadow, both personal and collective, is the Hyde to our Jekyll. As Jung so graphically states, "mere suppression of the shadow is as little of a remedy as beheading would be for headache."[3]

We tell our story, turning the details over and over, adding, subtracting and embellishing, until we find a way to tell it that holds the truth of our experience. Stories shape our perceptions of each other, our world, and ourselves, giving meaning to our experience, history, and our lives. Stories highlight our differences and serve as bridges to our common humanity. Within our stories are the places of our wounding, our longings, and the possibility of reimagining ourselves and our world. Family stories take on mythic significance, ground us in our being, and place us in relationship with the larger family of which we are all a part. From our stories we derive a sense of self and a sense of how and where we belong. We are, by virtue of the stories we tell.

An old Chinese proverb tells us, to forget one's ancestors is to be a brook without a source, a tree without root. A friend of mine was in an academic class sitting in a council circle with her classmates. Her ancestry is typical of many Americans—a melting pot of other peoples and cultures. Another member of her class was a Native American woman. (My use of the generic term *Native American*, rather than using the particular name of this woman's people, is in the service of protecting the identity of my friend and her classmate.) The Native American woman, holding the talking piece, shared her experiences of how difficult it had been, was, and continues to be, living in America. As my friend listened to her classmate's story, she saw that this woman knew who her people were. She knew the stories of her ancestors, and through these stories, her world, her history, herself and her place in the larger story of her people from their moment of creation through time. Her people's stories were her stories. Through the horror of dislocation, re-education, assimilation, and genocide, this woman and her people strove and often fought to remember and to stay connected to their traditions and their ancestors. Whether we are forced to or we make a conscious choice to break away and move from the land of our ancestors, that land, its history and peoples are still a part of us. We are, even when we find ourselves on new ground, rooted in psyche and in our bodies to our origins, our ancestry.

This Native American woman's story stirred a longing in my friend. As she sat in circle listening, she felt the absence of her own identity with a people, with their stories and traditions, with a land that connected her with her origins, with her ancestors. She felt a longing for this kind of connection which reached back through time and into the future, connecting individuals in a community to their roots. She recognized and longed for that same sense of belonging that her classmate had been born into. Her personal story and history had origins that were unknown to her, scattered across other continents. The indigenous ground of all the peoples she had a genetic and historical connection with had been transformed by civilization and progress. Her ancestors, with their stories and traditions, were absent from her conscious way of being in the world. Her longing, inspired by another woman's story, was an indication of their presence. Perhaps this longing for a sense of deep belonging is met from the ancestors with an equally compelling and insistent longing.

Where do I come from? How many of us can remember asking this question as children? How many of us have been asked this by our children and our grandchildren? To what tribe do I belong? And, how did *I* get here from there? Where do I come from informs the question, where am I going? Knowing where we come from and who we are related to informs how we are in the world and provides a foundation for our actions. These questions and the insistent "why," so characteristic of that time in each life when one's world begins to extend beyond the individual self and family, are deeply, commonly shared, human questions.

Some of us can trace our personal family trees through genealogical records. Many of us cannot, because records are inadequate; even those of us who can often find large gaps in our family trees. With current advances in genetic testing, we can now follow the trails of our ancestors through identifying markers on our DNA across continents and oceans, sometimes to very specific locations on the globe. Technologies exist which can tell us what percentage of our blood links us to other Asians, Africans, Native Americans, and Europeans.

Jung's conceptualization of the collective unconscious provides a psychological framework that, like genetics, allows us to trace the footprints of our ancestors across time and space. Rather than being derived from consciousness, the unconscious provides the foundation for and is the root of consciousness. According to Jung, the collective unconscious is "the mighty deposit of ancestral experience accumulated over millions of years."[4] "[A]ll human experience right back to its remotest beginnings" is contained here.[5] Universal, "it not only binds individuals together into a nation or race, but unites them with the men of the past and with their psychology."[6] This imperishable world is our psychic heritage, the legacy of our ancestors, "to which each century adds an infinitesimally small amount of variation and differentiation."[7] In his encounter with the unconscious, the spirit of the depths teaches Jung that the dead "bear the future and the past in the depths. The future is old and the past is young."[8] The unconscious, this land of the dead, is a world of accumulated and potential memory from the lives of our ancestors *and* descendants. It provides the psychological ground of our existence.

What would happen were we to listen deeply to our ancestors? Imagining this as a journey to the underworld, rather than entering the underworld like Hercules to capture its guardian Cerberus and return with him to the upper world, this is a journey like that of Ulysses' who entered the underworld humbly, approaching and making offerings hoping to receive help in his quest to return home. He meets his mother there, listens to her story and returns to the upper world with greater wisdom. Or it could be compared to the deeds of Aeneas, who makes offerings to Apollo seeking his aid in finding a new homeland for his people. Hearing Apollo's prophecy of great hardship and war, Aeneas wishes to enter the underworld to visit the spirit of his father and ask for his counsel. He begs for help and makes sacrifices to the gods. Receiving their aid he descends into the underworld and encounters a throng of the dead. Here he learns the fate of his yet to be born descendants. Or like the descent undertaken by Inanna, who leaves the upper world to attend the funeral of her shadow, underworld sister Ereshkigal's husband and grieve with her. The intention of this journey from the upper world of consciousness into the underworld, the land of the dead, the unconscious, is to approach humbly, to listen, seeking counsel and hoping to return with greater wisdom.

What is being asked from us in the present in relationship to the past and unfolding future? For Freud, it was the recovery of lost and repressed memories for the sake of healing and the adaptation of the instincts to the requirements of civilization. For C. G. Jung, it was facing and integrating the personal and collective pieces of the shadow in service to a sense of wholeness. For Malidoma Some, a Dagara elder who offers the wisdom of his African ancestors in service to the healing of people in modern Western culture, this same question—what is being asked in the present moment?—is critical not only to our personal well-being, but to the well-being of our family, our community, and the larger collective body of which we are all a part.[9]

The ideas explored in this book originate in my personal story. Recognizing that I was being addressed by the ancestors in the same way any unconscious aspect of psyche gets our attention—through physical and emotional symptoms, family patterns, synchronicities and dreams—I have spent the last ten years actively engaged in personal research, dialogue, and ritual in an attempt to come more consciously into relationship with these figures of my past.[10] Each of us, through our experience over time, will come to our own perspective regarding the nature of the "reality" of the ancestors. This book, through theory and story, will be an exploration of our relationship with them and theirs with us, with particular attention given to the influence of their particular past on our immediate present and imagined, hoped for, and perhaps dreaded possible future. It is not necessary to have a particular perspective regarding the nature of our existence after death to fully engage with what is presented in this work. What is required is curiosity.

Depth psychology has its foundation in the personal stories of its theoreticians, practitioners, and their patients. Through the individual stories of men and women, analysts and patients, depth psychology has illuminated and brought many of us in Western culture back into a more conscious relationship with the world of the unconscious, those parts of our psyche, our experience, lying outside of our conscious awareness. Our personal relationship with this "invisible" world that is our inheritance is essential to our personal and collective well-being.

Jung's autobiography, told as his personal myth, is one of the stories of origin, one of the creation stories, of depth psychology. It is the myth of one of the founders of depth psychology and, I would suggest, one of its founding myths. Described within the pages of *Memories, Dreams, Reflections* are a collection of Jung's experiences, dreams, and visions that reveal some of the original material that provided the foundation for Jung's theoretical work. Many of Jung's stories, which will be discussed in greater detail in Chapter 4 are stories about the relationship between the here and the hereafter, the living and the dead.

In his autobiography in the chapter titled "Visions," Jung describes a visionary experience he had following a heart attack. In this vision he knew that his life was situated in the much larger context of those who had come before and those who would come after him. He writes,

> I had the feeling that I was a historical fragment, an excerpt for which the preceding and succeeding text was missing. My life seemed to have been snipped out of a long chain of events, and many questions remained unanswered.[11]

Each individual's story as described by Kimme Johnson, a writer and teacher who explores earth based healing traditions, "is at the center of a spiraling wheel of kinship" inseparable from that of the greater community of which we are all an integral part.[12] As "historical fragments" integral within "a spiraling wheel of kinship," each of our stories in its living and telling, carries a part of our shared collective memory and wisdom.

To understand Jung and the ancestors, which is the intention of this book, necessitates not only a close reading of Jung, but putting into practice what is learned from him through his theoretical work, his autobiography, and his imaginal dialogues regarding his and our relationship with the dead and the living. Jung's psychology, in my personal experience, as a clinician and a teacher, provides a broad enough theoretical ground to explore the reality of the ancestors' presence in the present. The dialogues in *The Red Book* provide insight into the direct experiences Jung had with the ancestors and "the dead." Theoretically and phenomenologically, Jung's work is complementary to what Gregory Cajete, Apela Colorado, and David Peat call Indigenous Science.[13] Vine Deloria's thorough comparison of Jung and the Sioux is an excellent example of the way that Native American understanding and Jungian psychology complement and inform each other.[14] Jung's psychology is the only one I've found that allows this bridge to be made between indigenous ways of knowing and understanding of the world and modern Western psychology. Bringing indigenous traditions into dialogue with Jung provides an expanded framework of understanding that establishes a solid foundation from which we can engage with and understand the stories that are shared in this book. The relevant aspects of Jung's work and Indigenous Science as it pertains to this phenomenon will be presented in detail in the chapters that follow.

While stories provide the basis for theory, it is the interplay between practice and theory that keeps depth psychology vital. To this end, theory and personal story, mine and those of the women who generously offered theirs, will be interwoven throughout this book. This blending of formal theory, using a more traditionally academic voice, and informal storytelling, using a more personal and poetic voice, is designed to bring theory and experience into direct relationship with each other. Bringing theory with its demand for intellectual clarity into the realm of personal experience with its non-rational insights creates the possibility for a deeper understanding of Jung and his relationship with the ancestors and of one's own relationship with the ancestors in a personally meaningful way. My hope is that you, as reader, will find yourself reflecting on your own experience of the ancestors. That is one of the goals of this book. Another is to offer practitioners in the healing professions new ways of understanding the nature and origins of individual mental, emotional, and physical disease, trauma, and vocation in the process of healing.

You can read this book objectively for the veracity of its content and its theoretical point of view. However, another possibility exists. This possibility requires a different attitude, approach, and way of listening than we generally associate with our reading of non-fictional works, one that is more congruent with the tradition of storytelling. Bill Plotkin, depth psychologist and wilderness guide, observes that storytelling "conveys meaning in a way a mere explanation never could."[15] Stories have the potential to touch both the heart and intellect of both the teller and listener or, in this case, reader.

David Peat describes his experience of listening to Danny Musqua, an elder and traditional storyteller of the Soto people. As he listened to Danny tell stories of his grandfather, he

> seemed to comprehend what was being said to me, not in an intellectual way, but directly in my heart. There were times when I was not sure if Danny was talking about his own particular grandfather, the historical individual who had brought him up, or about the Grandfathers themselves, the Old Ones, the ones who had come long before, the spirits who stretched back for hundreds and thousands of years, the Grandfathers who can be seen moving within the hot rocks of the sweat lodge, who appear in dreams, and whose voices can be heard at night. In the space of just a few hours and in what may have been a small way for traditional people—but was very important to me—I was taken into a relationship with spirits that could teach.[16]

I share Peat's story to offer his way of listening to the stories of Danny's grandfather as a way for readers to listen to the stories in this book. My intention is to tell the stories that have been shared with or experienced by me in a way that carries their spirit, speaks to the heart and transcends the boundaries of space and time. I invite each reader to find a quality of being present, a quality of silence into which these stories can "speak" and offer whatever knowledge they may contain. I invite you to risk being touched by these stories. The potential exists that something may be sparked that could open the eyes and ears of your heart to the voices of the ancestors in your personal story.

The Origins of This Work

My story finds its origins at any and many points in time. The ancestral thread of my life can be picked up in this moment in time and traced to one of the many points in time in the lives of my ancestors—to the early sixteen-hundreds, when some of the first Europeans began transplanting their roots from European soil to the continent of North America, and to a specific historical event in the history of this land. The date of my birth, March 29, is the anniversary of the date Providence, Rhode Island was burned to the ground in King Philip's War by the grandsons of the men who had given my ancestor, Roger Williams, this land thirty years before, when he was banished from Massachusetts Bay Colony by his contemporaries for heresy.

The effect of the European presence on this land was traumatic and devastating for the native people. The burning of Providence was traumatic for my ancestor. King Philip's War, the native people's attempt to rid the land of the English, was one of the most vicious and deadly wars on this soil. It was devastating to the English and Indians, to the land and the ecology of New England. This ancestral, historical, cultural, and ecological trauma would become part of the symptomatic landscape of my personal trauma. Without knowing my story, you must wonder about what I suggest in this last sentence. It certainly stretches the boundaries of our understanding of trauma. The understanding that my personal trauma in this time was a recapitulation of collective trauma from the time of my ancestor requires an expanded theoretical framework—one that could contain the complexity of my experience. As you continue to read, my hope is that the basis for this will become clearer.

My story also threads its way to the day my ex-husband's ancestor, John Cotton, and Roger Williams, my ancestor, met in England. As I learned more, it seemed that their mutual respect and their philosophical differences continued to exist in some way in my relationship with my ex-husband. Looking at the connections between my personal, familial, and ancestral biographies, and our collective biography, revealed the interconnected intricacy of the web of which each of us is a particular expression at any given moment in time. I began to see how the known and unknown stories of my ancestors were present in my personal symptoms, inclinations, dreams, and visions, and, ultimately, how the ancestors were deeply implicated in my fate. I wondered if and how our ancestral and cultural legacies continue living in our bodies, through our relationships, in both matter and the timelessness of psyche, as do other unconscious contents.

Tracing the origins of our symptoms to our personal and immediate family history is commonly accepted in depth psychology. As I researched the story of Roger Williams, I discovered that the origins of my symptoms, personal suffering and the teleological intention in my life had threads that tied me not only to his life, but also to the collective history of this continent and to the land on which he lived and in which his body was buried. The more connections I made between my life story and Roger's, the more I understood my complexes, inclinations, interests, fears, and choices. Ultimately, making and understanding these connections resulted in healing, transformation, and a clearer understanding of the telos of my life. Even though we may not be consciously aware of the connection between our life and the lives of our ancestors, our ancestral and cultural legacies continue living unconsciously in our bodies, relationships and in psyche.

Who am I? Who and how am I in relationship with the rest of the world? These are basic human questions. My initial interest began in response to my daughter's insistent and stubborn curiosity about the ancestor her grandmother, my mother, said we were directly descended from. Prior to her interest, I thought the story about our family's relationship with this ancestor was just a story. I discovered in doing research with my daughter that I was actually a direct descendant of this important historical figure. As this ancestral dialogue unfolded, I discovered that the ancestors who were speaking to me were not limited to my personal ancestry. They included ancestors from other people's lineages, the ancestral people indigenous to this land, a black robed priest who haunted the women in my mother's line for centuries following the spread of Christianity to the British Isles, and finally, the ancestors and elders of the rich academic tradition of which this work is a part. The more I understood the depth and breadth of these connections, which seemingly transcended time and space, the more what appeared to be random and unconnected parts of my life began to form a more coherent whole.

As I shared parts of my ongoing story with others, I found what resonated for them were not the particularities within my personal story. After all, I was not talking about an experience that was common for people in our culture, nor does anyone else share the particularities that coalesce to make my story uniquely mine. It seemed that listening to my story opened listeners to a new way of understanding her or his own story. Sharing my story served as a catalyst that evoked a desire in others to learn more about the lives of their ancestors. My story was like a spark that evoked questions within these listeners—questions regarding what lived within and behind what each individual knew consciously about their symptoms, family patterns, personal idiosyncrasies, inclinations, and purpose in life. Talking with others, I discovered a sadness regarding what was not known and had been lost and a longing to reconnect more consciously with the ancestors whose life anticipated theirs. Each person wanted to know more about the people and the stories of those who had walked this earth before they were born. People wanted to know more about my experiences and what I had learned from being engaged in this seven-year conversation with the ancestors. It seemed that my story was a not only a catalyst, but also a possible map for navigating this "new" territory. What do the dead have to do with the living? On what do our futures rest?

Unbidden Visitations

My maternal grandfather, who died when I was in my early twenties, returned to me on a wave of emotion. I was enraged, feeling the pain of the legacy of sexual molestation in my family. I was writing a letter to my sisters and mother that I never intended to send. I titled it, "the cost of abuse." I wrote as I felt the pain of all the losses associated with that initial trauma. Sobbing, screaming, writing, my bones shaking, I thought I could never forgive him, my grandfather, for what he had done to my sisters, my mother and me. Suddenly I felt a wave of pure love surround me. In that moment, it was incomprehensible. The love was so pure, so palpable, and in some way that I didn't understand, recognizable. I smelled cigar smoke and knew immediately it was my grandfather's presence. The psychologist in me reduced it to compensation, as if in response the love began to modulate. Surrounded in love, the rage and grief that I had never expressed to him when he was living gathered in my body, heart, and mind. He was a molester; he had no right to love me. I would never open to his love again. I would never forgive him![17]

The returning memory and lingering effects of my childhood trauma would be the portal through which, years later, I would return to a particular moment in the American pre-colonial history of this land that occurred in the life of my ancestor, Roger Williams. Four years after my experience of my grandfather returning on a wave of love we were asked as part of our dissertation work at Pacifica Graduate Institute in California to do four imaginal dialogues to explore the unconscious aspects of our work. Robert Romanyshyn, the instructor in this course, developed a methodology called Alchemical Hermeneutics.[18] As part of that method he created transference dialogues to differentiate and engage with the various levels of the personal and collective unconscious—the personal, cultural-historical, collective-archetypal and eco-cosmological.

As much as I love imaginal dialogue, I had great resistance to the cultural-historical dialogue. I waited until the last possible minute. I woke up that morning physically shaking and crying, my body, once again, symptomatically remembering the sexual abuse I had suffered. I wandered around the campus trying to trust the wisdom of my body and psyche, wondering why, after all the work I had done, a lifetime of work, this memory in my body and psyche would not come to rest. The pain was more intense than my body had ever felt during other moments of remembering. It was excruciating, unbearable. My mind could not comprehend what I was experiencing. I found myself walking to the chapel on campus. As I entered I noticed a small altar on my right with a few pews. Sitting in this chapel held by the gaze from their portraits on the altar, of Mother Theresa,

Martin Luther King, Saint Francis, Aung San Suukyi, and Christ, I gave in to the shaking of my body and a deep experience of grief.

With the intention of the exercise and my experience and trust in working in this way, I entered into the active imagination inviting the unconscious to speak to the cultural-historical aspects of my dissertation. I found myself at the top of a hill looking down. I both am *and* feel an American Indian presence behind me, within me, even as I am aware of my body on the bench in the chapel.[19] His heart is broken, shattered as he sees what has happened to the land. I cannot find words adequate to describe the intensity of this pain. It is utterly unbearable, a sorrow of sorrows. Afraid I cannot tolerate this much grief; I open my eyes and look up at the figures on the altar. The memory of who they are and the compassion they embody(ied) which held and can hold experiences of such deep, unmitigatable sorrow and pain, holds me in this moment of remembering. I close my eyes and return to the dialogue and the man standing on the hillside. This man feels the pain of the land as it is developed, walked on by ones who cannot feel its life through the soles of their feet. His body is the land's body. And my body, through my wound, feels the rape of the land as he feels it, as the land feels it. This kind of suffering and sorrow lives forever until it is deeply witnessed and heard. It is a cry across and from the land that travels across and through the generations.

As I sat both experiencing and witnessing this collective trauma, another presence came forward. He was a tall white man with a walking stick. Although there are no pictures of him, being a Puritan, he thought it vain; I knew instantly that he was my ancestor, Roger Williams. My experience continued as I felt and saw things through the presence of these two men. I wanted to disengage from this rage and sorrow, to dissociate from my body (a familiar feeling). Experiencing the feelings of the land, the "Amerindian" and my ancestor was more intense than anything I had ever felt personally as a result of the molestation.[20] The intense affect and physical memory that was part of the legacy of having been molested seemed to be a portal that connected me to a particular moment in my ancestor's life and to the place and time of an old and unreconciled cultural and historical wounding. "Tell the story, this story. That is all we ask," said Roger and this Native presence.

Jung suggests the following way of understanding the relationship between an ancestral trauma and disturbances in living descendants. It is based on an "energic" model of psyche—one in which affective energy cannot be created or destroyed, but can be transformed. Unlike Freud's understanding of psychic energy that is causal, Jung's conceptualization is acausal.[21] He writes,

The psychogenesis of the spirits of the dead seems to me to be more or less as follows. When a person dies, the feelings and emotions that bound his relatives to him lose their application to reality and sink into the unconscious, where they activate a collective content that has a deleterious effect on consciousness.[22]

On March 29 in 1676 during King Philip's War, my ancestor Roger Williams stood on a hill with Cuttanque, a Quinniticutt sachem watching the town of Providence burn. On March 29, 1952, exactly two-hundred and seventy-six years after the burning of Providence, I was born in Hanover, New Hampshire early in the morning, in the midst of a blizzard. I was born on the anniversary of this very significant date in the history of this land and its people, of America and in my ancestor's life, a date which represented a turning point for Indians and Europeans in what is now called New England. This synchronicity would be one of two dates that would link my life to the life of my ancestor and to the collective history of this land in which he played a significant part.

The pain that shook my body that day, almost to the point of breaking, connected me to a traumatic time in the history of the land and its peoples, to a place in the history of America one hundred years before it was named the United States of America, and to the particular life of an ancestor through my mother line. The experience in this imaginal exercise was evidence of the depth of the link between this deeply personal and traumatic event in my ancestor's life and my personal trauma. Traveling on this one thread within an intricately woven tapestry along the memory of trauma, I found myself at a place of intersecting origins.

Stories of personal trauma often remain isolated and split off from the rest of one's personal story. Untold and unwitnessed, these stories exist like islands of isolated memory separated from the rest of one's personal narrative, or, they may become the monument around which the story of one's life is centered to the exclusion of anything that isn't related to the trauma. Reaching backward and forward in time and through space, discovering the way one's personal story of trauma is connected through the lives of one's ancestors to the greater collective story, can contribute to creating an expanded narrative context. This more inclusive context has an emotional and narrative coherence that is characteristically lacking in the stories of individuals who have experienced trauma.

Through this imaginal exercise for the cultural and historic transference in the work of my dissertation I realized I had been addressed by my ancestral past from and in the moment of my birth. From a Jungian perspective, the coincidence of the dates of the burning of Providence and the date of my birth, March 29th, becomes synchronistic and meaningful. The concept of synchronicity was conceived of by Jung as a way to understand

and explain certain kinds of "remarkable phenomenon . . . of the uncon-scious" when the principle of causality is an insufficient explanation.[23] Synchronicity, as defined by Jung, is "the simultaneous occurrence of a certain psychic state with one or more external events which appear as meaningful parallels to the momentary subjective state."[24] Synchronistic phenomena, according to Jung, are evidence that psyche has a material aspect and matter a psychic one. These events, by definition, transcend the physical limitations of space and time, and are associated by meaning rather than cause and effect.

The experience in this imaginal exercise was evidence of the depth of the link between my ancestor Roger's life and mine. Making this connec-tion, first physically and emotionally, then cognitively, provided a context that revealed a deeper meaning in and understanding of the trauma in my life. Even after thirty-three years of conscious work on the physical, emo-tional, mental, and spiritual levels, I did not feel free from the effects of this trauma. The ancestral, historical, and cultural memories that are synchro-nistically linked to my memory of personal trauma informed and were an integral and necessary part of my process of healing. Seeing the relation-ship between my childhood trauma, my ancestor's trauma, the cultural-historical trauma and the trauma to the land made possible a more complete transformation of the pattern of abuse in my family.

CHAPTER 2

The Threads of Fate

Ancient notions of fate include an invisible thread woven through all the things of the world and throughout all the events of time. Fate appears as the original web of life, but also as the fine thread that weaves each soul into the world of time and space at birth.[1]

—Michael Meade

We are part of a family tree whose deep roots reach into the earth where the memories of our ancestors are held and whose branches reach into the sky with the budding of each new generation. Originating in what Jung refers to as the "mighty deposit of ancestral experience," each individual life originates in and is woven into this infinite ancestral story, this "original web of life."[2] The fine thread of our fate, woven into "all the events of time," is connected to the lives of our ancestors and our descendants. Each of us is a unique response to all that has come before and all that will come after.

It was a surprise to discover that there was a relationship between my personal trauma, the trauma of an ancestor who lived in the sixteen-hundreds, the trauma to the people native to this land, and the trauma to the land itself. Jung's differentiation of the collective unconscious into its various levels and his description of the nature of psyche provide a working model that allows us to see how our biography is part of a continuing story, part of a dynamic web of relations, which has its roots and telos in the stories of our ancestors and descendants.

Levels of the Unconscious

The unconscious is a universal aspect of the psyche shared by all of us. It connects us with the origins of our being and intimately binds us together in our families, nations, and with all of creation. In the reality of the unconscious we are also connected to the ancestors yet to be born. According to Barbara Hannah, in one lecture Jung differentiated between the levels of the unconscious.[3] (See Figure 1.) The uppermost level is the personal layer of the unconscious. Similar to Freud's conceptualization, it contains what has been repressed, discarded, or forgotten from everyday consciousness. Below that are ever more inclusive layers expanding from the personal to the family, to clan, into nation, and from nation into larger collective groups like Europe, West Africa, the Middle East or North America. While each of these layers is particular to one's individual ancestry, the level below this larger group is shared by all humankind. Jung referred to this as the level of "primeval ancestors."[4] Between this level and the lowest that provides the archetypal foundation for the entire collective web of being, is that of our animal ancestors. Every layer, even the animal, is part of our psychic inheritance.[5]

Following the path of our ancestors backward, crossing and crisscrossing oceans and continents we travel through levels of the collective unconscious—from the personal with its shadow of lost, forgotten and purposefully repressed pieces of personal experience, through the family, clan, and national levels, until we reach the deeper regions of psyche and our collectively shared history. There are, like the layers of civilizations visible in an excavated tell, levels and layers of complexity within each individual's ancestry.

Underlying and informing all of these layers is what Jung called the "central fire," the pure archetypal energy that provides the patterning for all of its varied expressions through the levels. According to Jung, a spark from this "central fire" that burns at the deepest layer of the collective unconscious runs through every layer. These energies take shape and are given form in ways that are particular to each individual, the family, the culture, and the times. Our images of Mother, Father, Hero, Warrior, Villain, Wise Old Man or Woman, and Beloved originate from the same spark but are shaped in ways that are particular to each individual through the levels.

For example, at the personal level the image of mother is formed out of our personal experiences of mother. At the familial level, she is the long line of mothers in our ancestral lineage. At the cultural level, she is depicted in movies, art, and literature in a variety of forms. We see her archetypal pattern depicted in the myths, fairy tales, and stories that have been passed down through the generations. Some of her mythic faces are those of Demeter, Mary, Isis, Yemaya, and Pachamama.[6] Jung's conceptualization of the collective unconscious provides the theoretical ground for understanding the ways in which the ancestors are a living reality in the present moments of our lives. Differentiating these levels helps us understand the nature and influence of the ancestors in the present. Using this

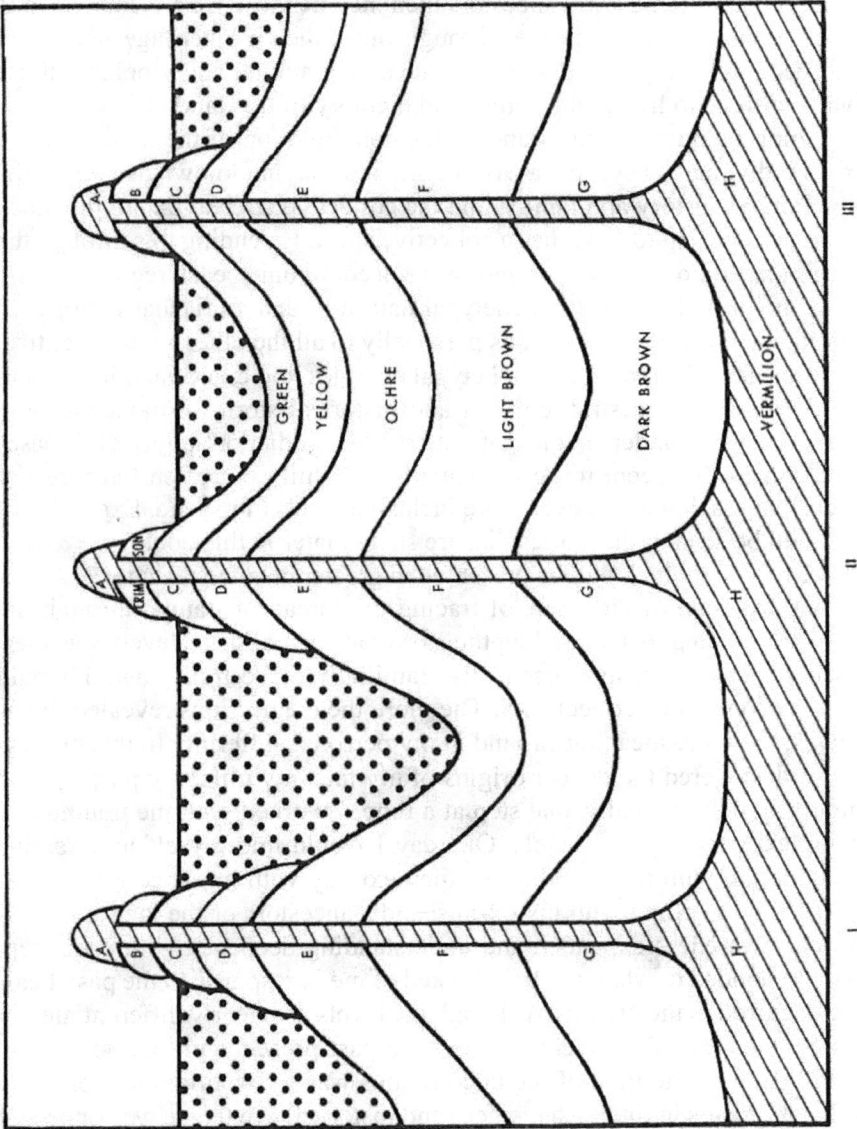

Key to Diagram

A. Individual (highest point)—Vermilion
B. Family—Crimson
C. Clan—Green
D. Nation—Yellow

E. Large group (e.g., Europe)—Ochre
F. Primeval ancestors—Light Brown
G. Animal ancestors in general—Dark Brown
H. Central fire—Vermilion

Figure 1. Levels of the Unconscious (from Barbara Hannah)

differentiated framework, ancestors then include those we are connected to through our personal lineage, through our collective heritage nationally and geographically, through our primeval and animal ancestors and those who continue to live in the nature and memory of this land.

Jung found that understanding the configuration of the national layer of an individual's psyche was as important as having knowledge about the individual's history and family, and the collective, archetypal myths. Each nation, according to Jung, has a collective spirit. Extending this through the levels one could say that each family, each community, each region also has its own spirit. There is an archetypal nature to that spirit that is threaded through and connects each of us personally to all the other levels. Identifying the particular way these archetypal energies find expression in our personal, familial, ancestral, cultural and historical stories provides a more comprehensive understanding of patterns like addiction, physical diseases and trauma that seem to be particular to a family but often have deeper roots that reach into the ever more inclusive levels of psyche. Examples of this will be seen in the stories that are shared later in this book.

My story, which will be presented in greater detail in Chapter 3, serves as one example of the value of tracing the thread of trauma through the levels. Listening to and tending the stories at each of these levels was therapeutic personally, interpersonally, familially, ancestrally, and I would hope in some way, collectively. The more the connections revealed themselves, the more meaning I found in my personal suffering. In this process I also discovered the deeper origins of my fate, my gifts, my purpose and my vocation. Gradually, one step at a time, I worked with the trauma and complexes through the levels. One day I would find myself in an active imagination with my grandfather, the next day with my ancestor and the next I'd be working with my ex-husband's ancestors or the land in Providence. Awareness expanded and understanding deepened with each step. As I responded to what was being asked of me in response to the past, healing occurred in the present. Although the levels are clearly differentiated in Jung's model of the psyche and in time past precedes present, engaging with this dynamic field of the unconscious was far from a linear process. What moments in time, what places and historical events are we connected to through the lives of our ancestors and how do they reveal themselves in our personal biography?

Personal and Collective Trauma

If we accept Jung's model of the collective unconscious, we are naturally and irrevocably connected to each other, to all of creation, in a way that transcends time and space. In its timeless nature, the collective unconscious is a remembrance of things past as they anticipate the future. Jung suggests that we have generally neglected taking into account the larger collective dimension of the psyche when looking at personal problems. In his autobiography he writes,

> It is difficult to determine whether these questions are more of a personal or more general (collective) nature. It seems to me that the latter is the case. A collective problem, if not recognized as such, always appears as a personal problem, and in individual cases may give the impression that something is out of order in the realm of the personal psyche. The personal sphere is indeed disturbed, but such disturbances need not be primary; they may well be secondary, the consequence of an insupportable change in the social atmosphere. The cause of disturbance is, therefore, not to be sought in the personal surroundings, but rather in the collective situation. Psychotherapy has hitherto taken this matter far too little into account.[7]

Understanding the nature and origin of our individual wounding, phobias, addictions, patterns of behavior, and inclinations as situated within this larger collective reality, allows for a depth of remembrance and healing that is more complete than if addressed only at the personal or family level.

From the perspective of Navajo, according to Jerome Bernstein, a Jungian analyst and author of *Living in the Borderland: The Evolution of Consciousness and the Challenge of Healing Trauma*, there is an intimate connection between each individual and the cosmos. For Navajo, an unnatural act—something that disturbs "the natural balance of the cosmos"—wounds the individuals involved, the community, the cosmos, and the universal psyche.[8] In Jung's conceptualization of the psyche each individual life is influenced by and intimately connected with the collective. A wound to one is suffered by the many. Bernstein goes on to say, "to heal the one—the individual psyche—is to heal the other—the universal psyche. They are not separable from the standpoint of Navajo cosmology and medicine."[9]

Following this logic, individual trauma in the present may reflect and be an embodiment of ancestral and cultural trauma. Addressing this trauma within the individual in the present, listening for the echoes from the past, may begin to restore balance and harmony within the collective psyche and cosmos, as well as for the traumatized individual. Following the thread through all the levels, discovering and remembering other places of origin of the trauma, and listening to what is being asked for in this moment in response, offers healing not only to the individual, but also to the family, community and the earth itself. Weaving the threads of the stories of one's ancestors with one's own, new meaning may be found within personal and collective suffering. Within the particularities of these stories the origins, nature and extent of what is out of harmony and what questions wait to be answered within and through time become clearer.

If we imagine at the deepest levels of the unconscious our collective roots, like the roots of Aspen trees where each individual tree within the grove of trees is connected through a shared root system, we might imagine the possibility that in those places where our roots connect a timeless resonance exists. Each individual story is connected through its roots to and is an expression of the collective story. As Daniel Taylor, American author and professor at Emory University, writes, "We are born into stories. . . . No one's story exists alone. Each is tangled up in countless others. Pull a thread in my story and feel the tremor half a world and two millennia away."[10]

Lucy, now the world's most famous early human ancestor, whose 3.2-million-year-old skeleton was recently discovered in Africa, captured my imagination in a way similar to that first image of the Earth from space. I felt a bone-to-bone connection to this ancestral human grandmother. I began to imagine that within the extraordinary diversity of life on this planet, somehow at the deepest level, at the source of our origination, we are related. Jung touches the core of this related quality in his autobiography:

> Our souls as well as our bodies are composed of individual elements which were already present in the ranks of our ancestors. . . . Body and soul therefore have an intensely historical character. . . .We have plunged down a cataract of progress which sweeps us on into the future with ever wider violence the farther it takes us from our roots . . . it is precisely the loss of connection with the past, the uprootedness, which has given rise to the "discontents" of civilization.[11]

Jung wrote these words in his chapter on the Bollingen Tower. The original structure was a round, two-story house built of stone that served as a sanctuary where he could be entirely himself. Its conception, crafting, and design reflected an intention to represent in stone his "innermost thoughts" and the sum of his knowledge. It began as a primitive one-story building with a hearth at its center: "I . . . had in mind an African hut where the fire, ringed by a few stones, burns in the middle, and the whole life of the family revolves around this center."[12] The tower was without electricity or running water. Jung chopped wood for fuel and cooked his own food over that central fire. He created a place which modernity did not touch, a place where time was not sweeping forward for the sake of progress, uprooting one from the past. He expresses his experience in this way: "In Bollingen, silence surrounds me almost audibly . . . . Thoughts rise to the surface which reach back into the centuries, and accordingly anticipate a remote future."[13]

Jung describes Bollingen as a place of timeless existence where one feels as if one lives simultaneously in many centuries. The absence of electricity and telephones provided a space where there was "nothing to disturb the dead."[14] The tower's timelessness and harmony with nature provided a place where Jung felt a connection with and the influence and living presence of his ancestors. Jung felt that his ancestors' souls were sustained by the physical structure of the tower. In the tower it was "as if a silent, greater family, stretching down the centuries, were peopling the house. There . . . I see life in the round, as something forever coming into being and passing on."[15] Here, unhindered by the confines of linear time and space or the intrusions of modernity, the ancestors could be welcomed, hosted and their voices heard. Here, he could hear their unanswered questions; questions that couldn't be answered by them in their time but could now be answered by Jung in his.

While working on the stone tablets at Bollingen, Jung became aware of the threads from the lives of his ancestors that were woven into his own:

> It often seems as if there was an impersonal karma within a family, which is passed on from parents to children. It always seemed to me that I had to answer questions which fate had posed to my forefathers, and which had not yet been answered, or as if I had to complete, or perhaps continue, things which previous ages had left unfinished.[16]

Jung devoted a lifetime to listening and being responsive to the voices of the dead in service to his time and the times to come.

Fate and Destiny

According to this particular passage it is fate that posed the questions to Jung's forefathers and fate that required an answer from Jung in his time. Fate is derived from the Latin word *fatum*, which translated means "that which is spoken."[17] In *The Soul's Code: In Search of Character and Calling,* James Hillman uses the analogy of the acorn for the seed that carries one's fate, the "secret plan in the heart."[18] It's important to distinguish fate from fatalism. In a fatalistic view of life, all is predetermined; there is no choice, implying every event is already written. Fate is more like an intention that is woven into the fabric of our being. Michael Meade, in his book *Fate and Destiny: The Two Agreements of the Soul,* writes, "Fate is the inner Koan, the archetypal pattern an enigma of each soul; it is the puzzling question that one's life secretly desires to answer."[19]

This archetypal pattern is given shape by each of our ancestries as it exists in very particular ways throughout the ages. As Jung discovered, the unanswered questions of our ancestors, give shape to our fate and the story of our life. Meade explains that

> Fate involves aspects of life that aren't freely chosen and plot lines that were well underway before we each came . . . upon the scene. We are each styled from within and woven into a story already underway in this world. Each occasion of fate reveals something that was in us all along and something that might distinguish us from others. In the crucible of life we can choose to learn about the fated elements and hidden qualities within us or else live our fate unwittingly, encounter it blindly, and act it out unconsciously.[20]

Our experiences in the present—personal trauma, addictions, physical and emotional symptoms, disease, or a sense that we are cursed or doomed— our sense of fate and destiny, may find multiple places of origin in the unconscious shadows of our ancestors. Destiny, according to Meade, is the "divine errand set deeply within us."[21] Finding and consciously embodying and giving expression to our destiny depends on our ability to listen and discern fate's hand in the events and circumstances of our life. Meade guides us saying, "Fate appears as whatever limits, restricts or even imprisons us; yet fate is the territory where we must go if we are to awaken to our inner destiny."[22]

My fate was revealed through the synchronicity of my birthday and the day Providence was burned and was woven into my personal experience of trauma. Feeling the echoes of my personal trauma reverberating through time and space, I was led to the deeper ancestral and collective origins of my suffering. Arriving at that time and place in my ancestor's life, I found new meaning in my suffering. I also discovered the gift of my destiny in the final words that were spoken to me by my ancestor and the Amerindian who stood with him on the hill—"tell the story."

My understanding of Roger's and the Amerindian's request of me to "tell the story" has revealed itself over time. At first, taking their request literally, I imagined these men were asking me to tell the story of the burning of Providence during King Philip's War. For a year I researched Roger's life and the particular moment in the history of this land referenced in this imaginal dialogue. That, however, was only the beginning of the journey and only one place in time where my story began.

As with many phrases which originate in dream and imaginal work, these words held a greater depth and breadth of meaning than I could initially comprehend. "Tell the story" is a theme that has been repeated in the years preceding and following this experience in the images of dreams, visions, and active imagination and through the words of others to and about me. I did not really understand the depth of meaning in the words of my ancestor and the ancestor of this land until someone asked a simple question about the meaning of those words. In looking for an answer to this question, I began to see the way "tell the story" threaded its way through my life, the way it is a gift and a calling. Those three words carry the essence of my gift—I am a keeper of the stories. My destiny exists in the origins of the trauma that seemed like a horrible fate. My ancestors' simple request served and serves as the circumference and the center point of my work and my life.

Our fate also reveals itself in other, seemingly arbitrary, non-traumatic ways. As I learned more about Roger, I understood my fascination with compasses.[23] When I was a child I would wander in the woods for hours, even in winter, compass in hand, exploring and making new paths, using my treasured compass to guide me. (Roger's compass is iconic.) My interest in and desire to learn about the people native to New England was insatiable. I played church and school enlisting my friends and siblings as worshipers and students. (Roger was a minister, teacher and prolific writer.) I wrote tomes of "scribble-scrabble" on blank pages creating books filled with stories before I could write a single letter or word, let alone an entire sentence. When I learned to write words and sentences I fashioned a quill to write with from a feather I found in the woods. All of these things seemed random until I saw my life as a living answer to Roger's. Discovering that my interests, passions, and inclinations, which were evident even in childhood, also had their origins in my ancestor Rogers's life allowed me to actively and creatively participate in more consciously actualizing my destiny.

We see the hand of fate in Jung's life and his work. His father and many other members of his clan on both his mother's and father's side, past and present, were ministers. As an adult he recognized the "overwhelming theological influences"[24] that had been present since childhood. His father was deeply rooted in Christianity. It seemed to Jung that his mother, although professing the Christian faith of her family, "was somehow rooted in deep, invisible ground. . . . It never occurred to me how 'pagan' this foundation was."[25] His life was a response to his parents, his clan, his Swiss heritage and "the spirit of the age."[26] These influences would have a significant effect on his life and his work. Looking backward from the end of his life, Jung saw the hand of fate in his work, the origins of which lay within his personal and cultural lineage. As he became conscious of these influences through dreams, synchronicities and visions, he fulfilled a rather remarkable destiny.

Jung observed that what remains unconscious will come to us externally as fate. He is quoted as having told students at the C. G. Jung Institute in Zurich in 1958, "If you are not interested in your own fate, the unconscious is."[27] Meade believes that recognizing the hand of fate in the events of our lives is the key to becoming conscious of and fulfilling one's destiny—that which is ours and ours alone to realize. Gathering pieces from the past we become more conscious of how the lives of our ancestors are implicated in our personal story in very particular ways. This allows each of us to come into a dynamically co-creative relationship with our individual fate, thus fulfilling our destiny.

CHAPTER 3

Beyond Biography

Every story has many beginnings; in any given moment we choose a place to start the telling.

—From a dialogue with the ancestors

Illustrious Origins

One of the family stories I grew up with was the story my mother told of our illustrious origins on this North American continent—that we were descended from Roger Williams, the man credited with founding Rhode Island. She was very proud of this. I thought this was just a story, one that gave my mother a sense of connection to the past and more meaning and purpose to our ordinary lives. It was my older daughter Melissa who picked up the thread of Roger's story from my mother and handed it back to me.

In a conversation Melissa and I had when she was about five years old, she told me that she had come here to get me on my path. In the moment, her words were out of context and shocking. They were clearly beyond her conscious awareness and outside of anything I expected to hear from my five-year-old daughter. I knew and felt the unconscious reaching out to me through her. Through her interest in Roger I discovered the truth in my mother's story and the deep roots of our family's legacy. Melissa did indeed get me on my path.

My family history and the past mattered little to me until I married and had two daughters of my own.[1] My older daughter Melissa was given a school assignment in the fourth grade to research and report on a famous Maryland historical figure. (We were living in Maryland at the time.) Having heard the story about Roger from my mother, she insisted on doing her report on our ancestor. She's very persuasive and got her teacher's permission to do her research on Roger. Synchronistically, the day Melissa received her teacher's permission, I received a complete genealogical diagram from my Aunt, my mother's sister. We were, I discovered, directly descended from Roger Williams. I am this man's great-granddaughter times nine. In fact, five generations back, two of Roger's descendants from his son Joseph married each other, bringing that original DNA together again in a new time and place. The connection I thought was imagined was in fact very substantial and real. Melissa and I began to explore the story of Roger's life. This was the beginning for me of consciously reconnecting with the origins of my fate.

The historical context for my life took shape with each new discovery and story. As my journey unfolded, I became aware that the ancestors who had a hand in my fate, whose questions were unanswered, were not limited to my personal ancestry. They included the ancestors of people indigenous to this land, an archetypal figure who haunted the women in my maternal lineage for centuries, and finally, the ancestors and elders of the rich academic tradition of which this work is a part.

The more I learned through historical and genealogical research and through imaginal dialogues, the more I became aware of the way the threads of my personal trauma were intricately woven into the history and memory of this land and the many-layered fabric of the collective story. My symptoms in the present, in the immediacy of somatic and emotional memory, "re-membered" a decisive moment in the collective history of the North American continent and a traumatic event in my ancestor's life. Over time I began to see that "my" trauma, "my" symptoms, the entire story of my life, was continuous with a much longer "chain of events" whose origins were multi-located.

Ancestral Legacies—Origins Without Cause

On March 29, 1676, after many years of conflict and negotiated peace, Roger Williams walked to the top of a hill overlooking Providence to meet with Cuttanque, one of the sachems who was leading the march of native people up the coast with the intention of destroying every European settlement in their path. King Philip's War had been raging for over a year, but Providence, excluded and separate from the Massachusetts Bay Colony, remained neutral. The Quinniticutt sachem told Roger that Providence was to be burned. Providence had been built on land that Roger and others lived on only by agreement with the Narragansett grandfathers and grandmothers of the men who were now destroying it. This land, although purchased from the Narragansett, was in Roger's words, "a gift of love."

In a letter written to his brother on April 1, 1676 Roger wrote,

> I asked them why they assaulted us with Burning and Killing who ever were kind Neighbours to them (& looking back) said I this Hous of mine now burning before mine Eyes hath lodged kindly some Thousands of You these ten Years.[2]

I have been told that Williams understood the gift culture of the Indians.[3] His relationship with the Algonquin tribes was unusual for a European of that time. Williams spent much of his time with the Narragansett and Wampanoag Indians. They considered him a man of integrity and wisdom, and a friend. Understanding the native languages and culture, he served as mediator in negotiations and treaties between Indians and Europeans in the northeastern part of what is now America for many years. Canonicus, a Narragansett sachem and one of the men who gave my ancestor the land that he would call Providence, and Roger remained neighbors and friends until Canonicus' death. When Canonicus was dying he sent for Roger and with "the last of that man's breath . . . [said he] desired to be buried in my cloth of Free gift and so he was."[4] Gaustad, in his biography of Williams, using quotes from Roger's letters writes: Williams attended Canonicus' funeral. His relationship with this man was founded on mutual respect. In one of his letters after the funeral he would write, "'when the hearts of my countrymen and friends failed me,' it was the 'infinite wisdom and merits' of Canonicus that sustained him. This sachem loved him as a son 'to his last gasp.'"[5] According to Gaustad, these two men shared the dream and hope that English and Indian could live together peacefully, generation after generation.

But times had changed since the grandfathers of the sachem he stood with on the hill had given Roger the land. For the people native to this land, King Philip's War was an attempt to rid the land of Europeans, the people who had taken their land and who had through trade and commerce introduced molasses, liquor, small pox, and influenza. Plagues had decimated entire villages. By the time this war began, trading no longer benefited the Indians. They gradually became more dependent on Europeans for their survival. Incurring debts for European goods, they traded more of their land.

For the Indians, Providence was just another English settlement, associated now with Plimoth and Boston, towns that had repeatedly broken treaties and appropriated land at will. Williams reminded the sachems that were present that day—Nahigonsets, Cowwesets, Wompanoag, Neepmucks, and Qunticoogs—that Providence was a "Throughfare Town" which "had never acted hostilily" against them. He told Cuttanque, that they (the Indians) had forgotten that "they were Mankind."[6] Cuttanque responded saying that "they were in a Strang Way" which they had been forced into by the English and that "God was [with] them and Had forsaken us [English] for thy had so prospered in Killing and Burning us far beyond What we did against them."[7] The argument heated up. Roger said that God favored the English and that "God would help us to Consume them Except they Hearkned to Counsel. I told them they knew how many times I had Quenched fires between the Bay and them, and Plimoth, and Quniticut, and them."[8]

LaFantasie, in his notes on this letter, finds this passage, along with other passages in the letter that express more conventional Puritan opinions on the war as "a sign of God's wrath and as divine punishment for the loss of faith," to be contradictory to Williams' understanding as expressed in his other letters and in historical documents. In the past, Williams ordinarily disagreed with the Puritans interpretation of events as god's will, whether punishing or providential.[9] He suggests that Williams's opinions might have changed or that he wrote this to meet his reader's expectations as he had done in other writings. He also notes that the way Williams expressed himself in this letter may more accurately characterize the "tone of his diplomatic encounters"—"more direct, forceful and even challenging" than the mythic, tactful and patient "roving ambassador" that many historians have portrayed.[10]

Roger was a complex, passionate, idealistic man of deep and strict conscience. Moreover, he was a practical man of vision. Over the centuries, he would become known for his ideas regarding "soul liberty," liberty of conscience and the separation of church and state. He was known as a pioneer of religious liberty, an irrepressible democrat, and a friend of the Indians. He had welcomed Indians into his home, had walked with them for hundreds of miles learning their language and customs. Yet, after the war, according to Patricia Rubertone, author of *Grave undertakings: An archaeology of Roger Williams and the Narragansett Indians,* he served on the committee that was charged with the task of "determining the fate of Indian war captives. . . . Although the enslavement of Native peoples was prohibited in Rhode Island, Williams, as a member of the committee . . . helped devise a plan for selling captives into 'involuntary servitude' for periods of years."[11] Rubertone believes that Roger took this war very personally—"a war waged directly against him and his idealism . . . in which he was badly defeated."[12] From my experience in dreams and imaginal dialogues I believe for my ancestor King Philip's War was deeply personal and painful.

As the story of that fateful day continues. Cuttanque came across the river to meet with Williams after asking him to show that he was unarmed. Roger wrote, "We had much repetition of the former particulars Which were debated at the Poynt."[13] Cuttaquene told Williams that they had broken their treaties and that "you have driven us out of our own Countrie and then pursued us to our great Miserie & your own, & we are forced to live upon you."[14] As they spoke, houses were already in flames. Roger "told them there were Wayes of peas [peace] . . . and planting time was acoming."[15] Cuttaquene told Roger "they cared not for Planting these Ten Years. They would live upon us and Dear."[16]

For these Algonquin, it was too late to negotiate a peace with Providence. There was too great an imbalance in power and resources between the English and Indians. English betrayal was now part of the pattern of colonization and broken treaties. Seeing the inevitable future, the only solution for the people native to this land was to drive the English from it. According to Roger's letter to his brother, the two men parted "civilly" and Cuttaquene advised him to go by the waterside and not near particular houses so he and his family would be safe. Roger, now in his seventies, watched as his neighbors were murdered and Providence burned. His home was not spared. I can only speculate as to the "truth" of other scholar's interpretations and understanding of Roger at this particular moment in his life. I can only imagine how the two men standing there on the hill that day felt in the midst of a war that both knew would determine the future of what is now New England. So much was at stake for both of these men, their way of life, and their people.

The consequences of European colonization of this land are still being felt and its echoes reverberate within the American collective psyche. This letter, excerpted above, represents one particular moment in a long complicated history, a moment which was fateful for Roger personally and for this country collectively. Many other conversations had taken place and much happened between the time Roger first set foot on this continent and the day he stood on the hill watching Providence burn. The conversation as shared in Roger's letter between these two men—one Native, one English—in some ways summarized the more complex "conversation" and interactions of that time in the history of this land and its peoples and reflected the complex nature of Williams' longstanding relationship with the Narragansett and other tribes of the region.

King Philip's War was devastating, brutal, vicious, and full of cruelty. The Indians burned more than half of the English colonists' towns and had pushed them back almost to the sea. Although the English suffered losses great enough that they were almost forced to abandon New England, Indian losses were even greater. According to Drake's account of this war in *King Phillip's War: Civil war in New England, 1675–1676*, looking at seventeenth-century New England as "America's origin," this war had the highest casualty rate per capita in America's history.[17] "Both sides suffered tremendous loss of life and property."[18] Thousands of Indians were killed or died of disease or starvation. Those who survived were enslaved.

Any semblance of equality between these two peoples vanished with the removal of a majority of the Indians from the territory. The losses suffered by the English were so great that they became more dependent on England for their survival. According to Drake, this war not only brought an end to a generation of co-existence between colonists and Indians, it fundamentally changed the political, social and economic landscape of the region. This war completely changed the face of the northeastern coast of this continent and the dynamics within the region. The legacy of this war haunted both Indians and colonists for many years. Many other battles and wars on the North American continent would follow.

The postwar reconstruction brought with it new struggles resulting in even more bloodshed and loss. In the ten years that followed, the last of his life, Roger would persist in his argument with other English settlers in Rhode Island who continued to expand the boundary lines of their property into Narragansett land. Roger stated clearly in letter after letter that this was Narragansett land, which the English had no right to based on their written agreement with the Narragansett. But the victors of the battle for land in New England had already been decided in the war.

A Wampanoag woman at the Plimoth Plantation, in sharing her personal story, told me the Narragansett and Wampanoag still suffer greatly from what began then. Her son was forbidden from speaking his native language in the public school. Sitting, talking with her, I witnessed the separation and discomfort felt by many of the white people visiting this Native part of Plimoth Plantation. The relationship between American Indians and the dominant culture in the U.S. continues to be complex and strained in many ways. Although given land as an act of restitution, she and many others had to sell their land because they could not pay the taxes. The "great Miserie" that Cuttaquene spoke of to my ancestor continues today. The European legacy in North America continues. I have been told for American Indians the conflict never ended. They have been resisting for over three-hundred years.

Reconciling Head and Heart

Ochwiay Biano tells Jung in their conversation at the Taos Pueblo that the "whites" think with their heads. When Jung asks what he thinks with, Ochwiay Biano responds, "We think here" as he points to his heart.[19] Centuries before this conversation, my ancestor, Roger Williams, in his encounters with the Wampanoag and Narragansett, experienced the split between "civilized" and "primitive" on an interpersonal and intercultural level. His book, *A Key into the Language of America*, creates a picture of his experience of two radically different cultures—one English, Christian and civilized, the other, Narraganset, pagan and "savage."[20] Within his depiction and juxtaposition of these two radically different peoples and cultures, the internal conflict and tension Roger felt personally "between the head and the heart" is poignantly expressed.[21] He could not reconcile the admiration and respect he felt for the men and women native to this land with what he believed theologically.

It seems trivializing to reduce Roger's struggle to reconcile his head with his heart to an unanswered question. Meeting him in dreams and through ancestral dialogues, I have felt his anguish, his desire, his despair. Roger spent his life negotiating peace between two radically different peoples. When Providence burned, his idealistic hope for peace and reconciliation between Europeans and the people Native to this land was reduced to ashes along with the homes and gardens that burned to the ground. This was a war that he couldn't imagine and thought should never have happened. His pain, grief and hope retained its affective potency in the unconscious as I experienced it standing on the hill with him in the transferential dialogue described in Chapter 1.

"This Uncompleted Work Has Followed Them . . ."[22]

On July 28, 1629, Roger met with other Puritans in England to discuss journeying to America to escape religious persecution.[23] One of the other men at that meeting was John Cotton. This was the first time Cotton and Williams met. My ex-husband Clark is a direct descendant of John Cotton through his mother's father. Unaware of our ancestry, three-hundred-sixty-one years later, my ex-husband Clark, and I married on July 28, 1990, on land given by King Charles to Lord Baltimore in 1634.[24]

Cotton and Williams, initially shared the same beliefs, dreams, and fears. As time went on they would ultimately find themselves in an ongoing and heated conflict over religious, civil, and political philosophy. Clark's ancestor was one of the men responsible for exiling Roger from the Massachusetts Bay Colony for religious heresy and for his public denouncement of the English for taking Indian land beyond what had been traded, sold or given. In this time, centuries later, Clark and I were married and living on land that he would inherit that had been given to Lord Baltimore not by the Indians of that region, but by the King of England. The past was present, the story in many ways the same, but with new possibilities as the times had changed and their conflict could be engaged with in the context of these times and our relationship.[25]

I discovered that the synchronicity of the dates of my birth and wedding anniversary are not uncommon indications of specific connections between an individual life and the lives of one's ancestors. Schutzenberger, a French Freudian psychoanalyst who uses a transgenerational approach in work with her clients, coins the term "anniversary syndrome" for the coincidence of dates which she discovered frequently become apparent in this work. She found that a date that is meaningful in the life of an individual in the present marks the anniversary of an event in the past that had a significant effect, positive or traumatic, on the family or a particular family member. She writes, "It seems that the unconscious has a good memory, likes family bonds and marks important life events by repetition of date or age."[26] A birth date is often coincidental with the anniversary of a specific event in the history of the family. Schutzenberger found that these coincidental anniversaries indicate a link between that individual in the present and the event in the past. Discovering this kind of synchronicity can reveal a dynamic and meaningful connection between the individual in the present and a specific event in the life of the historical family or with a particular individual in one's lineage, or both. Theoretically she defines these as expressions of the "family and social transgenerational unconscious."[27] This is similar but not identical to Jung's concept of the collective unconscious.

As a Freudian, Schutzenberger sees the coincidence of dates only as indications of repressed family material that must be made conscious in order for the individual to be free to live her individual life. This, in part, is true. Jung's work provides us with a broader perspective. These synchronicities may also reveal meaningful connections that carry more than repressed family material.

Recognizing the synchronistic connection between my birth date and my wedding anniversary was the beginning of a process that has involved more than bringing a repressed memory to consciousness. Bringing my story into relationship with the other stories which came to light through these synchronicities, Understanding our ancestors' relationship brought new understanding to my relationship with Clark. Situated within this ancestral and historical context, the unanswered questions and unresolved parts of this longer story, as they are specifically related to my life now, became more apparent. As time went on, I also began to see the way our relationship was an answer to the past in service to an ever-evolving story and the generations that would follow.

Even though the men and women who left England for this new land had seen and suffered from religious persecution themselves, most of them expected a uniformity of beliefs and worship in America. The Puritans who colonized Massachusetts in the seventeenth century, of which Clark's ancestor and my ancestor were a part, never intended it to be a place of conflicting opinions. They established a theocracy in which there was one church and religious law superseded and determined civil law. In the eyes of the Massachusetts Bay Company, a heretic was more dangerous than a murderer. The reason, according to Polishook; "the murderer destroyed a person in this life only, but the heretic killed a soul forever!"[28] Williams, unlike his peers, believed that governments, receive their power from the people, not from God. As a Puritan who disputed the sacred right of Kings and the sacred character of government my ancestor, Roger, was not welcome in England. After coming to this land, once again considered a heretic, he was soon not welcome in Massachusetts.

While Roger shared the fundamental principles of the majority of Protestants in New England at the time, his interpretation of the Bible led him to concepts that were in direct conflict with his contemporaries. Williams, unlike Cotton and other Puritans, had become a separatist, severing all ties with the Church of England. His ideas regarding "soul liberty"— that every man and woman should enjoy "liberty of conscience" and the right to worship as they chose—were in radical opposition to the ministers and government officials in Massachusetts. His opinions about the separation between civil and religious law, state and church, challenged the very foundation of the Massachusetts government and clergy. He considered the Indians to be the rightful owners of the land. His continuing declarations that the colonists had no religious or civil right to the lands of the Indians except through direct purchase just added fuel to the already blazing fire of a very public argument.

Cotton, on the other hand, advocated the commonly shared idea of most of his contemporaries of a union of church and state law. He and other Puritans believed that "the essential purpose of society was the glorification of God. . . . They feared the religious purity of the nation could not be achieved without state intervention."[29]   Along with most other English colonists of his time, he believed that the English had a sovereign and spiritually ordained right to Indian land. In one of their many public disagreements, Cotton denounced Williams' support of toleration and soul liberty. For Cotton and other Puritans, only one freedom was granted by God—the "freedom to accept His will."[30]

Over time Massachusetts Bay Company was fearful about and confronted with hostility from Indians beyond their borders. Their relationship with England also became dangerously strained. As these tensions mounted, Roger's public protestations and challenges became more and more problematic for the colony. Looking for ways to solidify the new government and the developing colony, the General Court decided to require that every colonist take an oath of loyalty. Williams objected to this oath on religious principles. His very publicly shared opinion was considered seditious. This was the proverbial straw that broke the camel's back.

Cotton, the most prominent minister in the colony, who had a very good personal relationship with Roger, was called in to help. He was certain that he could get Williams to publicly retract his statements and stop his public protestations. This issue remained unresolved for months. Williams, not surprisingly, refused. Considered to be dangerous to the peace of the colony and "beyond redemption," Roger was ordered to leave Massachusetts. Cotton was part of the company of ministers who, along with the General Court, made this decision. Even with these fundamentally different and publicly debated disagreements, Roger and John remained friends. Living a life of conviction and principle was something they shared and respected in each other.

In January of 1636, warned that the government was preparing to ship him back to England, Roger fled south from Massachusetts. Months later, having survived a New England winter "in the Wilderness," he made it beyond the borders of Massachusetts to Narragansett territory where he was given land by Canonicus and Miantonomi, Narragansett sachems. Money was refused in exchange for this land. Williams called this a gift of love and saw it as evidence of the divine providence of God. Thusly named, Williams founded Providence.

In Providence each individual was allocated the same amount of land and the right to worship as he or she so chose. He, along with others who followed him to Providence, created a community, an "experiment," where church was separated from state, and where decisions would be arrived at by mutual consent not dictatorial authority.[31] Founded on his concept of soul liberty, Quakers, Jews, and individuals who were considered heretics found a home there. The first synagogue on this continent was built in Providence. According to the Colonial Women's History Project, Providence was also where "the first legal decision in the seventeenth century New England colonies to uphold a woman's right to 'freedom of conscience,' that in matters of thought and belief, a woman could be seen as independent of her husband's control."[32] Following this momentous decision, Jane Verin's husband Joshua whisked her back to Salem, Massachusetts. According to the Rhode Island Commission on Women report, "Preliminary conclusions indicate that subsequently, Jane actively challenged the authority of the Salem Church and suffered admonishment, removal from church and corporal punishment for her beliefs."[33]

Until his death, Williams continued his argument with other New Englanders about their "right" to American Indian lands. Unlike most of his contemporaries and Cotton, Williams did not see the people native to this land as primitive savages. His friendship with Canonicus was one of the most important and meaningful relationships in his life. From his letters and books, it seems to me that he considered Amerindians equals. In his first published book, *A Key into the Language of America*, it is clear that he saw them as more authentically Christian than the Europeans who had been baptized as such. He writes,

> *Boast not proud* English, *of they birth & blood,*
> *Thy brother* Indian is *by birth as Good.*
> *Of one blood God made Him, and Thee & All,*
> *As wise, as faire, as strong, as personall.*[34]

Teunissen and Hinz, the editors of the 1979 edition of Roger's *Key*, differentiate this book from others that presented and discussed Indian language and culture. In other works there was a tendency to view the people native to this land as exploitable resources.[35] In contrast, *A Key* shows Roger's deep appreciation of these people.

A *Key* was not intended to be a simple dictionary of Indian language. In his introduction to the book, Roger wrote that he intended this book to be "[a] little *Key* [which] may open a *Box*, where lies a bunch of *Keyes*."[36] The book is written metaphorically. Williams uses language as a way of framing and contrasting Amerindians and their culture with that of the English. Each chapter begins with language translating Narragansett phrases and concepts into English words, then to cultural observations related to these phrases and finally to Roger's spiritual observations of the Indians. At the end of each chapter he took his observations further into spiritual insights. "Williams comes to the general conclusion that from the 'natural' point of view the 'savage' is in no sense inferior to the civilized European, and that in respect to natural virtue he is undeniably superior."[37]

In his encounters with the Wampanoag and Narragansett, my ancestor experienced the split between "civilized" and "primitive," Christian and pagan, non-native and indigenous, on an interpersonal and intercultural level. His book poignantly expresses the internal conflict and tension he felt between the head and the heart.[38] Fred Gustafson, a Jungian analyst who has "been ceremonially involved with the Brule branch of the Lakota people" for years, states that the "westernized form of the Christian Church" has contributed to separating God and us from the earth.[39] "Earth was not portrayed as our home but as a place to endure, to get through, to be done with. Further, there was no tolerance for the notion of spirits. They were driven away. Matter became inert—dead."[40] He suggests that our alienation from the earth as home is accompanied by an alienation and dissociation from the roots of our being, the roots of consciousness, the "Indigenous Ancestor," the archaic man of which Jung has written.

Roger's experiences with the people native to this land brought him face to face with this fundamental Christian separation of spirit and matter.

In the seventeenth century, at the height of the Enlightenment, Roger struggled with the irreconcilable nature of his theological understanding and his experiences of the people native to this land. He could not reconcile his admiration for these men and women and what he believed theologically.[41] Nor could he reconcile the differences between cultures. No amount of successful or unsuccessful negotiations would lead to the kind of peaceful co-existence Roger hoped for. His dreams for the way we could live in relationship with this land and its Native people have yet to be realized.

What Roger experienced as an irreconcilable conflict between cultures and between his head and his heart I experienced in the present as an intrapsychic conflict in consciousness. Born into a culture that is described by cultural historian Richard Tarnas as one that roots us to the limited consciousness of our egos even while it separates and isolates us from the rest of nature, including our own "primal" psychic roots, I found myself struggling with a split in my experience of consciousness that has existed for centuries between head and heart, right and left brain, Logos and Eros, modern and primitive, reason and instinct, evolved and primordial, masculine and feminine, science and art, human and nature, man-made and natural. I believe what Roger was unable to realize personally was the recovery of a spirituality that was more indigenous and of the heart, one in which Pagan and Christian are reconciled. That recovery and reintegration would continue through me.

According to Tarnas, in the worldview of modern Western culture, intellect reigns and effects have their explainable causes. The universe is defined empirically. The modern self and the human mind are "fundamentally distinct and separate from an objective external world that it seeks to understand and master."[42] Subject and object are split in a seemingly irreconcilable way. The world itself and the things of the world are viewed and experienced as impersonal, devoid of soul and without consciousness. The modern human split from the rest of the unconscious material universe, exists in a world which is "devoid of spiritual purpose . . . ruled by chance and necessity, without intrinsic meaning."[43] The world itself is merely and essentially a construct. This vision "emerged fully in the course of the European Enlightenment of the seventeenth and eighteenth centuries, though its roots are as old as Western civilization itself."[44] The emergence of this historical paradigm happens to coincide with the time my ancestor Roger Williams and other Europeans uprooted themselves and their families and traveled, partly out of necessity and partly out of a new vision, across the ocean to this, for them, "new world."

In this current age, which Tarnas characterizes as "an age between worldviews," our highly differentiated, Logos oriented, egoic consciousness is reconnecting with nature.[45] Jerome Bernstein identifies this as a necessary and compensatory evolutionary shift in the western psyche. This evolution is occurring within the consciousness of individuals who Jerome Bernstein refers to as "Borderlanders." According to Bernstein, "the western psyche is being forced to integrate the transpersonal and *transrational* dimensions of life from which I propose it split some three-thousand years ago."[46] (Italics added) Bernstein uses the term "'transrational' to refer to . . . observable phenomena and connections that do not 'make sense' by generally accepted scientific and rational criteria."[47]

Bernstein's conceptualization of the psyche was challenged as he listened to the experiences his patients shared with him. Their experiences did not fit into "our rational construct of the universe" or known psychological, clinical models.[48] It necessitated creating a clinical container that "was more accepting and less judgmental of transrational experience."[49] Working within Jung's description of and framework for the psyche, Bernstein describes the transrational consciousness experienced by Borderlanders as a dynamic process in collective consciousness "that is moving the Western psyche to reconnect our overspecialized ego to its natural psychic roots."[50] This evolutionary shift, as Bernstein describes it, is one in which the "runaway western ego" is not only reconnecting with its psychic roots, it is also reconnecting to its relationship to nature. As we evolve, we reconnect with what Jung calls the "Archaic Man," and Gustafson, calls the "the Inner Indigenous One."[51]

An experience of transrational consciousness rooted in our "Indigenous Mind" is available to each of us. David Peat describes his experience of his first Sun Dance at the Blood Reserve, with the Blackfoot Confederacy in Lethbridge, Canada. In this annual celebration of one part of the cycle of nature, he found himself led into a profoundly different reality from that which he encountered in his everyday Western world.

> To enter into this domain is to question what we mean by space and time, by the distinctions between the living and non-living, by the individual and society, by dreams and visions, by perception and reality, by causality and synchronicity, by time and eternity.[52]

Slowly his Western-oriented consciousness freed itself from its "rigidities and fixed patterns of response" and he opened, through his participation in this ceremony, to a different way of seeing.[53] He remembered the other times in his life when "everything was truly alive . . . vibrating with power."[54] As he sat in that Sun Dance ground, surrounded by people whose experience of the world had always been rooted in nature, he realized that

"we had all, as children, seen the world in that sense of numinous animation and direct connection of the cosmos that is hidden deep within us."[55]

Our conditioning and view of the world often limit our openness to
encounters such as this. Our beliefs about the nature of reality act as filters
which govern what we are open to noticing. Gregory Cajete, a Tewa
Pueblo, scholar and educator, describes "a worldview [as] a set of assumptions and beliefs that form the basis of a people's comprehension of the
world."[56] Our worldview pervades every aspect of our perceived reality,
inner and outer, and acts as a filter and interpretive lens for our experiences. Our worldview is embedded in the way we perceive, think about,
imagine, and story the reality of our world. It shapes the creation and interpretation of the stories we tell of our experiences. The stories that we tell
and how we tell them, our concepts of good and evil, of what is real and
what is not, our values, our concepts of what can be and is known and how
we know—all reflect and are reflections of our worldview.

Malidoma Some believes that pathologizing or explaining away the
kinds of experiences that Bernstein describes as transrational only serves
to reinforce the conceptual divisions Peat describes above. Rather than an
actual difference between what is real and not real, or imagined, these divisions are a result of the separation between the modern, logos oriented
consciousness and the archaic part of consciousness with its roots in nature.
If we approach experiences with an open consciousness, one that can hold
complexity, contradiction, and the disorientation of not knowing, it is possible to relax the constraints of our Western worldview. In doing so we
open ourselves to a different way of seeing and being in the world.

Peat's story is offered as an example of how transrational consciousness can be awakened in an individual, who is, in this case, a traditionally
trained Western scientist. Peat's participation in the Sun Dance allowed
him to reconnect with a way of perceiving and being in relationship with
himself and the world that compensated for and corrected the point of view
of his Western, differentiated, one-sided consciousness. Through the ceremony of the Sun Dance, he reconnected to a way of seeing that we all have
access to. In Jung's words, Peat connected with the "laws and roots of his
being."[57]

As a child the transrational, Borderland consciousness that Bernstein
describes was a natural part of me. However, with experience, I learned
that these experiences were not common to my family or peers. I learned
to keep experiences like this to myself at an early age. Studying psychology in college, I began to worry that these experiences were pathological,
regressive and compensatory. Like Roger, I found myself in unfamiliar
territory, looking for ways to live with two seemingly irreconcilable ways
of knowing and being—a rational and transrational consciousness.

My first awareness of the difference between the way I experienced reality and the way the rest of the world did, which at the time was my family, happened when I was 5 years old. I "stopped" the rain. My family; mother, father, younger sister and I were at the drive-in watching Bambi. It was pouring rain. My sister was whining, my mother was complaining and my father, unable to find a solution to make everyone happy, was getting more and more frustrated. Watching the drama in the car I very naturally thought, "Why don't they just ask the rain to stop?" Then I thought, I'll just do it myself. This experience occurred before I learned to read and write, and before I would have developed a strong, differentiated ego. I was connected to the natural way of things.

I will describe what I did from my adult perspective. However, what I did in the moment was as natural as breathing and required no thought about how to do it. I felt my heart, and with my heart, felt into the heart of the rain. When the connection was made I said out loud, "Rain Stop." At that moment the rain stopped. After a long time of a solid sheet of rain pounding on our windshield drowning out the sound from the speaker hanging from our car window, suddenly not a drop was falling from the sky. I held the connection with the rain easily and naturally, with reverence and gratitude. I didn't have the concepts of reverence or gratitude when I was 5 years old. It's only now, of course, as an adult remembering, that I recognize these qualities. My parents' heads turned toward me. I expected them to be happy. Instead, I saw the fear in the expression of alarmed astonishment on their faces. I thought I had done something terribly wrong and immediately released my heart to heart connection with the rain. Of course, the downpour began again. It was a confusing experience that eventually fell into the category of all the things I, according to my mother and teachers, only "imagined."

Some of you may be thinking that this was mere coincidence. I understand and appreciate healthy skepticism. I couldn't do this work if I didn't ask questions about the validity of my perceptions and experiences. What I can say to those of you who are wondering right now about my memory of a childhood experience, is that the connection I felt with the rain was so embodied and palpable, that I felt the rain stop in complete congruence with my request, and start again in complete congruence with the moment I thought I had done something wrong and I released it. I experienced this very physically in my heart. It was so natural; I would never have been conscious of this experience had it not been for my parents' reaction. It was completely unforgettable.

As an adult, Jung's recognition of an "archaic" aspect of human consciousness and Bernstein's conceptualization of Borderland consciousness provided the framework of understanding that I needed to accept and understand my experiences and to reconcile the split within my own consciousness. As a Borderlander, my process of integration of these two aspects within my own consciousness is an ongoing dialogical process in which I find that the center, as I perceive it, is always shifting. In my ancestor dialogues I have experienced Roger's rapt attention, enthusiastic curiosity and support, and his relief as I consciously engage this "conflict" intrapsychically and in my work.[58]

My understanding of and approach to this phenomenon of the presence of the ancestors in the present reflects my attempt to find ways to engage as a human being with the world from a more integrated consciousness. An integration of the modern rational aspect of consciousness with the "primitive" archaic aspect was facilitated by and necessary for engaging with the "brighter, more dynamic and expansive energetic world" of nature, which Some refers to as the place where the ancestors dwell.[59] In this way, what was irreconcilable interculturally and personally for Roger—the split he experienced between head and heart—begins to find its answer, reconciliation, expression, and application through me.

Ezechiel's words to Jung in *The Red Book* in Liber Secundus, Nox Secunda speak to the effect "the dead" have on us and the effect being in a more conscious relationship with "the dead" has on them. Ezechiel tells Jung that one of "the dead" stands behind him

> panting from rage and despair at the fact that your stupor does not attend to him. He besieges you in sleepless nights, sometimes he takes hold of you in an illness, sometimes he crosses your intentions.[60]

Jung is told that he must redeem "those roaming dead" and restore what was "created and later subjugated and lost. . . . Every step upward will restore a step downward so that the dead will be delivered into freedom."[61] Malidoma Some would put it more simply. We will see the ancestors smile when we are listening and being responsive to them in ways which restore balance and harmony.

From all the historical records and his letters, Roger seemed to be a highly spirited, vigorous and expressive man. This was not my experience of him in our imaginal dialogues until recently. When I encountered Roger for the first time as an imaginal figure in the transferential dialogue presented in the first chapter, he wore black, was old, haggard, lame, bent over and emanated a feeling of resignation—the kind of resignation one has when one is utterly defeated and without hope. He remained this way for over nine years. I don't know what Roger's relationship with God was after Providence was burned. I can imagine that he may have felt betrayed by God in the way Job had. I also imagine that his experiences during and after that war were far from experiences of divine providence. In fact, I would guess that he had a difficult time with theological ideas about the ways God demonstrated his favor in this world. I know that the story of Job was one that he spent a significant amount of time contemplating. When I entered therapy for the first time I realized at the heart of my suffering was feeling betrayed and abandoned by God. As I do this work of reintegration, Roger, as an imaginal presence, appears to be transforming. He is more joyful. I've even seen him dancing and smiling.

Stephen Aizenstat, who created the practice of Dream Tending, suggests that as we tend our dreams and the figures who inhabit that landscape, both we and the figures individuate.[62] Aizenstat states that these figures, in particular

> those who carry the intelligence of the ancestors, are at the core of our personal maturation. As they open to their own depth, we open to ours. As we witness their changes, we understand the forces that influence our behavior.[63]

The relationship between the ancestors and their living descendants, as Aizenstat observes, is reciprocal. If this is true it suggests that bringing consciousness to the ways my story is connected and an answer to Roger's, engaging in an ongoing dialogue and taking appropriate action in the present in response, is transformative for both of us. What is most important to me is that he is smiling for the first time in a long time as the weight of history is lifted.

Roger died sometime in the winter of 1683. He was buried in his family plot next to his wife Mary at his farm on the hill overlooking Providence. The Rhode Island Historical Society decided to exhume his body so they could give him a more elaborate burial befitting the man who they credited with founding Rhode Island. Great care was taken in this exhumation. They found greasy soil where Roger had been buried which indicated there had been human remains in the ground, but not a single bone or vestige of bone was discovered. Instead of a body there was the root of an apple tree. The root grew into the grave entering where Roger's head would have been and grew down through his remains. As documented in the historical papers of the Rhode Island Historical Society the root followed

> the direction of the back bone to the hips, and thence divided into two branches, each following a leg bone to the heel, where they both turned upwards towards the extremities of the toes of the skeleton.[64]

The body of this man, whose concept of Christianity and worldview were challenged in this new world, transformed into the root of an apple tree in the land that he perceived as "a gift of love." His body would gradually become one with this tree, literally rooted in this land. This root, severed and exhumed, is now on display in the carriage house behind the John Brown House, a well-known historical landmark and museum.

Malidoma Some describes the way Dagara ancestors are represented on their ancestor altars. The female ancestors are represented by a wooden stool, male ancestors by a wooden stick shaped like an upside down Y.[65] The root that stands in a case in the old carriage house, the root of the apple tree that incorporated itself into Roger's body, is in the shape of a male ancestor. For over a century and a half, his body went through a process of transformation in the land that had been given to him under the same kind of tree that Eve and Adam had eaten the fruit from in the Garden of Eden. His body naturally became, in the truest sense of nature-ally, the shape the Dagara use to represent and provide a place for the spirits of their ancestors. For the Dagara, an object like this tree root is not merely a representation of the ancestor; the spirit of the ancestor is actually in the root. From this perspective and given all that has been projected onto this root in the many times it has been viewed, I would imagine it is full of spirit.

His body becoming rooted in this land is a striking metaphor for being indigenous to the land. That it was the root of an apple tree is especially interesting given its association with wisdom, knowledge, the fall from grace, and expulsion from Paradise.[66] It is as if through his body, after death, the opposites he struggled with in life—nature and heaven, heart and head, "savage" and civilized, Pagan and Christian, good and evil—were symbolically and literally reconciled. For me, discovering the story of the tree root, given Roger's personal struggle between Pagan and Christian, was quite amazing in its metaphorical significance. Its shape, exactly formed by nature into the Dagara representation of a male ancestor, places this discovery in the realm of mystery. Roger was an important elder during his life. It would seem that in his death he became an ancestor not only in memory and spirit, but in the actuality of his newly formed "body."

This root remained in the basement of the Historical Society, unavailable for public viewing, until 2007. One hundred-and forty-seven years after it was exhumed from the grave, it was finally moved to the old carriage house behind the John Brown House and placed on display. The timing of this second "exhumation" from the underground part of the house that has the responsibility of gathering and holding pieces of Rhode Island History is personally meaningful. It occurred as I was writing my dissertation, becoming consciously aware of these previously unconsciously experienced ancestral connections, discovering and exploring the ways Roger's story was present in my own.

Many biographies have been written about Roger in the centuries following his death. Rubertone sees Roger as more than a historical figure, for he has taken his place among "folk heroes in American mythology."[67] His image would change over time, reflecting popular collective ideas and the interpretive needs of the times.[68] Tracing the cultural imagination of Williams over time, he has been identified as "the favorite son, the hero of the Revolution, the statesman of the Republic, the man of impeccable character to American Anglophiles, the ordinary person, the democratic visionary and the leader in the cause of freedom."[69] How he is remembered and how his story is told is mythic even in its depiction of his personal and America's cultural history. I would suggest that our family stories as they are created and shared and the stories of our ancestors as they are passed down through the generations become mythic in nature. They are in the particularities of remembered "facts," myths that are rooted in our personal and collective history.

Using Roger's story to understand and amplify my own, in a way similar to the way one would use myths or fairy tales, provides meaningful insight into my personal suffering and the questions that inform my life.[70] His struggle between head and heart, between "savage" spirituality and Christianity, his wish that two very different cultures could co-exist and benefit and learn from each other, couldn't be resolved peacefully in his time. Held in the unconscious, in the land of the dead, it found its way into this time through me.[71] What my ancestor Roger Williams began in his book, *A Key into the Language of America*, originally published in 1643, as a dialogue between two languages and cultures, exists now in me as a living dialogue of consciousness, as irreconcilable differences in my marriage and as a deeply rooted grief that is the legacy of a collectively shared history and cultural and ecological wound. Adding my life, my story, may contribute in some small way to the evolution of this deeply rooted conflict. My hope is that as our consciousness evolves collectively, the dream Roger had will also evolve and take root in this land much as Roger's body did.

I learned from Clark's mother that, following John Cotton's death, there was a comet in the sky for several days. She said people saw this as his soul, bright and shining, on its way to heaven. Cotton died on December 23, 1652. There was indeed a comet associated with his death. According to White, comets, from the point of view of the Bible, were seen by Samuel Danforth of Massachusetts as "portentous signals of great and notable changes."[72] The comet that appeared in 1652 was especially noted as such. Appearing just before Cotton became sick and disappearing seven days after his death, it was seen as "testimony that God had then removed a bright star and a shining light out of the heaven of his Church here into celestial glory above."[73] Cotton ascended to heaven and Williams became rooted in this land. It seems our ancestors had different paths in life that are reflected in the stories of their deaths. Their stories in life and in death, and now centuries later, continue to speak to aspects of the story of Europeans on this continent—historically, theologically, and psychologically, and to the evolution of consciousness that is occurring according to Bernstein.

The story of our ancestors in the actuality of its history is mythic even as this myth is rooted in history. These men were significant enough in their time to be remembered and written about centuries later by historians. After discovering Clark and I had ancestors who had known each other well and shared in a part of this country's history, I realized that their initial meeting and originally shared spiritual beliefs and vision as well as their eventual passionate disagreements were mirrored in Clark's and my relationship. Clark and I reenacted some of the spirit and substance of our ancestors' relationship.

Clark and I met each other through a spiritual group that was outside the mainstream of organized, traditional religion. It was based in California, a continent rather than an ocean away from where we lived. Eventually, Clark would decide to move to California to be closer to the center of this spiritual community. After our decision to get a divorce, we decided, for the sake of our daughters, that it would be best if I moved too. Clark stayed in Maryland for a time and I moved across the country to continue studying depth psychology at Pacifica Graduate Institute. I ended up living in a community called Painted Cave in the mountains within walking distance of many painted Chumash caves. My ancestor in exile moved to the land of the Narragansett. I found it interesting that after leaving Maryland and "Our Lady's Manor," the new home I found, after looking at many, was less than a mile from a preserved Chumash cave. I'm very grateful that I didn't have to spend months walking through the woods in the middle of a New England winter to get to my new home!

Just as our ancestors had, Clark and I initially shared the same beliefs, but, as time went on, our spiritual beliefs and political philosophies diverged. My roots in Christianity were authentically strong. After all, I was descended from a long line of ministers. Christ continued to appear to me in dreams, even as my spiritual practice became more and more rooted to the land and nature. Clark's spirituality remained rooted in transcendence. Although we do not share all the particularities of our ancestors' opinions or beliefs, of course, it seemed to me that something essential to the nature of the disagreements, which tied our ancestors together in the past, continued in the present in new ways through our relationship.[74] Using Jung's energic model of the psyche and the differentiated levels of the collective unconscious, it appeared to me that the emotional remnants of their relationship still had potency, which produced effects in the present in Clark's and my relationship.

Although I feel a personal connection with Roger Williams, Clark does not feel this with Cotton. It seems that what is most relevant for him in our ancestors' story is the interpersonal connection. If individual lives are informed by the unanswered questions of our ancestors, it is also possible that this is the case on an interpersonal level as well. When I was writing this book I discovered an interesting fact about the ongoing very public debate between Cotton and Williams. When Roger was writing his response to Cotton's *The Bloody Tenet Washed*, Cotton was in the last year of his life. He died before it was published. Gaustad believes "[had] it not been for his death, the argument might have gone on for another thirty years, each convinced of the rectitude of his own position, each convincing the other of very little."[75] It seems that their debate although temporarily put to rest by Cotton's death continued a few centuries later in Clark's and my relationship.

Our relationship was a new book being written about an old story or a revised edition of works, so to speak, that had been published over three centuries ago. Having this perspective made a difference in my experience of our marriage, separation, divorce, and our relationship in the years that have followed. I keep in mind the history that seems to be carried in our bones and psyches and hold an intention that in some way our relationship will move the story forward rather than unconsciously reenacting the past. even if past tensions have resurfaced in the present time.

"The Dead Need Salvation"[76]

I conducted many ancestor dialogues inviting both of our ancestors into the conversation.[77] I saw, imaginally, and felt the real substance of the ties that bound these two men. I felt bound to and by their history together. It seemed that in some way the process of our divorce was tied to their relationship. The divorce took time and seemed to move forward as I conducted the dialogues. I wondered what it was that was being asked of us by the ancestors at this moment in time in response to their past relationship. During one of our conversations about the specifics of our divorce agreement, I jokingly said to Clark that Roger had lost more than one home as a result of his ancestor's actions and that he owed me some kind of reparation for the losses. That day he was reading the *New York Times*, and came across a book review of a newly released book written about Roger. He considered it a synchronicity and called to tell me about it. Understanding the way our story was related to the story of our ancestors gave us a broader perspective from which to consider the choices we were making as we moved out of the marriage.

In an ancestor dialogue I conducted involving these two men as imaginal figures during our divorce negotiations, I stood facing the ocean, leaning for support against a large boulder. Objects from nature—stones, sticks, shells—representing various ancestor figures including Cotton and Williams were placed in a circle in the sand in front of me. I was part of the circle. During the dialogue, I experienced an intensity of feeling which I had come to know was ancestral and collective as well as personal. I brought my full attention to these feelings. As I did this, the feelings intensified. I closed my eyes, turning my focus to this very real imaginal reality. I saw our ancestors and I saw and felt the tie that bound them. I stayed with the complexity and intensity of feelings that seemed to connect them to each other and me to them as I leaned against the rock for support. In one moment, the tie broke and dissolved. It just happened. There were no actions, no particular dialogue was taking place, just my willingness to fully experience the nature and reality of their connection and my hope, intention, and prayer that somehow, by bringing conscious awareness to this, something in this centuries-old tie might be revealed that would help with the story as it was being lived in the present. As the tie between them dissolved, I felt a personal sense of release.

Skeptical, as always, I wondered if this was just my imagination. I heard "open your eyes." It was not a human voice, but the voice that I have come to know as an energetic, not physically embodied, presence. Still needing time to recover from the emotional intensity of the dialogue, I wanted to gain a sense of balance and return to full waking, daylight consciousness gradually. I heard again, "open your eyes." As I opened them, I saw a white Scottie dog walk through the council circle of objects. He moved toward the two stones that represented John and Roger. Brushing past them, "Roger" fell into the circle toward me. "John" fell out of the circle toward the ocean. No other object in the circle, even those that were beside the objects representing John and Roger, was moved. Shortly after this, Clark and I, four years after we had separated, signed our divorce agreement.

What do I make of this? Without moving into metaphysical territory but trying to stay within the context of depth psychology, and at the same time pushing at its edges, here is my current way of thinking about what this one example might suggest. Is it possible that there is a resonant connection between the emotional reality of our ancestors' past and our relationships in the present? And, if that is so, what is the particular nature of that connection and how is it expressed? Is there an ancestral level or component to our complexes? My experience of release suggests that this might be so. The integration of the unconscious, shadow aspects of complexes may be facilitated by bringing awareness to this level.

Going through the process of the divorce and in the years that followed, I wondered if my feelings of betrayal by Clark echoed those of Roger's by John Cotton. I discovered that just as my personal trauma was a portal into the historical and collective trauma, my personal sense of betrayal and loss in my relationship with Clark, was the portal and connection to Roger's sense of betrayal.

Roger hoped that the English and Native Americans could live side by side in a peaceful coexistence. This vision informed the way the division of land, the government and the right to freely worship which included non-conversion of the Indians, was conceived and implemented in Providence. He devoted much of his energy and time to negotiating peace between the English and Indians. He watched as treaty after treaty was violated and witnessed Europeans misappropriating more and more land. The conflict between the English and people native to the North American continent was at the heart of the conflict between Clark's and my ancestors.

While writing this chapter I reconnected with the betrayal Roger felt when he was exiled from Massachusetts. The dreams that came, the ancestor dialogues I conducted and what was actually occurring in my relationship with Clark while I was writing this chapter, all served to bring consciousness to the reality of that part of Roger's experience. Doing the psychological work at the personal biographical level was important. Connecting my experience of betrayal with Roger's and with the people native to this land was necessary for the multi-leveled aspects of this complex to be transformed. Until I experienced the ancestral and cultural level of this betrayal, nothing would have been enough to counter that centuries old wound. As the integration of the particular pieces of this complex occurred, more meaningful reparative and restorative actions could be imagined and taken.

I would guess that many readers have questions about whether or not this is mere fantasy and projection. It is a question I continue to ask. If it is, there is still therapeutic value in engaging in dialogue with the ancestors in this way. Personally, I have come to experience and understand the ancestors in a way that is similar to that of the Dagara or the Sioux, and, the way it seems that Jung experienced them as depicted in the dialogues in *The Red Book*. One of the questions people often ask when they begin to work with me is if their experiences of the ancestors are really real. There are many times when something comes to light in a dialogue that a person then discovers actually happened in the life of an ancestor. The are many examples of this in the other stories shared in this book. Each reader will have to come to a personal understanding from their own experience.

As of this writing, four more years have passed since the dialogue described above took place. Signing the divorce agreement, from this vantage point, appears to have been an ending as well as a beginning. While the tie that bound Roger and John was severed in an instant during the ancestor dialogue, the threads of those ties in the reality of embodied physical time and space have taken more time to be released and, I would suggest, reconfigured and transformed. In the process of writing this book, I've been revisiting the experiences I'm sharing on these pages. It is clear to me now that there was more work to do, more that needed to happen in this time, in response to what had happened between our ancestors in the seventeenth century. As I learned from Malidoma, a sacrifice was necessary—one which was proportional to the energetic "heat" that characterized the conflict between our ancestors and specific to the nature of the betrayal and wounding.

The details of this sacrifice are extremely personal. For many reasons I choose to keep them private. Through insights gained from ancestor dialogues and dreams, I have come to realize that the salvation for Roger, and, I would suggest, for future generations in my lineage, comes from making a willing sacrifice that is proportional and homeopathically formulated to the centuries old ancestral wound. In his dialogue with the spirit of the times and the spirit of the depths in *The Red Book*, Jung struggles with the split within the image of God, science, and faith. The spirit of the depths tells Jung, "Sacrifice is not destruction, sacrifice is the foundation stone of what is to come."[78]

Always the skeptic, I wondered if this notion of sacrifice was merely a rationalization that would help me deal with the necessary losses. A few months after writing this section, as I neared completion of the book, my younger daughter Margaret was in Detroit doing service work in community gardens. She called me late one night very excited and left a message to call her immediately. She had talked with a man who talks with the ancestors and wanted to share what he said with me.

Having just met her and without knowing anything about her family, he began talking about me. He identified some very specific things that were unknown to anyone except close family and friends. One of the things he told her was that the relationship between Clark and me had to be severed. He didn't understand why, if we were divorced, we were still so connected. He said that it was important and necessary that this be done completely and finally. He said it would require a sacrifice on my part. Once that was done and the ties that bound us were released, Clark and I would both be happier, life would be easier, and each of us would be more successful with our work. The information was synchronistic and stunningly validating.

Gathering Up the Loose Ends of the Ages

In *The Red Book,* in the section called "One of the Lowly," Jung encounters a man dirtily clothed, with only one eye and a black stubble beard. Regarding his "companion with feeling," Jung sees that "he lives the history of the world."[79] From the content of the conversation it appears that it is the history of the European world. I wondered if, would even suggest that, the figure of Roger as I first encountered and have known him over these last nine years, like this figure in *The Red Book,* was living the history of his times. Roger was an important figure in the seventeenth century in both England and New England. While a man of his times he also seemed to have ideas that have come to be associated with the ideals of the United States and democracy as well as its shadow. In the centuries that followed he, his ideas, and his story have continuing relevance and have become part of our collective story.

Ezechiel, in their dialogue in *Liber Secundus, Nox Secunda*, tells Jung,

> I see behind you . . . the crush of dangerous shadows, the dead, who look greedily through the empty sockets of your eyes, who moan and hope to gather up through you all the loose ends of the ages, which sigh in them.[80]

Perhaps "telling the story," as I was invited to do in that first dialogue, contributes in some small way to gathering up some of the loose ends of our collective story.

CHAPTER 4

Jung and the Land of the Dead

You are an image of the unending world, all the last mysteries of becoming and passing away live in you.[1]

—The spirit of the depths to Jung in *The Red Book*

In his autobiography, in the chapter "On Life after Death," Jung writes, "my works . . . are fundamentally nothing but attempts, ever renewed, to give an answer to the question of the interplay between the 'here' and the 'hereafter.'"[2] He devoted his life to trying "to see the line which leads through my life into the world, and out of the world again."[3] As Jung would come to understand, what is unresolved, unredeemed, and unanswered has continued vitality in the unconscious and can be heard in the moans, hopes, and lament of the dead. The stories that will be presented in the following chapters are illustrative of some of the ways the ancestors are dynamically involved in our personal and collective experience in the present from the perspective of Jung's work as it relates specifically to these dynamics.

The Red Book and *Memories, Dreams, Reflections* are the autobiographical bookends to Jung's life's work. His encounter with the unconscious, now visible in the text and images in *The Red Book*, would serve as the foundation for the theoretical work that followed. The *Collected Works* and the other volumes that have been published where Jung defines and elaborates the characteristics of and dynamics between consciousness and the unconscious, are framed by his encounter with the unconscious and his reflections on a life devoted to the exploration of the unconscious. *The Red Book* is a record of dialogues between Jung and the figures of the unconscious that presents a story about and an expanded picture of reality. While Jung's theoretical works remain within a medical and scholarly framework congruent with the times, *The Red Book* offers a broader perspective on the nature of being and what is real from the spirit of the depths. I will go into this in more detail in the chapters that follow. But first, let's start with

Jung's ideas as he presented them to the world before *The Red Book* was published.

This chapter provides a depth psychological foundation, from a Jungian perspective, for understanding the relationship between the living and the dead, specifically, the way each of our lives is part of a continuing story in which our ancestors and descendants are a part. The stories and ideas presented in this chapter provide information regarding the nature, dynamics and figures as it pertains to the ancestors. We'll look specifically at Jung's psychological understanding of the existence of consciousness after death and the relationship between the living and the dead. Included in this chapter are Jung's ideas about the evolution of the soul after death and the nature and dynamics of psychological inheritance. The chapter that follows will focus specifically on the relationship between the land and those who are born to, and, who live on that land.

Questions of the Soul after Death

The psyche in its deepest reaches, participates in a form of existence beyond space and time, and thus partakes of what is inadequately and symbolically described as eternity.[4]

—C. G. Jung

One cannot talk about Jung and the ancestors without talking about "the dead" and the experience of death itself. Jung's father died early in 1896, shortly after Jung began his studies at the University of Basel. Six weeks after his death he appeared to Jung in a dream. He told his son that he had recovered and was coming home. In the dream Jung felt ashamed for having imagined that his father was dead. Two days later, the dream returned. This experience was "unforgettable" and it "forced" Jung "for the first time to think about life after death."[5] In response to these dreams Jung would ask, "What does it mean that my father returns in dreams and that he seems so real?"[6] Thus began Jung's interest in the dead and their communications with the living. The experience of a dream figure as very real, in some way both dead and alive, would return years later during Jung's confrontation with the unconscious.

In his second semester at the University of Basel, Jung came across a book on spiritualistic phenomena. The stories he read were similar to the stories he had heard "again and again in the country since [his] earliest childhood."[7] Jung recognized the authenticity of material on spiritualistic phenomena but did not find information which answered the question of whether or not the soul or some part of one's consciousness has some continuity of existence after death. Being a scientist, a man of his times, and his father's son, this was an important, deeply significant and meaningful question. Being Jung, understanding the nature of these experiences informed and became a significant part of his life's work, which had as its "cardinal question—the objective nature of the psyche."[8]

The foundation of human consciousness, according to Jung, derives from hundreds of thousands of years of collective physical and psychological experiences. This shared foundation instills "into our inmost hearts this profound intuition of the 'eternal' continuity of the living."[9] Our sense of immortality is a natural activity of psyche which "transcends the limits of consciousness."[10] This sense of the eternal continuity of the self which

> embraces our whole living organism, not only contains the deposit and totality of all past life, but is also a point of departure, the fertile soil from which all future life will spring. This premonition of futurity is as clearly impressed upon our innermost feelings as is the historical aspect.[11]

Theoretically Jung distinguished between a metaphysical and psychological understanding of the meaning and nature of the soul. Jung answers the question about whether or not some aspect of consciousness is immortal from a psychological perspective concluding that

> the autonomy of the soul-complex naturally lends support to the notion of an invisible, personal entity that apparently lives in a world very different from ours. Consequently, once the activity of the soul is felt to be that of an autonomous entity having no ties with our mortal substance, it is but a step to imagining that this entity must lead an entirely independent existence, perhaps in a world of invisible things. Yet it is not immediately clear why the *invisibility* of this independent entity should simultaneously imply its *immortality*. The quality of immortality might easily derive from another fact. . . . namely the characteristically historical aspect of the soul.[12]

In 1958, three years before his own death, Jung visited a small psychology study group in Basel. He was asked several questions about whether or not individual consciousness continues after death. Jung responded saying that this is a very difficult question, one that was put to Lord Buddha twice. Both times Buddha left the question open, although it is well known that he was aware of 560 previous incarnations. Although the question of continuing consciousness after death can be understood psychologically, according to Jung, it is impossible to answer questions regarding immortality with any certainty. His response to the question:

> We are not in a position to prove that anything of us is necessarily preserved for eternity. But we can assume with great probability that something of our psyche goes on existing. Whether that part is in itself conscious, we don't

know either. There is also the consideration, based on experience, that any split-off part of the psyche, if it can manifest itself at all, always does so in the form of a personality, as though it possessed a consciousness of itself. . . . All split-off complexes speak in personal form whenever they express themselves. You can, if you like, or if you feel the need, take this as an argument in favor of a continuity of consciousness. In general one could say that since consciousness is an important psychic phenomenon, why shouldn't it be just that part of the psyche which is not affected by space and time? In other words, *it goes on existing relatively outside space and time, which would by no means be a proof of immortality, but rather an existence for an indefinite time after or beyond death.*[13] (italics added)

Jung had many personal experiences of the presence of the ancestors as evidenced in his encounters with the figures in *The Red Book* and in his dreams as described in his autobiography. The dream of his father in 1896 was the first of these encounters with the dead. This dream occurred seventeen years before Jung began recording his experiences of his encounters with the unconscious which later became the basis for *The Red Book*. Although the question of the immortality of the soul remains a question for Jung, his response to the study group in Basel suggests that some aspect of consciousness does have a continued existence after the physical body dies.

Whatever is actually so, his theoretical assertions provide us with a way to psychologically understand the "reality" of the ancestors. Based on Jung's description of the nature of psyche, the traces and echoes of our ancestors' consciousness exists within, beside, around, and through this three-dimensional existence, outside the bounds of time and space. Their presence is most frequently experienced as personified, autonomous figures in dreams, visions, and active imagination. Our collective history, memories of the past, and a potential future exist within these echoes.

The Collective Unconscious

And this structure tells its own story, which is the story of mankind; the unending myth of death and rebirth, and of the multitudinous figures who weave in and out of this mystery.[14]

—C. G. Jung, "The Role of the Unconscious"

The collective unconscious has and is its own story. Jung's conceptualization and experiences of the collective unconscious provides a model which serves well as a framework for understanding the ways in which the ancestors are a living reality in the present moments of our lives. Originally, his understanding of the unconscious was similar to Freud's. Two dreams in 1912 would change this. The first dream deeply stirred Jung and activated a series of fantasies. "One fantasy kept returning; there was something dead present, but it was also still alive."[15] This series of fantasies and the questions they provoked were resolved in a second dream. In this dream Jung saw before him a long row of tombs similar to the lane of sarcophagi in Alyscamps which went back to Merovingian times.

The dead lay on stone slabs, hands clasped, dressed in clothes from specific times in history. These figures, however, were not hewn in stone as in "old church burial vaults."[16] They appeared to be mummified. On the first tomb lay a man from the 1830s. Jung walked down the lane of sarcophagi, through the centuries, looking at each tomb, figure by figure. As he looked at each figure, its hands unclasped and the figure came to life until he reached the last figure, a man from the twelfth century. The twelfth-century figure was different than the others in composition. This man seemed to be carved from wood. Jung describes what happened. "For a long time I looked at him and thought he was really dead. But suddenly I saw that a finger of his left hand was beginning to stir gently."[17]

This dream challenged and changed Jung's understanding of the unconscious. The figures on the sarcophagi came to life as Jung viewed them. He would conclude that the unconscious is not merely the repository of "vestiges of old experiences" as described by Freud.[18] More than a collection of repressed memories which the conscious mind wants to be rid of, it is "a natural organ with its own specific creative energy."[19] Dreams as well as Jung's "actual experiences of the unconscious, taught [him] that such contents are not dead, outmoded forms, but belong to our living being."[20]

About a year after having this dream Jung would begin writing the Black Books which contained the material he used to compose *The Red Book*. Ezechiel's words to Jung in *The Red Book* convey the reality of the collective unconscious. He tells Jung,

> These figures are the dead, not just your dead, that is, all the images of the shapes you took in the past, which your ongoing life had left behind, but also the thronging dead of human history, the ghostly procession of the past, which is an ocean compared to the drops of your own life span.[21]

This ghostly procession of the past is a powerful image which represents the collective unconscious in a personified way. *The Red Book* provides a dialogical model for tending the figures of this land of the dead, the ancestors.

This experience, the dream following Jung's father's death, and the dream of the figures on the sarcophagi were experiences of the dead *and* in

Jung's experience, very much alive, very real, autonomous figures of psyche. The understanding Jung gathered from these dreams would provide the foundation for his concept of archetypes and the collective nature of the unconscious. Viewing the figures in this dream as archetypal presences allows for an expanded interpretive field and understanding of the origins of the psyche and the fundamental nature and purpose of dreams. This understanding opens and creates a framework for experiencing the actuality of the continuing presence of the ancestors in our lives. According to Smith in *Jung and Shamanism in Dialogue*, "Jung's understanding of a deeper collective dimension to the psyche brought him close to the ancestral soul theory of primitive psychology and shamanism."[22]

In personifying the unconscious, Jung imagines it as the quintessential, archetypal, ancestor. He suggests, we might think of the unconscious

> as a collective human being combining the characteristics of both sexes, transcending youth and age, birth and death, and from having at its command a human experience of one to two million years, practically immortal. . . . It would be a dreamer of age-old dreams and . . . an incomparable prognosticator. It would have lived countless times over again the life of the individual, the family, the tribe, and the nation, and it would possess a living sense of the rhythm of growth, flowering, and decay.[23]

Although, according to Jung in his essay "Archaic Man," the modern human has learned to differentiate "what is subjective and psychic from objective and 'natural'"[24] at the deeper levels of the human psyche we are archaic in nature. Our consciousness, rooted in the collective unconscious ties us to our human, ancestral, and "primitive," instinctual nature, to the animal ancestors, to the land, and to all of nature. According to Jung, the processes in the unconscious affect civilized humans as much as they do "primitives." Although our modern explanations and understanding of the world are for the most part based in ideas of causality and scientific reasoning, we are, in fundamental ways, not that different than "primitive" humans.

Our inheritance is composed of psyche, matter, and spirit. The matter of our bones and the contents of the psyche are a result of, and connect us to, our origins. Through our birth we are each related to a family, a place, a nation, a time, and to that "mighty deposit of ancestral experience" described above. Our physical and psychic heritage has deep roots. Our individual existence, through our collective heritage, reaches back millions of years. There are those ancestors from whom we are physically descended, ancestors who appear in a variety of forms in accordance with particular familial, national, and cultural milieu; there are archetypal ancestors that are part of our common human heritage; there are ancestral presences that are specific and particular to a place and there are our animal ancestors, as well as ancestors of particular scholarly and spiritual lineages.

In 1944 Jung had a heart attack. In coming close to death himself, he experienced visions and hallucinations in the weeks that followed. During one of these visions he saw an illuminated room where he knew he

> would meet there all those people to whom I belong in reality. There I would at last understand—this too was a certainty—what historical nexus I or my life fitted into. I would know what had been before me, why I had come into being, and where my life was flowing. My life as I lived it had often seemed to me like a story that has no beginning and no end.[25]

In meeting these people to whom he belonged, these "illustrious ancestors," Jung knew he would find answers to his questions regarding the way his life fit into a flowing continuous story informed by "what had been before and what would come after."[26] He knew this with certainty. In meeting these people, Jung knew he would have a more comprehensive understanding of the "particular assumptions" that accompanied him into and informed his life and the ways in which his individual life served as a link in a chain of questions, answers, and intentions which both preceded him and would continue evolving after his death. He became conscious of the way his life existed within an ever evolving larger ancestral and collective story.[27]

Jung and the Spirits of the Dead

The psyche might be that existence in which the hereafter or the land of the dead is located.[28]

—C. G. Jung

Descriptions of experiences in which the dead or ancestral figures break through into consciousness in dreams and in visionary experiences are found throughout Jung's autobiography. The experience of spirits and a spirit world, according to Jung, is not an invention "in the sense that fire-boring was an invention."[29] It is, he claims, "one of the earliest and most universal acquisitions of humanity: it is nothing less than the conviction of a spirit world" based on the experience of and "conscious acceptance of a reality in no way inferior to that of the material world."[30]

From his personal experiences and those of his pupils and patients, Jung postulates that lying behind or beneath our three-dimensional world there is another order of things which operates outside of the laws of cause and effect and in which time and space are relative. In his lecture to a study group in Basel, Jung is quoted as having said:

We must reckon with the fact that this empirical world is in a sense appearance, that is to say it is related to another order of things below it or behind it, where "here" and "there" do not exist; where there is no extension in space, which means that space doesn't exist, and no extension in time, which means time doesn't exist.[31]

In a letter written in 1939 to Pastor Pfafflin, Jung writes that "psychologically and empirically, [the unconscious] results in manifestations of the continual presence of the dead and their influence on our dream life."[32] In a rather poetic passage Jung describes the collective unconscious as

the mysterious background, which from time immemorial peopled the nocturnal shadows of the primeval forest with the same yet ever-changing figures, seems like a distorted reflection of life during the day, repeating itself in the dreams and terrors of the night. Shadowily they crowd round, the revenants, the spirits of the dead, fleeting memory-images from the prison of the past whence no living thing returns, or feelings left behind by some impressive experience and now personified in spectral form.[33]

Aniela Jaffe, a student of Jung's, wrote a book about the experiences people have of ghosts and spirits. The material that provided the basis for Jaffe's exploration came from over 1200 letters written in response to an inquiry in a popular Swiss journal, the *Schwiezerisher Beobachter*, in 1954 and 1955 about such experiences. She notes that the experiences described in these letters "have been recorded at all times and all over the world in a similar way."[34] Civilization and the development of a differentiated ego may result in changes in our worldview and our perception of ourselves in relationship with the spirits of the dead, but psychologically and phenomenologically their presence continues to have its effects. Although we may not see our ancestors in the mountains or trees or a hawk, in the way the Dagara or Sioux see them, they exist as personified figures in the reality of the unconscious.

Originally Jung attributed the parapsychic phenomenon of communications from spirits to spontaneous irruptions of collective, unconscious contents, personifications of powerful affect. He states:

These phenomena exist in their own right, regardless of the way they are interpreted, and it is beyond all doubt that they are genuine manifestations of the unconscious. The communications of "spirits" are *statements about the unconscious psyche*, provided that they are really spontaneous and are not cooked up by the conscious mind.[35]

In a footnote Jung added fifty years later to his essay, "The Psychological Foundation of Belief in Spirits," Jung states that he is no longer as certain as he was in 1919 about "the whole question of the transpsychic reality immediately underlying the psyche."[36] By the time Jung writes

his autobiography, his observations have led him to conclude that the figures of the unconscious are often indistinguishable from the "spirits of the
departed."[37] After years of experiences with many people and many cultures the question still remains for him as to "whether the ghost or the voice
is identical with the dead person or is a psychic projection, and whether the
things said really derive from the deceased or from knowledge which may
be present in the unconscious."[38]

One such irruption of the collective unconscious into consciousness
occurred on a warm summer Sunday afternoon in 1916. Everyone in Jung's
household heard the front doorbell ringing frantically. Jung, sitting near the
doorbell, not only heard it ringing, but saw the doorbell moving. When
they all looked to see who was there, there was no one in sight. Days before
this event, Jung had "the strange feeling that the air was filled with ghostly
entities."[39] His daughters, independent of one another, experienced haunt-
ings in the house in the days preceding this event. Jung's son had an anxiety dream the night before. At the moment the doorbell rang, Jung described
the atmosphere as being so thick that it was almost impossible to breathe.
"The whole house was filled as if there were a crowd present, crammed full
of spirits. They were packed deep right up to the door." . . . [Jung exclaimed],
"For God's sake, what in the world is this?"[40] The ghostly procession, crying out in a chorus, replied, "We have come back from Jerusalem where we
found not what we sought."[41]

This experience directly followed Jung's experience as depicted in
The Red Book, of his soul, his anima, withdrawing into the unconscious,
the "mythic land of the dead, the land of the ancestors."[42] In this land of the
unconscious, according to Jung, the anima produces

> a mysterious animation and gives visible form to the ancestral traces, the col-
> lective contents. Like a medium, it gives the dead a chance to manifest
> themselves. Therefore, soon after the disappearance of my soul the "dead"
> appeared to me, and the result was the *Septem Sermones*.[43]

In the *Septem Sermones*, the dead "addressed crucial questions to" Jung.[44]
Reflecting on this experience while writing his autobiography much later
in his life, he described how it laid the foundation for and informed the
nature of his life's work. In his words:

> From that time on, the dead have become ever more distinct for me as the
> voices of the Unanswered, Unresolved, and Unredeemed; for since the ques-
> tions and demands which my destiny required me to answer did not come to
> me from the outside, they must have come from the inner world. These con-
> versations with the dead formed a kind of prelude to what I had to communicate
> to the world about the unconscious: a kind of pattern of order and interpreta-
> tion of its general contents.[45]

This was one of Jung's many visionary and dream encounters with "the dead." He would spend the next 45 years distilling and translating what he learned in these encounters into his theoretical, scientific writings.

Thinking about the experience of Jung's in light of what I was learning from my own and other people's dialogues with the ancestors, I wondered if the dead from Jerusalem and the figures in the dream of the row of sarcophagi were connected in any way with Jung's personal ancestry and the land on which he lived. Did these figures reference particular times or particular individuals in Jung's personal or collective ancestry, or both? Had the unanswered questions of these "dead" been carried forward through Jung's lineage by familial ancestors who had lived in the periods specifically referenced in each figure's clothing? Were the origins of the unanswered question(s) which would lead Jung to his understanding of the collective unconscious and archetypes in some way directly related to ancestors who were connected to and represented by that twelfth-century figure composed of wood? Were these figures actual ancestral presences located in the land which had been home to Jung's family for many generations?

While I couldn't find anything suggesting that Jung made a connection between ancestral spirits in the land in relationship to his dream of the tombs and the horde from Jerusalem who came ringing at his door, as described in *Septem Sermones*, as I worked with the material for this chapter I began to wonder about this possibility. Might the figure from the twelfth century in the dream and the figures of the dead come back from Jerusalem reference the Second Crusades which took place in the twelfth century.[46]

Early in the twelfth century the Templar Knights were created to protect pilgrims traveling to the Holy Land. These knights also fought to regain the Holy Land for Christianity throughout the Crusades. Their order, wealth, and power grew and declined moving with the fortune of the Crusades. The Templars were persecuted in the fourteenth century by Pope Clement V. It is thought that many fled to Scotland and Switzerland, territories outside of Papal control to escape persecution. Charles Baudouin, a professor at the University of Geneva and associate of Jung's, recounts a time when Jung told him about the ancestral spirits in the land. He remembers Jung saying that the ancestral spirits of one's birthplace "fall upon one on return." Listening to Jung, Baudouin recognizes the atmospheric weight of these ancestors in a way that is very similar to Jung's description of the atmosphere prior to and during the visitation from the dead come back from Jerusalem.[47] I would suggest the possibility that the figure in the dream and in Jung's waking vision could be the ancestral spirits of Crusaders, possibly Knights Templar, and that these spirits, like other ancestral spirits were present in the land where Jung was born and lived.

Continuing to explore the warp and weft of these ancestral threads suggests another possible connection. Although there is no verifiable documentation linking the lineage of the Templar Knights to the Freemasons, the Freemasons began using many of the Templar symbols in the seventeenth century suggesting a relationship between them that is archetypally based. Jung writes that his grandfather was "an ardent Freemason and Grand Master of the Swiss Lodge."[48] He mentions this not because it is of any consequence in itself, but "because it belongs in the historical nexus of my thinking and my life."[49] He does not say more than this.

If one looks at Jung's dream from an ancestral perspective with its many levels in the collective unconscious, there seems to be a thread that runs from the national, through the tribal and familial levels into the personal, which carries the unanswered questions that inspired Jung's life and work. Considering the dream in this multileveled, multi-dimensional and very personal way, we begin to see the interconnected and complex nature of the legacies that inform each of our lives. As evidenced in the dreams, Jung's experience with the dead come back from Jerusalem, and his dialogues with Ezechiel, however one interprets these figures, history and the ancestors, far from being dead and in the past, are alive and present, a living reality in the unconscious.

Although these experiences are of a transpersonal nature, Jung states that it is likely they also reference things that are subjective and personal. Whether dream or vision, Jung found that all of these encounters in which the unconscious breaks into consciousness were "ultimately directed at this real life of mine."[50] These figures of the unconscious, "the voices of the Unanswered, Unresolved, and Unredeemed," the ancestors from different historical periods who are still alive, haunt, orient, and inform our lives in the present.[51] Jung concludes that "inner peace and contentment" depends on whether or not one creates harmony between the "historical family" and "the ephemeral conditions of the present."[52] Developing a relationship with the historical family which is inherent in each individual, the contents of the unconscious, the mythic land of the dead and the ancestors, is the work of individuation and the way in which psyche is developed or transformed. Jung's psychology rests on this foundation.

Inheritance and the Debts of Our Forebears

The less we understand of what our fathers and forefathers sought, the less we understand ourselves, and thus we help with all our might to rob the individual of his roots and his guiding instincts, so that he becomes a particle in the mass, ruled only by what Nietzsche called the spirit of gravity.[53]

—C. G. Jung

Just as our body derives from the ancestors, so does the psyche. In *Nietzsche's Zarathustra*, Jung suggests that our minds as well as our bodies consist of Mendelian like units of inheritance, fragments of the past. Consciousness is based on the foundation of "many inherited units. They are what the primitives would call ancestral spirits, remnants of ancestral lives."[54]

Consciousness, from the deepest roots in our instinctual animal-like nature to our highly developed sense of ego, is a result of the evolution of the psyche. According to Jung, as a child develops, this development, which is a result of the accumulation of the experiences of our ancestors, is repeated and re-experienced.[55] Our minds and bodies, based in this collective ancestral psyche, are not a *tabula rasa* at birth. The personality, at first, is "an absolutely irrational conglomeration of inherited units" from both our mother's and father's sides of the family tree.[56] Reaching back through the centuries, just as we might inherit the characteristics of our nose from our great grandfather on our father's side, we also inherit certain qualities, abilities, and inclinations from those to whom we belong. We may have some idea of the origins of the particular inherited units which comprise the foundation of our psyche through stories and remembrances which have been passed down through the generations. But for the most part, the origin of many of our individual characteristics remains a mystery. Who we are is very complex and can be viewed and imagined from many perspectives from biology to metaphysics. Whatever one's perspective, each of us determines how even the most biologically predetermined characteristics are expressed.

Jung likens these inherited psychological units to pieces of a puzzle. Individuation consists of putting the pieces of this puzzle together. In one lecture he stated, "You are a collection of ancestral spirits, and the psychological problem is how to find yourself in a crowd. Somewhere you are also a spirit—somewhere you have the secret of your particular pattern."[57] Putting the pieces of this puzzle together is likened to an alchemical process in which a chaotic collection of disjointed and disparate elements are, in their original condition, contained within a circle. The task of the individual is to arrange these pieces in a way which "squares the circle." A quarternity is then created, which has, as its result, at its center, a fifth essence. This *quinta essential* "is again that circle of the beginning but this circle has now the anima mundi, the soul of the world, which was hidden in chaos."[58]

Jung also likens this process of integration to his understanding of the way healing is imagined and accomplished by healers whom he refers to as "primitive medicine men." A medicine man, according to Jung, must be able to talk to the dead, must be able to reconcile them. For the dead are the makers of illnesses, causing all the trouble to the tribe . . . [the medicine man] is supposed to be able to . . . make a compromise with them, to lay them or to integrate them properly. He has to collect these spirits and make them into a whole, integrate them; the integration process, is called the carrying of the corpse of the ancestors, or the burden of the ancestors.[59]

In his introduction to Frances Wickes's, *The Inner World of Childhood*, Jung wrote, "the things which have the most powerful effect upon children do not come from the conscious state of the parents but from their unconscious background."[60] The unconscious of the parents, as discussed above, is comprised of many levels. The roots of an individual's psychological foundation are deeply interwoven into these levels. The unlived life of a child's parents, which extends into and through these levels, has the strongest effect on the child's psyche, "for we are dealing here with the age-old psychological phenomenon of original sin."[61] Jung disputes the concept that a child's identity is explained merely by a causal relationship with the parents. However, he writes,

it is not so much the parents as their ancestors—the grandparents and great-grandparents—who are the true progenitors, and . . . these explain the individuality of the children far more than the immediate . . . parents. In the same way the true psychic individuality of the child is something new in respect of the parents and cannot be derived from their psyche. It is a combination of collective factors which are only potentially present in the parental psyche, and are sometimes wholly invisible. Not only the child's body, but his soul, too, proceeds from his ancestry, in so far as it is individually distinct from the collective psyche of mankind.[62]

According to Jung, along with our individuality, the sins of our ancestors are also part of our conscious and unconscious inheritance. It is the nature of our collective inheritance based on what Jung calls the "energic" nature of psyche. Living the unlived lives of our parents is a concept that comes from a natural ethos which is compensatory in nature. According to Jung, neither education nor psychotherapy will prevent this "fate" from being realized. Jung expresses this most clearly in the following passage from his seminars on dream analysis given between 1928 and 1930:

A human life is nothing in itself; it is part of a family tree. We are continuously living the ancestral life, reaching back for centuries, we are satisfying the appetites of unknown ancestors, nursing instincts which we think are our own, but which are quite incompatible with our character; we are not living our own lives, we are paying the debts of our forefathers. This is the dogma of inherited sin. So that man may go blundering on till he is a hundred. But if one gets into the history of the family, one will see. We know too little about our forebears. We go on in a terribly one-sided way sometimes, because it makes sense as a historical compensation for ancestors who lived a hundred years ago or more, though we think they have nothing to do with our lives. This corresponds to the primitive belief in ghosts; whatever is the matter, they say it is due to an ancestral spirit.[63]

Imagining the unlived lives from the timeless and spaceless perspective of the multileveled unconscious, these unlived and yet-to-be lived lives extend through the layers from personal to primal and exist in the vastness of the unconscious of our parents in the present as well as ancestors past and our future descendants. We are, as Jung so aptly put it, "historical fragments" in a much larger story. Each of us embodies and expresses, compensates for, and dreams forward our part of this seemingly infinite ancestral story. Our fate is a result of and response to what has come before and what will follow. How all of these pieces combine in each individual is unique. Each of us is vitally necessary to the entire web of being. What remains unlived, unresolved, unredeemed and unanswered will be passed on to future generations.

Is there an effect, and if so, what is the effect of bringing conscious attention to the "ghosts" of our ancestors? At a question-and-answer session conducted at the Basel Psychology Club, Jung was asked, "Can I help the spirit of my dead father by trying to live in accordance with the demands of the unconscious?"[64] Underlying this question is a question about if and how the actions of the living affect deceased family members. Jung replied with a qualified yes. He found the first question, with its reference to living in accordance with the demands of the unconscious, too general. It is the "urgent need of the father. . . . something the father has left unfinished," according to Jung, which should be compensated, not the unconscious.[65] These relationships with the dead are only satisfactory, according to Jung, when they "fit the real character" of the deceased.[66]

He offers two specific examples of ways this could occur. In one, the father appears in a dream and tells his daughter that she must give back property which was stolen, and in another, that a particular philosophy made him unhappy and he wants the daughter to think differently. In each example, the woman's father comes in a dream with a very explicit request. A response to what is being specifically called for rather than a generalized idea of what is needed is what, according to Jung, has a positive psychological effect. One's relationship with one's ancestors must be responsive to who they were and what they did in life. Understanding the unanswered questions of one's ancestors that are personally resonant, the ancestral echoes in one's complexes, the particular character and life of an ancestor, rather than a generalized view of working with the unconscious informs how we respond.

Whatever is so regarding the nature, existence, and reality of our ancestors, Jung suggests that believing in the reality of the existence and connection with, in this case, one's dead father, contributes to psychological health. For any response to have a positive effect on one's psychological health, the reality of the spirit of the ancestor, in this case, the woman's father, must be a living idea. Imagining one's ancestors are alive in spirit, although transcendent in nature, is reasonable, as it serves a purpose. According to Jung, if one assumes that the spirit of one's ancestor

> has a subjective existence, a consciousness of its own, then there also exists an ethical relation to what it is or what it wants and what it needs. And if I live in such a way that it helps this spirit, it is a moral achievement from which I can expect satisfaction.[67]

In her book on death, dreams, and ghosts, Aniele Jaffe gives many accounts of redemption and forgiveness in which the deceased individual appears to someone who is living and asks them for help. Jaffe found that in the majority of stories and legends redemption happens as the result of the relationship between the "spirit" and a living person.[68] The following passage from her chapter on ghosts beautifully conveys what is at the heart of being in a more conscious dialogue with the ancestors. "What the legends and the letters seem to convey is the need to make peace with these powers, to listen to them, to admit them to our lives and our consciousness."[69] Only then, she says, "can the process of integration become a work of salvation for ghosts, gods and men."[70] We each only have to do our part with this one life that is ours to live in relationship with the past with an ear to the future as consciously as possible.

Unanswered Questions, Unfinished Work

I feel very strongly that I am under the influence of things or questions which were left incomplete and unanswered by my parents and grandparents and more distant ancestors.[71]

—C. G. Jung

The unanswered questions of his ancestors inspired and directed the content and course of Jung's work. Jung recognized that the ideas which came to him from his earliest childhood were both "spontaneous products which can be understood only as reactions to my parental environment and the spirit of the age."[72] In his autobiography he writes: "The meaning of my existence is that life has addressed a question to me. Or, conversely, I myself am a question which is addressed to the world."[73] It is difficult, according to Jung, to know if these unanswered questions that inform our lives are of a personal or more collective nature. I would suggest from my personal experiences and my reading of Jung that these unanswered questions often, maybe always, have both personal and collective origins.

Wondering about the more collective and ancestral origins of these unanswered questions Jung writes:

> Perhaps it is a question which preoccupied my ancestors, and which they could not answer. Could that be why I am so impressed by the fact that the conclusion of *Faust* contains no solution? Or by the problem on which Nietzsche foundered: the Dionysian side of life, to which the Christian seems to have lost the way? Or is it the restless Wotan-Hermes of my Alemannic and Frankish ancestors who poses challenging riddles?[74]

Specifically, Jung would ask and struggle with questions regarding the nature of the soul. His father's understanding of the soul was taken on blind faith—a faith that his father desperately and valiantly struggled to keep. When Jung's father was living, their discussions about matters of the soul and of faith exasperated them both. What came naturally to Jung in dreams, what he saw in "the beauty of the sunset or the terrors of the night," his father sought in theology and took on faith.[75] The "arch sin of faith," Jung writes, is that it "forestalls experience." "Blind acceptance never leads to a solution; at best it leads only to a standstill *and is paid for heavily in the next generation.*"[76] These statements seem to express the burden, the weight, Jung felt as the son of a man of unquestioning faith. What was unquestioned, out of necessity, became the burning question that underlies all of Jung's work: what is the relationship between the here and the hereafter? Blind acceptance is contrary to Jung and to his psychology. Always the scientifically oriented phenomenologist, Jung sought the answers to questions about the soul in direct experience.

Jung's professional exploration into the nature of psyche and soul would move forward significantly after his father's death. Following the death of his father, Jung's mother would speak to Jung from what he called her unconscious personality. He described this part of her personality, which appeared only now and then, as "unexpectedly powerful; a somber, imposing figure possessed of unassailable authority."[77] Following his father's death, his mother said simply, "He died in time for you," implying that the death of his father allowed Jung to move into his work in a way that wasn't possible when his father was alive.[78] The unconscious would speak to Jung again in the dream of his father returning home that is described at the beginning of this chapter.

It is interesting that Jung's father appeared to him in a dream, an experience that Jung had more than faith in. From this dream, dreamed twice, a question formed that would move the course of his work into an exploration of spiritualistic phenomena. The frustration Jung experienced in conversations with his father regarding the nature of the soul when his father was alive seemed to transform into inspiration after his death. The seeds of Jung's work were planted in this struggle. After his father's death, these seeds, watered by the unconscious, sprouted, broke through the ground and began to grow in ways that hadn't been possible when he was living.

As Jung's understanding of the relationship between the here and the hereafter deepened through his encounters with the unconscious, he developed working and evolving theories regarding the relationship between the living and the dead. For Jung, central to this relationship, were the unanswered questions asked by his "spiritual forefathers, in the hope and expectation that they would learn what they had not been able to find out during their time on earth."[79] Although, according to Jung, unlimited knowledge is present in nature, what can be known at any particular time can only be known when the time is ripe.

During the writing of *Symbols of Transformation*, Jung had a dream while on a bicycle trip. In the dream Jung is in the presence of "distinguished spirits of earlier centuries," who he refers to as the "illustrious ancestors."[80] One of these figures asks Jung a question in Latin. Not being proficient enough in Latin and unable to answer this distinguished ancestor's question, Jung felt profoundly humiliated. Upon waking, he had a sense that his work on the book would answer this man's question. His feelings of inferiority were so intense he decided to cut his bicycle trip short in order to immediately return home to continue his work on this book. Only many years later did Jung understand this dream. "The bewigged gentleman was a kind of ancestral spirit, or spirit of the dead, who had addressed questions to me."[81] The questions of these "illustrious ancestors" could not be answered in their time. They could only be answered centuries later, when the time was right. "These figures from the unconscious," Jung concludes, "are uninformed too, and need man, or contact with consciousness, in order to attain knowledge."[82]

He recounts a dream of one of his pupils as an example that supports this conclusion. It also serves as an example of this dynamic relationship between the living and the souls of the dead. His pupil's dream occurred two months prior to her death. The dreamer was in the landscape of the Hereafter. She saw several deceased friends sitting on a bench. There was a class taking place and she was looking for a teacher. Finding none, she realized that she herself was the lecturer and that she must give an account of the total experience of her life.

According to Jung, the dream indicated that "the dead were extremely interested in life experiences that the newly deceased brought with them, just as if the acts and experiences taking place in earthly life, in space and time, were the decisive ones."[83] For this audience, existing in a state that is outside the confines of time and space, even the most mundane details of the dreamer's life were interesting. Whatever knowledge individuals have attained and bring with them after their death is very important to those whose existence by nature is timeless.

One of Jung's key ideas regarding the relationship between the living and the dead is expressed in the following passage from his autobiography:

> The souls of the dead "know" only what they knew at the moment of death, and nothing beyond that. Hence their endeavor to penetrate into life in order to share in the knowledge of men. I frequently have a feeling that they are standing directly behind us, waiting to hear what answer we will give to them, and what answer to destiny. It seems to me as if they were dependent on the living for receiving answers to their questions, that is, on those who have survived them and exist in a world of change.[84]

Jung offers a psychological and theoretical way of understanding the relationship between this world and the world of the ancestors with regard to the evolution of consciousness. The souls of the dead are dependent on the living for attaining knowledge beyond what they attained in life. The unconscious, the "land of the dead," exists outside the bounds of space and time. According to Jung, the embodied, physical world is a world bounded by time. Jung describes this world as one of clashing opposites. Knowledge is generated out of this dynamic opposition in a way that Jung believes is not possible after the death of the physical body. Jung's name for the reconciliation of this dynamic opposition, this clashing of opposites, from which knowledge is generated, is the transcendent function.

The theory of the transcendent function provides the foundation for Jung's theory about psychological growth and the evolution of individual and collective consciousness. The theory of the transcendent function is at the heart of the process of individuation. The "'transcendent function' arises from the union of conscious and unconscious contents."[85] By nature, the unconscious holds a complementary, counter-position to consciousness. It serves a vital compensatory function to the ego's, one-sided standpoint. Listening to the unconscious speaking through dreams, synchronicities, symptoms, spontaneous fantasies, slips of the tongue—and, I would add, the voices of the ancestors—is essential to psychological well being. Bringing consciousness into relationship with the unconscious is vital "because the constant flow of life again and again, demands fresh adaptation."[86]

Jung further suggests that "man needs difficulties; they are necessary for health."[87] These "difficulties" are situations and experiences—physical or emotional illness, difficulties in personal relationships or at work, failures—that result in personal discomfort and suffering for which there is no rational solution. The resolution to these very human problems results from the clashing of opposites—consciousness and the unconscious—by maintaining the standpoint of the ego while allowing the unconscious its say. Jung likens this to a dialogue taking place "between two human beings with equal rights, each of whom give the other credit for a valid argument."[88] "The confrontation of the two positions generates a tension charged with energy and creates a living, third thing . . . that leads to a new level of being."[89] With regard to the "souls of the dead," Jung concludes that this dynamic tension doesn't occur in the unconscious, in the land of the dead, or for the soul after death. It only happens in this embodied reality. This conceptual understanding and way of being in relationship with the unconscious is an essential aspect of working with the material that comes up as a result of listening to the voices of the ancestors in the present. I think, for many people, *being in a conscious relationship with the ancestors is an integral and necessary part of the process of individuation.*

Several months prior to his mother's death, Jung's father returned again in a dream. Jung had not dreamed of him since his death 26 years earlier. His father appeared rejuvenated, "as if he had returned from a distant journey."[90] He had come to Jung to consult with him on marital psychology. Jung did not understand, until his mother's sudden death four months after this dream occurred, that this dream presaged her death. While acknowledging the value of interpreting this dream subjectively, Jung did not see this dream as compensatory to his conscious awareness. Instead, he saw this dream as reflective of his father's soul's need for an updated understanding of marriage prior to his wife's death. His father sought an understanding of marriage which he had not gained from his own life experiences and apparently he could not now find in his experiences in the timeless reality of the soul after death, whatever the actuality is of any existence consciousness after death.[91] He thought that his father evidently had "acquired no better understanding in his timeless state and therefore had to appeal to someone among the living who, enjoying the benefits of changed times, might have a fresh approach to the whole thing."[92] The answer to his question could only be obtained with his son's help. Jung's experience of his father's presence in the dream, as an actual visitation of his father, framed his interpretation of this dream. His father's question inspired Jung to write the essay "Marriage as a Psychological Relationship."

Mysterium Coniunctionis, Jung's last major work, was also heralded by dreams. He notes one in particular in which both his father and mother appear. In these dreams and others, his parents seem to embody something of their essential nature as described by Jung in his earlier memories of them as a boy and young man. Who they were when living and who they are in their essence are represented and recognizable in these dreams. In the dream, both of his parents "appeared burdened with the problem of the 'cure of souls,' which in fact was really my task."[93] He writes, "Something had remained unfinished and was still with my parents; that is to say, it was still latent in the unconscious and hence reserved for the future."[94] The relationship and dynamics between one's ancestors, and specifically one's parents, and the questions that inform our lives, is illustrated in Jung's interpretation and understanding of this dream.

We can surmise, if Jung is right, that the questions that were his to answer remained latent in the unconscious until the time was ripe for them to be answered. Jung's parents embodied these questions in their lives. They continued to embody the symbolic essence of these questions as dream figures after their deaths. These particular dreams provided Jung with insight into the questions that were carried through his lineage, deepened his understanding of these questions, and contributed significantly to the progression of his work. These dreams, and Jung's understanding of them, provide insights into the familial, ancestral, and cultural origins of Jung's work.

An evolution of consciousness, which occurs as a result of the relationship between the ego and the unconscious, and the relationship between the living and the dead, is implied throughout Jung's work. It is as if the questions within a lineage are carried forward through the generations. These questions are held by the ancestors in a symbolic and essential way for the living who, in this world of clashing opposites and change, can answer them and continue the story in their time. Expanding on these ideas, the ancestors seem to embody and represent who they were and the knowledge they had gained in life. They return in dreams as expressions of this knowledge, bringing questions, offering keys, and providing inspiration to their descendants.

Through his observation of dreams Jung came to the conclusion that the evolution of the soul, of consciousness, continues after death. He shares a dream that serves as an example of the way the consciousness of an individual can, and may need to, learn what it did not learn in life. In the dream, Jung was visiting a friend who had died a few weeks earlier. His friend, now physically dead but "alive" in the dream, is listening with rapt attention to his daughter, who is still very much alive. She had studied psychology in Zurich. In Jung's dream, she is telling her father about the reality of his psychic existence. Her father, who had "never espoused anything but a conventional view of the world, and had remained stuck in this unreflecting attitude," was fascinated by what his daughter was telling him.[95] Jung thought the dream indicated that his friend's soul was now required to understand what he hadn't been able to in life. Jung concludes that this man after death "was required to grasp the reality of his psychic existence, which he had never been capable of doing during his life."[96]

He reasons:

> If there were a conscious existence after death, it would, so it seems to me, have to continue on the level of consciousness attained by humanity, which in any age has an upper though variable limit. There are many human beings who throughout their lives and at the moment of death lag behind their own potentialities and—even more important—behind the knowledge which has been brought to consciousness by other human beings during their own life-times. Hence their demand to attain in death that share of awareness which they failed to win in life.[97]

Another of Jung's dreams also suggests that, if there is some conscious existence after death, the soul continues its development. About a year after his wife Emma's death, Jung had a dream which touched him deeply. He awoke knowing that he had spent an entire day with her in Provence where she was engaged in studies of the Grail, which she considered her life's work. Emma died before completing her work on the Grail Legend. Interpreting this dream subjectively, as his unfinished anima work, yielded nothing of interest for Jung. He knew consciously and "quite well" that he was not done with that.[98] Knowing that Emma continued her work after her death was deeply meaningful and reassuring for Jung. Jung's understanding of this dream and those described above suggest that the relationship between the living and the dead, with regard to unanswered questions and the generation of knowledge, is interactive and mutually transformative.

An experience Jung had prior to his wife's death alludes to the reciprocal nature of the relationship between the living and the dead. In a letter to Erich Neumann following his wife Emma's death, Jung describes a

> great illumination which, like a flash of lightning, lit up a centuries-old secret that was embodied in her and had exerted an unfathomable influence on my life. I can only suppose that the illumination came from my wife, who was then mostly in a coma, and that the tremendous lighting up and release of insight had a retroactive effect upon her.[99]

Two months after the death of his mother, Jung began building the tower at Bollingen. After his wife's death, he added an upper extension to the tower. For Jung, the tower was a "concretization of the individuation process."[100] It was a womb in which he could be reborn. The upper story, built after Emma's death, represented his ego-personality and was inspired by "an inner obligation to become what I myself am."[101] The deaths of Jung's parents and wife seemed to open new possibilities in Jung's life, to open him to parts of psyche which had previously only been there as potential.

His personal process of individuation and his theoretical work progressed in significant ways following the death of his parents and wife.

Jung spent a lifetime developing an understanding of the relationship between the here and the hereafter, the living and the dead. His thinking deepened, and his understanding changed, and evolved over time. I am deeply appreciative of Jung's openness to and understanding of experiences such as the one's shared in this chapter. His attitude and approach toward and his conclusions about the infinite reality of the psyche provides a foundation on which each of us can build.

Based on my own experience and Jung's understanding of the psyche, I would suggest that the relationships between one's self, one's parents, one's ancestors, and one's descendants are ever evolving and reciprocal in nature. The spirits of the dead, as figures "alive" in the reality of the unconscious, inform and inspire the lives of their descendants. The living, existing in a world of "clashing opposites," can engage the unanswered questions of previous generations bringing what is conscious into relationship with the unconscious in ways that contribute to the evolution of consciousness and our collective wisdom.

CHAPTER 5

Between Life and Death

Several years prior to my mother's death, I had a dream in which she lay on a table in a sleep or coma-like state. I wondered if she was close to death or even dead. My father, who had died years before, was with her. He was standing beside the table wrapping my mother in what appeared to be a kind of cocoon made from fine filaments of light. There was one window in the room. All the light in the room came from the daylight that streamed through this window. Looking through the window I could see a large, open, grassy field bordered by dense forest. My father was intent on his task. He seemed so much more alive and vital than my mother. I had a sudden insight as I watched him in the dream. I knew that he was preparing my mother's soul body for a new birth after the death of her physical body. I felt an absolute certainty about this in the dream. However, upon waking, given that my mother's death didn't seem imminent, I wondered if my understanding in the dream was accurate.

Jung's dream of his father suggests that the dead prepare for their loved one's arrival. The dream of my parents seems to suggest that the dead may also help the "soul body" of someone who is living prepare for its transition from a physically embodied state to one which is not. It's important to point out that finding a language to describe and interpret this kind of dream without implying any metaphysical truth is somewhat challenging. The figures of the unconscious always appear in personified forms. They often appear so real as to be indistinguishable from the person we knew in life. Whatever is so, these figures have psychological and archetypal weight. Dreams and imaginal dialogues may reveal certain dynamics between the ancestors and the living that are meaningful.

On the other side of reality, in this world, several years after the dream shared above and a year before my mother's death, I had an experience that seemed to be part of the process of my mother's transition from life into death. Early one morning I was shocked awake from a deep sleep. Without my conscious awareness or thought, I sat bolt upright in bed from a deep sleep, propelled by the feeling of a dark, living substance being expelled from the center of my chest. As my consciousness returned to waking, I saw a black, feminine figure above me. I knew her immediately. She was the essence of the negative, annihilating mother, an archetypal figure that was at the heart of an ancestral and cultural complex. This figure was part of the legacy of the women in my maternal lineage.[1] She circled above me in ever-widening spirals, finally disappearing as my consciousness returned fully to waking.

Death and the Complex

For many years prior to this experience I had a series of dreams in which a wound in my heart, which was filled with black, tar-like material, was being healed in a number of different ways. These dreams, although intermittent, were clearly connected through the images and feelings associated with them. In every dream my heart was wounded and a black substance was being removed, sometimes being coughed up, sometimes cleaned out by a white cloth, sometimes cleansed by special machines or by shamanic dream figures. I was told in the first dream in this series that I had been shot in the heart in a war between good and evil, another common theme for many years, and that removing the bullet too quickly would kill me.[2]

Later that day, after the experience of this black figure erupting out of my chest, I was driving down the California coast taking my daughters to visit their father for the weekend. As was our ritual during this weekly drive, we called my mother. This time she did not answer. Instead, we got a recording telling us that the phone had been disconnected. I called the phone company to find out what had happened. All they could tell me was that the phone line was disconnected. I tried calling my sisters who lived on the east coast closer to where my mother lived to alert them. They did not answer. Four days later I would finally hear from my sister. The day of the dream, the day that my daughters and I called my mother and heard that the phone line had been disconnected, she had fallen to the floor unconscious and had been rushed to the hospital with a serious, nearly fatal, case of pneumonia. At the time, we were told she would die within days. My daughters and I flew to the east coast to see her the next day. The cause of the disconnection of her phone remains a mystery. The phone company never found anything wrong with the line.

I wondered about the relationship between my visionary experience and my mother's fall to the floor which brought her close to death. Did one cause the other? While I don't know the answer to that question, what I do know is that these two events, have both psychic and material reality and weight. They *are* connected coincidentally and acausally through meaning. Jung suggests that events like this point to the underlying "unitary aspect of being which can very well be described as the *unus mundus*."[3] The *unus mundus* is the "original, non-differentiated unit of the world or of Being." According to Jung, "while the concept of the *unus mundus* is a metaphysical speculation, the unconscious can be indirectly experienced via its manifestations."[4] Jung recognized mandala symbolism as "the psychological equivalent of the *unus mundus*" and synchronicity as "its para-psychological equivalent." This underlying unitary aspect of being is apparent in my personal experiences and in the experiences of the people I work with who consciously engage in dialogues with the ancestors. The interrelated reciprocity between the psyche and physical reality, and, the dead and the living becomes visible in these experiences.

After visiting my mother for a few days, my daughters and I returned home thinking that we had seen her for the last time. A few days after returning to California, I created and opened the space for a dialogue with the ancestors outside in a natural setting in the woods. I placed objects in a circle to represent the ancestors and other dream figures.[5] I was still in shock from the events of the previous week and had a lot of questions about the relationship between my dream experience and my mother's condition. I had barely finished the opening prayer when the imaginal figure of my father appeared. He told me that it was not yet time for my mother to die. Based on what I knew, I doubted the truth of his communication. At that moment a real, not imaginal, dog entered the council circle and walked right to the spot where the stone representing my father was placed. The dog paused, and then moved to the stone which represented my mother. He paused again and then moved away from the circle and went on his way.

The two stones representing my parents were in a circle of stones along with other objects from nature used to represent various ancestors, figures from dreams. Whether or not these experiences were real or just my imagination is a question I continue to ask myself. More than healthy skepticism, in that moment, the question came from the doubts I had about my perception of reality. The dog's presence at that moment served to remind me that this process of dialogue has its own objective reality which is beyond my conscious intention or design. With regard to the truth of my father's communication, I thought, time will tell. My mother lived for another year, but never returned to live in our family home.

I remained skeptical about the reality of the soul after death for many years after this dream. Doubt about my perception of reality was a constant companion. At the end of my mother's life I had an experience in a dialogue with her that left no doubt that individual consciousness has a continued existence after death. I would suggest further, based on the dream of my father wrapping my mother's body in a cocoon, that the "soul body" exists in the psyche while we are still living.

A Parting Gift

On a Saturday morning, I received a phone call from my sister telling me that my mother was in the hospital. My mother's bowel had burst and she had been rushed to the emergency room and into surgery. Machines were now keeping her body alive, and, as per her wishes, she would be taken off the machines within an hour or so. I began to think about making plans to fly with my daughters across the country for her funeral. However, I received another call from my sister a few hours later. The hospital was not allowing hospice to step in. For legal reasons the hospital staff insisted on keeping our mother on life support. We didn't know when my mother would be allowed to die. After talking with her, I immediately went to my ancestor altar, frustrated and grieving.

Turning the corner into my home office, at the first glimpse of the altar, I saw my mother dancing, a glass of champagne in her hand. I heard laughter and music. She told me that everyone was there and it was a big celebration. It was wonderful, she said, to be free of the pain of her body. She was happier than I had seen her in decades. I couldn't help but laugh with her. I told her I was concerned about making arrangements to travel to the east coast for her funeral. One of my daughters had a week-long school trip coming up, the other had exams, I had appointments with clients, and . . . I asked her if she could tell me when she was going to die. Twirling on one foot, glass held high, she said 2 o'clock on Monday. I asked her if that was east-coast or west-coast time. She laughed and danced off, out of imaginal sight. Skeptical and doubting I wondered if this experience was really real or just a compensatory fantasy.

When I was a child, my mother repeatedly asked me, in response to stories I would tell her of my experiences, "is this real or is this your imagination?" As a child, I heard her question as a challenge to my experience of the world; of what I perceived and knew to be real and the way I knew it. It was very difficult to understand why no one else saw and heard the things I did. Although my experiences were very real to me, I very quickly became aware that my experiences were different than those of my family and friends. I learned to differentiate and separate two realities—one that was "really real" and one that was "just my imagination."

Needless to say, the ability to differentiate between what was real in this world and the imaginary world was invaluable. My mother's questioning helped me develop a strong and differentiated ego, to function in this culture and ultimately to develop the skills that are so necessary for me to do this work.

A few days later, at 2 p.m. on Monday, west coast time, I received a call from my sister. She told me that my mother had died. I thought, ah, my mother meant that she would die at 2 o'clock west coast time. My sister continued, "I didn't call you right away. I just wanted to be with Mom after she died." I asked her what time mom had actually died. She said about 2 o'clock—that would have been east coast time. My mother had managed to "die" at 2 o'clock on Monday on both coasts. Her actual death occurred at 2pm east coast time. She was "dead" in my life at 2pm west coast time. My experience of my mother in the dialogue a few days prior to her death was validated. The way my question was answered—what time was she going to die—was impossible to imagine and it was really real. It was a perfectly timed parting gift from her. In her death she affirmed the "really real" reality of those "imagined" experiences. And so she stepped out of real time into soul time.

These experiences of my mother's life and her death are examples of the connections which exist beyond the boundaries of space and time. They also demonstrate the way psyche and matter, psyche and body are intimately intertwined. The mystery of my mother's near death and the archetypal negative side of the mother complex as it lived in me remains somewhat of a mystery. I have had only one dream of my heart since that time. In that dream, water was being removed from around my heart and put back into the earth. I knew that this dream referred to the grief I was carrying.

My experience reveals some of the nature of the relationship between the various levels of the unconscious and the complexity of relationships within families. I imagine the shadowy figure as an aspect of a mother complex which lived as a wound in my heart. This complex was formed out of my conscious experience of my mother as well as her unconscious annihilating envy. It is most likely, given what I know from my experiences, dreams, and the stories that were told about my grandmothers and their grandmothers, that the complex, with its archetypal core of Mother, existed at the personal, familial, ancestral, and cultural levels of the collective unconscious. With every generation the energetic power of this complex intensified. My dreams indicated that work devoted to healing this wound had been going on in the psyche for years. As I worked consciously with these dreams and conducted ancestor dialogues, the negative aspect of this complex was released psychically and physically. The transformation of this complex occurred not only in my personal psyche, but, based on my imaginal experience of the women in my mother line, in our matrilineal psyche. The coincidence of this release with my mother's physical collapse is an indication of the depth of connection between mother and daughter and psyche and matter within this complex collective web.[6]

My mother's question about what was real and what was my imagination, while invalidating, also served to bring my attention continually to my perception and experiences of the world. In the last moments of her life, my experiences provided validation in a way that removed the doubt I had about these kinds of experiences being "just my imagination." I would suggest that the process of my mother's death, which occurred during the writing of my doctoral dissertation on this topic, liberated both of us from some of the ties that bound us and, it seemed to me, returned a way of knowing and being that had been lost to consciousness in our maternal lineage centuries ago. These experiences solidified the new ground of a more integrated consciousness on which I stand in this world; one which is differentiated but no longer split.

The Ancestral Faces of a Complex

The wounded heart in my mother line was not healed at the moment the black figure flew from my heart or at the time of my mother's death. After her death I continued to experience the annihilating aspect of the negative animus in the mother complex in a variety of ways.[7] While I still experienced this in relationship to the ancestral figure of my mother, it was as a memory. The pattern was no longer being enacted in this world. My personal memories of mother were the portal into the ancestral and cultural wounding. This was the same experience I had when I encountered the trauma and grief in the transferential dialogue described in Chapter 1.

I have encountered figures from my personal, familial lineage, as well as archetypal figures who seem to be related to a particular cultural/historical piece of my lineage, and ancestors who are indigenous to this land that I live on. Each of these figures has a different feeling tone and imagistic quality. The figures who are mother, father, grandfather, grandmother, those people I have conscious memories of, carry the archetypal spark of mother, father, grandmother and grandfather from the deepest layer of the collective unconscious. They are connected by this spark to all mothers and fathers, but, as figures within the psyche, they seem to carry the soul essence of the actual people I knew in life. Jung recognized this difference in his dreams of his parents and wife. Some figures originate in the ancestral, collective unconscious of the land I was born from and live in relationship with. These figures are, as they call themselves, Indians and animals and other aspects indigenous to this continent. Although these levels can be differentiated, in my experience, working with the ancestors is not a straightforward, linear process. It is labyrinthine, moving away from and towards the center in a path connected through meaning and relatedness as it exists in any particular individual at any given moment in time. The spark within each complex almost always has referential figures within all the levels.

One particular archetypal figure, who has haunted my lineage for centuries, presents himself in my dreams as a black-robed minister. Many of my ancestors were ministers and pastors. Roger, given the choice of studying the law or ministry, chose to be a minister. My great-great grandfather built a church which still stands in Rhode Island. This black-robed figure appeared in my dreams for many years. Self-righteous, judgmental, punishing, and shaming, he was horrific and terrifying. He appeared to me in dreams, but had "haunted" the collective psyche of my family for generations. I heard his voice in the stories of my great-grandmother chastising herself for her sins as she looked in the mirror. I saw him in my mother's idealization of and unquestioning faith in ministers and doctors. I believe this figure is the negative animus within the mother complex as he is personified in my lineage. As I came to know the black-robed figure, to begin to face him in the mirror of psyche, I discovered he sought redemption— from the striving for and failure to achieve God's perfection on earth, the demonization of women and of all that is earthly, and the separation of matter and spirit.

I recognized the archetypal energy of the figure of the black-robed priest in the dream figure of my ex-husband. This archetypal energy also appeared as a male figure wearing black in modern dress performing ancient, sacred rituals. This particular figure was reminiscent of the Greek god Dionysus. The energy is recognizable and the figures are distinct. Each embodies the energy in a very particular way. As one works with each figure, the psyche seems to weave in and out of the levels, referencing different times, places, and people. Just as there is value in understanding the archetypal nature of figures in dream through myth, there is value in understanding the ways one's specific ancestry is referenced. The spark from the deepest level of the unconscious, which connected these figures to each other archetypally, was a shadowed aspect of Christianity.

My experience and the experience of others I've worked with indicate that the transformation of an ancestral wound does not happen as a result of one dream or imaginal dialogue. However, I am sure that it is possible for these patterns to be transformed in an instant, especially in ritual time and space. A dream, an illness or an experience in a ritual can open an ages old wound. When this happens, it is essential to be aware of the psychological implications and to address them responsibly. For most people in modern western culture, especially those who have experienced personal trauma or who are dealing with significant ancestral trauma, this process usually takes time and careful psychological tending.

CHAPTER 6

Reimagining the World—Reimagining Ourselves

The image of the world is half the world.[1]

— Jung finding his Soul again

We see and hear what we are open to noticing.[2]

— Jerome Bernstein

The belief in other cultures that ancestral spirits play a significant part in the daily life of the tribe, as well as in causing and curing illness, has been well documented.[3] In other societies with a worldview that is not predominantly modern and Western, being in communication with one's ancestors is a normal part of life. In other cultures, ancestors are integral to the health of each individual, family, and community. In cultures where this is so, the ancestors are respected and looked to for the origins of problems and sought out for their guidance in solving them.

The belief that a consciously sustained relationship with the ancestors is critical to one's wellbeing is more common in cultures still connected with their indigenous roots such as that of the Dagara in Africa. For Malidoma Some, born into the Dagara tribe in West Africa, and an initiated Dagara Elder with Ph.Ds. from the Sorbonne and Brandeis University, the ancestors are always available just on the other side of this reality. Actively soliciting guidance from the ancestors is part of daily life. According to Some, the ancestors are always "available to guide, to teach, and to nurture" and "embody the guidelines for successful living."[4] He reminds his readers that this is true in many cultures.

For the Dagara, keeping the relationship between the living and the dead in balance is essential to the wellbeing of all. Ancestor altars and rituals are common practices used among the Dagara to tend this relationship. When there is trouble of any kind, it is seen as an indication from the ancestors that some ancestral law has been broken, some abuse has happened for which amends must be made. They believe that when something is out of balance it is the responsibility of the living to heal the ancestors.

For the Dagara, "If these ancestors are not healed, their sick energy will haunt the souls and psyches of those who are responsible for helping them."[5] However, according to Some, even with regular and careful tending of our relationship with the ancestors some abuses remain buried so deep that they are no longer visible making it difficult to address them directly.[6]

In *The Red Book*, the words of three shades, whose chilling breath is evidence that they are dead, seem to echo what the Dagara believe. One of the shades, a woman, informs Jung that they have been left alone too long. They come seeking community with the living. It is what both the dead *and* the living need. Having been forgotten, the need of these shades is great and they now "demand" his service.[7] As Some suggests, and as this shade warns Jung, if the dead are not tended to "they are as malicious as the serpent, as bloodthirsty as the tiger that pounces on the unsuspecting from behind."[8]

Jung spoke about the dangers of becoming uprooted and detached from the past, of losing one's connection to the ancestors. He writes,

> If you give up the past you naturally detach from the past; you lose your roots in the soil, your connection with the totem ancestors that dwell in your soil. You turn outward and drift away and try to conquer other lands because you are exiled from your own soil. . . . That is the Will always wandering over the surface of the earth, always seeking something. It is exactly what Mountain Lake, the Pueblo chief, said to me, "The Americans are quite crazy. They are always seeking; we don't know what they are looking for." Well, there is too much head and so there is too much will, too much walking about, and nothing rooted.[9]

Some believes that "the present state of restlessness that traps the modern individual has its roots in a dysfunctional relationship with the ancestors."[10] Is it possible that our loss of connection with the past, our loss of connection with our roots in the psyche and in the earth, results in what Jung describes as the "discontents of civilization" and Some as our "restlessness?" And, even more specifically, does this loss of connection find expression in our personal and collective suffering?

Jung stated that in America the ancestors are not considered, nor are their values respected.[11] I believe he was speaking specifically about Americans who were of European descent. Today, people of many different cultures and traditions live on the North American continent. Some Americans can trace their ancestors presence on this land to the sixteen and seventeen-hundreds. Many of our ancestors immigrated later. Some of us are the first in our family to live here. Some of us came of our own free will; others as captives who were sold into slavery. In an effort to become Americans, some of our ancestors intentionally divorced themselves from the traditions of their native lands. Others maintained what they could of their traditions. And there are those who were here long before Europeans set foot on this soil. The First People of this land have fought and struggled to keep their connection to the ancestors and their stories, traditions and ceremonies.

As I write this paragraph, considering Jung's observation, I think about the upsurge in interest in exploring one's ancestry in America. The website Ancestry.com and the television program *Who Do You Think You Are?* are evidence that many Americans experience a great yearning to trace their ancestral lineage. I am always moved by the way individuals are touched by what they unearth. The discoveries that are made often lead to a deeper understanding of who they are and the choices they've made in life. I imagine that Jung, if he witnessed this renewed interest in ancestors in America, would wonder why now and ask what is changing in the individual and collective psyche.

Researching our ancestral lineages is the beginning of reestablishing a more conscious relationship with the ancestors. However, it is only a beginning. And, as is evident in Jung's conversations with the dead in *The Red Book*, it is not only Americans who have not considered their ancestors. As the shades tell Jung, who we know was Swiss to the core of his being, they have been neglected too long and demand his service. For the Dagara, tending one's relationship with the ancestors, feeding them and making a sacrifice, has to be done regularly. Malidoma acknowledges that "doing wrong is human, and it is with the ancestors, who never forget, that humans must make things right."[12] Within five days, things will go out of balance if a sacrifice hasn't been made. Making a sacrifice cleanses the negative energy.[13] Clearing the energy also involves taking action in the world that is reparative. All of this is done with the guidance of Elders. If not cleared, these "wrongdoings," these "unresolved errors are passed on to surviving relatives."[14]

Imagine, given what the Dagara believe to be true and the neglect of the ancestors that Jung identified, what memories and unearthed abuses have been buried, no longer visible to consciousness within the psyche of many Americans and many others in modern Western culture. These memories, although forgotten, have a continued existence in the present affecting us in unconscious ways that not only impact us personally, but also have a wider, deleterious effect in the world. If Some and the shades who speak to Jung are right, these forgotten pieces of our heritage sit, latent, haunting us through symptoms and in dreams, waiting to be remembered consciously and addressed. In this remembering, it becomes possible to directly address and heal the wounds of the past in the present.

These ideas, this way of imagining the presence and direct influence of ancestors in the present, may stretch the belief systems of many of us in modern Western culture. Even those of us who believe in some kind of continuing existence after death rarely consider the role the ancestors play in our lives in the here and now, much less communicate with them. Many people believe that communicating with the dead just isn't possible, and, among many professionals in the field of psychology and medicine, communicating with the dead is seen as pathological. To provide a foundation for this work required expanding a traditional depth psychological framework with what Jung would have referred to as a more "primitive" and what Some refers to as an "indigenous" way of knowing and understanding the nature of reality.

Beneath the Surface of Consciousness

Ralph Metzner, a German born American psychologist, through the experiences of his students and psychotherapy clients and his own inner work, came to the understanding that

> while the origins of many disturbances can be found in patterns of relationship with one's parents (who are, after all, ancestors too), one often needs to go beyond the biographical factors to perinatal and prenatal conditions, to multigenerational family patterns, and to ethnic, cultural, racial or national influences.[15]

As a psychologist, I too see that the problems my clients seek my help with have origins that include but go beyond the patterns that can be seen in the immediate family.

Without a worldview that incorporates the role of ancestors, personal and collective, in the present moments of our lives, we remain inattentive to their presence, ascribing our symptoms, inclinations, and dreams instead to those things that fit within our known frameworks of understanding. They return to us in unconscious ways, that appear to be random and meaningless or are ascribed simply to our personal family history. This is evident in my story. For years my understanding of my personal trauma was limited to my personal family history. However, the ancestral trauma, unconscious for so many generations, was "remembered" and was being acted out in the relationships in my family. There are many other examples of this in the stories that are shared later in this book.

Without a framework that allows for the possibility of the reality and existence of our ancestors as more than pieces of DNA and bones in the ground, their presence fixed within our personal, conscious memory, we are limited in our ability to listen and to respond to the ways they address us. Our ability to respond, to continue what previous generations left unfinished, to heal the sick energy which haunts us, to listen for the ancestors' guidance and benefit from their wisdom, to explore their unanswered questions, I would suggest, depends on reconnecting with the origins of our shared human consciousness.

Jung's work establishes the idea of a shared collective unconscious that is unfathomable and seemingly limitless in its relationship with time and space. His conceptualizations of a personal and collective unconscious allow us to entertain the possibility that forgotten memories from previous generations, especially those that are affectively charged, are still present and accessible in this land of the dead. In his second essay on Analytical Psychology Jung shares,

> I must confess that I have never yet found infallible evidence for the inheritance of memory images, but I do not regard it as positively precluded that in addition to these collective deposits which contain nothing specifically individual, there may also be inherited memories that are individually determined.[16]

While remaining purely phenomenological with regard to his theories, Jung didn't rule out the possibility of inherited memories that are particular to an individual and their lineage. As the stories presented later will demonstrate, that pure archetypal energy is expressed very particularly within each individual through the various levels of the collective unconscious.

The Dagara belief that "unresolved errors" are passed on to surviving relatives,"[17] one that Jung would consider "primitive," can be understood psychologically within Jung's theory as inherited units of consciousness. In other words, one's personal complexes carry within them affective memories and the "unresolved errors" from the lives of our ancestors. There is also evidence for the inheritance of ancestral memories and patterns from the field of pharmacology. Candace Pert's work on the molecules of emotion is very interesting in this regard. She suggests that emotions, like all information, exists "beyond time and place, matter and energy" belonging to a non-material realm that we cannot apprehend with our senses, "one that we can experience as emotion, the mind, the spirit— an inforealm!"[18]

Jung, as a phenomenologist, while affirming the reality of "inner," psychological experiences, did not use this data to make any conclusions concerning reality or the world's natural constitution. Tarnas, in *The Passion of the Western Mind: Understanding the Ideas That Have Shaped Our Worldview*, acknowledges that Jung, although more metaphysically flexible than Freud, was more exacting epistemologically.[19] Tarnas continues: "Whatever the human mind produced could be regarded only as a product of the human mind and its intrinsic structures, with no necessary objective or universal correlations."[20] Although Jung attributed a psychological, inner reality to ancestor spirits, according to Smith he "did not address whether or not they *are* spiritual realities, having an objective status outside any presumed personal mental structures."[21] Peat, from his understanding of the "Native mind," recognizes the limitations within Jung's psychology with regard to indigenous people's experience of reality. Archetypes, to the native mind, are not images or representations of reality, "they *are* the reality itself. . . . Jung's archetypes are too limited, too literal, and too impoverished to account for the vitality of Native American imagery.[22]

Smith notes that although Jung affirmed the reality of what could be characterized as spirits and ghosts, he interpreted them in a purely psychological framework. He observes that Jung did not "address the possibility of independently existing spirits, nor did he speculate on the relationship between such spirits and the archetypal structures of the shaman's mind."[23] According to Smith, in the shamanic view, "spirits are a *sui generis* reality; they simply are what they are, and should not be reduced to other terms.[24] From a shaman's perspective, spirit beings are real. This was the window of perception that opened for Malidoma Some in his initiation. While these beings may appear to us as illusions in an ordinary state of consciousness and be identified from a Jungian perspective as an archetypal pattern or the projection of a complex, "in the shamanic state of consciousness, they *are* spiritual realities, having an objective status outside any presumed personal mental structures."[25]

For the Dagara of Western Africa, the ancestors and other beings that live on the other side of this reality "are not considered mere metaphors or abstract representations of intangible concepts. These beings simply live in a different time/space continuum and perceive us as much as we perceive them.[26] According to Vine Deloria, Jr., scholar and author of *Jung and the Sioux Traditions: Dreams, Visions, Nature and the Primitive*, for the Sioux, "the physical and spiritual are explicitly intertwined."[27] In *God is Red: A Native View of Religion,* Deloria describes the Indian experience of Spirit:

> Whenever we find Indians and whenever we inquire about their idea of God, they tell us that beneath the surface of the physical universe is a mysterious power which cannot be described in human images that must always remain the "Great Mystery." There are on the other hand, many other entities with spiritual powers comparable to those generally attributed to one deity alone. . . . In addition, all inanimate entities have spirit and personality so that the mountains, rivers, waterfalls, even the continents and the earth itself have intelligence, knowledge, and the ability to communicate ideas. The physical

world is so filled with life and personality that humans appear as one minor species without much significance and badly in need of assistance from other forms of life.[28]

According to Jurgen Kremer, a clinical psychologist who is involved with indigenous peoples and their traditions, Jung's interpretations of native myths and healings do not reflect the reality of the tribal mind. "What may be a good starting point for the western mind would split and dissociate the indigenous mind."[29] Jeff King, a member of the Muscogee Creek and a clinical psychologist, in his article critiquing Western psychology from an American Indian perspective, discusses basic concepts that are embedded in Western psychology and accepted as the truth about reality, the individual and the world. Of particular note is the concept of "self." The Muscogee, Lakota, Navajo, and Pueblo do not have a word for "self." He writes, "the self is construed as encompassing family, community, and even the land."[30] His "Native American clients". . . over the years, have reported visions, contact with spirits (including deceased relatives), and experiences of entering the spirit world—sometimes voluntarily, sometimes not."[31] These descriptions of the tangible nature and reality of the invisible world that exists just behind the veil of physical reality, and the other beings who exist beneath the surface of our consciously perceived reality, illustrate the differences between Jungian psychology and the Dagara and American Indian worldviews.

Ancestors in the Land

In 1925 Esther Harding wrote in her notebook that Jung said many interesting things about the ancestors in one of his lectures. She made particular note of one—that the ancestors "seem to be in the land."[32] Continuing the dialogue between Jungian psychology and the understanding of the Dagara and Native American people as it relates to our relationship with the ancestors wouldn't be complete without looking specifically at Jung's understanding of the relationship between the body, the psyche, and the earth, and, in particular, the presence of the ancestors in the land. As Jung's understanding of the unconscious developed beyond Freud's, he recognized a "quality in man which roots him to the earth and draws new strength from below."[33] Jung recognized what many indigenous cultures have known for many generations—that the land and its people are intimately connected in body and psyche.

In his autobiography Jung expresses the depth of connection he felt with the land and with nature.

At times I feel as if I'm spread out over the landscape and inside things, and am myself living in every tree, in the splashing of the waves, in the clouds and animals that come and go, in the procession of the seasons.[34]

Barbara Hannah recognized the importance of Jung's connection to nature and the land and the way this influenced and informed Jung's personal and professional life. She chose to begin her biography of Jung with a chapter devoted to the nature and history of Switzerland to provide the ground for telling the story of his life. She describes Jung as a man who "belonged organically to Switzerland, just as much as the famous mountains, and was just as rooted in Swiss soil."[35]

In 1934 Charles Baudouin writes about a conversation he had with Jung in which he realized the substantial nature of the connection Jung felt to his ancestors and the land of his birth.

When he was talking with me the other day, at Dr. von Sury's, about these "ancestral spirits," which fall upon one on return to one's birthplace, and which he himself feels whenever he returns to Basel, I recognized that these "spirits" had weight, like the atmosphere during a thunderstorm. And when he was led by this reflection to study, on the wall, the genealogical tree of the von Sury family, I realized how he felt those roots digging down and holding fast in an earth that was real and solid.[36]

In his essay on "The Role of the Unconscious" Jung discusses his observations about the effect the chthonic aspect of the land has on its inhabitants. He recognized that "the soil of every country holds . . . mystery. We have an unconscious reflection of this in the psyche: just as there is a relationship of mind to body, so there is a relationship of body to earth."[37] The mystery in the soil, the ancestral spirits, are inseparable from the collective unconscious. Far from disembodied, the archetypes, which are the basic structures of the psyche and the foundations of consciousness, are, according to Jung, "the roots which the psyche has sunk not only in the earth in the narrower sense but in the world in general."[38] To be connected with the roots of the psyche, one must be connected with the earth, or, when one is connected to the roots of the psyche, one is connected to the earth. Jung's understanding of the relationship that exists between the past, the ancestors, the earth, and those who live on it is expressed in the following passage: "The past is really the earth; all the past has sunk into the earth, as those primitives say. The ancestors . . . went underground."[39]

While Jung refers specifically to "primitives" in this passage, he states clearly that although this dynamic relationship between the people and the land is less conscious, or even completely unconscious, in modern humans, it continues to affect us. Jung suggests that separation from the land of one's ancestors, whether physically or psychically, results in detachment from one's instincts, a sense of uprootedness and a nagging restlessness. The development of the modern, Western, egoic consciousness is accompanied by separation from the more archaic part of the psyche. Separation from the land, from one's instincts and the archaic roots of the psyche leads to a dissociation between consciousness and the unconscious. Jung describes this dissociation in modern man:

> The unconscious is with the ancestors down in the bowels of the earth, and their [modern man's] consciousness is a head on two feet, constantly marching about in an awful restlessness. That is the restlessness of our time, always seeking—seeking the lost ancestral body. . . . *But they are only to be found on the spot where they have gone underground.*[40] [emphasis mine]

Developing a relationship with the unconscious is one way of restoring a more conscious connection to the ancestors, the land, and the archaic roots of the psyche. I would suggest that it becomes increasingly important to find ways to establish and maintain this relationship as more of us travel and no longer live on the lands of our indigenous ancestors. Having moved many times in my life I have found ways to establish a relationship with the places I've lived. I've also found a way to stay in touch with the ancestors—those from my personal lineage who are from other lands and those who are present in the land I live in relationship with—wherever I live. Jung's psychological understanding of the relationship between the ancestors, the land and its inhabitants, serves as part of the framework of understanding that enables me to do this.

The living reality of the ancestors in the collective unconscious is complex. Just as the ancestors are in the land, they are a living reality in the psyche. Stanislav Grof's and Christopher Bache's work demonstrates that each of us has access through the collective unconscious to other times and places—past, present, and future—in our collective story.[41] These collective memories are accessible as part of our direct psychological experience wherever we find ourselves placed. While these experiences of collective memory do not necessarily come from the land, they do not discount what Jung recognizes about the nature of psyche in the land. Ancestral soul work grounds remembering and experiencing collective memories in one's personal ancestry in relationship to specific times, events and *lands.* I will offer two stories that illustrate what Jung recognized as the intimate relationship between the ancestors and the land. The first is from Jung's autobiography, the second is from my personal biography.

In his autobiography Jung shares an experience that is one example of the way he experienced the presence of the ancestors in relationship to the land. After finishing the Bollingen tower in 1924, he had a dream experience in which he was awakened by the sound of soft footsteps. However, he was still asleep and dreaming. He awoke to stillness, not even the wind was making a sound. Returning to bed, he wondered about the strong sense that this had been real and that he had been awake when he heard the footsteps. He fell asleep again, and the same dream began. Once more he heard laughter, talking, and music. This time he saw the spirits of several hundred dark-clad young peasant boys who had come down from the mountains and were now "pouring in around the Tower, on both sides."[42] It seemed to Jung that these peasant boys had come out of curiosity to see the Tower. He describes the dream as being "insistent on its reality."[43] Different than an ordinary dream, this dream seemed "bent on conveying a powerful impression of reality to the dreamer."[44]

He would discover a historical referent for this ghostly procession in a seventeenth-century Lucerne chronicle. It was an account by Cysat, who, while climbing a mountain that was known for being inhabited by ghosts, was disturbed in the night by a procession of men playing music and singing. The next day, a local herdsman offered Cysat the following explanation—it must have been "Wotan's army of departed souls. These, he said, were in the habit of walking abroad and showing themselves."[45] Jung asks, "Do we know what realities such stories may be founded on? Is it possible that I had been so sensitized by the solitude that I was able to perceive the procession of 'departed folk' who passed by?"[46] Jung also discovered a direct historical parallel. In the Middle Ages, such gatherings of young men actually took place. They marched from their homeland in Switzerland to Italy where they served as mercenaries. He concludes, "My vision, therefore, might have been one of those gatherings which took place regularly each spring when the young men, with singing and jollity, bade farewell to their native land."[47]

Explaining these kinds of experiences as psychic compensation for the solitude he experienced in the Tower was unsatisfactory for Jung. Rather than being compensatory, Jung describes this experience and other premonitions and visions like this one as synchronistic, where psyche and world touch, where "the same living reality [is] expressing itself in the psychic state as in the physical."[48] In this case Jung found a recorded account of an experience that was similar to his in which the spirits of departed souls were seen walking the countryside. These experiences suggest that there is a psychic reality particular to the location of the Bollingen tower. That psychic reality, experienced by Jung in a dream state, had been experienced by others. The spirits, the psychic presence of those young boys who were now ancestors, and the memory of a yearly ritual were ever-present in the land.

After realizing that the ancestors were "alive" and producing effects in the present in very specific ways, I decided to travel to the land where the original ancestral trauma had occurred on March 29th in the sixteen-hundreds and where ten generations of my ancestors' bones were buried. It was my first visit to Providence in thirty-seven years. I wanted to visit the places where Roger had lived, the graves of my ancestors and the historical sites where many of the events that were personally and collectively consequential occurred during his lifetime. I decided to do this as a "walkabout." I listened to the soles of my feet and followed the promptings of dreams and synchronicities. At the time I hadn't yet read what Jung had to say about the ancestors in the land.

I found myself in a park at the side of a river. I walked to an open area and sat down on a small boulder. As I sat, resting from a long day, wondering what I was doing, if what I was intuiting and experiencing was merely compensatory and a good story, I became aware of a feeling that was not, at first, easily identifiable. Moving from my mind to a more embodied consciousness as I opened to the experience, I realized that I felt a sense of belonging that was very unfamiliar. I had felt connected to landscapes and mountains and creeks and oceans and animals and trees before, but this was different. I felt as if my body was part of and was recognized by this land. I felt "known" by this place, body to earth. I began to sob. I "heard," "You and your kin are welcome here." Even as I opened to this deep sense of recognition and belonging body and soul to this land, I was utterly shocked. I would never have presumed to be welcomed on land that had been colonized by Europeans from who I was descended. I felt recognized and known in some essential way that was qualitatively different than other experiences I've had. I had never experienced this sense of belonging to a place in any of the other places I had lived or traveled to. It was as if the land remembered me. Was it the ancestors in the land who spoke to me? And, if it was, which ancestors spoke—the Narragansett, the 10 generations of my ancestors whose bones were buried there, both?[49] Whatever was so, I experienced the living consciousness of the land as I sat on the boulder looking out at the river.

Jung's understanding of the relationship between the land and psyche approaches that of the Dagara and Native American. It is difficult to even write about the relationship between indigenous people and the land they live in relationship with from the point of view of Jungian psychology. In Native cultures, people are inseparable from place and the relationship between people and place is reciprocal in nature. From the perspective of Native cultures, as described by Cajete, place is "a living presence."[50] He continues,

> the inner archetypes in a place formed the spiritually based ecological mindset required to establish and maintain a correct and sustainable relationship with the place. This orientation was, in turn, reinforced by a kind of physical

"mimicry" a "geopsyche" or that interaction between the inner and outer realities that often takes place when a group of people live in a particular place for a long period of time. Our physical makeup and the nature of our psyche are formed to some extent by the distinct climate, soil, geography, and living things of a place. . . . their landscapes became reflections of their very soul.[51]

Further on he writes, "in the same fashion as myth, land becomes an extension of the Native mind, for it is the place that holds memory."[52]

In *God is Red* Deloria writes about the Indian sense of identity its relationship to one's homeland.

Most tribes were reluctant to surrender their homelands to the whites because they knew that their ancestors were still spiritually alive on the land, and they were fearful that the whites would not honor the ancestors and the lands in the proper manner. If life was to mean anything at all, it had to demonstrate a certain continuity over the generations and this unity transcended death.[53]

For Indian people, death and the ancestors are understood in the larger context of life. For many Indian people, according to Deloria, "the next life [is] a continuation of the present mode of existence."[54] "The souls of people often remained in various places where they had died or suffered traumatic events."[55] He offers several examples. The cries of the men and women massacred at Sand Creek have been heard by people visiting the site. "Indians receiving bones from museums for reburial tell about spirits of the departed speaking to them during the reburial ceremonies and thanking them for helping to get their bones from the museums so they can rest in the Mother Earth."[56]

For Indian people, Cajete explains, the effect of moving either forcibly or willingly from the place of one's ancestors, from one's homeland can "lead to a deep split in the inner and outer consciousness of the individual and group."[57] Jeanne Lacourt, a member of the Menominee Indian tribe and Associate Professor of American Indian Studies at St. Cloud State University, in her article "Coming Home: Knowing Land, Knowing Self," writes, "Native people's revelatory experiences with the land echo the workings of the unconscious, failure to acknowledge this fundamental attitude is to alienate oneself from the unconscious."[58]

The focus in this section is on the relationship between the land and the ancestors. Jung seemed to recognize some of the same characteristics of the relationship between self and place that Cajete, Deloria, and Lacourt describe. He came to understand what Native Americans and other indigenous peoples have known for generations—that the land from which we are born, in which our ancestors bones are buried, on which we currently live, is part of our psychic landscape. The ancestors, present in relationship with the land, are a living presence in the land and in the psyche of its inhabitants.

Jung's comparison between and description of the European and American psyche illustrates his understanding of the presence and effect of the land in a psychological framework. While his ideas are based on a world that existed a century ago, his assertions are useful in understanding the unconscious aspects of the relationship between the land and the people who live on that land. In her biographical memoir of Jung Barbara Hannah notes having

> been struck, during [her] long experience of the many people of different nationalities who were drawn to Jung, and who still come to the C. G. Jung Institute in Zurich, by how necessary it is to have at least some knowledge of the national layers in order to understand the individual.[59]

Europeans, according to Jung in an article published in the *New York Times* in 1913, identify with the country they are from. The Swiss, he said, "must be Swiss, because we won't be Germans, and we won't be French, and we won't be Italian."[60] The ancestors and the ancestral shadows share the same origins as the body and psyche of individuals born in places where the bones of their ancestors have been buried for many centuries. The land, the people, the history, folktales and stories, and the unconscious have a collective, cultural, and historic congruence consciously and in the unconscious of each individual. Barbara Hannah remembers Jung saying that within the European psyche there are a set of clear steps which descend from the door which opens to the shadow. Opening that door and following those steps downward, if he or she chooses to, is quite safe.[61]

The diagram of the differentiated levels of the collective unconscious sheds light on Jung's understanding. One level of the collective unconscious is comprised of the expressions of the pure archetypal energy as experienced and expressed in a single country like France. The level below that is regional in nature. In this example the region is Europe. Remembering that the same archetypal spark infuses and threads through each level becoming more differentiated the closer it gets to the familial and personal unconscious, it is understandable that Jung would imagine there was a level of the psyche that was European in its character and that there was also a level that was particular to each country within that region. The psychological landscape and contour of individuals who live on the same land their ancestors have lived on for many generations has a natural continuity that comes from the congruence that exists between the levels of the unconscious from the archetypal to the personal. How are these levels of the psyche patterned and experienced in the psyche of an individual who is living on land that is not the land of their birth or the land of their ancestors?

Jung uses the words *assimilate* and *permeate* to describe the way the land affects the unconscious psyche of anyone whose ancestral origins are foreign to that land. The foreign country, according to Jung,

> gets under the skin of those born in it. Certain very primitive tribes are convinced that it is not possible to usurp foreign territory, because the children born there would inherit the wrong ancestor-spirits who dwell in the trees, the rocks, and the water of the country. There seems to be some subtle truth in this primitive intuition.[62]

Many Americans are descended through our blood from ancestors who lived for centuries on other continents. Through our bodies and psyche we are also related to a land whose ancestors have particular local and regional indigenous heritages that are different than those of our own indigenous ancestors. In the Houston film interviews conducted in 1957, Jung noted that "American life is, in a *subtle* way, so one-sided and so *déraciné*, uprooted, that you must have something to compensate the earth."[63] [italics added] This uprooted, one-sidedness, leaves the unconscious in "an absolute uproar."[64] However uprooted American life was as observed by Jung in his time, however disconnected we may or may not be from nature and the "living presence" of ancestors in the land, we cannot escape their influence in our lives.

Jung was struck by the differences between the Americans he analyzed and Europeans. In Hannah's biographical memoir of Jung, she recalls Jung's warning to his pupils. He advised being more careful in approaching the shadow of Americans whose ancestral roots originated in European soil. The European has a door into and a reasonable flight of stairs leading through the collective unconscious, where he will encounter a shadow that is familiar and related to his own country and region.[65] For Americans, opening the door to the shadow is more complex. Rather than a flight of stairs one can negotiate step by step, there is a "dangerous gap," a drop of hundreds of feet. From analyzing the dreams of Americans Jung discovered that if one can negotiate this drop successfully, the face of the shadow is either "an Indian" or "Negro."[66] While these terms and the idea of race that underlies Jung's assertions are problematic, the phenomenon itself is interesting. What Jung observed about the American psyche may have relevance and value in this time for those of us who have a complex ancestral heritage and for those people who find themselves living in places that are not the lands of their ancestors.

Times have changed dramatically in the one-hundred years since Jung developed his theories. Many of us are living on land far from the lands of our ancestors. Many of us have or will move at least once and often several times in our lifetime. We are increasingly globally oriented. However,

Jung's observation about the relationship between the unconscious and the ancestors as configured and experienced by an individual in relationship to place is an important one. Each place has a particular history and indigenous quality. Whether or not we live on the land of our ancestors, our self-identity, the characteristics of our personal, cultural and collective shadow are derived from and related to the lands our ancestors are from, the land we are born to and the land we currently live on.

Living on land that is the native soil of other peoples, our consciousness attempts to integrate the diversity that exists in the deeper, increasingly inclusive levels of the unconscious psyche. As I wrote this last sentence, a band of coyotes began yipping and howling. They continued until I finished the last sentence of this paragraph. They are adding their voice to this dialogue. Their voices are part of and seem, in this moment, to be speaking for and affirming the presence and complexity of the psyche, at this moment in time in this particular part of the American landscape. Jung identifies a layer of the collective unconscious that lies between the "primeval ancestors" and the archetypal central fire as the level of the "animal ancestors." In *Animal Speaks* Ted Andrews observes that coyotes form a very close-knit family unit. They are keenly intelligent and adaptive. As I listen, I am reminded that the ancestors in this land include the animal ancestors, and, that we are all kin. I am also struck by the quality of adaptation that coyote brings. That is certainly a valuable quality to have if one is attempting to integrate disparate aspects of the collective unconscious.

Jung states that every country, or collectively identified people, is characterized by a collective attitude, the *"spiritus loci."*[67] He characterizes the *spiritus loci* of America as heroic. From his experience with American analysands, most who were of European descent, Jung found that "the American hero-motif chooses the Indian as an ideal figure."[68] According to Jung, the unconscious psyche chose the figure of the people native to this land to represent the character of its collective attitude. Mythologically, one function of the hero is to journey down into the underworld, reconnect with the totemic ancestors, and bring them back for his people. Perhaps the national American collective psyche constellated around the hero as compensation for the loss of connection with its collective roots. The hero is archetypally prepared to negotiate the "dangerous open gap" which exists in the American psyche and bring individual and collective consciousness into relationship with the ancestors indigenous to this land.[69] Keiron Le Grice suggested another aspect of Jung's understanding of the hero that seems particularly relevant to this discussion of the underlying archetypal motivations and desires in the American psyche. The hero is also a wanderer whose wandering originates in his or her yearning for the Great Mother.[70]

In an interview with one of his American pupils, Carol Baumann, Jung commented:

> The American unconscious is highly interesting, because it contains more var-
> ied elements and has a higher tension, owing to the melting-pot and the
> transplantation to a primitive soil [true of much of the world now], which caused
> a break in the traditional background of the Europeans who became Americans.
> On the other hand, Americans are in a way more highly civilized than Europe-
> ans, and on the other hand their wellspring of life energy reaches greater depths.
> The American unconscious contains an immense number of possibilities.[71]

Perhaps Borderland consciousness is one of the immense possibilities that originates in and is a result of the complexity of the American collective psyche.

Vine Deloria's son Phillip wrote a book entitled *Playing Indian*. It is a book about the narratives that have formed the national identity of non-native Americans. He proposes that this identity has been created "around the rejection of an older European consciousness and an almost mystical imperative to become new."[72] It began, according to Deloria, with the first story of the Boston Tea Party when colonists dressed up as Indians raided cargo ships in the Boston Harbor and dumped the valuable cargo of tea overboard in protest of the exorbitant tax levied by England. Deloria cites D. H. Lawrence who saw the American dilemma as one that wanted to "savor both civilized order and savage freedom at the same time."[73] Deloria contends that Americans "lost in a (post)modern freefall . . . have returned to the Indian, reinterpreting dilemmas surrounding Indianess to meet the circumstances of their times."[74]

In Native cultures, a natural ethos based on the continuity of life, har-mony, and sustainability results from having a conscious connection to and relationship with the ancestors, with place, with the land, with the earth. Jung's understanding, broadened by that of Native understanding, may be even more critical now than ever as we face an ecological crisis of global proportions. Thinking globally, of the earth as our home and basing our actions on our relationship with the specific places where we live—acting locally—with the understanding that the ancestors are in the land and part of what Cajete calls our "geopsychic" landscape, may result in a more deeply informed ethic on which our actions are founded.

Bridging the Dangerous Gap

Besides the story of Roger Williams, only one other story of my ancestors from my mother's side of the family survived. It was a story about my mother's grandmother who died before my mother was born. The only memory my grandmother shared, maybe remembered, was seeing her mother standing in front of a mirror chastising, berating and beating herself for her sins. My grandmother's mother was "taken away" shortly after this when my grandmother was still very young. They never saw each other again. It was the only memory that was consciously passed on from my grandmother to my mother to me and, from me, to my daughters. If that story was any indication of the experience of the women in my mother line, there was much that was too difficult to remember. Except for that one story about her mother's mother and our ancestor Roger Williams, there was a vacuum in our lineage, void of tradition, ceremony, stories and ritual. The uprootedness and lack of connection with our ancestral and psychic roots as is common in many Americans and many other people around the world according to Jung, was true for us.

My acceptance to Pacifica Graduate Institute, in the Depth Psychology doctoral program where this research originated, was met by the unconscious with two dreams. Although I did not know this at the time, these dreams heralded working with the ancestors. They contained information and reference points that were revealed over time as a result of engaging with this topic. The second of the two dreams would clearly show the gap in my lineage, the point where the connection between the women I was descended from had been severed from our origins. This dream occurred during the time I was preparing for my first quarter of classes. In the dream I am in a beautiful forest landscape. There is an area which is like an open glade surrounded by trees. It is not day. It is not night. I am barefoot and can feel the earth touching the soles of my feet. I hear a man standing next to me say, "You are descended from a long line of Indian princesses." As I hear his words, I know who I am. I feel it in every cell in my body. I respond by immediately rushing forward, running ahead into the future. I know who I am and now can move into my destiny, my work, my future. I am very excited as I head off.

My forward motion is stopped when the man places his hand firmly on my left shoulder. He turns me to face him, a quarter of a turn to my left. He places both of his hands on my shoulders, looks into my eyes, and says three times, "You are descended from a long line of Indian princesses." The last time he says this he adds, "Look this way" and turns me another quarter of a turn to my left. In front of me I see my mother, behind her, her mother, and behind her, a long line of women reaching back through countless generations. I see a place in the line of my mothers where there has been a break of some kind. The women in front of the break have a different quality of presence and being than the women behind it. The women behind the break are vital and have a strength that is missing in the women who are their descendants.

As I look at the women behind the break in the line, they look back at me with recognition and welcome. As I look down this line, my vision is drawn to a tree that is directly behind the last woman in this long line. It is as if the line of women moves aside and my body is drawn by the force and intention of this tree. I am suddenly in front of and face to "face" with a feminine fiery figure who sits in and is part of this tree. She is an absolute, somewhat personified, force of nature. I am in complete awe and terrified. The force of this figure, the absolute truth of her being, stripped my sense of myself to its core. The terror and shock of coming face to face with this formidable figure woke me from sleep, and I sat bolt upright in bed. I had reconnected with the indigenous origins of my mother line.

There was a break, a tear, a discontinuity in my lineage. I am not certain where this break in my lineage occurred, at what moment in history, on what soil. What was clear, however, was that whenever and wherever this break occurred there was a loss of vitality, a loss of connection with something that had deep roots from which the women in my lineage gained a power—the kind of power Jung describes as emanating from the soil itself. I could feel this archetypal, ancestral fiery figure's roots in the earth and her branches reaching into the sky. She was the origin of my being—the chthonic source in which the wisdom and power of the grandmothers of my grandmothers originated. Jung uses the phrase "central fire" to describe the lowest level of the unconscious. This would be the most primal, undifferentiated level from which a spark flows into every other level of the unconscious. At whatever point the break in my lineage happened, the line of women born after this break were disconnected from that central fire particular to our lineage and lacked the vitality that was carried in its spark.

For generations the women in my lineage have been separated from their indigenous roots. It was not only the women in my line who were haunted by this legacy, Roger, a descendant in this lineage of mothers, also struggled with the legacy of being severed from our indigenous roots. The time was now ripe to restore the connection with my indigenous origins. Following psyche's lead through dream and synchronicity and actively participating in imaginal dialogues with the ancestors, this connection has been restored intrapsychically and intergenerationally. My daughters are rooted through the heart of our mother line to the deepest origins of their being and to the earth.

This dream was chosen by my classmates to be enacted in a class that explored the connections between psyche, self, and world. Several classmates took on the role of the figures from this dream. The eldest woman in our class, coincidentally and without conscious intention, was chosen to represent the fiery figure in the tree. She sat in a chair at the end of the long line of women represented by a few of the women in the class. We reenacted the dream. At the moment when the long line of women moved aside and I and the class looked upon this elder woman, there was a collective gasp. Several of the women in the class had tears in their eyes. Afterwards, several women in the class said they felt as if this had been a ritual of initiation for them into a deep place of connection to some part or place of their origins. The man who played the role of the male figure in the dream felt that he had participated in a sacred ritual. There was something in this dream which held the potential to open some of the women in the class to a reconnection with their ancestral lineage and the origins of their being.

Jung writes about the psychic connection that exists between mother and daughter:

> Every mother contains her daughter in herself and every daughter her mother, and that every woman extends backwards into her mother and forwards into her daughter. This participation and intermingling give rise to that peculiar uncertainty as regards *time*: a woman lives earlier as a mother, later as a daughter. The conscious experience of these ties produces the feeling that her life is spread out over generations—the first step towards the immediate experience and conviction of being outside time, which brings with it a feeling of *immortality*. The individual's life is elevated into a type, indeed it becomes the archetype of woman's fate in general. This leads to a restoration or *apocatastasis* of the lives of her ancestors, who now, through the bridge of the momentary individual, pass down into the generations of the future. An experience of this kind gives the individual a place and a meaning in the life of the generations, so that all unnecessary obstacles are cleared out of the way of the life-stream that is to flow through her. At the same time the individual is rescued from her isolation and restored to wholeness.[75]

This restoration to wholeness is the aim of individuation, according to Jung. Specifically, in the experience in the dream, and the reenactment of the dream in a group, looked at from the theoretical understanding of Jung, this restoration of wholeness, for women, can come through a conscious reconnection with the ancestors in her maternal lineage and the mystery within the experience of mother and daughter that Jung describes so beautifully above. Jung ends the above passage stating, "All ritual preoccupation with archetypes has this aim and this result."[76] I would suggest that for those of us whose indigenous origins can be traced to ancestors from a variety of different lands, reconnecting to one's indigenous origins through one's lineage is an important part of the process of individuation for both men and women.

Now, many years after dreaming this dream, considering what Jung had to say regarding the ancestors and the American psyche, my understanding of the dream of my mother line has deepened. I knew the break in my lineage was a severing of the connection from the deeper, instinctual, nature-based origins of being, to the deepest archetypal and primal, archaic level of the origins of the psyche. Originally, I interpreted the break as a result of the influence of Christianity on paganism. Now, additionally, it occurs to me that the break that exists in my mother line could also have occurred when my ancestors left England, immigrating to this new land, which would become home for the generations that followed. From the perspective of the collective unconscious which is not bound by time and space, both ways of understanding the origins of the break in my lineage can be true, each an echo of the other. Being in the tenth generation to live on this continent, the particularity within the levels of the collective unconscious as I experience it has ancestral, cultural, collective origins in both lands.

The words in the dream were interesting: "You are descended from a long line of Indian princesses." (And the bell just rang on the clock as I typed those words adding its own punctuation to that statement.) I have never felt comfortable using either of those words to identify any part of myself—Indian or princess. I am even less comfortable with the juxtaposition of those two words. The phrase, *Indian princess*, unexpectedly juxtaposes two cultures. The words *Indian* and *princess* could reference the ancestral aspect of both England, the land my ancestors immigrated from, and the collective unconscious in the land to which they immigrated ten generations before I was born.[77] *Indian princess* holds the tension between cultures with their very different worldviews and ways of knowing and being. With this simple phrase, two lands with their distinct histories and particular collective landscape are brought into relationship.

Returning to Our Indigenous Roots

According to Tarnas in *Cosmos and Psyche: Intimations of a New World View*, "ours is an age between worldviews, creative yet disoriented, a transitional era when the old cultural vision no longer holds and the new one has not yet constellated."[78] He proposes that the "pivot of the modern predicament is epistemological."[79] Specifically, our capacity to know is shifting from the perspective of a "coolly self-aware rational ego radically separate from a disenchanted external nature." to a more "unitary consciousness" reminiscent of the *participation mystique* formerly attributed to primitive consciousness.[80]

In the past century, largely as a result of the capacities inherent in this differentiated subjectivity, "long established assumptions and strategies of the modern mind" have been challenged as new data and perspectives have emerged within every field and discipline.[81] The telos of the Western mind, according to Tarnas, is to "reconnect with the cosmos in a mature *participation mystique*."[82] This reconnection is a marriage between modern, egoic consciousness, and a way of knowing and being in the world that was familiar to our ancestors and which still exists in the archaic part of our human consciousness.

To engage in a more conscious dialogue with the ancestors assumes that in some way the ancestors exist as very real and vital presences in the present moments of our personal and collective history, that they are indeed "speaking" to us and that listening and being responsive to their voices is the necessary and correct stance to take in relationship to the ways we are addressed. Most of us easily allow for the inclusion of family stories, heirlooms, recipes, anecdotes, and other consciously held pieces from the lives of our ancestors as part of the ways they "speak" to us in the present. Jung's psychology opens the possibility that they are speaking to us through synchronicities, physical and emotional symptoms, and in our dreams. From my experiences personally and with others, I would suggest that listening to the ancestors speaking using imaginal dialogues, ritual and ceremony necessitates *and* facilitates a reconnection with what Jung refers to as our more "archaic," "primal," "original" mind.[83]

My experiences of the ancestors and the world in which they existed, during the time I was doing the work this book is based on, stretched beyond the bounds of Jungian psychology. The figures I encountered in my dialogues certainly had the psychic weight and substance that Jung describes. However, as my work developed over time, I came to experience them as really real in the way described by Some, Deloria and Elijah. The reintegration of the archaic aspect of consciousness with our modern egoic, logos oriented consciousness that Tarnas describes was facilitated through this work. As my personal dialogue with the ancestors continued over time, I found myself returning to my personal and our collective roots, to a way of seeing and knowing that is a natural part of our consciousness that Jung refers to as "Archaic Man" in his essay *Modern Man in Search of a Soul*.[84]

"Archaic Man" as described by Jung is an archaic aspect of consciousness that still exists within every "civilized," modern human being. According to Jung, this aspect of consciousness, which is common to and shared by all humans, is not something that existed only in a distant past. It exists now, in modern humans. Jung uses the attributes of the mind of "primitive" humans to describe this archaic aspects of consciousness. The concept of primitive as used by Jung is contradictory and problematic in many ways.[85] However, his description of a more primitive, primal and original aspect of consciousness is valuable with regard to our relationship with the ancestors in the present. *"Participation mystique"* is "the outstanding trait of archaic man. . . . [who] projects psychic happenings [unconscious psychic contents] so completely that they coalesce with physical events."[86] What is important about the concept of "Archaic Man" with regard to understanding and, more importantly, experiencing the ancestors, is that Jung recognizes that modern human consciousness has separated itself from the aspect of consciousness that is an integral part of the consciousness of the Dagara and American Indians.[87]

Modern humans have "learned to distinguish what is subjective and psychic from what is objective and 'natural.'"[88] For modern humans, "it is a rational presupposition of ours that everything has a natural and perceptible cause. . . . Causality, so understood, is one of our most sacred dogmas. . . . We distinctly resent the idea of invisible and arbitrary forces."[89] This logos centered, rationally based, egoic consciousness limits our ability to perceive, interact with and understand the effects of the ancestors in our lives in the present in the fullness of the actual phenomenon.

Our task, according to Jung is to return to our psychological roots, to reconnect with that archaic part of our psychological inheritance. Jung, in Miguel Serrano's recounting of their talks in 1959, is attributed as having said, "What is needed is to call a halt to the fatal dissociation that exists between man's higher and lower being . . . we must unite conscious man with primitive man."[90] Halting this "fatal dissociation" by reconnecting with the ancestors also connects us consciously in the present to an inherited wisdom that exists in the deeper levels of psyche.[91] Reconnecting with forgotten aspects of our psychological and cultural heritage is at the heart of this work.

Izdubar, a figure Jung encounters in his confrontation with the unconscious seems to embody this archaic aspect of consciousness. In "Liber Secundus, First Day," in *The Red Book*, Jung encounters Izdubar.[92] He is a force of nature! Despite his gigantic presence, Izdubar's face "speaks of consuming inner fear, and his hands and knees tremble" when he sees Jung.[93] He experiences Jung's understanding of the world as poison. Jung responds saying,

> Oh Izdubar . . . what you call poison is science. In our country we are nurtured on it from youth, and that may be one reason why we haven't properly flourished and remain so dwarfish. When I see you . . . it seems to me as if we are all somewhat poisoned.[94]

As the conversation continues, Izdubar tells Jung that it is science that has lamed him.[95] Jung defends science, stating that whatever has been lost as a result of the laming poison of science has been compensated for and rediscovered through mastering the forces of nature. Izdubar draws his own force from the force of nature. He embodies a way of knowing different than one that is situated in logos or reason, one that is more connected with nature, one that is archaic. At the end of this part of their dialogue, Jung and Izdubar both say that they long for each other's truth.

This theme of recognizing and longing for, needing to reconnect with a more archaic, natural aspect of consciousness seems to appear again for Jung in his experiences in Africa. He writes:

> These seemingly strange and wholly different surroundings awaken an archetypal memory of an only too well known prehistoric past which apparently we have forgotten. We are remembering a potentiality of life which has been overgrown by civilization, but which in certain places still exists.[96]

In *The Healing Wisdom of Africa*, Malidoma Some tells a story that speaks to the relationship between what is considered by Jung to be a more archaic aspect of consciousness and one that is more scientific and logos oriented. The story he recounts is of a conversation between a shaman and a villager about the relationship between the indigenous world and the West. Westerners had been enticing the children of the village to leave for years. In the eyes of the villager, Westerners must have powerful magic. The shaman's response caught Malidoma's attention. In his training as a shaman he had learned that the "white man" searches the world and came to Africa to heal himself, not steal children from the villages. The shaman continued saying that the Africans also need healing from the white man. That is why their children leave the villages. As in Navajo, the shaman reminds Malidoma that it is one world, one community, and when one person is sick, everyone is. "We are together in this struggle. All our souls need rest in a safe home. All people must heal, because we are all sick."[97]

It appears to me that Jung's experience in Africa and his conversation with Izdubar recognized this same truth. In *The Red Book*, the first part of his conversation with Izdubar, in which he recognizes that Izdubar has been wounded by science, is followed by a description of Jung's continuing journey on a path that led him "beyond the rejected opposites."[98] This is the point—beyond the rejected opposites of science and magic—where Izdubar can be healed. This encounter also has a profoundly transformative effect on Jung in the present.

Regarding the Split

At the age of four Malidoma Some was taken by a priest with his father's blessing from his village in Burkina Faso to be educated in a Jesuit school.

He was not only separated from his indigenous community and culture, he was also not allowed to speak the language of his people, practice his peoples' rituals, sing the songs of the culture he had been born into, participate in ceremonies, or tell the stories that had been told for generations by the Dagara people. His stories of origin and creation were replaced by the Christian myth of Adam and Eve and the Garden of Eden. His ways of being and knowing, considered primitive and demonized, were literally beaten out of him. His view of reality was severed in two. As he absorbed a "Western consciousness" and gained literacy, he began to see experiences that would be considered normal to his people as "primitive trickery unworthy of civilized thinking. . . . [His] 'Western trained mind' regarded such experiences "as an alien with hostile intention."[99]

At the age of 20, fleeing the mission school, driven by the fear of consequences he might suffer for striking a priest, Malidoma traveled many miles by foot back to his village. Upon his return, his Uncle Guisso tended "the wound of [his] psyche."[100] Although Malidoma was much older than other young men undergoing initiation, it was decided by the elders that he would undergo this series of rituals. The objective of this undertaking was to "restore the damaged regions of [his] psyche."[101]   In his initiation he would have encounters and experiences that challenged his Western mind and opened him to a broader understanding of reality. Undertaking this initiation was not to be taken lightly. Being initiated, especially at his age, meant putting his life at risk.

The initiation was designed to help Malidoma learn how to open to "all the realms of knowledge" that his Western education had left unexplored. In this initiation Malidoma struggled with the effects of his Western education. He felt that literacy, learning to read and write, had its own logic and perception of time that was different than and "incompatible with the logic innate to the Dagara and other native peoples."[102]

His "civilized mind" struggled with the "sweeping powers of the Other World."[103] As a result of this struggle with perception he experienced an "aligning" of his "physical vision and his spiritual sight."[104] Gradually awakening to these realities "would help [him] reconcile [his] educated self with the culture of [his] ancestors."[105] As he explained:

> I call my initiation a radical healing. My angry, vicious self was quieted, intimidated by the sweeping powers of the Other World. Something like a new person was born in me. The region of my psyche that had been put to sleep at the schools of Western thought was suddenly restored. I was reconnected to the deep regions of my psyche and to all living things.[106]

Malidoma's personal story is a familiar one, for in its telling it reveals the experience of the ubiquitous effects of contact between Western "civilization" and indigenous peoples around the world. I believe it also recapitulates the modern Western individual's experience of moving away from the indigenous roots of our shared human consciousness and the painful return home to those collective roots Jung refers to as "archaic." After his initiation Malidoma continued his Western education receiving doctorates from the Sorbonne and Brandeis. Valuing both educations, Western and Dagara, he came to realize that his civilized mind was limited and limiting, leaving "a wide range of experience unexplored."[107]

A New Cosmological Ground

Jung's work is fundamentally about our relationship with the unconscious, "the land of the dead," the "spirit of the depths." With the publishing of *The Red Book*, Jung's direct experiences of the unconscious are now available to the public. *The Red Book* is a series of dialogues with "the dead," which presents a story about and a picture of the nature of reality, one in which the ancestors are very real presences who are seeking salvation and redemption. Sonu Shamdasani, historian and editor of *The Red Book*, describes it as "Jung without concepts." He believes that Jung's concepts "were a makeshift. . . . an attempt to try to translate as much as he felt he could get away with to the medico-scientific audience of his time."[108]

While Jung's theoretical works remain solidly within a phenomenological and medico-scientific rather than metaphysical framework, congruent with the rational and empirical orientation of the times, *The Red Book* offers a different, broader picture of these figures of the depths and the nature of the reality they inhabit than the one presented by Jung in the Collected Works. I would suggest that *The Red Book*, if viewed as part of the creation story of Jungian psychology, offers an expanded view of reality, one which is more congruent with the Dagara and Indian worldviews.

Elijah in Liber Primus in *The Red Book* informs Jung that he and Salome are "certainly what you call real."[109] Rather than being mere psychic realities, these figures of the unconscious, according to Elijah, are as real as we are.[110] Elijah and the spirit of the depths challenge the ontological ground of depth psychology in ways similar to American Indian and Dagara perceptions of reality and worldviews. *The Red Book* was published as I was finishing writing my dissertation that this book is based on. It seems that the time was ripe for us to understand our relationship with the ancestors in new ways.

The Red Book opens the ontological ground of depth psychology. Shamdasani and James Hillman discussed the implications of *The Red Book* for the field of psychology. Their conversations were recorded,

transcribed and published in a book aptly titled, *The Lament of the Dead*.
In their first conversation Shamdasani states unequivocally that these figures are "the ancestors. It is the dead. This is no mere metaphor. . . . When
he [Jung] talks about the dead he means the dead. . . . They still live on."[111]
In a later conversation he states that this land of the dead depicted in *The
Red Book* is not merely "an abstraction, the collective unconscious. One is
dealing quite specifically with the dead of human history."[112] Hillman
believes that *The Red Book*

> is crucial because it opens the door or the mouths of the dead. Jung calls
> attention to the one deep, missing part of our culture, which is the realm of
> the dead. The realm not just of your personal ancestors but the realm of the
> dead, the weight of human history, and what is the *real* repressed, and that is
> like a great monster eating us from within and from below and sapping our
> strength as a culture.[113]

The Red Book begins with Jung struggling to resolve the "spirit of the
times" with the "spirit of the depths." Through his encounters Jung learns
that in addition to the spirit of his time—and, I would add the spirit of his,
our, and any time—there is another spirit at work, namely "that which
rules the depths of everything contemporary."[114] While the spirit of the
times "changes with the generations," the spirit of the depths has existed
from "time immemorial."[115] In his encounter with the spirit of the depths
Jung will come to understand that, "The image of the world is half the
world."[116] This is reminiscent of the understanding and experience of the
world of the Dagara and Indians as described by Some and Deloria among
others.[117]

As one explores the underlying assumptions within the Western
worldview, as one listens more deeply to the voices of the ancestors,
developing, in the process, a more conscious relationship with both, the
telos within this remembering becomes more apparent. In this looking
backward, the opportunity exists to create new ways to move forward. In
the words of "the dead" themselves, as told to Jung by Ezechiel: "The new
will be built on the old and the meaning of what has become will become
manifold. Your poverty in what has become you will thus deliver into the
wealth of the future."[118] In other words, the unanswered questions,
unhealed traumas, unlived aspects, longings and lamentations of our
ancestors are the "poverty" which haunts us and, which, as we attend to
them contribute to the "wealth" of knowledge and consciousness for what
is to come.

The vast expanse of the psyche with all of its dimensions and complexity in its challenge to consciousness necessitates an ongoing reimagining of our understanding of ourselves and the world. My personal

experiences and the experiences of the people I've worked with have not only given me insight into the dynamics, nature, and the complexity of the relationship between consciousness and the unconscious, it has required a re-storying of the nature of reality and the ways in which we come to know what we know.

CHAPTER 7

Following the Path Backward to Create a New Forward

Come to me with the eye of your heart, the ear of your heart.
Take in the deep beauty of your soul,
through the sea lion's song,
the rain's dance,
and the shadows cast by the sunlight herself.
Let your eyes and ears feast on it all
as you remember a time
of long, long ago
and of not yet.
Let the pulse of life enter here now
as you take your next breath and listen.

—Grandfather's Blessing from the Dream Time

Coming into a more conscious relationship with the ancestors involved opening and listening to the ancestors with an imaginal and physical heart. As I opened to the actuality of the presence of the ancestors in the present, an ever evolving and expanding conceptual framework of reality took shape. One of the key concepts at the heart of this work is that we must follow the path backward to create a new forward. This phrase came to me in a dream many years ago. Little did I know at the time the profound implications of this statement.

I wrote the preceding paragraph in 2008, prior to the publishing of *The Red Book* and *Lament of the Dead*. Two years after finishing my dissertation, I read these words in the latter: "What he [Jung] grapples with is the weight of human history and ancestry. He realizes *he can't move forward without going back*, without understanding the implications that the past weighs on him."[1] [italics added] This is not Freud's past of personally repressed memories. It is the cultural historical past of our ancestors. Implied in the phrase from the dream is that one *can* move forward without going backward. However, what the phrase suggests is that a *new* forward can be created by following the path backward, one that is a response to rather than an unconscious re-enactment of the past on an all too familiar personal and collective path.

The actual instruction, invitation in the dream was to "follow the path backward to create a new forward." Understanding the truth in this simple statement has been, for me, a process of what Peat calls "coming-to-knowing." In Native science, knowledge is an ongoing process that unfolds out of an active and reciprocal relationship with the world, a continuing and on-going process of "coming-to-knowing."[2] Coming-to-know, a Native way of creating knowledge, entails a journey. It is not a linear path. It is a process with a meandering path that "occurs through fields of relationships and establishment of a sense of meaning."[3] Jaenke in her doctoral dissertation, *Personal Dreamscape as Ancestral Landscape*, explains that coming-to-know involves "personal engagement, direct experience and personal transformation."[4]

A Story about Causality, Time and Space

As the truth in this simple phrase revealed itself, I realized that my understanding of the communication and intention offered in the dream from which these words originated was limited by my linear concept of time and history which rests on and is rooted in the foundation of our Western worldview. I will share some of this story of coming-to-knowing the meaning of this phrase as an example of the transformation of consciousness that can occur when we listen deeply and tend the promptings and invitations of the psyche. What I came to know provides an expanded foundation for understanding the stories that follow.

A relationship with time that is linear and evolutionary is, for most of us who have been educated and live within the context of modern Western civilization, an accepted and familiar concept. This way of conceptualizing time and history is part of our collectively accepted and tacitly agreed upon framework. It influences the way we see our world, our relationship with place and the land we live on, the questions we ask, the way we ask these questions, the way we listen, the meaning we ascribe to our experiences, and ultimately, as a result, our experience and understanding of all the phenomena which form the basis of life on this planet. Tied to this conceptualization of time is our understanding of causality. In his essay "Archaic Man," Jung writes:

> It is a rational presupposition of ours that everything has a natural and perceptible cause. We are convinced of this. Causality, so understood, is one of our most sacred dogmas. There is no legitimate place in our world for invisible,

arbitrary and so-called supernatural forces. . . . We are now surrounded by a world that is obedient to rational laws.[5]

Experiencing the nature of time as linear, a concept that is not only part of my culture's worldview but organic to the language from which my thoughts are formed and expressed, affected the way I understood the phrase from the dream. The experiences I'll describe below that occurred at a workshop I attended in Santa Fe as part of the book launch of Vine Deloria's book *Jung and Sioux Traditions*, and continued as I wrote this section reveal some of the underlying assumptions that affected my interpretations and understanding of the world, assumptions that are part of the Western, modern worldview as described by Tarnas among others.[6]

The "myth" of modern culture, hidden and revealed in these assumptions would prevail were it not for the challenges implicit in the worldview of other cultures. These experiences by themselves, prior to being subjected to a particular worldview and language, have a phenomenological purity. What follows serves as one example of the ways opening our perception beyond our commonly held Western, modern worldview opens us to noticing in ways we may have forgotten as we differentiated ourselves from the rest of nature.

The essence of Western European identity is founded on the assumption that time proceeds in a linear fashion. This is, according to Deloria, the fundamental philosophical distinction between European and American Indian experience. Imagining time in a linear, sequential, and evolutionary way with history and the ancestors behind us and the future ahead, in different places, and in different times, influenced the way I understand the guidance within the dream.[7]

Through this work I had come to know that the traumatic experiences in the lives of my ancestors were a significant cause of personal and collective suffering in the present. When I began this research I believed that the *sole* reason and purpose in the process of remembering the unconscious traumatic influences of the ancestral, historical, and collective past and taking what restorative and reparative actions I could in the present was to create the possibility of moving forward into a future that was less determined by unconscious complexes from the past. This is an important understanding and approach to healing trauma. However, the relationship between past, present and future, between the ancestors and the living, is more complex.

A perspective of time and space that rests on the cause-and-effect nature of the relationship between past and present has value. It offers a particular way of understanding and relating to personal suffering. A causal perspective, which includes the stories of our ancestors, allows the overwhelming nature of trauma to be understood in new ways and to be broken down into more discrete processes. It opens new possibilities for reparation and restoration in the present based on a more conscious and deeper understanding of one's ancestral past. However, this understanding is limited and limiting.

Following the path backward provided an orientation, a direction and a place to begin. It was an important correction to my conscious attitude and relationship with my parents, grandparents, great-grandparents, and further back through many generations. For most of my life I had been moving forward, away from the past, away from my family and any direct experience or memory of the pain I suffered at the hands of my grandfather. The message in the dream was clear—to create a new forward, which I had been desperately trying to do my entire life, I would have to follow the path backward and reconnect with a traumatic past to discover the deeper roots and origins of this pain.

The dream in which this phrase was offered, as is characteristic of dreams, placed my personal story in relationship with other stories, other times and places, and with an archetypal aspect of reality. In following the path backward through dreams, active imagination, and visions, I was brought through my mother line to a particular time and place in my ancestral and our collective history during King Philip's War. My story and this more inclusive collective story also threaded its way into and through my marriage and divorce. I thought if I could identify *the* original cause across time through the levels of the unconscious, I could address and remediate my personal suffering, at the least, and at best, free my daughters and future descendants from this legacy. As you can see from my story, that was an important part of the process. However, there was more to be seen and known.

A linear, historical, causal concept of time is not the only perspective from which to view the world and our relationship with the ancestors. Deloria reminds us that our concepts of space, time, and matter are how we describe the universe but are not part of its eternal, underlying structure.[8] In his autobiography, Jung uses strong language regarding our relationship with and understanding of our world. He writes,

> We must face the fact that our world, with its time space and causality, relates to another order of things lying behind or beneath it, in which neither "here and there" nor "earlier or later" are of importance. I have been convinced that at least a part of our psychic existence is characterized by a relativity of space and time.[9]

Jung suggests that the possibility that the psyche "touches on a form of existence outside space and time presents a scientific question-mark that merits serious consideration for a time to come."[10] With the concept of relativity and experimental findings in the field of quantum physics our Western ideas regarding the nature of reality are moving beyond many of the boundaries that we have taken for granted.

At the workshop in Santa Fe, which, when I originally wrote about this experience was just yesterday, I listened as a Navajo elder described his and his peoples' concept of time as circular, not linear. I heard him say, there is no distance between the creating and this moment or any other moment in time. Even though I had read about this many times, understood it with my mind and felt resonance in my heart and body, as he talked I experienced a different consciousness of time and its and my relationship with the nature of matter and space. The truth of his experience was communicated through his words, his presence and the presence of "nature" around and within us all. I listened to his words and felt the deep knowing that originated in his personal experience from which his words were created. As I opened to the sympathetic resonance that exists within all of nature, I experienced a shift in my understanding that was bone deep. My way of thinking about time and space began to catch up with the actuality of the way I was experiencing myself in relationship with the world. The truth in what I had been reading regarding the concept and experience of time and space from an Indigenous Science perspective became an embodied knowing.[11] As I listened to this elder I knew with certainty in my mind, heart, and body that the traumas, wisdom, and dreams of our ancestors exist in the moment in the matter of our bodies and the land. The split between mind and body, spirit and matter, time and space, primitive and modern, past and future did not exist.

Leroy Little Bear, trying to explain to David Peat the "sense of movement within time that most Native American societies share," told him that

> within this metaphysics of time and reality the buffalo are still present. It is as if, to use images from our own Western view of science, other spaces and times interpenetrate and coexist with our own. To traditional people this is no mere metaphor or poetic image but the reality in which they live, and since to The People time is a great circle, the time of the buffalo will return again.[12]

Deloria describes the American Indian understanding of the nature of reality in *Spirit and Reason:*

> [I]f there were other dimensions to life—the religious experiences and dreams certainly indicated the presence of other ways of living, even other places— they were regarded as part of an organic whole and not as distinct from other experiences, times, and places in the same way that Western thinkers have always believed.[13]

The schism that exists in our worldview between matter and spirit is also experienced and viewed differently by the Dagara people of West Africa.

Some writes that matter and Spirit are two sides of an interdependent reality that are manifestations of each other. Balance and stability are achieved through a constant "stream of interaction" between the two.[14] This way of seeing the world is very congruent with Jung's theory of synchronicity. He states, "psyche and matter exist in the same world and one partakes of the other."[15] Moments of synchronicity reveal this relationship between psyche and matter pointing "to a profound harmony between all forms of existence."[16] For the Dagara, matter is viewed as a veil which obscures "the brighter world of Spirit." Some likens this veil to a permeable skin that creates a boundary between the worlds of Spirit and matter.[17] According to Some, beings, such as the ancestors, who exist in other worlds, are not merely personified aspects of psyche. They are as real as we are, just living in a different time/space continuum.

Although the landscape from which these concepts originate is separated by an ocean, this way of viewing reality within Dagara culture has much in common with the ideas and practices in American Indian cultures. According to Peat, within an indigenous, American Indian perspective, symbols are reflections of reality, not mere abstractions. Through these "symbols" one can connect directly with "the energies, spirits, and animating powers of nature."[18] Indians, according to Deloria, are aware that there are other dimensions of reality and think that the experience in these other realities is not much different than what they experience in the reality of the senses.[19]

Returning to the day I listened to this Navajo elder speak, I remember hearing him say that accessing the wisdom within the natural world is not about remembering something that has been lost. It is all here, now, in the wind, the animals, the plants, the sun, the thunder . . . The question is not what have we forgotten, but how do we connect with what is right here, right now—that which has been with us, of which we are a part, since the beginning. As he spoke about this, the wind blew strongly into the room through the open doors, gusting with a punctual resonance congruent with his speaking. It is important to note that although much of this natural wisdom is available in the present, much has also been lost. As tribes have been decimated and dislocated from the land of their ancestors, many of the rituals, songs, ceremonies, and indigenous languages have been forgotten and have not been passed on through the generations.

I had been writing about the ways the ancestors were present in our symptoms and dreams. I had an altar devoted to the ancestors, which, much like Bollingen but on a much smaller scale, provided a space where the "silent, greater family, stretching down the centuries," unhindered by time and space could be heard.[20] I understood from a Jungian perspective that time and space are relativized in the unconscious. I had experiences of the ancestors through visions, active imagination, and dreams. However, until that moment when the wind blew vigorously through the door as the Navajo man spoke, the fundamental foundation on which my understanding of time and space was based had remained firmly fixed in a modern Western worldview. According to Some, for most indigenous people, learning is simply "remembering what you already know."[21] In that moment I experienced a sense of the ancestors being present right here, right now, *and* within time, history, and the future with all of its distinct moments. I experienced and knew that the ancestors and their wisdom are alive, accessible, and present in every "new" moment throughout time, as some aspect of our consciousness is always ever-present with them. My experience, opened by listening to and being in the presence of the Navajo man, of the present in relationship with the past and future, unlocked time from its linear and causal anchors.

"The historical now" is one of the four dynamics of Native science: Apela Colorado, Founder and Director at Worldwide Indigenous Science Network, describes this concept beautifully. "Today, every day, we see our ancestors making the trail for us as we work and move about the face and surface of our mother, the earth. Past present, future perfect and future exist at this moment."[22] Peat describes the Native American's experience of time in this way,

> To the Native mind time is alive, and, if it must be pictured as a flowing river, then it is a river in which the mind is free to swim and move. Time does not exist apart from, and independent of, the spirits of nature and the lives of the people; its processes must be constantly acknowledged and renewed.[23]

Writing specifically about the Sioux universe, Deloria informs us that some of the ideas of time within that worldview appear to be "reasonably close" to those within the Western universe. However, there is

> also an apprehension of time among the tribal/primitive peoples that another dimension of time exists over and above or within ordinary time. This time is sacred; that is, spirits who have their own chronology inhabit it and are bound by it. Yet this time dimension also contains human destinies and therefore is able to intrude upon secular time in order to accomplish a larger task.[24]

There is the sense of an eternal "now" where and when all generations are present and simultaneous continuity exists between the living and non-living. As in the Dagara worldview, in the Sioux universe, the spirit and earthly worlds are reflections and extensions of each other.

> Sioux people frequently suggest the oneness of time in generational terms, from Black Elk's observation of a multigenerational process of Sioux people to the Ghost Dance's dream of re-engagement with ancestors and landscapes

out of historical time. These various examples of the apprehension of time suggest that, despite their inevitable linkage, time may be more complex than space, and that we are subject to the timeline of another dimension that is itself unfolding to accomplish a specific goal.[25]

An African sangoma told me that the ancestors are in front of us suggesting the teleological nature of their presence.[26] In the past, their lives were lived in distinct historical moments that preceded and continue to co-exist with our personal and collective lives in this present moment consciously and unconsciously. These events, which occurred in the lives of our ancestors, cannot be changed. Their trauma, unlived dreams and unanswered questions live on in the reality of psyche in each of us in deeply personal and particular ways. Their stories continue living in the land and in the earth of our individual bodies. In the present moment we are formed from the DNA of our ancestors who have traveled across continents and centuries carrying in their DNA an evolutionary history and ancestral story which is particular in its expression through each of us. And, they are indeed before us in the questions we are compelled to ask and in the eyes and dreams of our children. As Colorado explains, the ancestors are making the trail for us in the historical now.[27]

This perspective fits within Jung's experience of and theoretical description of the psyche. Throughout his work, in a number of places, Jung writes about the "relativization" of time and space with regard to the collective unconscious. His experiences with and observations of the unconscious were rich with examples of ways psyche is not limited by or within space and time. For Jung

There is no trouble with time in the unconscious. Part of our psyche is not in time and not in space. They are only an illusion, time and space, and so in a certain part of our psyche time does not exist at all.[28]

The nature of the unconscious psyche is trans-spatial and trans-temporal. In its deepest reaches the psyche "participates in a form of existence beyond space and time, and thus partakes of what is inadequately and symbolically described as eternity."[29]

Following Jung through his theoretical examination regarding the relationship between spirit and matter, Deloria concludes that the conceptual and theoretical "Jungian universe" is "compatible with the worlds in which many tribal/primitive peoples live and have lived."[30] Within these two different, but compatible worldviews, time and space are intertwined and flexible. He concludes that "[t]here are at least two time dimensions intertwined and moving in the same direction that we can experience. One we can observe, and one we find through mystical and unusual experiences."[31]

American Indians, according to Deloria, think in terms of space. Their lands, the places they live, are the central reference point for their thinking and being. The Sioux understanding of space can be summarized as "a collection of knowledge, and of experiences of events occurring at specific locations, that appear to violate the normal expectations of secular space and distance."[32] The "sacred manifestation of space" included "expansive and relative space, simultaneous material/spiritual space, and even material/spiritual movements across space."[33]

For "primitive peoples," the naturally intertwined nature of space and time is not split either conceptually or as a way of understanding the world.[34] Within a "primitive" worldview as described by Deloria, experience is unified "in a continuum that transcends traditional Western divisions of time and space."[35] From this perspective, our understanding of any given event or experience in its immediacy and particularity is a manifestation of the unity of the natural world of which humans are an integral part. Experiencing and sharing experiences seen and articulated from this perspective relieves it from the imposition of cause and effect.

The Dagara believe the spirits of our ancestors reside in nature. For indigenous people, according to Some, the divine, rather than separate from nature and heavenly, rises from the ground beneath our feet.[36] Nature and place host spirit and memory in a way that is both located and experienced in the present that also transcends time. Nature does not and cannot forget or ignore the wounds that are inflicted by humans. In the Dagara worldview nature is a hospitable place for our spirits after we die.[37] From this perspective, the ancestors are more than autonomous complexes or projected unconscious contents. They are a living reality residing on the other side of ours, always and ever present in nature.

The subtle difference between objects representing an invisible presence and being an embodiment of presence is a distinction that affects the way being in dialogue with the ancestors is experienced and understood. In a lecture, Some stated that from an indigenous perspective, a piece of carved wood such as a mask is not just a representation of the ancestor, it *is* the ancestor.[38] The spirit of the ancestor is in the mask. To be in relationship and dialogue with the ancestors requires, according to Some, moving from "a state of cognition" in which this is not just an idea but is "a reality." Some explained that when the Dagara say ancestors exist it's not a subjective thing or figment of their imagination.

For those of us educated in a modern, Western perspective, to experience the presence of our ancestors in this way requires allowing ourselves to suspend our rational mind and engage with the eye and ear of our hearts. Listening and seeing with our hearts enables us to experience the spirits of our ancestors in a stone, or hawk, or mountain crag. In my experience and as will be seen in the stories in Chapter 10 and Chapter 11, the ancestors "speak" to us through nature. I encourage people to spend time in nature. In my experience, nature, as container and facilitator, aids the healing process that is such an important aspect of this work.

As I wrote this section, a day after listening to this Navajo elder, crow perched above me, standing at the edge of the open skylight cawing away. At first I found crow's cawing to be merely part of the annoying and intrusive noise I was trying to tune out. As I re-read what I'd written above, remembering that this crow, like the wind rushing through the door as a Navajo elder spoke about nature's presence in the present, was part of this larger conversation of which we are all a part, I stopped writing and listened. Opening myself to and acknowledging crow's presence, I was pulled into the present moment. I laughed out loud, certain that I was being directly addressed. Although I do not understand this crow's language, although I lack a cosmological context in which to place this experience, out of my listening, out of being in relationship with crow sitting at the edge of the skylight cawing, listening with both my heart and mind, I experience something of the nature of the paradigm shift that I am trying to express with the words on these pages. As I placed the period at the end of the preceding paragraph, crow stopped cawing and flew away. As I acknowledge him now and thank him, heart-to-heart, for his persistent presence as I write these words on this page, he caws from a distance one more time.

Ted Andrews in *Animal-Speak*, tells us that crows are the smartest of birds and enjoy that to the fullest. They have a remarkable voice range and a complex language. They are actually a member of the songbird family. There are many stories and mythologies involving crows. When crow appears it may reflect a connection to past-lives placing one in relationship with different times and cultures. As symbols of creation and spiritual strength, crow's presence may also connect us with archetypal forces. Andrews suggests that crows

> remind us to look for opportunities to create and manifest the magic of life. They are messengers calling to us about the creation and magic that is alive within our world everyday and available to us.[39]

I will let his words speak for themselves with the hope that some of the mystery in this experience is present for the reader in this moment.

Stepping outside of a linear concept of time allows an experience of the present as it co-exists with and originates from the lives of our ancestors in any given moment. Future also exists within these moments of connection out of the actuality of the present. The lives of our ancestors root us to our origins and carry within them a future necessity. Reconceptualizing the trauma and the dreams of *my* ancestors and *the* ancestors themselves as present and available in any and each given moment in time through a connection with nature and place affects the ways I understand the nature of the phenomenon, and how I hear and respond to what is being asked for in the moment. Rather than trying to fix what is wrong, I come into relationship with what was and is so. It then becomes a question of listening into the disharmony and dis-ease in relationship with all things and asking what is needed to restore balance.

Experiences of trauma to the land, to other living creatures, to entire peoples, and to specific individuals have occurred throughout history. According to Deloria, the souls of people who have suffered traumatic events remain in those places where they died.[40] Initially, following the path backward on a wave of resonant affect placed me in relationship to a particular and traumatic moment in the history of this land in the life of my ancestor. Asking whether or not my personal trauma originated in and was somehow caused by the events in 1676 when Providence burned becomes too simple a question within the context of this expanded framework.

The opportunity to connect with and know is a matter of how one listens. Understanding this, knowing more consciously the nature of the ancestors' presence in the present connected to place and experiencing the relationship between the past, present, and future as a "historical now" opens new possibilities for understanding and addressing trauma. There is no past tense in the Lakota language or in many other Native American languages. Fred Gustafson, a Jungian analyst who has been studying Lakota for years, shared with me that in the Lakota language the past is implied in phrases like "a long time ago" or "yesterday." In the English language we would say "many years ago our people **were** killed at Wounded Knee."   In Lakota—"many years ago our people **are being** killed at Wounded Knee. Yesterday is still happening today. In an email to me Fred wrote, "If the world can come to see this, it would open up an entirely new way of relating."[41]

Healing in the present is connected across and through time and space. Opening in any given moment to the ancestors, their presence and their stories, which exist in our physical and psychical landscape, informs an ethical responsibility to a multidimensional relational, co-creative process. The stories and experiences of my ancestors inform the nature of what is out of balance and in need of restorative action in my experience of the effects of trauma in the present. Standing in the present, my ancestors before me making the trail, the path opens and a new forward is co-created.

Part of the significance of this experience is that the ancestors are inseparable from the experience of the physical world, nature and our bodies. Their presence was not "as if" or a result of active imagination, ritual or an altered state of consciousness, but of an altered worldview. My experience of the presence of the ancestors resulted from opening my perceptual boundaries to what is actually, already, and ever present in and part of the sensual, physically and psychically embodied world. From the new perspective, which came through this experience of listening, imagining time as a flowing river and symptoms having various points of interconnected temporal and spatial origins rather than causes, I understood how the traumas of the past as well as the wisdom of our ancestors are present and available in each moment in a substantial, embodied way. Feeling a direct connection with the ancestors in, not through, the landscape in which time was relative, in which past, present and future exist simultaneously, opened an ontological and epistemological window that had been gradually opening, through engaging in a more conscious dialogue with the ancestors. Through this window, the world reveals itself in previously unnoticed ways.

As I wrote the sentence about an ontological and epistemological window opening, the wind blew fiercely through the open living room window, rattling the vertical blinds that stretched across the entire width of the picture window. I would like to say that I knew I was being addressed, but old habits and ways of being in the world are easier to write about than to embody and live from. I continued to read, re-read, and edit this section on time and space, deepening into my understanding of Sioux, Dagara, and American Indian concepts and experiences of the world. I did not notice when the wind stopped blowing. I also did not notice until I got up about an hour later that the blowing wind had pulled the blinds aside along their track exposing a foot and a half of open window while I sat trying to tune out the noise and concentrate on writing. It was only when I walked from the bathroom on my return to my chair that I saw the opening in the blinds. My first thought was to wonder when I had pulled them back. Then it struck me—and crow flies by the window cawing as I write this—the wind pulled the blinds aside, opening my view to the landscape outside of my window as I was writing about a window opening to a new way of seeing and understanding the world. In the several months I have lived in this space, window open, wind sometimes blowing, this had never happened before.

This experience occurred several months after writing the paragraphs that describe my experiences of crow cawing. It happened in a completely different home—one without a skylight. As I write these words I am experiencing a sense of awe, gratitude, and humility at the way in which the world continues to meet me as I look for ways to put into words and adequately express this emerging perspective which has its origins in both Western depth psychology and the "primitive" forgotten depths of psyche. By opening to nature's voice and attempting to give expression to my experience, a more active and conscious integration of my modern and archaic consciousness, of self with world, of my human nature with nature and spirit and matter is taking place. Different ways of thinking, of imagining time, of knowing, of listening and memory come together through experiences of crow, wind and the wisdom embodied in the Navajo elder.

My individual experience of trauma exists as both a single point and as "the universe" of affectively resonant traumas of my ancestors, this culture and the land with which we live. Its origins are both individual and collective as evidenced in the particularities of my story. My personal wounding, through an experience of resonance in the present, places me in relationship to other particular ancestral, collective, and ecological traumas. The visions and dreams, the wisdom, the stories, the questions left to be answered are present in the landscape of my body and the land from which I was born. All wisdom, all trauma, exists and can be heard, felt and known right here in the embodied now.

Cajete explains that "Indigenous logic moves between relationships, revisiting, moving to where it is necessary to learn or to bring understandings together. Eventually this process, a synthesis, leads to a higher reflective level of thinking."[42] The date of Providence burning and the date of my birth places two distinct times and two separate places in relationship with each other. Somehow these experiences belong together, not causally, but through meaning. These events would fit within Jung's definition of synchronicity. Jung proposes, given what is known from parapsychological events, that "all reality would be grounded on an as yet unknown substrate possessing material and at the same time psychic qualities. . . . It affords us an opportunity to construct a new world model closer to the idea of the *unus mundus*."[43]

Peat comes to the same conclusion. Synchronicities indicate "that a mutual process is unfolding out of the same ground and that this ground must therefore lie beyond the individual consciousness that is located in time and space."[44] In Deloria's reading of Jung, he suggests that an accumulation of synchronistic events reveals and is evidence of the actuality of this underlying "personal, intelligent, constitutive energy" of the world, the "great mysterious" that is just beneath the surface of physical reality.[45] Indigenous, scientific and psychological perspectives begin to mirror each other in their view of reality. As bridges are made between perspectives, a solid theoretical foundation is created for those of us in modern, Western culture to engage more consciously with the ancestors in the present.

Honoring the nature of these kinds of experiences necessitates a wide angle of interpretation, a way to read the world which widens our traditional modern, Western point of view, our ways of being in relationship with the world, our perception, and our experience and understanding of personal and collective suffering. When faced with this nonrational dimension of reality, the ground on which our identification with our egos and our faith in rationality begins to shift with uncertainty. We can find these experiences annoying, fearful, dismiss them as mere coincidences, define them as projections, and identify them as pathological. And, we can open the windows of perception and see and listen in a different way. It's equally important as we open to listening in a new way that we not see these experiences as extra-ordinary. As remarkable as they are, they are within the normal range of human experience.

Well-Being

The Red Book depicts Jung's direct experiences of the living reality of the collective unconscious. It provides us with pathways and road signs that can help us negotiate this territory. In Hillman's conversations with Shamdasani about *The Red Book*, Hillman observes that "These fantasies didn't concern himself alone. That goes back to the voices of the dead. There's a collective strength, and collective message, a collective importance in what is coming up."[46] In a later conversation Hillman describes it in this way,

> It's the weight of human history, the voices of the dead, opening the mouth of the dead and hearing what they have to say, not just the deep repressed or forgotten, it's the actual living presence of history in the soul, the past in the soul.[47]

Jung's dialogues with the figures in *The Red Book* are also prescriptive. They provide insight and direction for how to be in relationship with "the land of the dead," the unconscious. These figures also offer insight and direction regarding how to be in relationship with the world as a human being. It is good medicine. The spirit of the depths teaches Jung, "there is a knowledge of the heart that gives deeper insight.[48]

Jung continues scribing what he has learned from the spirit of the depths. Knowledge of the heart is attained by living one's life to the full—not a life that is directed only by the spirit of the times, but an authentic life that results from being in relationship with the unconscious, the spirit of the depths. What then informs how one lives one's life? The spirit of the depths tells Jung, "Well-being decides, not your well-being, not the well-being of the others, but only well-being."[49] The spirit of the depths teaches Jung that he is a servant, rather than the image he had of himself as "a leader with ripe thoughts."[50]

Cajete uses the phrase "spiritual ecology" to refer to a way of living which is reflected throughout native understanding and ways of being.[51]

Mutually reciprocal relationships exist within and between all of creation, of which the ancestors are a part. The familiar concept often associated with American Indian philosophy that we are all related has deep meaning within which is an implied ethical responsibility—a natural result of seeing the world this way. Humans are one expression of nature, equal with all others and part of a complex, differentiated and integrated whole. Harmony among all is the guiding principle. Humans are responsible for their role within the larger cosmos.

It seems the spirit of the depths offers Jung a guide for living that is similar to the idea of spiritual ecology which is part of the foundation for living for Native people as Cajete describes above. This new understanding reflects a view of reality which rests on the wider epistemology of the heart Tarnas describes, one which is no longer exclusively rational but imaginal, revelatory and epiphanic; one which is a result of deep empathic listening.[52]

To serve in maintaining what Colorado refers to as "the Great Peace" in each moment in relationship with personal trauma necessitates placing one's story in immediate relationship in the present with the collective—familial, ancestral, national, cultural and ecological—stories.[53] Following the path backward to create a "new forward" from a perspective in which the origins of trauma from different levels of consciousness and different historical times co-exist in the present, informed by spiritual ecology and maintaining the Great Peace, makes "healing" a process of restoring and maintaining balance and harmony in the moment in relationship with the past and an emerging and co-created future. The concept of well-being offered to Jung as the guiding principle from the spirit of the depths, serves as the compass.

CHAPTER 8

A Shared Collective Legacy

Phantoms of generations past are in our bodies. These explain us to ourselves.[1]

—Linda Hogan

I wondered if my story was unique in the way it appears to demonstrate the intimate connection between personal, ancestral, and collective trauma. I discovered it was not. Kat Duff, a Jungian analyst, and Linda Hogan, a writer and teacher, have stories which, like mine, reveal the depths and multi-located origins of suffering in their personal story.[2] Placing our stories in dialogue with each other reveals the way the long history of genocide, dislocation, and trauma to the people native to the North American continent continues to haunt the bodies and psyches of individuals in the present.

There are limitations in the presentation of their stories. I used written texts. The process of editing and publishing Kat's and Linda's books, from which their stories in this book are derived, influenced the way their stories were originally told. Additionally, I've chosen to retell only parts of their stories and have chosen only some of their words. What is shared on these pages is taken out of their original context. Their stories have gone through another level of editing and are now seen through my eyes, witnessed and re-presented. I have chosen particular quotes and parts of their stories which are particularly relevant to the theme of this book. It would be impossible to do justice to the depth and complexity of each of their stories in these few pages. If you find yourself interested in or touched by Linda's and Kat's stories in this selectively abridged presentation, I wholeheartedly encourage you to read their books.

When I discovered these stories I read them without a preconceived idea of what I would find. As I read their stories, more than once I might add, particular aspects began to stand out revealing not only similarities in the experience of trauma and the process of recovery, but an underlying commonality in the origin of our suffering that was ancestral, historical and cultural. Kat's and Linda's stories describe a journey into and through personal trauma that, in their telling and their content, challenge the more commonly accepted cultural narratives regarding the history of this North American continent and the stories about the "founding" of America. Their stories also challenge and expand our understanding of the origins of personal illness and suffering.

For healing to occur, personal trauma and suffering needs to be witnessed. I approached Kat's and Linda's stories with the attitude of a compassionate witness. As I read their stories I experienced a witnessing of my own story through their words. This is the power inherent in testimony for the reader as well as the writer. Shoshana Felman describes testimony as a healing encounter, not just a historical transmission of events.[3] Our stories are not a statement of, but rather a mode of access to, previously buried truths. I humbly offer this retelling of their stories in service to the children of our children's children. If it contributes in any way to personal, familial, or cultural healing, I am grateful.

"The Alchemy of Illness"

Kat Duff, a Jungian analyst, writes about her experience of personal illness and ancestral trauma in *The Alchemy of Illness.* Her story is of a fall into the abyss of Chronic Fatigue Syndrome (CFIDS). Prior to her illness, Kat was very active, thinking ahead, always moving toward the future. Her disease announced itself one day after a counseling session with a client. Noticing for the first time the intricate patterns in the Persian rug under her feet, she felt herself sinking "like an anchor at sea, with exhaustion and decided to lie down for a few minutes."[4] She woke up an hour later to the sound of her doorbell ringing. She was too exhausted to get up. Although she was eventually able to get up off the floor, she says that she "never really got up again."[5]

She remembers little of the first months of her illness. Exhausted, she was unable to move. Her previous way of living, of dashing around in her Toyota, from one task and event to the next "with such fervent zeal" became a memory difficult to reconcile with the contrary experience of her illness.[6] Chronic Fatigue Syndrome (CFIDS) turned her world upside-down, reversing the assumptions she had about her daily life. Like the patterns in the Persian rug, things she couldn't see before become painfully apparent.

Her forward movement halted, her story turned upside down, repressed memories of the sexual abuse she had suffered as an infant rose to the surface. They returned like clips in a movie, out of context, devoid of sensation or feeling. Recovery from her illness was inseparable from recovery from her abuse. Van der Kolk and van der Hart write about this inability to arrange traumatic memory into comprehensible words and symbols. Unlike a normal memory, traumatic memories become "organized on a somatosensory or iconic level: as somatic sensations, behavioral reenactments, nightmares, flashbacks."[7] Like her fall onto the Persian rug, CFIDS carried Kat down into the intricate patterns of the symptomatic landscape of her past.

Freud's and Jung's understanding of the psyche, phenomenologically informed and grounded in experience, attest to its timeless quality. From a depth psychological perspective, the past is always present; personal, ancestral, and collective memories are preserved in the unconscious energetically and, as in Kat's case, may find expression symptomatically in our bodies. There is a story that is told about Jung's response to the question— where is the shadow? He took his index finger and laid it on his cheek. The shadow, although not conscious, is written into the lines and contours of our face on "the other cheek." For Kat, the personal, ancestral, and collective shadow was written on her body.

The iconic bits and pieces of the memory of Kat's sexual abuse lived in the physical terrain of her illness until they could consciously find their place in her story. As Kat began to experience her buried personal memories, she discovered a connection between her personal wounding and the suffering of the Sioux at the hands of her ancestors. Her ancestors had settled on Sioux land, displacing the native Minnesota who had lived on the land for countless generations. The well being of this Sioux tribe was intimately intertwined with this land which fed them and held the bones, stories, wisdom and memories of their ancestors. Driven from their land by Kat's great-grandfather in the name of progress, many Sioux suffered and died from sickness and starvation. The shaman she worked with as part of her process of healing explained to Kat that those deaths "made a gash in the land, and your body is the wound."[8]

Her illness became a portal into the unearthed abuses of forgotten and repressed parts of her personal story, her family's story, and her ancestral story. The painful truths that were excluded from the family narrative, that remained unacknowledged in the past or the present, were inscribed symptomatically on Kat's body. She writes, "Our bodies remember it all: our births, the delights and terrors of a lifetime, the journeys of our ancestors, the very evolution of life on earth."[9] Helene Lorenz, a Jungian analyst and teacher, states that symptoms, addictions, and illness may be the only markers of the historical event, and these cannot be given up, because without them there would be no recognition of what happened.[10]

Traumatic memory cannot find its place in the overall narrative of an individual, a community, a culture, or a historical period. The story, unhinged from its moorings in time and space, is frozen, remembered out of context in its insistent, intrusive repetitions. In her book on trauma, Cathy Caruth, an analyst who specializes in trauma, explains that "the traumatized . . . carry an impossible history within them . . . . They become themselves the symptom of a history they cannot entirely possess"[11] Trauma by its nature is an experience that one is unable to experience fully at the time or assimilate. It returns in very particular ways as an unwanted symptom, compulsions, or vivid and intrusive memories, suffered over and over again.

CFIDS literally froze Kat in her tracks and made it impossible for her to continue to push herself forward with her will. Her illness was a frozen record of very specific parts of her personal and ancestral story. Her body "remembered" the events which had occurred in her childhood abuse and the marginalized pieces of the story of the trauma that resulted from the actions of her ancestors. Kat's experience in the present was not merely a reenactment of a dislocated piece of history. Carrying the emotional force and weight of her personal and ancestral traumatic experiences, her symptoms bore witness to a past that was never fully acknowledged or experienced. Kat's physical symptoms serve in some way as a counter memorial to her great-grandfather's actions. Peter Homans, a religious scholar who devoted his life to exploring the process of mourning, writes:

> Unlike the traditional monument, the countermonument does not console or reassure—it does not heal. On the contrary, it torments its neighbors . . . the monument is a bearer and carrier of viewer's memories, imaginings and fantasies about the events it represents.[12]

Kat's chronic fatigue, like a countermonument to an unacknowledged and unspeakable past, bore witness to the personal, ancestral, and cultural trauma that had remained buried in the shadows for four generations. This unassimilated piece of her personal and our collective history became an insistent and intrusive presence in her life in the form of her illness. CFIDS was an unspoken record of the events which occurred in her childhood and served as a symbolic and literal re-experiencing of the repressed and traumatic pieces of the story of her ancestors. The official recorded history and the history told by her family had been written selectively by those in power. It did not include the collective and individual trauma suffered by an entire tribe of displaced people. This part of our collective story endured and was remembered in the present through Kat's body.

Her individual suffering and well being were woven into the story of her ancestors and the history of this land and its people, her body a memorial to and a remembering of a forgotten and unrecorded history. Unable to fully heal using medical and psychological treatments, Kat sought help from a shaman. To heal herself, she would have to honor those who had died as a result of her grandfather's actions and make offerings to them. As she consciously researched this history, remembered, and honored these forgotten and exiled people, she felt as if a weight which she had carried her entire life was lifting. Remembering, witnessing, honoring, and making offerings were integral to her process of healing. Finally, addressing the deeper levels of collective suffering that lived in her family story, she knew she would get well. She offers this perspective on illness in this culture.

> I would suspect the psyches and bodies of twentieth-century Americans are crowded and overflowing with these ghosts of memory so implicated in disease, because we as a people are so oriented toward progress and eager to escape the burdens and complications of continuity. It is the American way (as exemplified by my ancestors, but also by my own life) to leave one's home and past behind to start a new life on the great frontier, leaving a terrible—and toxic—trail of unfinished business.[13]

Gathering the Pieces of "Fallen Worlds and People"[14]

Linda Hogan's personal suffering was a result of the devastation of American Indian communities. Her Chickasaw ancestors were forcibly removed from Mississippi and Tennessee by federal legislation. They walked the Trail of Tears. The cost of their journey west was immeasurable. "We were broken, almost forever, by grief and betrayal."[15] This traumatic legacy continues. Linda's personal suffering is a continuation of the story of her people.

Linda grew up in Oklahoma, Germany, and Colorado. She describes herself as painfully shy and vulnerable, depressed, and neglected as a child. Her teeth had rotted, and were black and decayed. Other students taunted her and called her names. Her life was shaped by "a poverty of the heart."[16] Her mother cooked for her family providing nutritional sustenance, but could not touch or express any love. At the age of 12, living with her family on a military base in Germany, she met a man who took care of her, who loved her in ways that filled some of the empty places in her heart. For all intents and purposes this was a marriage. The relationship ended when she was 15 and her family moved back to America. Crossing the ocean, making her journey home, she writes, "as an Indian girl, I was moving toward my own continent, my place, bound to the American continent and all that transpired before my birth. This time my own story was added to it."[17]

Her parents' unspoken and unwitnessed histories filled their home with their silence. It was a place with no words, an absence of narratives for their suffering. As a child in this family filled with silences, Linda could not find the words to speak. The stories lay buried, untold and unknown. The grief of her family and her people remained unnamed, their stories untold and buried in the silence. She

> grew up with girls who cut or hit or burned themselves, as if it was a way to kill the self or to trade the pain of what resided within for external pain. There was never a language to say it, to form a geography or map or history, but to ourselves. We grew in a silence. In those days there were no songs, no incantations, not even any prayers that would lay it out before us. We hurt ourselves; our own bodies became our language.[18]

As a young woman she describes herself as lost. She drank suicidally. She wanted to "fall, to jump out of, or perhaps into" her own life.[19] Linda's father and grandfather were alcoholics. Her grandfather had done well as a rancher and cowboy. But in the Depression, losing all of his assets, betrayed even by his family, he gave up and fell into poverty and alcoholism. She describes herself as a drunk, not an alcoholic. There is a difference she says—a drunk wants to forget, to not remember every day of their life. Being a drunk was her way of escaping the collective pain of our American history. To stop drinking meant feeling the terrible grief of her people and this land. She writes, "Later I would fall through a life, fall as my grandfather did upon the sharp fences and boundaries of an America whose dark ongoing history is still unbearable."[20] She wanted to, needed to fall to the earth to heal her broken heart.

She remembers reading about the Sand Creek Massacre. The men returned to their camp to find their women and children killed and mutilated. Their despair was so great, words so inadequate, that they took the pain into their own bodies stabbing and cutting themselves. "There was not a language, even then, for such pain. That was the reason they hurt themselves. And the distance of this history still reverberates, entering into this and every day."[21]

The dislocation of native peoples and the destruction of the land on the North American continent share a coincidental history. Although the stories and history of suffering of the people native to this land are written in the geography of each individual and the body of the earth, the stories of the lives of American Indians are still missing from the American collective narrative. Linda inherited the trauma and wounds of American history. Her personal trauma originates in the collective trauma of American Indians. This unspeakable trauma lived in her bones, could be heard in the silence within her family, was carried in the scars on her body, and, I would suggest, possibly in the neuromuscular disease, she suffers from as an adult.

Carrying the wounds of a silenced history she descended into alcoholism and drug abuse. Attending an AA meeting, she heard the stories of other Indian people. For the first time she saw that her personal pain and problems were mirrored in the experiences and stories of others. This was when she knew

> History is our illness. It is recorded there, laid down along the tracks and pathways and synapses. I was only one in a lineage of fallen worlds and people. Those of us who walked out of genocide by some cast of fortune still struggle with the brokenness of our bodies and hearts.[22]

Families and tribes were uprooted from the land of their people, forced to relocate far from the places which held the bones of their ancestors and the memory of their people in the land. Their rituals, dances, stories, and even their languages were outlawed. The richness of cultures and languages shattered and broke into pieces with each loss. The transmission of memories and wisdom that had been passed from one generation to the next for centuries, no longer grounded in the places of their origin, were splintered and scattered along with the people.

The genocide of Indians was the "most massive and long-lasting genocide in the history of the world. Between 1520 and 1620, seventy million people throughout the Americas died.[23] There is an impossibility, an unimaginability, and unspeakability to the suffering in the history and the memories of the slaughter of Indians on the North American continent. The decimation of entire peoples and their ways of life, the stories of the Sand Creek Massacre, of King Philip's War, the Battle of Slim Buttes, and the massacre at Wounded Knee, haunt the body of the land and the bodies of the people who belong to this land. The memories of the trauma done to the people native to this land, although buried below consciousness, are remembered in the land, in the psyche and in many of the bodies of many of us who are connected to this collective trauma through our ancestry in very particular ways. These splintered memories of trauma to the collective fabric of our being continue to haunt us until they are remembered, re-collected, witnessed and honored, the losses grieved and reparations and offerings are made.

In his article on trauma and community, Erikson distinguishes between individual and collective trauma. Individual trauma is experienced as "a blow to the psyche that breaks through one's defenses so suddenly and with such brutal force that one cannot react to it effectively."[24] Collective trauma is a blow to the social fabric of a community. In collective trauma the bonds of communality which hold people together slowly and insidiously erode. This is the legacy of genocide on the North American continent. This legacy also haunts other lands where indigenous people and their way of life have been and are being colonized and annihilated. A wound to one is a wound to the collective body of which we are all a part. Unconscious, this unbearable pain is remembered and finds expression in physical symptoms, addictions, physical and mental illness and abuse, synchronicities, and dreams. When even one individual remembers and responds accordingly, the well-being of the collective is restored one piece at a time. When stories are shared, it touches the shared collective memory of each listener in ways that can be transformative. Linda's life and the lives of other Indians are a living testimony of a painful part of America's history. They exist as a parallel and separate stream of reality from the dominant cultural narrative of the history of the American soil.

Searching for the story of her mother's life as an adult, Linda put together the pieces she could gather from photographs, cards, and from other objects that had been collected and stored. Finding only bits and pieces, she realized the puzzle of her mother's life would remain a mystery. What she did find and remembers from her childhood tells a story of a disturbed daughter and a mother who feared phone calls, walking past windows and going out in public; a mother who believed that everyone would steal from her or would hurt her. Linda inherited her mother's fears. Her mother's pain did not find expression in words, nor was it ever spoken about. Whatever abuse or injury her mother suffered went unacknowledged, except for one time when her father told Linda that her mother wasn't stable enough to drive a car. The silences within which this pain lived were so deep that these simple words from her father were a gift. His words finally acknowledged that something in their lives was not quite right.

Linda and her father, searching for themselves "as individuals and tribal people," went back to their homeland in Oklahoma in search of their world, their histories.[25] Reconnecting with the land "the place I lived before I was born." with tribal dances and ceremony, learning the history of her family and her tribe, she began to collect the fragmented pieces of the story of her life and the lives of her people.[26] Linda's journey of personal recovery was tied to the threads of her people's tribal and ancestral memories.

Returning to her father's mother's house, which was now burned to the ground, Linda looked at the ruins:

There were broken dishes I remembered, lying on the ground alongside other discarded, burned, or otherwise broken goods. An instant tea jar still contained brown crystals of tea. I picked up a chip from one of the dishes and put it in my pocket along with the plant fossils from the "tanque," our name for the man-made waterhole. I carried away mementos not only for the memory and connection, but as if these things would prove my life, my tribe, my worth.[27]

Her father, after gathering these pieces of memory from their families and their peoples' past, was transformed as the "generations of anger and hurt" found expression.[28]

Linda adopted two daughters, both Lakota children. Their birth mother had abandoned them. The girls, once found, were placed in foster care. They came to Linda's home with unwritten, unspoken stories. In time, their stories would slowly be revealed. Before being adopted, before she was six, her older daughter, Marie, had suffered horrible things that most of us would find hard to even imagine. Over twenty years later she is "still a tangle of threads and war-torn American Indian history."[29] Her younger daughter came into her home unable to speak. She would eventually be diagnosed with attachment disorder. She hardly slept and repeatedly hurt herself. Linda's older daughter's pain was directed outward, onto others. Her younger daughter's pain fell inward.

"Along with the girls, history came to live with us, the undeniable, unforgotten aspect of every American Indian life."[30] Their abuse and lack of bonding mirrored the experiences of other American Indian children who were taken from their homes and put into Indian boarding schools. These children were separated from the land which gave birth to them, from their people and language, from the stories and ceremonies which came from living in relationship with the land. They were purposely separated from their origins to be assimilated into the White American culture. For Marie, their older daughter, the legacy of nonattachment and abuse would continue. She grew up to be a mother who would severely abuse her own children. Jeannette, as a result of the commitment and dedication of her parents and Z therapy,[31] would eventually speak and would, years later, become a loving, caring, and affectionate mother.

Linda knew her healing was connected to her family's and other people's healing. "We are together in this, all of us, and it's our job to love each other, human, animal, and land, the way ocean loves shore, and shore loves and needs the ocean, even if they are different elements."[32] Gradually, the legacy of silence, of unspoken pain, transformed. By following the path backward, Linda's life became a life filled with expression. She articulates this beautifully. In her words:

As time has passed, things in me have been burned away and I see my life more clearly, more cleanly, than I had ever seen it before. And in that vision of my past, my history, my body, I also saw there was something inside me that had survived and not merely survived but had done so whole and nearly intact. . . . Fire like pain, like love, is a power we do not know. Yet from the ashes of each, something will grow. No one knows if it will be something beautiful and strong. But in our lives, it is sometimes a broken vessel, as writer Andre Dubus calls it, that spills light.[33]

Linda sat down to write the story of her life, about the pain and suffering she, her family, and her people had endured. It became a story about healing, history, and survival. Her autobiography is "a book about love."[34]

Personal history and belief, I think, are not so far away from the histories of land, time and space, water, and exploitation. . . . We Indian people who inhabited the land of the fountain of youth had not been meant to survive and yet we did, some of us, carrying the souls of our ancestors, and now they speak through us. It was this that saved my life, that finally contained me. Or better said, I contained it. . . . it was knowledge of the depths, and this is what stories try to teach us, even our own; that what's below and beneath and inside is a generative, life-giving power.[35]

CHAPTER 9

Unearthing Abuse—Collective Grief

What happens in the collective is also taking place within us.[1]

—Sonu Shamdasani in conversation with James Hillman about *The Red Book*

Malidoma Some tells us that the ancestors, having a much broader perspective than the living, remember "unearthed abuses" that have been long buried and are no longer visible to the living.[2] And, as Ezechiel told Jung, the dead look to the living for salvation hoping to gather up through each of us all the loose ends of the ages.[3] From both the Dagara and Jungian perspective, there is a reciprocal relationship between the living and the dead.

In the Dagara tradition and in other indigenous cultures, when an individual suffers, the community suffers. For the Sioux, each injury "becomes part of the community memory."[4] When wrongs are not righted, personal and communal harmony is lost. This disharmony can lead to disease that can, from one individual's actions, extend to and affect that person's family and the entire community. The Dagara believe that any unearthed abuses that remain unresolved in a person's lifetime are passed on to living relatives.

Kat's, Linda's, and my journeys into and through the memory of our personal trauma brought us into the stories of our families and the story of the land to which we were born. It is as if our symptoms were expressions of the unearthed abuses of an inadequately remembered ancestral past. These long buried traumatic events in our family and collective history were remembered in the reality of the psyche. The moans of the dead could be heard in the present through our symptoms, in our dreams and synchronicities. Our suffering may also have a purpose, an intention, a telos that anticipates an unfolding future.

Michael Meade, in *Fate and Destiny: Two Agreements of the Soul*, says this poetically.

> The child of the future has already been bitten by the snake of the past. It may be our fate in life to be present when the long-festering poisons that trouble the world become undeniable. . . . Can you face the painful issues within and

make an act of truth that helps remove some of the poison from the current situation? . . . In the twists of fate that entangled you in the troubles of the world did you find the thread of destiny intended for you? [5]

The threads of our fate are woven into the fabric of ancestral, cultural, historical, and ecological memory. The memory, consequences and effects of these traumas linger in our bones, in our hearts, and in the land. As Hogan says, this kind of history "lives in the body and . . . is marrow deep."[6] Picking up the threads from our personal story, feeling the emotional resonance and allowing the images and figures of the past to come present, can reconnect us to the "unearthed," long-buried abuses of communally shared, unreconciled, historical/cultural traumas and to the ancestors' broader vision of the future.

Cultural Complexes

Joseph Henderson built on Jung's model of the psyche by positing a cultural level that lies between the personal and archetypal levels. The concept of a cultural unconscious, first identified by Henderson and expanded on by a variety of scholars and practitioners, is invaluable for understanding the influence of the ancestors within the individual in the present.[7] Samuel Kimbles, whose work is based on Henderson's, introduced the concept of the cultural complex. Kimbles and others have been developing this idea and exploring cultural complexes by applying Jung's complex theory to this intermediate level of the psyche.[8]

Complexes, according to Jung, are emotionally charged "bodies" with an archetypal core.[9] They are a normal phenomenon of life. A complex

> is the image of a certain psychic situation which is strongly accentuated emotionally and is, moreover, incompatible with the habitual attitude of consciousness. This image has a powerful inner coherence . . . a relatively high degree of autonomy, so that it is subject to the control of the conscious mind to only a limited extent.[10]

Jung likens complexes to partial personalities, which, when they are activated, easily overpower our ego's best intentions. When we experience feelings and behave in ways that seem foreign to the way we see ourselves or want to behave, this is a complex at work. Complexes often originate in response to an emotional shock or trauma or moral conflict that cannot be reconciled with the ego or consciousness. This results in part of the psyche being split off from the rest of consciousness. In his essay, "A Review of the Complex Theory," Jung refers to complexes as "skeleton[s] in the cupboard."[11] Physical and psychological symptoms are often expressions of unconscious complexes. They are "the real focus of psychic unrest" with far-reaching repercussions.[12] Jung's theory of complexes and its therapeutic application was primarily focused on the individual.

Contemporary Jungian scholars Singer and Kimbles, editors of *The Cultural Complex: Contemporary Jungian Perspectives on Psyche and Society*, stress the importance of including the collective aspect of the unconsciousness in complex theory.[13] According to Singer,

> As personal complexes emerge out of the level of the personal unconscious, in their interaction with deeper levels of the psyche and early parental/familial relationships, cultural complexes can be thought of arising out [of] the cultural unconscious as it interacts with both the archetypal and personal realms of the psyche and the broader outer world arena of schools, communities, media, and all other forms of cultural and group life . . . it is a description of groups and classes of people as filtered through the psyches of generations of ancestors.[14]

Cultural complexes are as important to our understanding of individuals as is our understanding of the influence of that individual's personal experiences of mother and father. Cultural complexes exert their influence as powerfully and unconsciously as personal complexes. Individuals in a cultural group "in the grips of a particular cultural complex automatically take on a shared body language and postures or express their distress in similar somatic complaints."[15] Singer and Kimbles explain that in most cases

> These complexes have to do with trauma, discrimination, feelings of oppression and inferiority at the hands of another offending group—although the "offending groups" are just as frequently feeling discriminated against and treated unfairly.[16]

When there has been repetitive trauma over centuries the emotional force of a cultural complex is particularly potent. Although a cultural complex may have remained hidden in the shadows, like a land mine, when activated it can capture the imagination in ways that can be as or even more destructive than personal complexes.[17]

Trauma

What is trauma? According to *The New Oxford American Dictionary*, it is a deeply distressing or disturbing experience that derives from the Greek word literally meaning wound.[18] The dictionary identifies two kinds of trauma—physical and emotional. The word *wound* defined is an injury to living tissue caused by a cut, blow, or other impact, typically one in which the skin is cut or broken. Tracing the etymological roots of this word one travels through Old English, German, and Dutch, reaching the German word *Wunde*, which translates—"of unknown ultimate origin."

Trauma is a wound to living tissue. Through bruising, tearing, breaking, or severing, it is an opening into the fabric of our physical and emotional being. When we think of trauma, we imagine emergency rooms, physical, emotional and sexual abuse, tsunamis, war, torture, the Holocaust, and 9/11. Whether we are victims, perpetrators, or witnesses, trauma affects the fabric, the living tissue of one's family, community, and environment. A deep gash to the skin or the severing of a limb opens a view to the depths of the physical body that are usually hidden from sight. Emotional trauma opens us to the depths of our own humanity.

These depths of "unknown ultimate origin" found within the etymological origins of the word *trauma*, if traced, may open our eyes to the points of intersection between our personal traumas and wounds and collective traumas. As individuals we are part of a larger fabric: our families, our communities, our countries, and the land on which we live. On the physical level there seem to be patterns of disease that run in families— genetic propensities for breast cancer and liver disease, for example. Sexual and physical abuse and alcoholism are often intergenerational. When individuals are diagnosed with cancer or recover memories of sexual abuse, the fabric of both their psychic and physical body feels the blow. We can see these effects in the simplest way by thinking about what happens when just one person in a family gets the flu.

Understanding the nature and origins of the wound is integral to the treatment of both physical and psychological wounds. We have many ways to look deep within the physical body—microscopes, x-rays, MRIs, sonograms. We have the capacity and tools to view matter at sub-atomic and quantum levels. Dreams and active imagination reveal what is concealed from our everyday conscious perspective. Like x-rays, what is seen using these imaginal ways of knowing can give us insight into our wounds and access to a greater psychic and physical reality than what we are consciously aware of.

Pioneering research in behavior epigenetics, the process by which environmental factors can alter the expression of genes, suggests that traumatic experiences in our past, or in our ancestors' past, leave molecular scars that adhere to our DNA. These scars are like biological memories which hold fast to one's DNA carrying the effects of alcoholism, sexual and physical abuse, genocide, living through war, as well as more nurturing and loving experiences. Life experience can affect the epigenome in ways that result in emotional tendencies.[19] It appears that what Jung theorized about the dynamics and reality of the psyche has a basis in biology.

Our Collective Inheritance

Fred Gustafson shares a dream he had four months prior to the centennial memorial of the Massacre of Wounded Knee. In the dream he found himself in a place "of too many deaths."[20] He became aware of the deep grief in the American psyche that results from the failed relationship between the people native to this land and the dominant culture. This dream was more than personal. It carried the reality and memory of the collective and tragic story of this land. In psyche, nothing is forgotten. The ancestors, the memories, the stories "soak the American soil."[21] The story of our American legacy on the North American continent, as yet not fully acknowledged, witnessed or integrated, haunts the bodies and psyches of all who live on this land. The ancestors, ever present, lament and moan, waiting to be heard. It is up to the living to restore what has been lost, atone for their "sins" and redeem them.

In this case, the culture Gustafson is writing about is American. I'd like to address those who are living on other lands and in other cultures before continuing with Gustafson's work. As described in detail in Chapter 6, Jung came to an understanding that the mystery in the soil is reflected in the collective unconscious. Jung also identified an "archaic" aspect of consciousness that is common to all humans. Whatever lands one's ancestors are from and whatever land one is currently living on, from this perspective two things are true. The first is that the land one lives on has a presence in the collective psyches of those living on it. And, secondly, every human being has an indigenous aspect of consciousness.[22]

It follows from this that whatever land we're living on and whatever land(s) our indigenous ancestral roots originated in, the land we're living on now and that archaic aspect of consciousness is present within the levels of the collective unconscious in each individual. Further, our personal and cultural complexes are given shape, along with many other factors, by these aspects of consciousness. I would suggest that what Gustafson is writing about the American psyche specifically, is also applicable to people from other lands living in other cultures. I invite you to consider this possibility and to imagine how what is presented in the sections that follow may expand your understanding of your life and your personal and our collective story.

Gustafson's dream brought him to Wounded Knee. My personal trauma brought me to Providence, Rhode Island on March 29, 1676 during King Philip's War. Kat's Chronic Fatigue brought her to the land of the Minnesota people in the eighteen-hundreds. Linda's story brought her home to the home of her grandmother, "the place [she] lived before [she] was born."[23] The stories of her daughters show the continuing effect of

America's legacy of colonization on individuals, families and communities in the present. Like Gustafson, for Linda, Kat, and me, the re-experiencing of these traumatic moments in our collectively shared history was more than personal. Our traumatized and wounded bodies and psyches connected us to and were implicated in collective suffering. Carrying the memory of the failed promises, massacres, hatred and fear of a tragic history, our stories are a living history. Moving through layers of pain into the deeper layers of ancestral and collective trauma, experiencing the grief and rage of this American legacy through our individual wounding, a history which had been remote became deeply personal.

Gustafson suggests that the kind of grief that he felt is a collectively shared "fundamental sadness" for all that has been lost. This grief "lies buried in the collective American psyche."[24] When I touched that grief in the cultural/historical transferential dialogue described in Chapter 1, it was almost unbearable. Gustafson is clear that it is necessary for reparations to be made for the violations done over this long history of violence and oppression. He suggests that a fundamental part of a restorative personal and collective transformation is "seeing, admitting, and weeping" this part of our cultural legacy.[25] Doing so, according to Weisstub and Galili-Weisstub,

> takes a strong ego, personally and culturally, to contain the opposing poles of a cultural complex, and to enable the necessary working through of the depression and mourning entailed in giving up archetypally based projections and possessions.[26]

Experiencing this grief serves to counterbalance and compensate for the dominant collective narrative. Gustafson suggests that while most of us know this history, we don't realize the "force of the grief behind it."[27]

> It is a hidden and silent grief barely visible, pushed aside and buried layer upon layer by the cultural and personal justifications for survival. It is a grief that binds victim and perpetrator in an unconscious alliance. Beyond the hatred, beyond the blame, beyond the guilt is a sense of mutual sharing— namely that both are victims of a common grief that can only be healed when acknowledged.[28]

In his conversation with Ezechiel, Jung learns that the dead are dependent on the living for their salvation. We must "turn to the dead, [whose companion you are] listen to their lament and accept them with love. . . . this uncompleted work has followed them. A new salvation is always a restoring of the previously lost."[29] While Jung writes about the way in which consciousness evolves through the experiences of the living, he does not directly address the way the ancestors' laments and suffering can be healed in the present through consciously acknowledging, witnessing, grieving and taking reparative action.[30] From a close reading of Jung, I would imagine he would tell us that our responses would and must be unique to each individual and the particular circumstances that are calling for our attention. And, that our responses, originate out of a relationship with and deep listening to the unconscious, to the psyche. Kat's, Linda's and my stories serve as examples of the way we, as individuals, are being addressed and can address collective suffering in a personal way. Whether or not one's ancestors were directly involved, we can all, as Gustafson suggests, allow ourselves to bear witness to our history, feel the grief that soaks this land and offer our tears.

Our understanding of the origins of trauma is informed by our perspective. In order to "heal," I would need to sit at the center of my ancestral home tracing what went wrong within the complex web of relationships over many generations, spanning centuries of time. I found myself in a circular, labyrinthine process of returning, and returning again following the psyche's lead with an intention of restoring harmony and balance. Each step I took brought more insight and awareness. Each new awareness and experience of the presence of the past in the present brings with it the opportunity to acknowledge and address the lament of the dead. I have found that experiencing and being responsive to the emotional reality of these experiences is not only a key into understanding, but, as Freud's and Jung's work demonstrates, a key to healing. Working within this broader perspective, as we more consciously address the multi-levelled nature of our suffering, healing can extend from the personal into the deeper collective levels of the psyche reaching into the past in service to the future. I would discover that the key to healing and the underlying purpose of being in a more conscious dialogue with the ancestors, as I would come to understand it, was opening the way for love to flow within, through and between the generations.

Seeking an Alternate Route

On my fifty-fifth birthday I made a trip to Providence, Rhode Island from the West Coast. It was the third trip I'd taken there after recognizing the depth of connection between Rhode Island's history, my ancestor's story and my own. I visited the places where Roger and many of my ancestors had lived for generations. I tried to go to the site of the Great Swamp Massacre. The Great Swamp was the site of a Narragansett fort, a sanctuary during King Philip's War for women, children and the elderly. The Narragansett initially remained neutral in King Philips War. However, as tensions mounted and the fear of all Indians increased, the "United Colonies" of Plymouth, Massachusetts, and Connecticut decided to attack the Narragansett.[31] The English descended on the Indians in the fort at the Great Swamp slaughtering most of the Indians who sought refuge there. Causalities were the highest of any battle in the war. Seventy colonists died. One hundred and fifty were wounded. The losses for the Narragansett, mostly women and children were devastatingly higher—"97 warriors and between 300 and 1000 women and children."[32]

I had attempted to make my way to the stone that memorialized this horrible tragedy on my previous visits back East. I hadn't been able to find the site. This fifth time, I was prevented from doing so by rain and lightning.[33] I was determined to find it, to humbly bear witness and offer my prayers. I climbed over a locked fence and trudged along a muddy dirt road into the woods as the rain, accompanied by thunder and lightning, poured down soaking through my clothes. When lightning struck the ground a few feet in front of me, I decided to take the not so subtle hints the place seemed to be giving me, didn't walk but ran back to my car and began the drive back to Providence. As I approached the main street in Bristol, right in front of Roger Williams University, a very large road sign flashed the words, "Metacom and Gooding seek alternate route." It was a detour sign. The roads with those names were closed.

Metacom Street was named for the Wampanoag Indian leader who began attacking English towns on June 24th in 1675. Earlier that month, in 1675, three Wampanoag had been convicted of murdering John Sassamon and were hanged.[34] Thus began what is called King Philips War.[35] Philip was Metacom's English name.[36] Over time Metacom has become iconic in the story of Rhode Island. Gooding is a common English name in Rhode Island history. The first Gooding arrived on this continent in the sixteen-hundreds. Metacom, who is iconic in Rhode Island history, and Gooding, one of the first Europeans to come to this land and establish a life and lineage here, now, according to the sign, sought an alternate route.

Over the next several years, in the course of writing my dissertation, that particular "sign" would reveal its meaning. It was time now, in the present, to seek an alternate route to the irreconcilable differences between cultures which resulted in the war named after Metacom. I encountered this sign after spending a year revisiting the past, becoming aware of the horrible genocide and unfathomable horror and losses that occurred during King Philip's War. Learning the stories, visiting the places of history and the graves of my ancestors, I felt the grief I felt in that initial transference dialogue and wept. I wanted to heal this cultural wound. My wish to heal this wound was understandably proportional to my experience of the trauma. It was also inflated. It took a lightning bolt from the sky to stop me in my tracks and a detour sign to point me in the right direction. What was being asked of me in the present in response to this collective trauma? What alternate route was I being directed to seek?

Following the signs, I decided that rather than trying again and again to return to the trauma of the past, to the war and genocide, I would open myself to an alternate route—whatever that might mean. As I contemplated an actual alternate route back to Providence, the rain ended and the sun began to come out. (This is an unexaggerated, true story, even as the details seem to carry the metaphoric and archetypal characteristics of a good folktale or myth.) I decided to follow the arrows. Rather than going back to Providence the way I had come, the signs directed me to a bridge. As I drove onto the bridge I saw a rainbow over the river. It was breathtaking. I was stunned into joyful laughter.

I returned to Providence a year later, to the place where my ancestors' remains are now buried, and sat in the rain looking at the state capitol building and the river. I sat there heartbroken, pleading for some insight, some answer about what I was to do in response to the trauma that I felt on so many levels. I smelled smoke. Looking around I saw there was nothing actually burning. I knew part of my consciousness was reconnecting with the memory of the day Providence burned, and with the memory of sitting in my grandfather's lap. He always smelled like the cigars he smoked. As I felt the pain of that history, I also felt a presence, one which I had come to identify as Roger. His answer to me was simple. "Live *your* life. The past is the past. There is nothing you can do to change what happened. Live your life. That is all the ancestors want."

I could not change history, this country's or mine. Having followed the path backward, having read the stories and grieved the personal and collective losses, it was time to seek an alternate route. The road sign stopped my forward movement and called into question the way I was approaching my experience of personal, ancestral and collective trauma. I had tried unsuccessfully to get to the place where there was a simple stone memorializing what had happened at the Great Swamp to offer my tears and prayers. The sign offered a direction that was an alternative to the one I had imagined with regard to the trauma. Rather than continuing to return to the trauma and trying to heal it with traditional psychological methods, my task was to continue to seek peace between "primitive" and civilized," Pagan and Christian, Indian and European, heart and head as Roger had done and to answer the questions that were so central to his life that couldn't be answered in his time. An alternate route for consciousness was sought; an integration of egoic, rational, differentiated consciousness with its archaic roots. The time was now ripe for these questions to be answered.

The story would evolve and Roger's questions would be answered as I held the opposing poles of the cultural complex and integrated and embodied Borderland consciousness. The "war" between perpetrator and victim, head and heart, European and Native American, Christian and Pagan began to be reconciled in me. To transform this multi-leveled story in service to creating a new forward I would also have to address the interpersonal aspect of this story, the one which originated with John Cotton and Roger, in a way that was responsive to the direction of the unconscious, the ancestors, the land of the dead. To bring an end to the war, to stop unconsciously reliving and perpetuating the old story required "telling the story" and consciously responding to what was being asked for in response. All of this is in service to bringing balance and restoring harmony within the complex web of relations of which we are a part.

My childhood trauma brought me to the deeper, more complex origins of the archetypal impulses and patterns that formed my personal complexes. My experience of the cultural complex that Gustafson identifies is specifically configured at each of the levels of the collective unconscious by the stories, experiences and figures that are particular to my ancestry. Following the path backward, learning and responding to what was being asked of me in the present, rather than being at the whims of an unconscious fate, I began to live *my* life in response to the past in service to creating a new forward.

As I sit at my desk editing this section of the book it begins to rain. California is experiencing a serious drought as I finish writing this book. We have gotten very little rain for quite a long time and it is unusual for it to rain in this area of California at this time of year. This rain is accompanied by thunder and lightning. I am deeply moved by this synchronicity. As Malidoma suggests, the ancestors are present in and speak to us through nature. I will take this as an affirmation that I am, through this work, listening to the laments of the dead, responding with love and creating a new forward. I am humbled and grateful.

Collective Origins of Personal Trauma

Linda Hogan's story shows the way personal and familial suffering is a result of collective trauma. Her story, her mother's, father's, and daughters' stories, were a living memory of their peoples' suffering. Each individual story was a continuation of the long history of genocide, dislocation and trauma to the people native to the North American continent. Her healing really began when she discovered that she "was only one in a lineage of fallen worlds and people."[37] If Linda's or her daughters' symptoms were seen only from the personal and family of origin levels it would have per-petuated the legacy of colonization and genocide. The voices in the cul-tural shadows would have continued to be silenced and remain unheard.

Kat's healing was dependent on becoming conscious of an event that was traumatically devastating for a tribe of Sioux. Her illness originated in the trauma suffered by the people her great-grandfather drove from their land.[38] Recognizing that her physical symptoms carried the memory of a particular historical event and place, she made offerings to heal the wound that had been inflicted on the Sioux by her great-grandfather. If she had worked with her memory of childhood sexual trauma without including the ancestral and cultural/historical origins of her suffering, her healing would have been incomplete. Healing herself was interdependent with healing within the ancestral and national levels of the psyche.

My story illustrates the relationship between the various levels from personal to archetypal. My childhood trauma tied me to the memory of a cultural, historical, ancestral and ecological trauma. How to respond to and address this trauma was related to and informed by the particular story(ies) that were associated with each level. As I engaged in ancestral dialogues, research and rituals, the archetypal thread that ran through each level slowly revealed itself. I would recognize the underlying pattern as one of "failed coniunctio." At the personal level it was the "failure" to integrate Borderland consciousness with the more rationally centered modern, egoic, western consciousness. At the ancestral level it was a failure to integrate head and heart, Christian and Pagan, masculine and feminine. At the inter-personal level, which I see as tribal in Jung's model of the psyche, it was a failed marriage which reflected and reenacted the story of our ancestors. At the cultural and historical level, it was an unreconciled conflict between two peoples with different worldviews and cultures.

Healing from my sexual abuse required understanding its origins and its archetypal nature and taking reparative action with medicine specifi-cally formulated for the wound at each level. While there are similarities in Kat's and my stories, there is no one-size-fits-all formula or approach for healing inter-generational cultural trauma. How one heals and transforms the patterns is unique to each individual.

Restoring Balance and Harmony

At the heart of this work is the concept that all of creation is interde-pendently related. Native cultures' foundations are based on this natural democracy. According to Apela Colorado, *Skanagoah* is the goal of Native science. For North American forest and woodland dwellers this term is used to describe the "great peace." [39] It is, according to Colorado a "feeling or state of balance" which is "at the heart of the universe."[40] This state of balance is a dynamic harmonic present within and between all aspects of creation. Within the Native American understanding of the underlying interrelated nature of all things Peat explains that each aspect of creation has a particular role to play "in renewing and ensuring those alliances and relationships that lie behind the movement of seasons and the rising of the sun."[41]

The story of the rainmaker, well-loved and so often told by Jung, is an example of this dynamic harmonic and its effect within one community. It is an example of how being out of harmony with the unconscious has a disintegrating effect intra- and interpersonally and in the world. It is also a story that demonstrates what occurs when one is once more, as the rainmaker expressed it, in Tao. The story of the rainmaker also seems to be a story about "well-being," the guide for living described to Jung by the spirit of the depths in *The Red Book*.[42]

As the story is told, there is a great drought in the village. Everything known to the community is tried: processions, prayers, burned joss sticks, and shooting guns to frighten away the demons, all with no result. Finally, a rainmaker is summoned. He settles himself in a quiet little house and on the fourth day there is a great snowstorm which produces an unusually large amount of snow at a time of year when it does not snow. When the rainmaker is asked *how* he produced such a large amount of snow he says he is not responsible for making the snow. He explains that in his country things are in order. In this village things were out of order, "not as they should be by the ordnance of heaven."[43] As a result, the entire country was not in Tao. When he arrived, he, like this country found himself "not in the natural order of things."[44] Alone in the quiet little house, he waited, until he was back in Tao. It was then that the snow came. This story is inconceivable, according to Jung, only if one thinks "along the lines of causality." However, if one thinks psychologically, "one is absolutely convinced that things quite naturally take this way."[45]

How does this story relate to trauma and cultural complexes? Trauma disrupts, unbalances, and creates disorder within the individual, the family, and the community. If we can imagine the fabric of life from a quantum point of view we include in this fabric of living tissue our ancestors, our descendants, the land we live on and all of its creatures, the air we breathe and the soil beneath our feet. As my daughters delighted in discovering and sharing with anyone who would listen, when we are drinking water from our tap, we are drinking dinosaur "peepee." I love their understanding of our interconnectedness in and through time. It's very simple and concrete. Finding the threads of connection between our personal story and the

stories of our ancestors—remembering, acknowledging, witnessing, grieving—contributes to the ecology of this web of interrelatedness, to Tao,
Skangoah, well-being and making the ancestors smile.

The issue of peace and reconciliation between the people native to this
land and those who have come here from other lands is beyond the scope
of this book and certainly well beyond what I can address in my life in any
significant way. My story and the stories shared in this book may, however,
offer some keys into what we as individuals can do in the present moment
that may in some small way contribute to our collective healing.

I want to emphasize the importance of reparative action as part of this
work. Doing the inner work of restoring balance as is evidenced in our
stories is very important. However, it is only part of what is being asked of
us by the dead. As evidenced in Kat's story, it was necessary for her to
conduct ceremonies that honored the people who had suffered at the hands
of her ancestor. Linda's adoption of her daughters is a way of changing the
legacy she had inherited of fallen worlds and people. I joked with Clark,
about what was being called for in the present to address the ways his
ancestor had contributed to Roger's suffering. But as time went on, it
became clear that the actions of our ancestors in the past necessitated
reparative actions in the present. Our marriage and divorce and the raising
of our daughters brought opportunities for reparation.

These stories are not a statement of, but rather a mode of access to
deeper and more complex and complete truths. As our stories meet each
other on these pages, as each reader's story finds its place in relationship to
the stories that are shared, a dynamic dialogue takes place through what is
consciously expressed and is unconsciously written between the lines. In her
novel, *Ceremony*, Leslie Silko writes that Auntie, hoping desperately to reconcile a family plagued by the legacy of genocide and dislocation from the
land of their ancestors and the roots of their tradition, sought to "gather the
feelings and opinions that were scattered through the village, to gather them
like willow twigs and tie them into a single prayer bundle." This task would
not be a simple one, for the roots of these feelings "were twisted, [and] tangled . . . buried under English words, out of reach." Peace would only come
when these entangled roots . . . "had been unwound to the source."[46]

As Ezechiel told Jung, it is the task of the living to "gather up the loose
ends of the ages."[47] Gustafson believes that all of us who live on this land
need to "dare to listen" to the stories, suffering and worldview of the ancestors of the North American continent.[48] Perhaps our personal stories in
dialogue with each other can serve to untangle the twisted and tangled
roots of our personal and collectively shared history.

CHAPTER 10

Five Intergenerational Stories

Stories are medicine. . . . Stories set the inner life into motion. . . . Story greases the hoists and pulleys, it causes adrenaline to surge, shows us the way out, down, or up, and for our trouble, cuts for us fine wide doors in previously blank walls, openings that lead to the dreamland, that lead to love and learning, that lead us back to our own real lives.

—Clarissa Pinkola Estes, *Women Who Run with the Wolves*[1]

This chapter contains the stories of four women, who, for a month, explored being in a more conscious dialogue with the ancestors. Their stories are written to convey their experiences in a way that is faithful to the depth and breadth of their experience. Each woman whose story is shared participated in an Ancestral Soul Work group. These groups are offered to individuals as a way of discovering the deeper ancestral, historical, cultural, and collective patterns that inform their lives. Personal and communal ritual is an integral part of this process. Creating and using an ancestor altar, conducting imaginal dialogues with the ancestors, and the process of council provide the ritual containers necessary for this work. Ritual opens us to an expanded awareness of the existence of reality beyond the sensible, everyday world we live in and provides a structure for containment of the intense emotions that may be experienced while participating in these ancestral dialogues. The containers used in Ancestral Soul Work provide a sacred space in which one's awareness can move within and through time and space as the veil between the worlds, between consciousness and the unconscious, becomes more permeable. In this field, the voices of the ancestors can be heard in a more conscious and direct way. Together and individually, reaching deeply into our personal and collective history, participants through sharing story in sacred space listen and remember.

The process of council serves as the foundation for the group work. The council circle creates a sense of immediate community that supports each participant in accessing and expressing their deepest truths. Council circles facilitate deep listening with the eye and ear of the heart. This creates a temenos, a protective circle, that facilitates deep reflection and sharing. In this communal mirror we see into the depths of ourselves and the psyche. In council, a ceremonial object is used as a talking piece. This talking piece is held by the person who is speaking. The council process is framed by four intentions and shared agreements: (1) speak from the heart, what is true, has heartfelt meaning, and about what truly matters; (2) listen with one's heart, feel what the other person is saying; (3) be lean of expression; and (4) be spontaneous.[2]

This tradition, which is assumed to have originated with Native Americans, is, in fact, found in many cultures and can be traced back to the Stone Age.[3] Speaking and listening from the heart, especially for a sustained period, increases one's capacity for empathy for oneself and others. This creates a dynamic group field that is potentially transformative. The council circle serves as the space into which our stories, memories and experiences of the ancestors are spoken, heard, mirrored, and held. As part of an interconnected, interdependent spiraling wheel of kinship, finding the threads of connection between each individual story and our collective story does not happen in isolation. Each person's process of discovery, remembering, and healing is dependent on others.[4]

Schutzenberger, a Freudian analyst and author of *The Ancestor Syndrome*, prefers to conduct ancestor work in groups rather than individually.[5] She finds that individuals in groups often share similar problems, traumas and family patterns. It is also common for members in a group to discover that their ancestors were involved in some way in similar political, sociological, economic and historical periods. Schutzenberger has found that each time someone remembers it "adds to and awakens the memories of other participants."[6] These personal and collective echoes within the group "allow each . . . person to delve deeper and deeper into his or her discoveries."[7] Within the resonant echoes of other people's stories, one discovers new truths and gains a deepened perspective on one's own story. Our group found this to be very true.

In ancestral soul work groups, between the times we gather together as a group, each person creates a personal ancestor altar, and spends time at least twice a week in relationship and dialogue with the ancestors using the altar as the focal point and container for the process. The basic idea for this altar comes from the Dagara tradition as described by Malidoma Some.[8] An ancestor altar is a ritual container that provides a place of continuity in the nonlinear, labyrinthine process of reconnection, remembering, and transformation. Holding the chaos and complexity of this dynamic relationship, it serves as a space where the relationship and dialogue between the ancestors and those who are on this side of the veil of reality can be opened and closed. The council circle and the ancestor altar, like Jung's

Bollingen tower, allow life to be experienced "in the round" reaching forward and backward through time.

The form of an ancestor altar is as unique and as individual as its creator. The altar can consist of a simple photograph of one's family members who have passed through the portal of death. It can be as elaborate as an entire room devoted to one's ancestors. It may contain photographs, heirlooms, genealogical charts, books written by and art created by one's ancestors . . . anything that represents and carries the psychic energy and reality of their presence. Using the ancestor altar, each person conducts dialogues with and "feeds" the ancestors. Genealogical research and talking with living relatives is encouraged as a way to provide grounding for the experiences and information that is gathered through imaginal dialogues and dreams. Each person is encouraged to keep a record of and reflections on her experiences. Ongoing support and guidance is offered as is appropriate and necessary.

Ancestral soul work is a practice that is devoted to being in a sustained, ongoing, imaginally based, consciously engaged dialogue with the ancestors. This dialogue is based on Jung's use of active imagination and utilizes techniques from Dream Tending as described by Stephen Aizenstat.[9] Dream figures, and, in this case ancestors, are assumed to be autonomous figures who "live" in the reality of the psyche. The technique of animation, as described by Aizenstat, allows us to interact with these figures much in the same way Jung did in his encounters with the unconscious as depicted in *The Red Book*. Rather than a symbol for something, these living figures of psyche are experienced as autonomous presences with their own, innate intelligence. This way of seeing and listening to imaginal figures is an approach, that invites and allows their natural intelligence to be expressed and perceived in a way that is image and psyche rather than ego centered.

I wrote each of the stories in this chapter using the information gathered from initial interviews, notes I kept of our time together as a group, personal conversations I had with the women between group sessions, the journals each woman kept during the time she was engaged in this work, and a final interview that took place a few months following our month together as a group. Dreams and experiences from other times and places as they are related to each woman's story are also included. To write these stories I used my ability to listen with my heart and discern and discriminate using my analytical mind. Listening into each woman's story and to the particular way it was expressed by her, I looked for the landscape from which her personal story originated, a landscape that provided the ground for her story. I listened and looked for the phrases, words, and images which, from my felt sense and analytical discernment, carried within them the deeper meaning within each woman's story. Using resonance as a measure, I wrote each story with the intention that it would carry some of the living meaning that is the breath of expression.

When I had finished writing the first version of each woman's story, I sent it to her to review. Each woman was asked to check it for accuracy. I wanted to know if it was an authentic representation of her experiences. Changes were made in response to their feedback, comments and reflections. This process of writing, review, and re-writing continued until each woman and I were confident that the story accurately reflected her experiences.

An aspect of this process involved discussions between each woman and me regarding some of the material that had been quoted or included. It is not always easy or comfortable to hear oneself quoted. Honoring and respecting that these stories are based on a process in which a deep trust was established between us was important. We worked together to create a final version of each story, which carried the raw veritability of her experience and was true to her personal voice and expression. Some statements and experiences were removed out of respect for the deeply personal nature of the material and the reality of its public presentation. These omissions did not affect the stories in a significant way. Although each woman was given the choice of using a pseudonym, each wanted her name to be used. I have been and continue to be moved by the courage, honesty, strength and vulnerability of each of these women.[10]

Also included in this chapter is the part of my story that occurred during the time this particular group met, which is a part of and integral to the whole process that occurred in this group. While each woman's story is written in the third person, mine is written in the first person using the same techniques as described above. Since this part of my story had been shared with and witnessed by the women in this group, I wanted to get their feedback. After receiving and incorporating their feedback, I wrote a final version that is presented in this chapter.

A few months are a short period of time to explore one's relationship with the ancestors. In my personal experience, it takes years of picking up and holding the iconic bits and pieces and looking for the threads of connection, or more accurately, allowing the threads to reveal how they are woven together, before the tapestry, or, as one of the women I've worked with named it, the quilt, comes together in a coherent way. Needless to say, working with the issues from one's immediate family or on the relationship with one's mother or father can itself take years especially if there is significant trauma.

I have also included the story told by JoEllen Koerner in *Mother Heal MySelf: An Intergenerational Healing Journey between Two Worlds* in this chapter. JoEllen's and her daughter Kristi's story is an extraordinary example of the relationship between personal, familial, ancestral, tribal and cultural wounding and trauma. The stories of the women who participated in this group carry the immediacy of experience within the process of group council and dialogues with the ancestors. JoEllen's story offers insight into the dynamics of placing one's story in relationship with and in the context of the stories of one's ancestors that can only be gained over time. I have only told a small part of her story in my words. I highly recommend reading her entire story written in her words as it is presented in *Mother Heal MySelf*.[11]

There is another story included in this chapter. It is the story of the hawks who were present at the moment in time when this work, my work, began. Hawk is a constant presence in my life, companioning me as I bring this work into expression in the world. Hawk was part of the story of this particular group and so, I include it as a prelude to the other stories. I capitalize the word hawk to recognize and acknowledge my experience of it as the archetypal and essential essence of Hawk, "a representative of the Great Mystery" as the Sioux regard them, even as each hawk is individual and unique.[12]

Our Stories

Hawk

Five years ago a young hawk circled overhead every day as I worked on the first public presentation of the experiences and ideas that seeded this work. This hawk was a constant companion. Anytime I worked outside, he would glide and swoop overhead, sometimes screeching loudly. One day after my morning walk, having had the familiar conversation with myself about my doubt about the reality of what I was experiencing, instead of walking on the road to the walkway that leads to the front of my home, I turned onto the hillside in front of my home. It's covered with honeysuckle and filled with trees and bushes, along with several varieties of weeds. I stepped from the paved road through the thick oleander onto the hill. I looked down to find a good place for my next step. There was a hawk feather lying at my feet. It stopped my thinking and questioning and brought me into a different way of listening and being in the world in the same way crow's cawing did in Santa Fe. This gift from Hawk at that particular moment affirmed that I could trust my experiences and ways of knowing—that, indeed, the right action, the one that would be in service to "well-being," was to step off the road that had already been conceived and paved by modern Western culture and Jungian psychology. I had never found a hawk feather before nor have I in the ten years since. I knew then and know now that I, as we all are but sometimes doubt or forget, am accompanied and guided on my path.

How we understand this is a matter, as Bernstein reminds us, of what we are "open to noticing."[13] In the world of the Sioux, Dagara, and many other peoples around the globe, animals and all beings are regarded as equals to humans. Deloria offers many examples of the way animals provide guidance for living life.[14] The Sioux understood that bonds of friendship could be formed between animals and human. These relationships are beneficial and reciprocal in nature. The friendship is most often initiated by the animal. It is the responsibility of humans to nurture these friendships. Deloria makes an important point about the human-animal relationship: "the point is not whether people talk to animals and plants, but the validity of the messages that are given and received."[15] This feather now sits on my ancestor altar. It is a constant reminder that nature and the ancestors through nature are listening and speaking. I have learned to listen to Hawk by paying attention to synchronicities and being open to the images and thoughts that occur to me when he is around.

While I was writing my dissertation, most of the homes on my street and the surrounding area were burned to the ground in the Tea Fire—one of two major fires in Santa Barbara that occurred between the fall of 2011 and spring of 2012. My home was only partially burned. A grove of eucalyptus trees in my backyard had been partially burned. The fire department suggested that all the eucalyptus trees be removed as they were extremely flammable and served as easy fuel for fires. A hawk's nest was discovered when these trees were being taken down. The nest and the trees immediately surrounding it were not cut down because it is the law. My neighbors and I were hopeful that the pair of hawks whose nest it was would return.

Shortly after I returned to my home, a year and a half after the fire, the hawks did return to their nest. In the spring, three eggs hatched and three eyas joined the neighborhood. The women in the research group and I could hear the constant screeches of these hungry hatchlings as we sat in our circle on the first day we all came together as a group. During our first break, we used my grandmother's binoculars to look into the nest. There were two adult and three downy, very hungry hawks. The parents worked constantly to feed their hungry offspring. The day before our second gathering, the young hawks took their first flights out of the nest. By the time of our last gathering, all three had flown from the nest and had successfully learned to hunt for food and were feeding themselves. Occasionally, one of the young hawks would sit in a tree in my back yard and screech for help from its parents, to no avail. Having flown out of the nest, it was time for each hawk to learn to survive as hawks do. In search of food, their territory expanded. All five were a constant presence for the entire month we met. Hawk would hold a very special significance for one of the women in this group. All of us felt companioned and accompanied by these hawks on our journey into a more conscious relationship with the ancestors. The nest was empty soon after our last group session. However, when I began writing the stories in this chapter as part of my dissertation, I heard the familiar screech. One of the hawks had returned.

All five hawks returned in a dream while I was working on the final chapters of my dissertation. In the dream I was in the yard on the west side of my house. There was a man there, not someone I recognized from life. He was a familiar dream figure, the kind who comes in dreams as a guide to open our eyes and bring our awareness to something that we wouldn't have noticed without their presence. He pointed to the trees on the other side of the fence, in what would be my neighbors' yard. The actual fence had burned in the fire. I built a new one as part of the process of restoration. Following his outstretched arm, I saw one hawk sitting in a tree. As I looked, I saw another and another flying in, landing and perching in one of the trees. The trees were a brilliant, luminescent white. There were no leaves on any of the branches. They looked like bleached bones. The hawks, with their red shoulders and tails, stood out against the bone-white trees. In the dream I was so excited and deeply moved that the five hawks had come back—that they indeed had actually never left my home. In the dream I knew, felt, and sensed that Hawk was my companion for life. Fences define boundaries and borders; they separate things—one neighbor's yard from another, head from heart, consciousness and the unconscious, the living and the dead, matter and spirit, domestic and wild, science and art, civilized and indigenous. These dream hawks are just on the other side of the fence sitting in trees that look like white bones. It seems that hawk exists in the reality of both worlds, the land of the dead—white bones—and the land of the living—in their nest in my backyard. While differentiated, there is no real separation.[16]

Diane's Story

Diane worked as an accountant for most of her adult life. Eleven years ago on the Day of the Dead she would enter a sweat lodge in Oaxaca and her life would begin to move in a new direction. In the sweat lodge the medicine man asked her what had happened with her father. She would "see her father's face" and get in touch with how she and her father didn't have much of a relationship with each other when he was living. As she felt the reality and pain of this she would also feel "his energy coursing through her body." This experience, three years after her father's death, opened Diane up to a broader perspective of reality. It would be the beginning for her of being in a more conscious relationship with the ancestors. It would also be the experience which would serve as a reference point for and the beginning of her journey into her own work as a shamanic healer.

Diane is one of two children born to Bill and Nancy. She knows little about her family's origins. Her father's mother's maiden name was Bozeman. This grandmother was a descendant of John Bozeman. The town of Bozeman in Montana was named after him. Bozeman left Georgia, moving westward in search of gold during the height of the gold rush. Unsuccessful as a miner, he sought other ways to make his fortune. Seeing the opportunities in providing services to the miners, he created a trail which originated in Montana, establishing a route that would connect with the Oregon Trail. This route went right through the Sioux, Shoshone, and Arapaho Nations, violating treaties these nations had with the United States.

The use of this trail would eventually lead to Red Cloud's War. For a time, the trail and the forts along the trail were abandoned by the United States, and the treaties were honored. However, Bozeman ignored the closure of the trail. Traveling with a friend along this route in violation of the treaty, Bozeman was murdered on the trail. Whether it was by Blackfoot or by his companion is not certain. The trail would be reopened during the Black Hills War and used by the U.S. Army in violation of the treaty once again. As was the case throughout the expansion of the United States into the west, the Sioux would not prevail. Although her father didn't carry the Bozeman family name, he seemed to carry the masculine, pioneering spirit, which Diane describes as being "from another era." He grew up in Texas and his collection of Bowie knives was renowned.

Diane's mother's family came to this land from Norway in the 1800s. When she looks in the mirror she sees her Norwegian nose. Her mother's father was a first-generation-born American. Diane was four years old when both of her grandmothers died within two months of each other. Her mother's father lived longer, and Diane had time to get to know him and to establish a relationship with him, one which would continue after his death. Both of Diane's parents were only children. She is one of two daughters born to them and has no cousins. Diane has no children of her own. Her sister has two sons. She has a very close relationship with her nephews.

In witnessing the way each of her parents experienced the process of death, Diane saw more clearly who they were in essential ways. Their deaths were initiations for Diane into a deeper expression of her own life. Her father died in his bed surrounded by his Bowie knives. She had the following dream right after her father died:

> In the dream I was in the hospital with my father and we were rushing him into emergency. He was on a gurney and I was at his side. I was freaked out and calling for help. He calmly reached out and took my arm and said, "Everything will be o.k. You just need to be strong."

She felt the reality of her father's presence and considered this experience to be a visitation from his spirit.

She has a deep sadness about not knowing who her father really was and about not being known by him when he was alive. They did not really see each other in life. Her father "raised her to be a boy." She never felt as if she could be herself with him. Her voice and individuality were sacrificed. Her creativity and femininity were feared and so Diane suppressed them and became one of the boys. In our initial interview Diane, describing her relationship with her father, would say, "What he took from me when he was alive he gave back to me after he died." The sale of her father's Bowie knife collection and her parents' estate provided the financial resources that would support her in moving into a new direction in life.

About a month before our group began, shortly after Diane decided to participate, she had a dream. She shares her experience of the dream as she wrote it in her journal:

> My father came to me in a dream. He gave me a clear plastic bag. In the bag there was a package of colored pencils, a package of regular pencils and a pad of paper. He said to me he was sorry that he hadn't been able to give me more gifts when he was alive. He was humbly coming to me now to give me this gift.

She wrote: "To me, this represented him giving me a gift to support my creativity, colored pencils to draw with and regular pencils to write with. This seemed clear as the gifts were given in a clear bag." Her father has deeply informed her changing path in life since his death. She was told in one of her first dialogues that doing this ancestor work would help her receive the gifts her father brought to her in this dream.

About one week after her mother died, on her way to see the attorney who was handling her mother's will, Diane stopped at Summerland Beach, a beach just south of Santa Barbara, California. She was very upset and sought solace walking by the ocean. About a half an hour into her walk, she found a beautiful rock. She picked it up. As she stood up, she heard something behind her. Turning, she saw a little girl with a bouquet of yellow flowers. The little girl held out the flowers and said, "This is for you." Diane took the flowers and handed her the rock. The little girl then ran off. It was a perfect moment of beauty, which "so embodied" her mother. She knew it was a gift from her and felt comforted. After her mother's death Diane took responsibility for sorting through all of her family's belongings. While her sister lived in her mother's house, it fell to Diane to carefully go through and determine what would be done with each item. Some items would go to auction, some Diane and her sister would keep, and some would be recycled or thrown away.

She discovered photographs of her grandfather and many relatives, some of whom she knew and others whose identity and stories would remain a mystery. She experienced excitement and sadness as she came into relationship with all that had been collected and saved over the years. In the bedroom she and her sister had shared growing up, she found the box that her father had gotten in the District of Columbia after his own father's death. His father had died when he was 13 years old. When Diane was a young girl, her father told her the story of the box and how it had been broken. As she held the box for the first time, the memory of her father and that moment touched her again. Discovering and sorting through the things her family had collected over the generations, which held the memories and images from her parents, grandparents, great-grandparents and beyond, was like a journey through both the collective conscious and unconscious of her clan.

Diane had begun remodeling her house a few months before she became a participant in this group. She was in the midst of it for the entire time she participated in this group. Her home was completely torn apart. Her books, the entire contents of her kitchen, her clothes, artwork, and furniture were all stored. She lived on the futon in the room she used for her shamanic healing work. This would become her "life raft" in the midst of the process of constructive remodeling. Pieces from her ancestor altar, which had also been taken apart and moved from its home, lay around her life raft. Her marriage of 22 years was also in a process of transformation. Her husband had found his perfect job in the San Francisco Bay Area. The necessary move from Santa Barbara for her husband brought questions about the relationship to the foreground. The months preceding, during, and following our group were characterized by deconstruction and reconstruction. During this time, the external remodeling seemed to mirror and be mirrored by the process of being in dialogue with the ancestors. If a house is seen as a representation of one's life, Diane's remodeling was occurring internally and externally. Her ancestors provided insight and gifts into both aspects of this process.

Diane's father, mother, and maternal grandfather were and are the ancestors with whom she has an ongoing relationship. Although she is connected to and aware of the larger collective field of which they are a part, her strongest relationships are with these people from her lineage whom she knew and was closest to in life. Their relationship with her continued through dreams and imaginal and synchronistic experiences after their deaths. Her experience with her father, described above, opened her to a different way of viewing and being in relationship with her ancestors and other figures from what had previously been a less visible reality. She experiences their continuing presence in her life. As her relationship with them has developed beyond their death, her dialogues and dreams of them inform the choices she makes. When they visit her in dreams, which is not often, the messages and gifts they bring are meaningful, especially with regard to her identity and the direction of her life. She knows and feels that her ancestors want her to be and express who she is in the most authentic way, to follow her own path and to be happy. Both of her parents have, after their deaths, guided her in the journey from accountant to shamanic healer. Her father's presence opened her to a different experience of reality. Her mother's presence, though less direct, has appeared at significant moments through synchronicities.

When she was living, Diane's mother bought three sets of very unique napkins with a distinctly indigenous South American pattern. Diane had never seen any other napkins like these in the many places around the globe that she had traveled to. Each of her daughters received one of the sets. One she kept for herself. After her mother's death, Diane inherited her mother's set. On Mother's Day, the day after participating in an Ayahuasca ceremony in the Amazon, Diane saw napkins with the same pattern as those her mother had given her in the market place. On another occasion, she went to see a healer in Oaxaca, someone she did not know and was not certain about; she saw napkins exactly like those she had inherited. She interprets these as signs of her mother's presence in her life and as affirmations of her choice to do shamanic work.

When Diane left her job as an accountant to take art classes and devote more time to developing her healing practice, she had a dream of her grandfather, her mother's father. In the dream she saw him walking across a plank that went over a ravine. Seeing him get up on the plank she wanted to yell to him, "I love you!" but did not. She was afraid if she yelled that he would be startled and fall. She watched him as he moved across the plank doing acrobatics and "walking it in his own way." It was dangerous, but he had no fear. For Diane, his message was clear; walk in your own way and have no fear. She honored this dream and her grandfather's message by making a teapot in her ceramics class with a plank that went down its side.

In her first ancestor dialogue, Diane's father and mother's father visited her. Her father reminded her of the gifts he had given her in the dream. He told her to use them. He also told her to support her nephews. Her grandfather told her to walk the path as he had showed her. He reminded her that there is a direction to her life and that things are moving. He asked her questions about her situation with her husband, her home, and her life that served to bring her awareness and focus to some of the lessons and information that were available in the experiences she was having in the present. At the end of this dialogue, these men were massaging her neck and sending their love and nurturing energy to her.

Her father, grandfather, and mother continued in their dialogues with her to offer guidance and support for the work on her house and all the decisions regarding the choices she was facing. From her choice of bathroom tiles to advice about how to be with herself through this time of transformation, her ancestors were a constant support. They reminded her to nurture herself, to take time to be alone, and to create a concrete vision for her life. Some of her father's words to her were:

> "You have been sad for so long. You don't need to be sad anymore. I see much beauty in your life. Patience. Take time for your own creative process. This will nurture you now. Buy the best you can afford."

When she asked her father what he wanted from her, he responded saying:

> Live your life with passion. Stand up for yourself and do what you want. Once the time is gone, it is gone and you will never have it back again. Don't limit yourself. Don't forget your dreams. Your life is going to change dramatically. Don't forget your dreams. It is easy to get distracted, but what are your dreams?

As the dialogues progressed, her father's message became simple and clear. He appeared as an imaginal presence on a beach in Baja, Mexico, with a stone in his hand. Placing the stone in her hand he told his daughter: "Live your own life."

Her mother encouraged her to do more with her shamanic work. She asked Diane, "What would make you happy?" Her mother told her to sit and observe and to be yin and the woman. She encouraged Diane to do her artwork and to let people support her. The *I Ching* reading Diane did as part of one of the dialogues supported and highlighted some of her parents' messages to her: take time for yourself, seclude yourself, embrace the feminine, and bring together what belongs together.

Diane asked for a dream about halfway through our month of research. She had the following dream: "I was in a river in Mesopotamia. I found a beauty pack floating in the river. It was made of skin and had three bulges in it. Each represented a different item for beauty." She woke up and then fell back to sleep and had a vision of a Persian carpet in powder blue and beige. She knew this was a dream from her mother. The dream offers gifts from her mother and also seems to reference what her father said to her in one of the dialogues; there would be much beauty in her life. Following this dream, another gift would come to her. She found the book that had been published about her father's renowned Bowie knife collection that she thought she had lost.

In addition to the emphasis on living her own life, one of the other consistent themes in Diane's dialogues involved supporting the next generation. Her father encouraged and directed her to support her nephews. Although Diane does not have children of her own, the daughter of one of her close friends has become very dear to her. During her month in this group she was moved to give her grandmother's ring to this young woman as a graduation present. At the end of our month together she went to Cambodia to celebrate her nephew's wedding. Coming back from this trip she talked about the incredible beauty she experienced in the people and the place. She felt that trip brought her into a deeper and more conscious relationship with the beauty and femininity her parents and grandfather had been bringing to her in the dialogues and dreams.

As our work together ended, Diane would live with the question of what to do with the treasures and gifts she had been given. She would ask for the courage to do what she needed in order to "live her own life" in ways which seemed to be presented to her through these dialogues and dreams. The work on her house continued. A few months after this work, after her husband had moved to Berkeley, California, and the work on the house was nearing completion, Diane attended a mythic writing workshop. She felt it honored the dream gifts of pencils and paper given to her by her father. The night before this workshop, she had the following dream: Her parents were standing by a pool of water. It seemed that they were alive. She hoped, in the dream, that they would stay around for a long time.

Janis's Story

Years before this group began; I sat talking with Janis's mother. She is a beautiful, deeply caring woman with rich blue eyes and pure white hair. At the age of 75, she has experienced many losses, joys, and disappointments. She is in constant physical pain. The sweetness, humor, and strength of her spirit are clear to everyone who knows her. On that particular day she was in Janis's office, helping her daughter with administrative work. Janis's mother and I were talking about being mothers and the relationship between mothers and daughters. Although I didn't record our exact conversation and I can't remember the specific details as I write today, I will never forget one thing she said: she didn't know the stories of her mother, her grandmothers, or her great grandmothers. As she spoke, her eyes filled with tears. Their stories had not been told and would not be passed on. What they had learned from life, what they knew, died with them. Her words and tears, in their simplicity, expressed the immeasurable value of what had been lost. Her longing to know these women, to know their stories, and to be able to tell their stories to her grandchildren touched me deeply. This loss is a particular kind of orphaning.

Janis's father's family came to this land from Germany in the 1800s. Her father was born in Nebraska. Her father's mother was a Gilmore. The Gilmores were originally from England. Her mother's mother, Grandma Clarice, was a first-generation American. Clarice's parents had come to Minnesota from Sweden and Norway in the 1800s. Her mother's father, a Waldon, traces his origins back to England. Janis's mother and father were still living at the time she participated in this group. She knows little about her family's origins or their stories. She knows they left Europe to come to this country seeking a better life. She describes the lives of her father's and grandfather's families as ones of "following the work," just to survive. Her family worked hard.

Janis was closest to her Grandma Clarice. Both of Janis's parents worked long hours, and she and her brother were left to take care of themselves. Her Grandma Clarice checked in on them. Janis remembers her as being somewhat distant in her care and doesn't feel as if she was raised by her. As Janis grew older, she became very close to her Grandma. She has heard stories of her Grandpa Ellery, her mother's father, but has few memories of him. He died when Janis was three. One memory stands out for her. She was seated on the couch with him. She remembers that her feet didn't touch the end of the cushion. She looked over at him and thought to herself, "That's my Grandpa." She writes, "Even at such a young age, I felt such love for him and I will never forget the emotion that came over me."

In anticipation of our first group gathering Janis wrote:

> I had initially thought all of the pictures, the memorabilia, the treasures remaining from my ancestors were buried deep in storage. Can their stories ever be buried or tucked away in storage? There, upon opening my chest of drawers (my heart?) lies the treasure trove of pictures and trinkets I thought were hidden away. The pictures of my Mom's side of the family slide easily into the velvet bag I am using to take with me to the workshop. Two pictures snag on the opening, almost hesitant to be placed within the bag. I realize the two pictures are of Dad and his parents, Grandma and Grandpa Hammers. Is it a message from them to me, or me to them? The discovery begins.

Janis brought all of these pictures to our first gathering. She placed them on the ancestor altar we were creating together that sat in the center of our circle. Each of us had one or at the most two photos of our ancestors to place on the altar on that first day. Janis placed each photograph carefully, telling us what she knew about each of the people in the photos. These photos held many unanswered questions, unknown names and places and forgotten stories. She placed a photograph of her father's grandmother on the altar. It had been taken at the 50th wedding anniversary celebration for her father's parents. Janis was in her twenties at the time. The day after this family gathering Janis asked who the woman was who was sitting alone at the table. It was her paternal great-grandmother. They had never met. Looking at the photographs of her father, his parents, and her great grandmother, she described a feeling of resistance from and towards them and a sense of secrets. As her relationship with these people developed, she would describe them as "shrouded."

Janis found more photographs of her family following our first gathering. She took them to her "Mom" and learned who these people were and some of the stories her mother remembered about them. As her process of discovery continued, the feelings of resistance increased. She didn't know if the resistance was hers or was coming from the ancestors. She described her relationship with the ancestors as "rocky" and "hesitant." Although sensing there was importance in understanding her connections with the people in these photographs, she couldn't "find a thread [she could] hold onto to draw them into her world." She had no sense of where and how these people fit into her understanding of herself.

The distance she felt was reflected in something "she learned from a shaman" she consulted for a reading. Her ancestors, according to him, were present, and one in particular was standing back and observing her. He encouraged her to be open to any communication from any of them. Soon after her visit to this shaman, she was looking for a new office space. Seeing a "for rent" sign outside of a beautifully renovated building, she went inside to inquire. The owner showed her the office and talked about the care that had gone into the renovation. As he showed Janis the historical photographs, he mentioned that the building had been built in 1902. She writes: "Shivers went down my spine. 1902 was the year of my Grandma Clarice's birth. I felt myself nod and found myself thanking Grandma for her guidance."

In between our second and last group gathering, Janis moved for the fifth time in three years. In that time she had gone through a divorce and survived two bouts with breast cancer. During this entire time she continued to take care of her mother. In a dialogue with her ancestors during this time she experienced feelings of anger coming over her. As she felt more deeply into the emotion, she felt a sense of release. She wrote that it was as if "we came to an agreement . . . perhaps condolences." Condolence is an interesting word, because it is an expression of sympathy for someone who is grieving. It also means to suffer with another. She continues to ask: "what difference does it make who I came from?! I am the result of people having sex. It wasn't for the conscious purpose of having me. I never felt a sense of family, of anyone caring for me. A sense of belonging never held any meaning for me, nor does it now." When she spoke with me, she talked about feeling very alone in her family. She said it was not her responsibility to heal them. This is *her* life. This was, in her words, "a crisis of faith." As she spoke those words, a hawk flew overhead.

We had to stop our conversation for a short time. When it resumed, Janis asked, "What is a family?!" I heard grief in her voice. As she asked this question, a hawk flew overhead. Answering her own question, she stated that family is whatever we choose it to mean. She has had and currently has close friends in her life to whom she is closer than she is to anyone in her biological family. Several of these people, "the family of the heart," as she calls them, have died in the last two years. She questioned whether she was turning away from the ancestors out of pain and bitterness. She asked: does being in relationship with the ancestors matter? What does it matter? These questions, the resistance she grappled with, the anger and grief, would continue. In our last group Janis talked about her "chosen family," her "heart family" which included those people who meant the most to her in her life. She said, "We are all family, we are all connected."

One of Janis's "family of the heart" died very recently. Janis felt her presence, her spirit, and wrote this song:

Once More, Once Again
A song sung by a friend
Is carried in the wind
From just across the way to me

A song of hopes and dreams
Of life and all its schemes
Of love and memories we've shared

I listen and I hear
Your voice, your heart my dear
So sing it once again for me

Once more, once again
Please sing it once again
Once more again to me
Sing it loud and clear
Let everybody hear,
Once more, once again, to me

But now my friend, you're gone
You've left me on my own
I long to hear your song again

I listen, I don't hear
Your sweet song fills the air
There's only emptiness for me

Please sing it once again
Once more, once again
Once more, once again for me
Sing it loud and clear
My heart longs to hear
Once more, once again for me

A song sung by a friend
Echoes in the wind
From somewhere far away for me

It lingers in the air
I listen and I hear
A haunting melody for me

Sing it softly in my ear
My heart once more can hear
Sing it once again for me
Once more, once again
Once more, once again
Forever once again for me

In our final interview she expressed her sense of guilt about not feeling closer to her family and her ancestors. She expressed how painful it is to know that in reality they were all "shrouded" and "fucked up." When she looked to them for guidance and wisdom, she had no sense that anything was there. She feels as if she can't reach out to them and learn anything from them. Neither does she feel the ancestors reaching out to her. This echoes her mother's grief at the stories that have been lost with the death of her mother and grandmother and all the women in her lineage, and, her wish for their wisdom gained from what they had learned in life. Janis doesn't want to reach out and be disappointed . . . again.

Janis has stayed with this process, with the questions and feelings of resistance. She knows that as hard as this has been, there is something valuable and very real going on in her relationship with the ancestors. Healing is a process that takes its own time. Being in a more conscious relationship has brought out "all of the emotions and longing." Her mother's longing for the lost stories of her mother's mothers and the grief she expressed in that conversation years ago seem to be mirrored in Janis's longing for wisdom and guidance from her family and her ancestors. She called me a few days after our final interview and said that the word *elder* had come to her. She wanted elders in her life. She did not and had not experienced this with her biological family.

Janis experiences her ancestors, especially her father's mother and grandmother, as being "shrouded." She describes her father as "shrouded, ignorant, and living his life in an unknowing place. No light of awareness penetrates through." I remembered that she told me about a year ago that an astrologer described the Sun in her chart as unrelated to any other planets, isolated and shrouded. Imagining the Sun as a character on a stage, the King in the play, the ego and one's sense of oneself, we can imagine Janis's Sun, shrouded and unrelated, does not know what is going on in the story nor does she understand her part in the "play." The other people on the stage are not related to her and do not see her. I shared this with her. She was stunned as she remembered what the astrologer had said. Something seemed to open. After a few moments Janis said, "Maybe I'm the first one who will be able to shed this shroud."

In our final interview I asked Janis if she had noticed any changes in her family since she began her dialogues with the ancestors that she thought or felt were related to the work she had done. She said, as open and optimistic as always, "It hasn't been revealed, and I am holding out hope." As I was writing her story, I received this in an email from her:

> I'll share with you that while I was waiting for a flight out of Sacto that I noticed I had received a call a couple of hours earlier today while in the seminar. It was a number I didn't recognize and the voicemail was from my Dad . . . he never calls, as you know. I finally reached him and he was very distressed, as was his wife, and had been waiting for me to call. He has been in the hospital several times this year and just came home from a week long admittance. His emphysema is so bad he can barely breathe and is unable to do anything. He told me all of his family has moved away, he has no one and he just needed to talk to me and my brother; he doesn't even know where anyone is, then he broke down while talking to me. I know he is close to the end of his time here, I can feel it.

After years her father reached out to her. On the stage of her life, Janis and her father are relating to each other.

Kathryn's Story

Each of us chose a journal on the first day we met. Each journal had a different image on its cover. The image on the journal Kathryn chose was of stones. There was an arch composed of gray stones perfectly placed beside each other to form the arch. On top of and supported by the arch of stones was one single stone.

Kathryn is the last in her line. She was unable to have children, and her only sister did not have children of her own and adopted a son. She is the aunt to her adopted nephew. In our group Kathryn asked: after I am dead, who will remember me, who will do ancestor work for me, who will show pictures of me and say this is my grandmother, who will heal me? She described herself as the weakest link in a chain, a pearl dropped from a strand. Seeing people who are sustained by family and community, she asks, why not me? She felt and feels like an orphan. The connections Kathryn does have with people have not been given to her. From early in her life, her girlfriends have been her "chosen family, sisters of the soul." She has worked hard to forge and maintain these relationships. "Many of these relationships prevail 45 years later." She writes that "her work as a psychotherapist and healer has also brought her to a pure state of love for her clients." For belonging, she looks "for sustenance not from the human world, but within the larger and more embracing realm of nature." "If belonging is for the human world," Kathryn asks, "does it mean anything that I was born into this human family?"

The objects Kathryn brought to be part of our collective ancestor altar for our first group were more archetypal than personal—a bone, an Egyptian cat, the Virgin of Guadalupe, a shaman figure, beach glass, a red square, and a photograph of her parents. Looking at the objects, she asked why these particular objects and what do they have to do with her lineage. They are "loose little threads" that she was able to find, "literally grasping for any shred of connection." She asks, "How do I make sense of my own life from the artifacts I have constructed from these threads?" Contemplating this question, some of her associations with these figures follow.

The Egyptian cat represents and holds the protective spirit and wisdom of cats which would be so important to Kathryn growing up and throughout her life. Looking at her daughter, "the baby she had birthed," Kathryn's mother knew intuitively that cats would be important in her daughter's life. However, in order to affirm this truth for her daughter and bring cats into her life, her mother would have to overcome the fear and conditioning that had been passed down through her lineage. Her mother had been raised on stories of black magic from the Black Forests of Bavaria. "She was taught that witches shape-shifted into cats, un-natural creatures that served the devil." Kathryn is grateful that her mother recognized her daughter's truth, her need, and that she loved her enough to overcome her fear of cats.

The Virgin of Guadalupe "stands as the good mother, the Goddess and the one that protects the feminine." She came into Kathryn's life "after much damage had already been done." The bone "stands for the wearing down" of Kathryn's "egoic identity." It is a "humble reminder to not seek truth in false idols." "Seeking a substantive belonging to this life", Kathryn acquired things, experiences, and knowledge, and held them close, seeking communion with the quality of the things she loved. The bone is a reminder that nothing can be "grasped with any permanence." She writes, "In the end I belong to no one and no thing that I can touch or taste or smell and my body grieves from the pain of this loneliness." The ancestor altar is her attempt to fashion a home, "a place where [her] heart can be seen and held in love."

Although she has good memories of her early childhood that involved intimacy with her mother, she writes that "her mother was unable to protect her . . . from the emotional abuse perpetrated by her father. [Her mother] tried to control and use [Kathryn] to meet her own emotional needs." Kathryn has been angry with her ancestors "for the poverty of spirit that produced parents such as mine." She knows and acknowledges that her parents "loved [her] in their way," and gave her life, an appreciation for beauty, a creative nature, and a good intellect. "They did the best they could, but my parents were too damaged to embody enough cherishing to sustain a sensitive child." She "receives their gifts with gratitude even as [she] enacts an alchemical prayer that the poison inherent with these gifts be purified." She writes that she is

> saddened that many of the latent talents within my genes did not fully manifest into their potential expression in this lifetime due, primarily to a lack of emotional nourishment. My life energies have been so consumed by the demands of survival that I have become simply strong rather than fulfilled. This is not to denigrate my many accomplishments, the wisdom I have acquired or the good person that I am. I only mean to say that it has been a lonely path and never once have I felt my ancestors walking beside me. I ask now, where are you?

In Kathryn's first dialogue she heard the voice of her paternal grandmother (the woman whose name she carries), her paternal grandfather, and her paternal great grandmother—the "French Grand Dame." In her journal she writes:

> *My paternal grandmother* informs me through these writings that I should be thankful for the freedoms I enjoy. "Living within the constrictions of convention strangled my soul," she explains. I wasn't like them and was meant for a different life. It was all wrong, even the clinging of my only child that grew up to be your father." I was not equipped to be a mother. Be glad you never had children; they are lead weights around your ankles. My so-called husband was of no use, a weak man, emasculated by that insufferable French Grand Dame, his mother, and my nemesis.
>
> Please believe me that I did my best to find my place within that family. You know nothing about where I came from, so I will say that like you, I have always suffered from not belonging. I did not even belong to myself, a desperate state that was my undoing. My "nervous disorder" worsened with the change of life and I went quite mad. You see, this was my deliverance, and the final solution for the family. My

poor son was but eleven years old and it broke my heart to see him suffer, but there was nothing I could do.

I was removed to the sanitarium and left in peace for the remainder of my days to write my music and to perform for the other patients. I gave singing lessons and my music was even published.

My son gave you my name. Perhaps he meant to honor or to reclaim me in some fashion, but my name has been the burden you have carried. Even as a small girl you were bewildered by his hatred of you and could not imagine what you had done.

Your father inherited my nervous disorder, as have you. He drank spirits for relief and his mind became dark and twisted. Some of this is my fault for not having been a proper mother to him. The greatest gift I gave him was my love of beauty and you were his beauty, and his dark elements determined to destroy you. Why? When he sees you he sees me and while I may deserve his hatred you do not. It never belonged to you and I beg of you to lay that burden down.

Be free, I say to you. Don't wear the yoke of this dead lineage around your neck. Free yourself and leave the madness for me.

My paternal grandfather speaks in such a soft voice I can barely hear him and must read his thoughts. He is concerned about propriety and a Victorian ethos of heroic manhood that flourishes in his imagination, alone. He values intellect, honor and appearances, but he is also insecure and often wonders if there is really any meaning to life.

He is caught in an untenable power struggle between his domineering mother with her French arrogance and his unpredictable Irish wife with her dark depressions and dreams. He can't reach his wife, or control her and he lives in constant fear of an embarrassing scene. It is his mother who prevails, wielding scathing criticism to rein the Irish woman in.

All he ever wanted was a noble and genteel life, but here he finds himself, captive in a feminine maelstrom of hysteria and oppression. He looks upon me with wistful disinterest. He doesn't have enough fire in the belly to connect across the generations. Does he even care about my existence?

He remembers only his small son demonstrating intellectual and artistic promise, so young. He does not look deeply enough to see the wound cleaved across this boys heart, nor did he have the where-with-all to do anything to protect his child. He gave him instead, words, ideals and a piercing intellect that refuted the existence of God and harbored contempt for any human weakness.

The French Grand Dame (paternal great grandmother) is a force of nature, an imposing presence, willful and superior like her name,

Madame Grand. As a young woman, she has a fine lace shop in a good neighborhood in Paris. She hires girls to do the work, but is also known for her own, exquisite fine lace work. Perhaps I inherit some of my manual dexterity and love of craftwork from her. Madame Grand had two husbands thus creating a branch in the family tree. Some of her descendants carry the trait of arrogance, including my contemporary French relatives. Let's see what Madame has to say.

"Stop feeling guilty for wanting fine things. Taste is a natural expression of refinement. Our blood is refined and class can't be bought it can only be bred. Your breeding has been tainted, but that's not your fault, you just have to live with it.

There are right ways and wrong ways to behave. I am appalled by your generation's heathen behaviors and I find it un-lady-like that you prance around like savages. Remember your heritage and act like a lady.

You have good hands you should put them to some good use. Stop complaining about having to work hard. Stop waiting for someone to do it for you. Demand it, take it, work for it, but it is up to you. I had my lace shop because I was the best lace maker in Paris. Don't dishonor me with lassitude or mad dreams like that Irish woman my son insisted he marry, polluting our pure French line with that bad Irish blood.

The children I had with my first husband carry the pure blood and all those fine qualities. Your line carries madness because of the Irish woman. I'm not saying she had no redeeming qualities, she did love music, after all, but her character was weak and she produced a somber child. My grandson showed promise, so perhaps he inherited some of my blood, but it's a travesty that he named you after his mother. I say, better it all ends with you.

Listen here. Don't you dare judge me! You know nothing about my life or my heart aches. You will never know. Fine, let it die with me and let the bloodline die with you. Just remember this, I was a business woman and an artist, a fine lace maker, the best in Paris so shame on you if you don't do something worthwhile with the skills I have passed on to you."

Kathryn wonders where this "channeled writing" comes from. Is it the voices of her ancestors, her imagination, her projections? What is the truth, and how can the truth be known?

Kathryn's father, the son and grandson of the ancestors who spoke to Kathryn in her first dialogue, was an illustrator. He was talented, and became well-known, but his illustrations were often dark, brutal, and predatory. She believes she inherited her artistic abilities, extreme shyness, introversion, and sensitivity from him. "It is bewildering to me that my father seemed totally disinterested in who I was, and rather than fostering my development, he withheld approval, or worse, denigrated me." His objectification of her as a woman also left its painful mark. She describes her father as cynical and nihilistic. He eventually succumbed to "the darkness of addiction." Although this was devastating for her, Kathryn felt that "there were moments when I could sense that he and I were alike, that we could have been kindred spirits, that he could have taught me so much, if only he had cultivated and supported my own latent talents."

Kathryn's feelings of disconnection and her longing to belong were a theme in her life and throughout this process. Her mother had nine brothers and sisters. From these aunts and uncles, Kathryn has seventeen cousins. While her mother was alive, Kathryn had some connection with her cousins, but nothing that proved sustainable.

> Most of my life I dreamed of what it would be like to be a part of a big family, like the one my mother grew up in. I always loved to receive invitations to friend's lake houses for gathering of the clan, because for a little while I could pretend that I belonged to a family. I have had moments of literally looking through windows at neighborhood family gatherings and celebrations and feeling absolutely bereft to not have this experience in my own life.

Kathryn discovered that her mother also felt "a type of loneliness and sense of not belonging within the community of her own large family." Her mother, the middle child, felt displaced. She also was the black sheep of the family. In our first group Kathryn had a sense that the bitterness she feels may have resonance and origins in her lineage.

Kathryn's existence was compromised "from the beginning" by the diethylstilbestrol her mother took when she was pregnant with Kathryn. Kathryn feels that her body does not support her as a home. Three years prior to this group, Kathryn was treated for breast cancer. She also suffers chronic pain from Lyme disease. At this time, she feels in transition. She feels as if she has yet to recover from the emotional and physical toll, "these assaults on her body." She has not been "able to retrieve herself." Recently moving from the east coast of America, to Santa Barbara on the west coast, "in an attempt to begin life anew," she carried boxes of photographs and other family heirlooms that had been collected and saved over the generations and left to her. What she has of the family legacy sits in boxes stored in a room in her home. She had not been able to bring herself to go into and through those boxes.

It was suggested in our first group gathering that, as part of being in a more conscious relationship with the ancestors, one should feed them.

After creating her ancestor altar, Kathryn fed them well. In one of the pictures she shared, there is an orange, a glass of brandy, chocolate, salt, a dried fruit and nut sweet, and a rose. Her loving care is expressed and clearly visible in these offerings, which are abundant and abundantly beautiful. Feeding them "created a context of nourishment and nurturing." She told us it felt good to have a family to take care of and to nourish. She writes:

> In inviting my ancestors to the table (altar) and feeding them, a pathway of nourishment opened. I cared about what they each might like or enjoy, as if they were actual guests in my home. This graciousness is closer to my true nature than the bitterness I have carried.

Between our first and second group gathering Kathryn began the process of opening and going through everything left to her by her family in the boxes. Beginning the process of "unearthing her ancestors," she encountered them in photographs, handwritten notes, newspaper clippings, and other memorabilia. She immersed herself in these iconic bits of her ancestors' lives. Some mysteries were solved, new stories were discovered, and some history was corrected. These archives also held new mysteries and led to more unanswered questions. She found evidence for the family myth that, from her father's side they had Mongolian blood. The dark skinned woman in a photograph of her great, great paternal grandmother did not look Irish or French. Her features and coloring suggested a different lineage, possibly Mongolian. Kathryn thought her parents had eloped, but discovered that they were married in a civil ceremony with her maternal grandparents present. It was her paternal grandparents who had in fact eloped and married against the approval of Madame Grand, her father's mother.

From a cryptic note written on the back of a photograph, she discovered that her father had an infant brother named Eugene. The note read, "they stole him from me." Kathryn wondered if her father's brother had died or if he was taken from his mother as she went mad. Was the note an indication of her grandmother's increasing paranoia? Her understanding of her father deepened as she encountered him through what had been passed down to her in the contents of these boxes. Her father appeared to be an unhappy child who "created a fantasy-laden world of daring heroes. As a college student his romantic objectification of women was gradually eroded by a cynical distrust of love." Reading her father's writings from that time, she "uncovered the origins of his contempt for women and sensed the pervasive low self-esteem that her father attempted to disguise with his bravado." As her understanding of the origins of his contempt for women deepened, her compassion for him grew. One of the most touching discoveries she made was a letter that her father had written to his mother when she was placed in a sanitarium.

> Discovering and reading his letter to his mother, written at age nine with a schoolboy's formality, bereft of any closeness or affection, was one of the most poignant moments I've experienced in this process. In reading between the lines, one feels strains of his broken baby heart, trying so hard to act grown up.

Initially Kathryn thought the voices of Madame Grand and her paternal grandparents in her first dialogue were pure imagination and conjecture. As she encountered them through the memories in the contents of the boxes she saw that, in fact, these dialogues had an uncanny accuracy.

> As I gaze upon the earlier generation of ancestors, I see people going about their lives. I try to see into their hearts and minds, but I can only guess at the contents. There really is no way to separate the hunches; myths and projections from the realities of whom they were. Truth be told, I don't know them any more than they know me. There are, however, some discernable themes that catch my attention. Repeating trends like artistic talents, a fascination with the occult, religious and spiritual devotions, a genetic predisposition toward cancer, a valuing of education, hints of aristocracy, strong women and hints of madness, all are woven into the histories I am able to glean from my explorations of the archives.

Kathryn brought a bag full of photographs to our last group gathering. We all laughed at the remarkable difference between what she brought to share with us this time and what she brought to our first session. She is creating albums from these archives, which she will ultimately bequeath to people she has chosen. She wants her ancestors, through these albums, to have an "honorable place." She feels it is the least she can do for them. Handling every piece in each of these boxes with great care, listening to the stories in the photographs, discovering unknown relatives, honoring each memory and each person, and finding a place for them in good hands is a daunting task. She writes, "I must be resolute in finishing what I started so I can finally lay this burden down." The room that housed these boxes, once emptied, will become Kathryn's art studio, something she has wanted for a very long time.

She sees her parents and other ancestors more clearly now and relates to them more as human beings rather than characters in a story. She is humbled as she realizes she had a lot of assumptions about who they were that have been dispelled. She is more aware of the victim mentality that has been an underlying theme in her life. With this deeper understanding Kathryn feels more compassion for her ancestors and herself. This is accompanied by an increasing sense of liberation. She has learned that the bitterness she embodied has "contributed" to her isolation, that her anger towards the ancestors and God only reinforces her sense of exile. When lived from a place of bitterness, "life becomes a lament instead of an authentic experience of living." She feels she is living the life that is hers to live more now than before rather than "lamenting" that life was not what she "hoped it would be." She writes, "I feel that understanding my parents as people has enabled me to be more of an adult, that it is incumbent upon me to take full responsibility for my own life." She accepts "the creation of who [she is] for better or worse" more now than before.

She still feels alone. It is hers to bear the reality of what this feels like. Kathryn "feels distressed by the cancer gene [she] inherited." She "accepts it is her karma to bear the reality of this." "Perhaps most painful of all" is that Kathryn does not feel loved by God and does not understand the purpose in her suffering. After reading a book on Mother Theresa and prayer, Kathryn realized that her maternal grandmother had probably been very spiritual. She had previously written her off as "a German catholic." Her mother grew up being abused by nuns and "ex-communicated herself from the church at 18." Her father "was a rabid atheist and her mother rejected organized religion and replaced it with a fairy tale fantasy world, that while enchanting, had little commerce with reality."

Kathryn is "acutely" aware of the need to repair her relationship with God. She "struck out on her own in search of sustenance," "a spiritual seeker since childhood." Even after all of this work, the ancestors are not a source of sustenance for Kathryn. She reflects on the way in which everything that she grasps for in this world dissolves. Her longing for a sense of belonging and meaning here always seems to slip through her grasp. The question now is what does sustain her. She says it is the earth, nature, animals, an invisible connection to Spirit and Source and the ocean. For Kathryn, "the ocean that she has waited a lifetime to live near is now her church and access point where she seeks a relationship with God."

After our last group together, Kathryn had an experience of healing and release. She wrote in her journal:

> My dear friend came to visit as I was concluding these writings. I shared with her some of my experiences with my ancestors. I felt compelled to show her two photographs; one of my father enacting a scene for one of his illustrations and looking positively demonic, and another of my aunt Anita who died at age 33 of breast cancer. I felt haunted by these two images and my friend offered to do a healing to help me.

Neither of us had any idea what to expect but the healing unfolded in a rather deliberate way. I began to speak as I lay on the healing table, as if I was speaking for Anita. I sensed that her experience of going through chemo, while pregnant, at a time when cancer was something to be ashamed of, was a wretched and lonely experience that she bore in an isolated silence.

As I felt the deepest empathy and compassion for her, my friend observed cords binding Anita and I together. It appeared that Anita was so grateful to find someone who cared and understood what it had been like for her, that some of her suffering melded with my own cancer experience. There was a silent acknowledgement of the truth of this between Anita and I and I felt a weight lift from me. Then I saw Anita turn and walk out a door. At that same moment my friend spoke and said she saw Anita leave and walk out my front door. My friend then offered that I no longer needed to carry Anita's suffering.

I lay on the table contemplating what had just occurred as my friend did some energy work. My thoughts turned to my father and memories of what it was like to live in the same space as him during the darkest hours of his drinking. I remember that it was actually hard to physically move sometimes, because the air felt so dense with negativity.

It occurred to me that my father had so misused his mind to entertain hateful thoughts that this activity eventually attracted a dark entity from the astral realms. That entity lurked about in my fathers' consciousness, preying upon the brightest and most vulnerable being in the vicinity, me. It had been trying to destroy me for most of my life, but I somehow managed to ward it off. Then for reasons I am still sorting out, I lost most of my protection when my marriage ended ten years ago and I started to get sick and finally succumbed to this curse.

I recall mumbling something about all of this to my friend, thinking I must sound really crazy. As she started to do some kind of shamanic work, I suddenly felt myself in the jaws of a serpent of black smoke, just like in the series "Lost." This smoke monster battered me about mercilessly; its dark tendrils invading deeply into my body. Then it suddenly stopped and pulled back and withdrew down a hole, again just like in "Lost." I was both horrified and profoundly relieved when this ended. When my friend and I spoke again, she reported seeing the same thing and made the same reference to the black smoke in "Lost." She told me she thought it was gone for good.

I am praying that the healing that took place at the conclusion of this Ancestor Work will indeed be lasting and true. I hope that I will learn to love my self and others in a way that will rectify history, burn karma and send ripples of healing back in time. I hope that as my days draw to a close I will feel I have been worthy of the gifts I've inherited and will have succeeded at doing some good for this world. With my last breath my lineage will flicker and then cease to be. May it go with God and may all beings be free from suffering.

After sending this story to Kathryn for final review, I received a call from her. She told me that her cancer had returned and metastasized. Once again she finds herself "confronting her mortality." When she first heard the news she thought, "Maybe the struggle is finally over." A tidal wave of feelings followed this thought. First, "a sinking disappointment as [she] faced the stark possibility that all [her] unfulfilled dreams might never come to fruition"; then, a wave of "immense gratitude for each breath and an acute awareness of all the beauty and abundance surrounding [her]." She has had "moments of so deeply penetrating the Now that it becomes eternal." She does not want to die. She does not want more pain. She finds it "hard to accept that this is God's plan for [her]."

During the month we met as a group, Kathryn went to a lecture given by a Himalayan monk, "a holy man," in Santa Barbara. As a result of this man coming into her life, she committed to going to India "on a healing and spiritual pilgrimage." She writes:

> As an uncanny twist of fate, I will be seeing one of the leading Ayurvedic cancer physicians in the world while there . . . . I had also sought out the counsel of a holy woman before the cancer diagnosis and she told me this; "When we lose our connection to God, pain then becomes agony. She said that everything that has occurred in my life is God's plan for me and to stop fighting it. While, my most recent quest for healing invoked my ancestors, it was now time for the divine conversation to begin and for offerings to be made, and so my walks on the beach have become prayers. The first time I prayed I found only one feather to give as an offering to the ocean. The next time I return to the beach, an amazing phenomenon has occurred and the ocean had returned, literally, hundreds of feathers to the beach. So it is now time for me to stand before my creator, just as I am, and to give and receive the love that has *always* been there. As I walk the beach, the counsel of the holy woman echoes in my mind, especially her parting words to me; "This is your last invitation."

As of this writing Kathryn has joined the ancestors. May she indeed be blessed and embraced in "the love that has *always* been there."

Tracy's Story

Tracy's father died when she was 16. He was only 37 years old. Tracy was sick and stayed home from school that day. It was January, and the apple orchard her family owned was dormant. A few years before he died, her father, a successful businessman, decided that he wanted to go back to the land. When Tracy was 12 years old, he quit his job and bought an apple orchard on 60 acres of land where he built a log cabin for his family.

Tracy's father loved hunting and fishing. For as long as Tracy can remember, there was venison in their freezer. The night before he died, he was out playing poker with the other farmers in the area.

Her father had Parkinson/White syndrome, an inherited condition. His heart had a valve which had the potential to remain open, resulting in tachycardia. He had been on medication since he was 18, and had never had any symptoms before this particular morning. That morning Tracy asked him if he was feeling all right. He told her that his heart was racing faster than normal that day, but he assured her that he would be fine. Tracy gave him a big hug and went downstairs to the basement to take a nap. At around 3:30 that afternoon her mom and brother woke her. They told her that her father was gone. While Tracy was sleeping in the basement, her father had died in her mother's arms during lunch while talking with the doctor on the phone. Tracy's mother thought it was a miracle that Tracy had slept through it all. Tracy awakened into a nightmare. She remembers feeling as if she were in an altered state. She was in shock. A week after his death, everything "returned to normal."

For months after her father's death, Tracy told herself that her dad wasn't dead; he was just on one of his hunting trips and would be coming back. She told herself this story for a long time. She refused to cry in front of her mother, believing that if she didn't cry her father's death wouldn't be real. About four months after his death, in the spring, Tracy had a dream:

> I am very cold. I realize I am underwater. It's very green and murky. I look around and realize where I am. I am in the pond in front of the cabin. [Tracy's father also built the pond.] I am dropping through the water, sinking, falling down, deeper and deeper. Drowning. I can see sunlight above coming through the water but I am going deeper. Then I realize my Dad is there in the water with me. It is like he's jumped into the water. He has his clothes on. He starts pushing me up toward the sunlight. I realize he's come from the other side of the pond and is pushing me away from that side onto the other side, away from where he came. He is not pulling me back toward him, but away towards the water's surface. I can see hazy figures through the water. As I surface I see mom and my brother standing there. When I realize I'm now saved and safe I have a huge sense of relief. I am glad I didn't drown. Everyone is relieved. I am happy because I realize my father is not dead but alive and there. When I turned around to acknowledge him, to thank him for saving me, he wasn't there.

This was a pivotal dream for Tracy. She began to let herself feel the loss and grief. It also brought Tracy's father back into her life. He returned to her in dreams and through experiences she had in nature.

On January 11th in 2010, the 31st anniversary of her father's death, Tracy, with her therapist, created a small ceremony in honor of his memory. This was the first time Tracy had ever done anything more than call her mother on the anniversary of her father's death. On this anniversary, she placed a beautiful yellow flowering plant, a large feather and a few rocks together. Her therapist added two candles. Tracy was comforted by the feather. She asked what kind it was. Her therapist said she thought the feather, was from a red-tailed hawk. The feather seemed to be very apropos and connected to Tracy's experiences in nature over the years following her father's death.

Every time Tracy saw a red-tailed hawk she thought of her father. Although she made this association, it was outside of her current understanding of reality to think that these hawk sightings really were indications of her father's continuing presence in her life. Having finished creating this collection of objects in honor of her father, Tracy looked out the window which faced the mountains and gasped. Soaring high over the mountains were two red-tailed hawks. Later that day she wrote to her mother and brother about seeing the hawks in that moment, "They were amazing, dancing and soaring and playing together. I was overcome with emotion. . . . We watched them until it was time for me to go."

Walking to her car, she felt blessed and watched over. Her radio came on when she started her car. It was tuned to the NPR station she often listens to. A beautiful song, sung by a woman in French, was playing. Tracy thought it would be interesting if it was a song about losing someone who was deeply loved. Her skepticism about whether or not the hawks were somehow related to her father, possibly an indication of his continuing presence in her life, disappeared when the announcer came on the radio after the song finished and said, "that was Lhasa de Sela, a beautiful voice recently taken from us much too soon. She passed away on January 1st of this year. She was thirty-seven." Tracy's father died on January 11th at the age of thirty-seven. When the clock said 1:11 each day, Tracy's brother would think of his father.

The hawks stayed in sight for most of her drive home, even though she lives on the opposite side of the mountain from her therapist's office. She decided to go on a long walk near the ocean. On this walk she caught another glimpse of a hawk. Even with these experiences or maybe because of them, Tracy didn't want hawk to leave. She wanted clear affirmation that when hawk appeared it was in fact her father letting her know that he was still there. She asked silently for more affirmation and validation of her father's continuing connection through hawk in the present, in her life. As she neared her home, arriving just at the end of her driveway, she looked up and saw two hawks soaring above her. She watched them for a long time until they flew so high they were out of sight.

Tracy had carried rose petals from her father's funeral with her since his death. After thirty-one years, she decided to create an altar in her home dedicated to her father's memory. She placed the rose petals on this altar. Tracy wanted a hawk feather of her own to place on the ancestor altar she had created in her own home. About a month after her experience with hawk on the anniversary of her father's death and a few days before our first group gathering, Tracy found three baby hawk feathers. She had anticipated finding them and was actually looking for them that day. She wrote, "They were in plain sight." On another day, standing outside of the office of the graduate school she attends, she noticed black crow feathers raining down onto the street from some eucalyptus trees. She followed the trail up to the eucalyptus trees and saw a red tailed hawk's nest with a mama bird feeding her babies fresh crow. She felt as if she was in the nest with them. She kept some of the crow feathers.

Tracy's first dialogue began with one of the parent hawks flying directly overhead and unusually close to her. She continues to see hawks flying every week since her experience on the anniversary of her father's death. Most recently, during a visit to her mother in Eastern Washington, "the home of my adolescence and the land where my father died," hawk appeared again. She and her mother were leaving to go to her father's gravesite. As they reached the end of the driveway, Tracy looked up and saw a beautiful hawk, "soaring above and watching over us." She had never before seen a hawk at her mother's home before or during any visit she made to the land where her father had built a home and had died.

Home and a sense of belonging to the land became recurring themes during Tracy's reconnection with her ancestors. A small replica of Stonehenge sits on her ancestor altar along with several crystals and stones—all matter of the earth. Having moved many times in her life, she has never had a sense of rootedness. As her dialogues with her ancestors developed and she gathered genealogical information, she traced her ancestors' ceaseless movement from Europe to and across this continent. As her relationship became more conscious, she felt an increasing tension between wanting to put down roots and a sense of having to keep moving. This, as she experiences it, is one of the unanswered questions of her ancestors – when and where to put down roots?

In her genealogical research, Tracy learned that many of her and her husband's ancestors began their journey from the Alsace Lorraine region of Europe. Although she and her husband have bought and sold several homes, they have yet to establish roots in one place. Tracy found a sense of resonance with the ancestors in her longing to buy a home and settle in one place. She asked in one of her dialogues, "What would the ancestors do?" Their response was simple, "exist on what is in front of you." This is the way of life her father had returned to with his family when he bought the apple orchard. As more and more ancestors wanted to be placed on her ancestor altar and became part of the dialogue, Tracy realized that she and her husband continued the nomadic journey of their ancestors looking for the right place to finally put down new roots. Currently renting, they are now looking for another home to buy.

As time went on and Tracy and her husband continue to look for a home to buy, she gains ground in her understanding of her experience of not feeling rooted to the land, to a place, to some place. Walking by a house she and her husband had considered buying but did not, Tracy felt the anxiety of not having a home, not having roots. Her longing to put down more permanent roots was met with reassurance from the ancestors and a response from nature. She looked down and at her feet was a perfect bird's nest. As she picked up the nest she heard, "Mother cry to me, hear my words softly spoken, lost but not forgotten." She knew it was a gift of acknowledgement and reassurance through nature, from her ancestors.

Tracy's connection to nature has always been important to her. As her relationship with the ancestors developed, she wondered about her own indigenous origins. Her father's deep connection to nature and to the land traces its roots to a "Black German" great-grandmother and great great-grandmother.[17] In a photograph Tracy has, her great-grandmother looks strikingly aboriginal. After a dialogue with the ancestors, Tracy shared these words in our council circle: "the sounds of nature do not change. The sound of hawk, hummingbird, beetle, dove, the wind – these are the sounds that our ancestors heard." She senses and knows that her ancestors heard these same sounds and are also immanent and present in these sounds. What has been, is, and always will be is present in these sounds of nature. Lying on the earth, listening to these sounds, feeling the presence of nature, feeling the deep connection through the generations past and future in the present moment in the presence of nature, she is at peace. Before this work, she thought her longing would be satisfied by owning a house. She realized that her longing, like her father's, was for a sense of connection to the land, a sense of belonging to the land, a grounding in nature in which roots can take hold.

Tracy's sense of abandonment was also a recurring theme. Tracy's mother was unconscious during Tracy's birth, in a twilight sleep which was a common birthing practice. Tracy spent the first 24 hours of her life "banished" to the nursery. When she became pregnant with her first son, she was clear that she wanted to give him the best start he could have in the world. She wanted to deliver him naturally and keep him with her so the natural process of bonding between mother and child could occur. Twelve hours after her son was born, he developed a fever and was taken to ICU. In one of her dialogues, re-experiencing her sense of abandonment at birth, she realized that the birth of her son was a recapitulation of her own post-bonding experience. She feels the presence of her ancestors and knows she is connected to the history of conception and birth in the women in her lineage. She hears them tell her, "be gentle."

In this dialogue she lies down to listen to them and realizes she is in the supine-birthing position. Her cat climbs onto her belly, and she holds him. In the first picture taken of Tracy with her parents upon her arrival home from the hospital after being born, her father holds her and her mother holds their cat. She hears again, "be gentle." She feels strength and calm flowing from them to her. A horrible image of a woman anticipating birth "flashes" in her mind. She then sees the birth from the doctor's perspective. "Whose birth, whose body" she does not know. It is horrible and painful to experience this "memory." She wonders about her grandmother's experience of giving birth to her uncle and mother. At that moment of wondering she hears a crow outside of her window "making quite a racket." Her grandmother had tried to self-abort her first child, Tracy's uncle. Tracy hears, "be gentle," again.

Her maternal grandmother's marriage to her grandfather was a secret. Her first pregnancy would have exposed the relationship, so she tried to end it. The son her grandmother attempted to abort, Tracy's uncle, was born in October 1938. Tracy's mother's pregnancy with Tracy was also a secret. After one of her dialogues with the ancestors Tracy wrote:

> Secrets in families need to be set free, to be known, seen and heard and forgiven. Do the words need to be spoken? Maybe not – maybe they just need to be felt and that is the healing. The healing works backwards from me—one point in time and then back through the generations and then back again.

The guilt Tracy feels about being separated from her older son at his birth is resonant with the guilt her grandmother felt. In one of her graduate school classes Tracy learned that her DNA code was present in her grandmother through the egg that became Tracy's mother. The links between the generations seem to have both psychic and physical origins.

Tracy's grandfather, her mother's father, joined the army in 1939. The family was constantly on the move and her grandfather was frequently absent. While Tracy's grandmother had an indomitable spirit, these experiences took their toll. Tracy wrote:

> Her drinking got out of control and my uncle and mother were sometimes unsupervised. Over the years the drinking became problematic and when her youngest child was around the age of three he was briefly removed from the home. . . . My grandmother continued to drink for many years although I remained unaware of this fact until my teenage years . . . she was as my mother called her, a highly functioning alcoholic.

Alcoholism was part of Tracy's family's legacy from her maternal grandparents. Tracy's grandmother's husband's grandfather, David, had been known as the town drunk later in his life. His son became a very religious teetotaler. Tracy's grandmother, now 96 years old, stopped drinking during the time Tracy was participating in this group. In the last several years her drinking was limited to two glasses of wine each night. As of this writing, years later, her grandmother has not had another drink. When Tracy asked her grandmother why she had stopped drinking, she said, "I lost the taste for it." This could be just a coincidence. But Tracy wondered if there was any connection between the work she was doing with the ancestors and her grandmother losing her taste for drinking. I had the following dream, which seemed out of context and made no sense to me until I heard Tracy's story in our circle that week:

> I dream of a man who is in our group. He is the fourth member of the group and a colleague. The other two members are women. With me, there are four. The man asks me if this kind of work with the ancestors can cure addictions. It's as if his question makes me aware that that this work can cure addictions. I know this to be true. However, as a psychologist I think—you can't put those two words together in a sentence that way. How do I know, how can I possibly say yes to this question? He turns and walks down the hall. I can't move forward. I have become frozen between the truth and what I have been taught about addiction. I want to say yes, but have nothing in my experience to back up the yes. I answer, telling him I don't know. He keeps walking, moving forward with certainty, knowing the answer is yes and waiting for me to catch up with him. I walk, following him, trying to catch up.

This does not indicate a causal relationship between doing this work and curing addictions. There is, however, a meaningful link between Tracy's consciously expanding work with the ancestors, her grandmother's new behavior and the dream which suggests that this work may have, can have an effect on the pattern of addiction within a family. There are patterns that continue and things that have yet to be done. She can see how she has gotten to this place and how the story is moving forward through her. She describes her life as one in which she is now traveling with her ancestors. Her ancestors have become her roots "in the divine sense." She is "in a struggle of birthing herself and finding a source of continuity with the ancestors and her roots." She "is coming home" to herself.

A few months after the group ended, while I was working on Tracy's story, she found a home not far from where she had found the bird's nest. Feeling this was the right home for them, Tracy and her husband decided to look at it. While they were there, she wondered if this was the home they would finally buy and move into, if this was the home that would be a place where she could put down roots and one which would serve her husband's wishes for a good financial investment in their future. As she stood in the kitchen she realized she could easily and comfortably see herself cooking for her family and friends in this home. At that moment she looked at the clock in the microwave. It read, 1:11 p.m. The actual time was 9 a.m. She and her husband went back to the house. The time on the clock still read 1:11 pm. Her husband, having read this story, said to Tracy, "here's your clock" as he opened the microwave door. The time disappeared from the display at that moment and did not appear again in all the days that followed. Their offer on the house was accepted.

My Story

One morning, during the time our group met, I woke up hearing these words: "in the end and in the now it is all about love." I went to the ancestor altar. As I looked at the collection of figures on the altar – photographs of my mother and father, grandparents and great-grandparents, a buffalo horn, objects from nature, coins, a red-tailed hawk feather and deer antler, a print of a buffalo from the caves in Spain, a photograph of Jung and of Vine Deloria, a picture of Bollingen, a map of the first settlement in Providence, Roger's book, a replica of his compass–I asked myself who and what are the points of love in my life. I was immediately drawn to the photograph of my father.

In this photograph I am about a year old. I am "standing" between my parents. My mother is on my right, my father on my left. My right arm is suspended in the air. The only contact I have with my mother's body is through her hand, which is barely touching my wrist. I am leaning against my father's leg, my body supported by his arm around me. My left arm rests on his leg. My hand grasps his index finger. My head rests against his shoulder. This photograph captured something essential about my relationship with my parents and theirs with me. As I look at this image I feel the presence of my father. I feel pure love coming from my father to me. It is all I can do to keep breathing and let it in. In this moment I see more clearly and feel acceptance of the natural closeness I felt with my father and the tentative relationship I had with my mother. Opening to and accepting the Love that seems to be coming from my father, I remember the birth of my older daughter and a kiss when I was 19—other points of love in my life.

My relationship with my father deepened and evolved at the end of his life and after his death. In the last year of my father's life I visited him several times. In the last month of his life, my mother, a trained nurse, insisted on caring for him herself. During my last visit, I heard my mother with him, asking him all night long to just sip some of the Ensure and ice-cream mix she had made for him. They met in high school and were the love of each other's lives. She loved him so much she did not want him to die. He loved her so much he held onto life. The next morning, I told her that I could stay home with him for the entire day if she wanted to go out. She was exhausted and needed a break. She was understandably reluctant to leave him. After she left, as my father lay in bed, I sat on the couch alternately knitting and meditating. My mother was gone for the entire day. The hospice nurse arrived just before she returned. The nurse was surprised to see that my father's condition had changed so dramatically since she had seen him the day before. Over the day my father had begun to ease toward death. He died a few days later.

About a year after his death, he appeared in a dream—the first dream I had of him since his death. In the dream the two of us were in the first car I ever owned—a red Volkswagen. His mother loaned me the money to buy this car after I got my first full-time job after college. He was driving. I was in the passenger seat. We were driving across an open field. The field was surrounded on all sides by dense forest. He stopped the car about halfway up the field, close to one side of the forest. He got out of the car. I got out of the car wondering why he had stopped in the middle of the field. He sensed my question and said to me, "I can only take you so far. You will have to go the rest of the way yourself." He handed me a walking stick. I stood barefoot on the earth, walking stick in hand, wondering what he meant. Half waking, the dream continued. I watched my father walk onto a small hill at one end of the field. There was a path between the trees that went over that hill. He stood at the top of the hill, turned, and facing me said, "I love you." A bright light filled that end of the forest and he was gone.

I have struggled with opening my heart to loving and being loved and accepting what is so. In a dream many years ago, I was in a war. Like many who have experienced trauma as children, I had many dreams of being in wars between good and evil. This was the last in the series. The war had been won. At the end of the battle I was relieved and thought I was fine. I entered the small cottage of an old man and an old woman to rest. They told me I had been wounded. They pointed to my heart and said I had a bullet in the middle of it. I felt the pain in my heart for the first time. I realized I might die. Until that moment I had been so intent on winning this war, the wound and the pain went unnoticed. It was now time to tend to the bullet in my heart. I lay down on the table in the middle of the room. Carefully examining me, the old man and old woman said that if the bullet was taken out too quickly I would die. The bullet lodged in my heart was also keeping me alive. Many dreams followed in which a black tar-like substance, like coagulated blood, was coughed up or pulled from my heart on white cloth. The final dream was the one in which the black figure who I identified as the Negative Mother flew from my heart described in the previous chapter.

A wound to the heart of one is a wound suffered by the many. As Jung states, we often identify a collective problem as merely personal. While these dreams of being at war are relevant on the personal level, they also reference cultural, historical and ecological traumas. As Gustafson writes about so eloquently, and as the Wampanoag woman I spoke with told me, the trauma done to the people of this land and the land itself continues and has yet to be fully acknowledged and grieved and, most importantly, reconciled. The battle between cultures and between Roger's head and heart raged on centuries later in me. It also references the many wars and the trauma experienced by the women in my mother line. I am not the first in this long line of women to experience betrayal and feel the need to protect my wounded heart. This dream of this final battle occurred at the time Melissa, my daughter, was writing her report on Roger Williams. It was the moment when I began to see that my story, as Jung says, was a historical fragment in a story which reached backwards and forwards through the generations. It would take time before the threads through the generations and levels of the collective unconscious could be connected and re-membered in the present, to witness and feel the pain and rage and grieve, before the bullet could be safely removed. Healing has its own "path" and takes time, sometimes centuries. There is an intelligence in psyche and nature which, if listened to and followed, will lead one through the labyrinthine process of "healing" from trauma.

Years later, my father appeared in another dream. This time he was wearing a white robe. I knew it was my father, but the shamanic power he embodied in the dream was beyond anything I had experienced when he was alive. We were in a simple room. I could see another room through a doorway. It was a long narrow room with a bank of windows opening to the forest along the far side. There was a sink, long counters and shelves which held a variety of containers with various kinds of substances in them. There were several women, assistants or apprentices, working in the room. They were preparing elixirs and other things. I knew I was dying. My father, sitting, held me in his arms. I felt *and* watched myself as I drew my last breaths. I had the sense that there were many people whom I was related to watching, holding, preparing for my death. I was afraid to let go, but knew it was inevitable. Feeling my father's presence, the energy of his arms around me, knowing he knew I was going to die and was there to facilitate this process, I surrendered. I breathed my last breath and died in his arms. At the moment I died I felt my body go limp. In an instant, in a surge of energy, my body became pure white light.

This dream occurred a few weeks after my divorce was final and during the time I was working on my dissertation. Although this is clearly a death-and-rebirth dream that relates to my divorce and earning my Ph.D., what was more significant for me upon waking was how real this dream was. Much like Jung's experience of his father, mother and wife in dreams, my father seemed very much alive. His shamanic nature seemed authentic and natural.[18] My memories of my father now made more sense to me in light of this dream. He worked very hard to support his family, but his real joy came when he was in his garden or at the ocean. He was deeply connected to nature. He was able to grow things that other people had no success with in the sandy soil of Cape Cod. My daughters still talk about their time with their Grandpa in his garden and his delicious raspberries. After these dreams and others in which I experienced him in a similar way, I began to think that being shamanic was part of my inheritance. My father, able to embody this gift more fully after his death, was assisting me in embodying it. He took me as far as he could. I have been walking the rest of the way myself ever since.

Back to the morning that began with looking for the points of love in my life – feeling and recognizing my father's love, remembering the feelings of love during my daughter's birth and that memorable kiss when I was 19, I was drawn to the photograph of my grandfather. He asked me if being molested was really that bad. There was a loud crack from the bookcase in the room. In response to his question I felt what I had felt when he was molesting me and was able to fully communicate the experience in a wordless, fully embodied way with all of the emotional and mental confusion and physical sensation. I knew he was feeling what I had experienced. It was like having an empathic channel which carried my experience, unedited, directly to him. My grandmother, who is next to him in the photograph, became present at that moment.[19] She was horrified. She said she had not known when she was alive. The love of my father held me in this dialogue as he held me in the dream. The conversation with my grandfather continued. In all the dialogues I've had with him, this was the first one I felt him witnessing and feeling the full reality of my experience of being molested. I felt no rage or grief this time, just the reality of what had happened. Suddenly, I felt forgiveness–for my grandfather, myself, my sisters, mother, father and the many others who had participated in this story. It was not an act of will. It was completely natural, spontaneous and sincere, a response to the dialogue. It was an action of the heart, as natural in that moment as breathing.

I told my grandmother that, indeed, this had happened to me and to my sisters. She said she wished she could have done something. The bookcase emitted a loud cracking sound again. I told my grandparents that I wished it hadn't happened and that I wondered what I would have been like had it not. I felt this question sincerely, not from a place of having been victimized by fate or robbed of the innocence of childhood and the discoveries of adolescence, but as a simple question, a wondering about how my life, how I, would have been different. I attributed my unhappiness, sense of broken-ness and continuing experiences of PTSD to being molested. I heard clearly as a chorus of ancestral voices – "you wouldn't be who you are." I felt and knew the truth of that statement, along with the pain of what had hap-pened and all that had followed. I have carried an imagination of me and my life and what could have been had I not been molested. That girl never existed and does not exist. She is not me. I experienced a profound sense of accep-tance of what was and what is so. In that moment I experienced a knowing and understanding of deep truth that was beyond words. I was completely aware of the reality of all that I had experienced, the full history of my life, but my perspective had changed. It could not have been other than what it was in every way. It was just so. I was and am just so. In that moment I felt myself connected to and continuous with all those to who I am related.

Today I asked, as I had asked many times before, what do the ances-tors ask from me in this moment? I felt a surge of love flowing from my parents and grandparents, from the field of the ancestor altar to me. I have been much more comfortable when given specific tasks to do by them— call your sister, go to Providence, talk with your daughter, bring more rasp-berries. It is clear, as Roger told me on my 55th birthday during one of my visits to Providence, that all the ancestors want of me is for me to live my own life. At this moment in time I am the reason for their existence. I pick an angel card. Three stick together: Expectancy, Play, and, yes, Love.

I woke up in the morning about a week after this dialogue feeling and knowing that life is a gift. As I write these words now, copying them from my journal, I am aware of how many times I have heard phrases like "life is a gift." Phrases like these are overused and often misunderstood and often become clichés. The experience of acceptance of my life and of feel-ing love and support from the ancestors could seem contrived to any reader—what one would hope to hear given my history. Phrases like this and experiences of forgiveness, acceptance, and love were prescribed to me by many well-meaning and not-so-well-meaning teachers and friends. In the past, I railed and raged against these concepts. They were far from my experience of reality, seemed impossible, were re-victimizing, and all too often added to my sense of shame. Experiencing love, support, acceptance, and forgiveness that is not an act of will but a spontaneous response of the heart, and knowing that my life is a gift in these dialogues while fully con-scious and awake is the result of over thirty-three years of conscious work.

On that morning, I went to the ancestor altar still feeling the reality of life as the gift that it is from the dreamtime. The photograph of Jung drew my attention. He reminds me that the animals on my altar are buffalo, hawk, raven, and deer. One is a predator. One is considered to be the smartest of all birds and is associated with magic. One has adapted to every sort of habitat, and the origins of its name mean wild animal. One is ancient and survived the ice age. He suggests I get rid of the rabbit statues around the house. They do not suit my nature. (Images and statues of rabbits are abundant in our home. My married name and the last name of my daughters is Easter. Needless to say, we have amassed quite a collection over the years.) He draws my attention to the card in the center of my altar which says "Be Kind to Everything that Lives."

I remember my vision of all the unkind actions I had taken in my life that happened when we were evacuating during the Tea Fire. In that moment in 2011, when the wind blew the doors of my house open and picked up the framed print of Chief Seattle's words—"Man did not weave the web of life, he is merely a strand in it. Whatever he does to the web he does to himself"—from the wall and placed it at my feet. I felt the effects of my unkind actions on others in my entire being. I committed on that day to the only thing I could commit to from this deep knowing—a practice of kindness.

In this moment years after that experience, Jung tells me, "that 'Everything' includes me. The world wouldn't be what it is without me, without each one of us. We are each a distinct expression of and within the undifferentiated whole. Read the Seven Sermons again. It is time to live, to live *my* life." His words hit their mark. I sit, feeling into what I have heard. I remember Roger's words to me on my birthday a few years ago—to live *my* life. This is the simple wish of the ancestors. Be who I am and live the life I was born to live practicing kindness. I can feel their love and their wish for me to be happy with a capital H.

The next morning, feeling for remnants of dream, feeling for the ancestors, I drift back into the dream time. I see an image and have a felt sense of pieces of broken glass coming together into a cohesive shape. I think, in the dream, the pieces of the puzzle are starting to come together. I feel the presence of the ancestors and then I feel the presence of another figure. I realize the figure is me. Recognizing it was me and not another was completely shocking. It was like those times I have caught my reflection in a window or mirror before I recognize it's me and before I am self-conscious enough to edit or judge what I see. I wake up with the memory and shock of seeing, feeling, knowing myself as I truly am. A sense of it remained but receded as I went to retrieve it. If I didn't focus on it but just focused on my breath and felt my body, I would begin to feel it as a fullness in my body pushing from inside out to the edges of my skin. I thought, this is what comes from being in relationship with the ancestors. One comes to know oneself, one's essential and distinctive nature in the mirror and love of one's ancestors.

I conducted the final dialogue outside, sitting on a boulder, facing the mountains in view of the hawks' nest. I arranged pieces of my ancestor altar on the boulder—a photo of Jung, a photo of my parents, of my great grandparents, a photo of Vine Deloria, the buffalo horn, deer antler, and my grandmother's binoculars. As I open the dialogue, hawk flies overhead screeching. The wind picks up the picture of Vine and places it right in front of me. The other photos were unframed and "should" have been moved by this wind too. I hear simply, "Embrace your intellect. Know your heart. Live from your truth." I laugh out loud, realizing that I have been projecting "Indigenous" onto Vine, continuing to split head from heart and Indigenous from Western. I have demonized intellect, my intellect and idealized indigenous ways of knowing and being. In the photograph I have of Vine he is sitting in front of shelves filled with books. We have a good laugh.

He continues with the lesson: "Being indigenous doesn't mean no mind, no intellect. Be embodied on this earth. This is not a war between head and heart. Stop the war between head and heart. Listen with your heart and speak your mind." As I listened, I felt a deep sense of gratitude. My heart was pounding. Recognizing my inherited gift of intellect along with a Borderland consciousness, I knew my parents had given me just what I needed, perfectly timed, in life and death. My awareness and acceptance of the necessity of each experience, even the trauma, flies in the face of my fantasy of a "happy family" and "good parents." It was not easy for them either. This work and living my life is one way of honoring their lives and the many lives of the ancestors whose love I am an expression of in this moment in time.

JoEllen Koerner's Story

JoEllen Koerner's story is interwoven into the threads of the line of grandmothers who began this journey in an ocean crossing and settled in the Dakotas in the 1800s.[20] Her people, Mennonites, depended greatly on the Sioux for their survival. For the women in her lineage, the struggle to survive was too great, leaving a legacy of motherless children. This is a story of five generations of women. Her story shows the way physical illness has its origins in an ancestral and cultural legacy of oppression. Like Kat Duff, the history of JoEllen's family, with its rich and complex heritage, would be remembered in the symptomatic landscape of her daughter's body. Their story is also a story of healing and love.

JoEllen's story, as she tells it, began in the late 1800s when her great-grandmother, at the age of five, lost her mother on their journey from Russia to America. JoEllen knew and loved her great-grandmother, who told her stories in their ancestral German language. Her family was deeply rooted in their Anabaptist Mennonite faith. Bringing their exceptional expertise as farmers to this land, her ancestors established new roots in what was then the Dakota Territory. JoEllen's paternal grandmother, born to first-generation American Mennonites, would also lose her mother at the age of five. JoEllen's maternal grandmother, her mother's mother, also died—from blood poisoning, ten days after her daughter's birth.

JoEllen's mother, grandmother, and great-grandmother shared a common heritage—all had been raised without a mother. During the seventh month of her pregnancy with JoEllen, *her* mother developed placenta previa. Her father was told he had to choose between his wife's and his daughter's life. Ultimately, against the odds, both daughter and mother survived. JoEllen Koerner was born into the rich lineage of her traditional Mennonite ancestors and into a family legacy of motherless daughters. Growing up, she was surrounded by the family clans of her father's and mother's relatives. Being raised in a culture that provided a rich and secure foundation allowed her to develop a trust in the process of life. However, the legacy of being orphaned and motherless would continue.

She attended a public school and eventually became a nurse and married her high-school sweetheart. After her husband graduated from college, they returned to his ancestral homestead and became the fourth generation of farmer-ranchers in his family. JoEllen became a farm wife, doing all the hard work involved in farming.[21] Her husband's heart was in the land. However, her heart was not in the work of the farm the way it had been in her career as a nurse. The Mennonite lifestyle and tradition felt stifling.

She and her husband decided to have a family. Miscarrying twice, they were told she might never carry a pregnancy to term. She did become pregnant again, this time with twins. They were born beautiful and healthy. Still, JoEllen's heart longed to return to nursing. She and her husband struggled to sort out what was best for them and their family from their Mennonite tradition and created a "tapestry that did not resemble the lifestyle of previous generations."[22] Her husband, moving in harmony with the land that birthed him, continued planting and harvesting. Once the twins started grade school, JoEllen returned to nursing, matching her work hours with her children's school schedules.

JoEllen's father had gathered thousands of pictures and stories of the German Mennonites who had emigrated from Russia. It was well known that JoEllen's ancestors had only survived through the help of the Lakota Sioux. JoEllen and her father wanted to tell and publish the stories of her ancestors and the people native to this land as a consciousness-raising effort. Her father died three months before the project began. JoEllen, in her grief, decided to write a new chapter rather than recording the history of her family. An important part of this new chapter would be her relation-ship with Wanigi Waci (Spirit Dancer), a Lakota Sioux spiritual healer, and the Wase Wapka Community.

JoEllen met Wanigi Waci through her work in Sioux Valley Hospital. He was hired by the hospital to work with the staff to co-create an approach to delivering health care within the hospital that honored and reflected the sovereignty and distinct differences of all of the cultures involved in receiv-ing and giving care. Wanigi Waci and JoEllen worked together at the hos-pital developing ways of bringing two cultures and two healing traditions together. As this conscious dialogue between cultures evolved, a friendship developed between them. JoEllen writes, "It was a rich time of learning and growing, and a shift in attitudes began. I felt that I was beginning to repay my ancestors' debt."[23]

Her daughter Kristi grew up, married, and became pregnant. The first six months of her pregnancy went well. During the sixth month Kristi began having problems. JoEllen tried to hold her fear—that the pattern of motherless children that had haunted the mothers in her family for genera-tions might be continuing in this next generation—at bay. The birth was an ordeal for both mother and baby. Kristi would eventually need an emer-gency C-section. Although their health was fragile, and her son Ethan struggled for his life after the birth, both mother and baby survived. Wanigi Waci told JoEllen that Ethan had made a conscious decision to be part of this family, had a strong warrior spirit and would be good medicine for their family.

Kristi became pregnant a second time and once again during her sixth month began experiencing severe problems. Western medical treatment was not enough for the healing that was needed. Weaving together Western and indigenous healing that had been taking place at work became critical for JoEllen's family and Kristi's health. Although many of her family members were disturbed by her move from tradition, JoEllen realized that if the outcome was to be different this time, the foundation on which heal-ing was taking place would have to shift. Wanigi Waci called and offered to perform a healing ceremony for Kristi. His community also offered a healing ceremony for her family. In preparation for this second ceremony, JoEllen made hundreds of prayer ties. She felt her grandmother's presence with her through the night as she wrapped these ties. Kristi's condition stabilized after the ceremony and a few months later delivered her second son, JJ.

Although JJ was healthy, Kristi's health continued to deteriorate. A CAT scan revealed several large kidney stones lodged in both of her kid-neys, five stones in all. One large stone was removed during surgery and a stent was placed in her left kidney. After weeks of enduring the nearly unbearable pain of the stent, Kristi underwent another surgery. The stones had not moved. She woke up from the surgery to find that she now had two stents, one in each kidney. Both stents would have to remain until the stones came out of their own accord. These five stones, JoEllen would discover as time went on, held particular meaning for the women in her ancestry.

Pain and suffering were her family's constant companions. Life and time as they had known it stopped. Her focus shifted from the outer world to a deep and profound place where questions about the meaning of life and death came to the foreground. Wanigi Waci met her in this place. He called to tell JoEllen that he knew that Kristi's heath wasn't improving and that he would make arrangements for her to meet with the Medicine Man on a nearby reservation. JoEllen prepared for the event: tying prayer ties, obtaining give-away gifts for the Medicine Man, and planning a feast of thanksgiving for those who would come to support her daughter in ceremony. When asked by the Medicine Man what she was seeking, she told him the story of the four generations of women in her family who had struggled with and died in childbirth, that she and her mother had almost died when she was born, and now her daughter had almost died giving birth to her second son and was seriously ill. Her prayer, if it was the will of the Creator, was that Kristi would recover and be healthy so that her children would not be orphaned.

The Medicine Man looked deeply into JoEllen's face. What he saw made his eyes grow wider and then draw back. She was terrified for her daughter's life. JoEllen and Kristi then participated in the healing ceremony.[24] Spirits came into the house where the ceremony for healing took place. After the ceremony the Medicine Man spoke to JoEllen and told her that the choice to heal or die was Kristi's. He assured her that all would be well. Although Kristi experienced relief and healing during this ceremony, this was not the end of her suffering.

Her spasms and intense pain continued. Wanigi Waci came to JoEllen's house and made medicine for her. After nine months experiencing unrelenting pain, Kristi was pain free. Wanigi Waci invited JoEllen and Kristi to sit down at the kitchen table and offered his explanation of their story.

> Kristi and Jo, you two come from a wonderful family, a family with a heritage of many good things. However, it is also a culture that has an oppressive history for the women who live within it. The women of your family lineage who died did so because life was simply too hard for them, and so they chose to leave it. The two of you agreed before coming to this earth plane to live through this time as a way to heal that deep cultural wound. When you heal, the healing will be extended to all the women in your lineage. Kristi, you

have manifested five stones. In our way a stone is a keeper of memory. These stones represent the five generations of women who have been plagued by death around childbirth; the stones hold their memory. Your earth body is the only thing you uniquely possess, a gift from the Creator. It is given when you are born and you leave it when you die. When people are oppressed they either turn outward or inward. The women in your lineage turned the oppression inward on themselves, and their bodies are destroyed. The key to healing this intergenerational issue is the notion of forgiveness. Jo, if you want Kristi to heal you must forgive all male oppression in this world.[25]

His words staggered JoEllen. She felt the weight of the legacy of pain and suffering of the women in her lineage. After Wanigi Waci left, JoEllen and her daughter began to see the threads of connection and patterns of suffering which were previously invisible. As they sat with each other and the unfolding understanding and insights, they saw the intention and purpose in their suffering.

Kristi's severe pain returned. JoEllen was gripped with terror as she remembered the Medicine Man's words – the choice to live was Kristi's. The pain was too great for Kristi to bear. She asked her mother if she would help her die if her pain did not end in a few days. As JoEllen looked into her daughter's eyes, she "saw visions of her long-suffering compliance with all the things imposed upon her or requested of her" and knew there was only one answer that would give her daughter hope.[26] She told her daughter that she was the most beloved being in her life and, if what she wanted was to die, she would help. As night turned into early morning, JoEllen, listening to Kristi talk about how she had not been there for her family as wife and mother for so many months, realized her daughter had made the choice to die. In that moment, a depth of despair and grief enveloped her. The grief she felt held the suffering and losses of the generations of mothers and children in her family through time. It was so profound she felt paralyzed and couldn't breathe.

She surrendered. In the clarity that came from no longer struggling, she spoke to her daughter. Affirming Kristi's right to choose, she also asked her to listen deeply to what she had been saying. She reflected to her that she was measuring her life based on what she did. "*That is the old way! That kind of thinking must die*"[27] It was time for this curse which had plagued the women in their lineage to come to an end. JoEllen realized and affirmed that life is not about doing, but about who we *are*. She told Kristi if she chose to die that she would love and take care of her children, *but*, no one could replace her.

She wrapped herself around her daughter's suffering body and began to pray with an intensity she had not known until that moment. Again and again she uttered the prayer, pleading with God, as a humble mother, for mercy for her daughter. As she prayed, holding Kristi and stroking her hair, she "felt a great warmth wrapping around [her[, and . . . sensed the spirit of [her] grandmother."[28] Kristi's breathing became slow and deliberate. Exhausted, JoEllen fell into a deep sleep and dreamt of her grandmother. A few hours later, feeling Kristi stir, JoEllen woke up. Looking into her eyes she saw new resolve and realized Kristi had made the choice to stay and face this difficult time. From that point on Kristi continued to improve.

In the months that followed, JoEllen had a conversation with her mother about her childhood and the loss of her mother. After her mother's mother died giving birth to her, her father's grief was unbearable. He left for California, leaving his newborn daughter with her grandmother. JoEllen's mother had been orphaned. JoEllen's mother told her what she knew of her mother's life. It had been hard. One day, she was told by her aunt, that her mother, JoEllen's grandmother, lifted her hands skyward and said, "Oh God, this life is too hard. Please let this house fall down and crush me. Take me home."[29] JoEllen talked with her mother about the many ways she had not repeated this pattern with her children. She had not abandoned JoEllen or her brother. She had loved and supported them every step of the way. JoEllen then told her mother the story of the five stones and what Wanigi Waci had said about their family. JoEllen's mother shared how seeing Kristi courageously face and endure her suffering in the last year had given her courage and the realization that she could do anything.

In the week following this conversation she received an email from a distant relative which contained a letter written by her father telling the story of his great grandmother's death at sea. JoEllen greatly missed her father many times during her daughter's crisis. She often called out to him at night. His words came to her now in this letter. This was the story of "the last stone."[30]

As Kristi healed, a sense of order and rhythm began to return to her family. However, this experience for JoEllen challenged her ideas about what was true and real. Her experiences with the Sioux awakened her to other dimensions of reality. Wanigi Waci told her that Kristi had lived because of her prayers, and now it was time for her to give back to the great Creator. She decided to go on a Vision Quest.

She carried in her heart Wanigi Waci's words to her and Kristi on that fateful day in her kitchen when he told her the meaning of the five stones. Her vision quest began when a "kind voice," that was "a voice, yet voiceless, "asked her if she was "seeking to understand for the purpose of retribution or reconciliation?"[31] She knew instantly that her intention was reconciliation. She found herself "at the opening of a cave" where she "was handed a candle to illuminate the darkness." There were many tunnels. She chose one and went down its "long slippery corridor." When the tunnel opened up she saw her "great-grandmother, [her] grandmother, and a host of other women in the dark clothing worn by Mennonite women of that era" sitting at a table. She writes,

> As I watched, what had been a sense of joy turned into a deep sadness as I realized what I was witnessing. "Oh!" I cried aloud. *How* can this be? It is the women who are placing fear into the hearts of the children. It is the women who are harshly punishing the children! How can this be?

The scene unfolded. She saw these women telling stories like the ones she was told as a child that "warned that hellfire was theirs if they entertained any unkind thoughts." There were serious consequences for any behavior that was on the long list of don'ts. She loved her grandmothers, but realized that "they were the ones who had planted such deep fears in my own soul." Feeling the weight of this, her vision opened to another scene. Above this table of women there was another, similar table. Her grandfather and the other men in her ancestral lineage sat around this table making "rule after rule." JoEllen explained:

> Each time there was agreement they would shout, "*Done!*" slamming their fists on the table and stomping their feet. As they did this, a large tuning fork moved between the floors and began to resonate deeply. I saw the energy of the resonance encircle and trap the women and children in a circle of fear.

Knowing these men loved them all, JoEllen asked her imaginal guide, the voiceless voice, why these men would do this? With this question her vision opened to "the space above the men. In it sat their image of God." This God was "a God of wrath and vengeance." Seeing this God clearly she understood, knew, "that the root of all oppression in my culture was its underlying notion of God and His love. It defined and dictated the interpretation and expression of love, permeated everything my people thought or did." As the reality of the effects of this oppression moved through her, she "cried out, "WHAT IS THE ANSWER?""

> And then a still, small voice whispered so quietly that I had to hold my breath to hear it. "Live authentically" was the soft and simple answer. At that moment my gaze was directed back to the ground floor where the women and children were housed. I saw a small girl off to the corner. She was by herself, just outside the reach of the band of fear that held the others hostage. Quietly playing with a small doll, she was singing a lullaby. I felt the sweet tenderness of her pure and innocent love. Waves of it moved towards the group bound by fear. As it tapped the rim of the circle, a tiny pinhole pierced its edge and slowly moved into the circle. Other small children saw the light and began to move towards the young girl. Slowly the circle began to enlarge, the edge softening and becoming porous. The older women also began to release

their hold, and gradually the whole scene shifted to one of joy, of laughter, of unconditional love.

As her vision quest continued she found herself in a different space working with her "professional family." Watching the nurses do their work, she realized that as nurses they did the "same thing to our patients that women do to our children!" Looking up she saw administrators and doctors sitting at a table. Like the men in her lineage, they made the rules that the nurses carried out. Above these men she "saw the God of Science sitting with the irrefutable Laws of Science and Economics." Her awareness of the male oppression Wanigi Waci told her she would have to forgive if Kristi was to live continued to expand until she "saw the oppression of the universe. A song of authenticity and love played in my heart, and a deep sense of forgiveness to all – including myself – flooded [her] soul." As she lay under the stars she heard Wanigi Waci singing "one of his ancient healing songs." Her heart opened. She felt joy beyond measure and felt as if "the song sang" her.[32]

The possibility existed in this moment in time for the transformation of an intergenerational legacy of oppression. This odyssey of healing would require JoEllen to embrace and move beyond the limits of her Mennonite tradition and her understanding of the genesis of physical illness. Seeing her life as part of a continuing story, she was able to reconcile the past with the present for the sake of the future and facilitate healing in the moment which extended beyond the bounds of time and space. Out of the depth and breadth of her forgiveness, which reached into the roots of the oppression in her cultural heritage and the present moments in her practice of nursing, she experiences an authenticity of self and an expanded capacity for love. A sense of loss and oppression is replaced by experiences of unbounded grace flowing in and through life. There is much more to this story—beautiful details which enrich its telling. It is well worth reading in its entirety.

Some Final Words

Exploring the depths of one's ancestry as it exists in relationship with one's personal story can be a lifelong endeavor. The stories of these women are a small part of, and open a window into, stories whose history and future span centuries of time. Even as I write, committing the stories to words on a page, freezing and immortalizing them in this expression of memory, each of these women's stories continues to unfold. The tangled threads of personal and collective suffering, the gifts and resiliencies that connect each of us to our ancestors through the generations past and future, take time to reveal themselves. These connections are buried within the unconscious and, like any process of the psyche, have their own way of and time for emerging into consciousness, unfolding, and transforming. The stage has to be set and the time has to be right for each insight, connection, and revelation. As is revealed in my dream, the "bullet," if removed too quickly from the wounded heart, can lead to death.

CHAPTER 11

Varieties of Ancestral Experience

The truth of an idea is not a stagnant property inherent in it. Truth HAPPENS to an idea. It BECOMES true, is MADE true by events.[1]

—William James in Pragmatism, Lecture VI

For the more a theory lays claim to universal validity, the less capable it is of doing justice to the individual facts.[2]

—C.G. Jung, *The Undiscovered Self*

Hence, it is not the universal and the regular that characterize the individual, but rather the unique. . . . I can only approach the task of understanding with a free and open mind.[3]

—C.G. Jung, *The Undiscovered Self*

Bringing our stories into relationship with the stories of our ancestors is archaeological and imaginative work. Our stories provide glimpses into what is unanswered, unredeemed, and unresolved in each lineage and reveals the way that each individual life also anticipates and is a response to the future. Each woman's approach to and experience of finding the threads of connection between her story and that of her ancestors was as individual as her personal lineage. True to the nature of the psyche, each woman's process moved in a non-linear, organic, and labyrinthine way that revealed the deeper relationship between her personal stories and the stories of her ancestors.

This process of reconnection and remembering was at times chaotic, sometimes ordered or repetitive, often unpredictable and surprising, as well as deeply moving and transformative. As we picked up and followed the threads of connection, each of us made discoveries that extended the boundaries of our story beyond our personal biography. Each discovery within this larger ancestral tapestry as it was woven into the levels of the collective unconscious carried information that was personally relevant and meaningful in the present. Gradually, through research, associative processes and the discovery of "coincidental" occurrences each of us began to develop a working theory regarding the significance and meaning of these connections.

Diane and I had been in dialogue with the ancestors for years prior to participating in this group. This was Tracy's, Janis's, and Kathryn's introduction to the idea that the ancestors may be present in the immediacy of their lives, inform their understanding of themselves and their fate, and, be implicated in healing physical and emotional dis-ease. Tracy was hesitant at first in approaching her ancestors using the ancestor altar as the medial space for her dialogues. As time went on, she began to trust what she experienced and heard. Kathryn's ancestors responded immediately with "channeled" monologues. During our time together as a group, Kathryn used her personal ancestor altar as a way of inviting her ancestors into her home and offering them the sustenance and nourishment she had not received from her family. Janis, although enthusiastic at first, experienced such resistance that she found it difficult to continue the process of dialogue.

Each woman's experience of being in dialogue with the ancestors seemed to unfold in a perfectly timed way, as if the process was being orchestrated from a deep intelligence. As Jung suggests, when the time is ripe, what has been latent in the unconscious crosses the threshold into consciousness. What is not as obvious in the individual stories is the way our discoveries as individuals seemed to be related to the discoveries of the other women in the group. In all the groups I've offered, there seems to be a natural synergy within each one in which each individual's experience is connected to, facilitated and enhanced by the other members' experiences and insights.[4]

Diane, who had been doing this work for years, had never worked in a group with this specific focus. She said that there were layers of understanding and things revealed that she would not have seen on her own. The capacity of the group to hold each other and each other's stories was substantial. There was enough space within and between us to hold and honor Janis' anger towards her ancestors and family and her questions about the value of this work. Sharing the story of my heart opening and spontaneously forgiving my grandfather was a particularly powerful experience for all of us. Something unimaginable had happened. It opened new possibilities for healing traumatic very painful experiences for the other women in our group. Everyone said that the depth of the work, the awareness gained, and the changes that occurred were very connected to the support and experiences in the group.

Our stories show the potential for healing and transformation that can result from being in a more conscious relationship with the ancestors. As we reconnected with painful memories, exploring and moving through this "field full of psychological ruins," new possibilities for healing also emerged. As Linda Hogan shares in her autobiography, memory is not only "a field full of psychological ruins," as described by Bachelard, it is "also a field of healing that has the capacity to restore the world, not only for the one person who recollects, but for cultures as well. When a person says 'I remember,' all things are possible."[5]

While each of our stories is unique, there are certain experiences and dynamics that are characteristic of being in a more conscious dialogue with the ancestors. This chapter presents a *descriptive* analysis of some of these patterns and themes. These observations are not meant to be an exhaustive and definitive analysis. In fact, examining our stories in this more analytical way leads to more questions than answers. My hope is that the stories and experiences of the women shared in this book will serve as inspiration for readers to begin their own journey following the path backward, listening to the laments and hopes of the dead in service to creating a new forward for the generations of ancestors yet to be born.

The Languages of the Ancestors

If we are to take Ezechiel's words to heart—turn to the dead, listen to their lament, and accept them with love—we need to understand the ways the dead, the ancestors, are speaking to us. The question of whether or not and how one knows an ancestor is "speaking" is fundamentally an ontological and epistemological question. As Bernstein says, we see and hear what we are open to noticing. The ancestors speak whether or not we are conscious of the reality, psychic or otherwise, of their presence. Jung's psychology and Indigenous Science when used together provide the ground for seeing and hearing the ancestors' speaking. Within this framework dreams, synchronicities, physical and emotional symptoms, and the sentient voices of non-human nature are seen as potentially valid and meaningful communications.

How does one know whether or not what one hears in a dialogue with an ancestor or in a dream, in one's symptoms, or a synchronicity is really that ancestor speaking as an autonomous presence? Is it just our imagination, it is a projection or wish fulfillment? One of the fundamental questions people have about their experiences is: are these figures and experiences "really real"? I continue to ask this question of myself and of my clients. This is a question that, like Jung, each of us has to ask and answer for ourselves.

However, even asking if the ancestors are "really real" perpetuates an artificial split between spirit and matter, and between the reality of this world and the world behind the world. Although they can be differentiated, each is an aspect of a single, unified reality, one mirroring the other. For the Dagara, we see the ancestors as "ghosts," but, from the perspective of the ancestors, we are "ghosts." Discerning between what is projection or fantasy and an experience of an ancestor speaking is essential to this or any imaginal work. Many people, learning about the work I do, tell me about a dream in which a deceased relative or friend appeared. They share that there was something different about this person in the dream from other dream figures they've encountered. Whether in a dream, a dialogue or a synchronistic experience, what is characteristic of an ancestor "speaking" is the autonomous nature of the the figure and the communication. It is often unexpected, shocking, and surprising. These experiences seem to have emotional and psychic weight.

There are many examples of the "really real" presence and communication from the ancestors in our stories. Sometimes unbidden, sometimes bidden, sometimes welcome, sometimes not, the ancestors spoke. Sometimes they "spoke" to us in response to a request, such as the request for a dream. Sometimes it was our deep need for connection or reassurance that engendered a response. Sometimes the ancestors were very direct, even intrusive, in their communications, sometimes metaphorical and mysterious. Sometimes, as in Janis's story, they are shrouded, watching, but do not reach out to us and are difficult for us to reach out to.

The ancestors appeared to us and communicated symbolically and directly through dreams and in our conscious, waking dialogues. They often spoke in a clear voice that was clearly distinguishable from one's inner voice or personal thoughts. Sometimes they were recognizable figures, sometimes archetypally essential energies. Synchronicities provided a bridge between inner and outer, this world and the world behind the world, that communicated the ongoing presence of an ancestor in our lives. These synchronicities were uncannily timed and communicated something specific in a very particular way. Physical and emotional symptoms and illness, like Kristi's kidney stones, carried the memory and told the story of our ancestors. Nature was often and most clearly the medium of communication. Something communicated in a dialogue, dream or synchronicity was often followed by the discovery of a photograph or letter which was directly related to and validated what was said.

Sometimes an ancestor's presence is accompanied by feelings of love and support. Sometimes a dialogue evokes anger, grief, fear, disappointment, bitterness, or feelings of betrayal. Whatever the experience, it was never emotionally neutral. Even as I write this, remembering what it feels like, remembering the times these stories were shared in our group, my heart is beating faster, and I feel deeply touched. (As I write this paragraph, hawk flies overhead whistling "kee-ahh.") One of the things that seems to be true of all of these experiences is the way an ancestor's presence touches the person in the moment of the communication and in the moment of remembering and sharing it.

Diane brought a bell that had belonged to her grandfather to our first group session to place on the ancestor altar. It was one of the objects that she kept on her personal ancestor altar. The bell was from India and was used to call the elephants. The talking piece in our council circle was passed to her. Before she spoke a word—before she spoke about her grandfather, about her relationship with him, his love for her and hers for him—she rang the bell three times. With the ringing of that bell, without knowing its story or its origins, each of us was moved to tears. In the absence of words, before we could engage this experience with our conscious minds, without knowing who or what this bell represented, we knew that an ancestor was present in our circle.[6] Certain things cannot be proven or objectively validated but can only be known from direct experience. It is striking that when these kinds of experiences were shared in the group or with me personally, the words "I knew" were used.

Symptoms of Ancestral Trauma

The ancestors spoke to Kat Duff, JoEllen's daughter Kristi, Linda Hogan, and me through the body. Our symptoms very specifically and concretely mirrored the trauma that was part of our legacy. The ancestral and collective trauma that lived in the silences and shadows was written on our bodies. Listening to our symptoms as a communication brought consciousness to our personal suffering in ways that allowed healing to occur not only for us in the present, but for those ancestors who had experienced the original trauma.

The clearest example of this is Kristi's five kidney stones which represented the five generations of women who died leaving their children motherless. Kat's and Kristi's illnesses were symptomatic of transgenerational wounds. Linda's alcoholism, her father's pain, and the silences and absences that filled her life were evidence of the dislocation and genocide of her people and her mother's pain. Our bodies symptomatically carried the memory of trauma. These memories had been preserved in the unconscious waiting until the time was ripe for them to be remembered, witnessed, and for reparative action taken.

Direct Experiences of the Ancestors

Awareness of the ancestor's presence when we are awake is often experienced somatically or through a strong emotion. Diane's first experience of her father's very real presence was during a ceremony in Mexico. She felt her father's energy coursing through her body in the work with the medicine man. She knew immediately and had no doubt that it was her father. This experience challenged her previous perception of reality and opened her awareness to new possibilities.

In one of her dialogues Tracy found herself lying in the supine birthing position on the floor re-experiencing a painful experience of giving birth from both the woman's and the doctor's perspective. She knew this was a memory of some kind. She wondered if it was connected to her grandmother's experience of giving birth. Bringing consciousness to the multilayered experience, Tracy became aware that this may have been her maternal grandmother's birth labor. She made the connection to her personal experience of giving birth to her first son and to being born herself. This ancestral memory "spoke" first through her body. Kathryn experienced the predatory, judgmental, masculine energy as a many tendriled smoke monster invading her body. It was as emotionally powerful and terrifying as it was physical. For Kathryn and Tracy, bringing consciousness to these experiences allowed for a deep sense of healing.

When my grandfather came to me on a wave of love, his presence was unbidden and unwelcome but undeniable. The love was palpable physically, emotionally, and mentally. Almost immediately, I recognized these sensations as the presence of my grandfather. It wasn't a thought, it was an undeniable knowing. With that recognition I felt intense rage. After that experience I started to find coins everywhere. I knew it was him letting me know in a gentler way that he was there. It would take years for me to open fully to experiencing his love.

Sometimes the ancestors speak and are heard as a clear voice. This was Jung's experience when the Anabaptists came knocking at his door. Tracy's re-experiencing and re-membering of birth traumas was punctuated by a feminine voice saying "Be gentle." I often awake hearing a phrase that seems to be from the ancestors, not one ancestor in particular, but from them all as a group, like "life is a gift," or "in the end and in the now it's all about love." These phrases serve as an orientation particular for that day and often for my life. There are other times when, before I even light the candle on my ancestor altar I will hear from my mother, "call your sister!" a very practical and concrete instruction. During her vision quest following her daughter's recovery, JoEllen sensed a voice asking her what she was seeking. It was a kind voice. She describes her experience of hearing this voice and seeing her ancestors as different from her experiences of people in this physical world. "It was a voice, yet voiceless. I 'saw' but not in the sense of material objects."[7]

In her first dialogue Kathryn's ancestors spoke to her in clear, distinct voices. She described them in the group as real presences, but also wondered if they were only conjured by her own imagination. She considered the possibility that the "channeled" voices she heard in her first dialogue were possibly reflective of or in some way the actual voices of her ancestors. She found validation for the veracity of these voices in the contents of the boxes she'd been carrying around for years. Finding physical and factual evidence that validated the particular characteristics of personality as well as the specific and particular communications from these "voices" in her first dialogue using the ancestor altar affirmed the autonomous and objective reality of the ancestors for her.

Most of Kathryn's direct experiences of her ancestors were a result of unearthing them from the archival boxes that were filled with photographs and other memorabilia from her ancestors' lives. She learned about them from notes, newspaper clippings, letters, other documents, and photographs. She found new information that sometimes dispelled an old myth or confirmed something she had known, suspected or had experienced imaginally and discovered ancestors she had never known. Her relationship with her ancestors developed as she let each photograph and note reveal its sometimes surprising story. As the contents from the boxes and the dialogues began to weave themselves into a more coherent story, some questions were answered, some remained, and new ones were formed.

Janis heard a song coming to her through a friend, one of the members of her family of the heart, who had just died. Tracy had profound experiences in nature and heard phrases in response to what she was experiencing and thinking in the moment. Some of her experiences of their presence were during her time spent in dialogue using her ancestor altar; some were spontaneous experiences of their presence at other times, often in nature. Diane and I experienced the ancestors directly as clear, identifiable presences and interacted with them as we would with anyone we were talking with using the ancestor altar as the medium for the relationship with them when awake just as the dream is during sleep. The conversations we had with them was as natural as any other.

Communication through Dreams and Visions

Another way the ancestors speak to us is in dreams. Malidoma Some says that this is a very common way for the ancestors to communicate with us.[8] There are many examples of this in Jung's autobiography and in the stories shared in this book. Diane's story is rich with examples. Her ancestors— her mother, father, and grandfather, the people she had been closest to in life—came to her in dreams with gifts and specific guidance for her life. Tracy's father appeared to her for the first time after his death in a dream.

My experiences in dreams of my father after his death and of my mother line are other examples of this form of communication.

During the time our group met, I found that the ancestors, as a collective body rather than a recognizable individual, were present each morning as my consciousness moved from dream to waking. Sometimes the communication was in words, sometimes a felt sense, and sometimes an emotion or an image. It seemed they came to me to offer a direction, thought, or focus from which the day, the ancestor dialogue for that day, and the work would develop. I opened the dialogue with the ancestors holding this thought opening to where it would lead. In response, particular ancestors came into the foreground in the dialogue that followed, grounding the general focus from the dream time in a very particular and specific way in this world.

Diane, Tracy, and I experienced ancestral dream figures whom we had known in life. These dream figures embodied the same quality of being very much alive that Jung experienced in the first dream of his father. These ancestors, in addition to being "alive," seemed to embody qualities that were essential and recognizable characteristics of the people we had known them to be in life. As one example, Diane always knew it was her mother when she experienced a particular quality of beauty. When Diane was recounting the dream of her grandfather walking across the plank, she told us that it was so like him to do that. Even though he had never done anything like that in life, his presence and actions in the dream reflected something essential and recognizable, a quality of his soul. Tracy, Diane, and I had no doubt about whom it was in the dreams. These dream figures brought perfectly timed experiences and gifts—just what seemed to be needed at the time.

According to Jung, if one's relationship with the dead is to be beneficial, the character of the dream figure needs to fit the real character of the deceased.[9] This seems to be especially evident in Tracy's dream of her father. Tracy experienced her father as very real, recognizable, and alive—so real, that she expected to turn around and see him standing there after emerging from the water. Paradoxically, this dream experience of her father as very much alive was the turning point for her in accepting and finally grieving his death.

In his autobiography Jung shares several experiences of waking visions in which the dead appeared. My experience in the transferential dialogue, as described in Chapter 1, is another such visionary, waking dream-like experience. In many of my visits to Providence, Rhode Island I had similar experiences in which the reality from the time of my ancestor seemed to co-exist with the physical landscape as it existed in the present. In my first experience of this nature I didn't understand what I was seeing.

I kept blinking my eyes, hoping to clear my vision. I didn't know until later, when I spoke with a local historian, that what I was seeing overlaying the present day landscape was an image of the land and river as it had been in the time of my ancestor. In visiting historical sites where genocide or significant battles had been fought in King Philip's War, I had visions of the ancestors from those times. These experiences were the clearest examples of Jung's recognition that the ancestors are in the land.

Synchronicity and the Land of the Dead

The concept of synchronicity is useful in understanding the ways the ancestors are present and "speaking" to us in the here and now. Jung uses the term *synchronicity* to describe a meaningful occurrence of two events, one outer and material, the other inner and of psyche, that are related to each other through *meaning* rather than cause.[10] Marie-Louise von Franz, who studied with Jung and became an analyst in her own right, who expanded on and deepened our understanding of Jung's work, describes a synchronistic event as a *"coniunctio of two cosmic principles*, namely *of psyche and matter. . .* in the process, a real 'exchange of attributes occurs . . . psyche behaves as if it were material and matter behaves as if it belonged to psyche."[11] The principle of synchronicity, Jung explains, "suggests that there is an inter-connection or unity of causally unrelated events, and thus postulates a unitary aspect of being which can very well be described as the *unus mundus.*"[12]

Experiences of synchronicity mediate between consciousness and the unconscious, opening a window of perception to the *unus mundus* in which all things are part of a non-random, unified reality rather than split into opposites. Synchronicity provides a bridge between inner and outer, this world and the land of the dead, body and soul, spirit and matter. One may experience a deep sense of understanding and connection with a kind of intelligence that is broader and deeper than the individual mind. As time and space are relativized through this acausal meaningful connection of two distinct events, future, present and past exist in the reality of the present moment.

The concept of synchronicity implies that on the other side of the physical reality that we perceive with our five senses is another "invisible" reality. This concept of an underlying unitary aspect of being corresponds with the Dagara and Sioux conceptions of the world.[13] For the Sioux, this is the "Great Mystery."[14] The concepts of the "Great Mystery," the *unus mundus* and the collective unconscious are different ways of describing and understanding the "invisible" reality that constitutes what Michael Mead calls the world behind the world. Seen from any of these perspectives the ancestors have some form of existence just on the other side of this reality. Malidoma Some, Deloria and the figures in *The Red Book* all maintain that the ancestors are available to offer guidance and support to the living. From any of these perspectives, synchronicities, which bring the "invisible" world and the physical world into direct and meaningful relationship through an association between a psychic and physical occurrence, can be perceived as communications from the ancestors.

Our culturally learned and accepted concepts of space, time, and causality are stretched by experiences of synchronicity. What makes it difficult for many of us to accept that two events can occur in the same moment that are related to but not caused by each other is our familiar and learned framework of understanding that is based on a "belief in the sovereign power of causality."[15] It is impossible to objectively verify or statistically validate synchronistic experiences. They are, as Deloria might say, part of the "Great Mystery," outside of human consciousness or control. Our experience of these events and the meaning we ascribe to them are, however, subjective in nature. This, according to Jung, makes it difficult to imagine or accept that meaningfully connected "causeless events exist or could ever occur."[16]

While Jung maintained a scientific approach to phenomenon, one of the most significant insights and foundational concepts of his psychology is the validity of subjective experience. Intuition, direct knowing, bodily wisdom, feeling states, and sympathetic resonance are subjective determinations of validity. Experiences of synchronicity can be accompanied in the moment by one of these other ways of knowing, which validates the "truth" and meaning of the experience. Opening to the meaning in the experience often leads to healing and transformation.

Our stories as told in this book contain an abundance of examples of synchronicities that were experienced as communications from and with the ancestors. Characteristic of these experiences was a sense of certainty about what it represented and meant. Rather than an interpretation of an event, these experiences were accompanied by a sense of the presence of an ancestor and an understanding of what was being communicated. I *know* or *knew* was used by each woman to describe these experiences of synchronicity. A perfect bird's nest found on the ground in front of a home that Tracy and her husband had made an offer on at the exact moment during a walk when she feared not having a place where she could put down roots was experienced as evidence of her ancestors' presence and reassurance. Standing in the kitchen of one of the homes that she and her husband were considering buying, wondering if this was the home where she could put down roots, Tracy's attention was drawn to the clock on the microwave. It read 1:11 p.m., the time of her father's death. The actual time of day was 9:00 a.m. She knew this synchronicity was her father's way of saying, yes, this is your home.

Janis had a similar experience when she learned that the building she was looking for office space in had been built the same year that her grandmother was born. When the owner of the building told her the date the building had been built, she felt the presence of her grandmother and took this synchronicity and sense of her presence to be a validating "sign" that this was the right place for her to rent.

Diane's experience on the day she went to see the attorney who was handling her mother's will is a very clear example of an ancestor communicating through a synchronistic event. As she was walking on the beach missing her mother terribly, a young girl came up to her and offered her beautiful yellow flowers. It was an unexpected and gratefully received gift. She "knew" this was a gift from her mother, just as she "knew" the napkins she saw on Mother's day and in the shaman's home affirmed her choices. Feeling her mother's presence that day through this experience brought Diane a much needed sense of comfort.

These synchronicities seem to reassure and affirm that the ancestors are in some way aware of the events of our lives, of our doubts and fears, and, that through their presence, as evidenced in each synchronicity, they are offering guidance and reassurance for our choices. For the Dagara, this kind of guidance from the ancestors is a natural part of life.[17] Diane's *I Ching* reading during one of her dialogues which supported and highlighted what her parents had just said to her is one of many examples in her story of a synchronicity which served as a guiding compass in her life.

Nature and the Ancestors

Experiences with nature—birds, the earth, animals—were abundant in our experience of the presence and voice of the ancestors and as an ancient presence. Jung's concept of synchronicity provides a theoretical basis for understanding these experiences within depth psychology. The Dagara worldview brings us closer to the experiences we had with nature. According to Some, nature offers a hospitable place where the ancestors can dwell.[18] The Dagara way of experiencing oneself in relationship with the ancestors' spirits in nature is similar to what the Navajo elder described in Santa Fe.[19] To see and hear the presence of the ancestors speaking to us through nature, of which we are a part, only requires listening with the eye and ear of one's heart.

Tracy's experiences with hawk are deeply moving examples of the generosity and responsiveness of nature to her immeasurable need to know that her father was still there for her even though his earth body had died. Her father was a hunter so it seems particularly fitting that hawk is the bird who consistently appears at times that are related to her father. Her experiences with hawks were abundant. The appearance of hawks seemed to affirm her father's continuing presence in her life. However, she continued to question whether or not this could possibly be true. Moved, but doubting each time hawk appeared, she created tests designed to validate her perception, her hope. Nature responded every time she asked. Her experiences are a moving demonstration of the interrelated nature of spirit and matter, the psyche and nature, the ancestors and nature, and, the ancestors and the living.

With time and with a framework of understanding that affirms her experience, Tracy begins to believe, to trust and to know, that her experiences are more than coincidental. I would suggest that her experiences with nature, especially those with hawk, were integral to her process of healing from the trauma of her father's early death. Hawk, like her father in the first dream she had of him after his death, assists her in stepping onto the shore. Feeling his support through the enduring presence of hawk, she stands more firmly in the world.

Hawk has been a continuing presence and companion as this work has taken shape and found expression in the world. Hawk appeared many, many years ago when I was participating in a ropes course in the Sierras.[20] As I spoke to the group, a red-tailed hawk circled over my head. When I ended, the hawk screeched and flew off into the mountains. I would not have acknowledged its presence were it not for the people in the group who pointed it out as I was speaking and talked about it for days afterwards. This was long before I was comfortable with acknowledging or sharing any aspect of my Borderland experiences. In fact, at the time, considering them pathological, I was actively denying them to myself and others. Following the path backward, I can now see that hawk has been a constant companion and ally at times when I am embodying and giving expression to my work in the world.

In *Animal Speak*, Ted Andrews describes hawks, whose eyesight is the keenest among the raptors, as "the visionaries of the air."[21] Specifically the red-tailed hawk "may reflect that the childhood visions are becoming empowered and fulfilled." He continues, hawk often appears at that point in your life where you "begin to move toward your soul purpose more dynamically."[22] Having five red-tailed hawks in the trees in my back yard during the time our group met, the same number as the number of women in the group, was remarkable. Like Tracy, I have my doubts about these kinds of experiences, especially when they are so meaningful. The dream that occurred in which they all returned "home," to roost in the white bone-like trees, seemed to indicate a homecoming. Homecoming is one way to look at the experience of strengthening one's connection to the ancestors.

In JoEllen's story, although it is not written about in the previous chapter, hawk appears when she is tying the prayer ties for the healing ceremony for her daughter. She knew it was the presence of her grandmother. What you can't see on this page, as I remember JoEllen's and Kristi's story, are the tears that roll down my cheeks. There is something profoundly moving in these experiences of synchronicity in nature.

While I was writing this section on hawk, I felt the presence of my maternal grandmother, Gladys Arnold Legg Carr. My connection to Roger extends to me through her. I saw her a few weeks before she died. She died many years before I was married and my daughters were born. She was in a nursing home being fed intravenously. My mother and my two sisters stood together at her bedside. As I held her hand she asked, "what have I done with my life?!" She was very upset and angry. I told her that she had given birth to and raised two daughters and now had six grandchildren. She got angrier and asked, *"but what have I done?!"* Her words were piercing as they found resonant chords and rang through my body. I felt the pain she felt as she came face to face with the end of her life. I did not try to reassure her again. What had she really done with her life? What had she not done?

Sitting here now, nearing completion of this book, writing about hawk, I feel her presence again. Without her stories, her playfulness, her mashed potatoes and never ending supply of ice cream, her love, her generous lap, I would not be who I am. Without her, I would not be. This book, my work, is in some way an answer to her question. My work serves as redemption for the women in the long line of women who were severed from their indigenous roots from whom she and I descend. It is the fulfillment of a promise I didn't know I made, the answer to a question that was a response to the generations of women in my lineage. She spoke for all of them to her daughter and granddaughters as she faced death and prepared to join our ancestors. As I accept and integrate the evolving Borderland consciousness, as I bring this work into the world, I can feel the connection with the vitality and gifts that come from my mother line being restored. Living my life and raising my daughters in the way I have is my gift to her, her grandmother's great-grandmothers, her daughter, my mother, and for the children of my children's children.

We are here as a result of the love of so many. We carry within our bones the memory of their pain and grief, their questions and their love. What I have come to know through my personal experiences and the experiences that others have shared with me is that as we listen to the ancestors, they are listening to us, supporting us, and counting on us for a response. Being able to hear the ancestors speaking doesn't require a belief in a continuing existence after death, or of an invisible world that is on the other side of the page of our reality. It is only a matter of opening to the possibility that they are.

Reconnecting with the "Inner Indigenous One"

Opening to the presence of the ancestors and listening for the ways they are speaking to us opens one up to that aspect of consciousness that Gustafson calls the inner "Indigenous One" and Jung calls "Archaic man." Coming into a more conscious relationship with the ancestors is a home coming, a return to origins, to a way of knowing, seeing, and being in relationship with the world that has been and is part of our collective inheritance.

Tracy experienced a connection with her ancestral, indigenous roots when she lay on the ground and heard the "sounds of nature," the "sounds that our ancestors heard." As time and space collapsed, she was aware that her longing for home and a place of belonging was a longing like her father's for a deeply rooted connection to the land and to nature. In that timeless moment Tracy reconnected with the archaic, primal, original aspect of her mind.

Diane's experience with the shaman in Mexico opened the path for her to pursue her vocation as a shamanic healer. In the years that followed she has recovered and reconnected with the archaic part of her consciousness through ritual, ceremony, dreams and dialogues with the ancestors. "Original mind" and modern consciousness are now integrated in her being and an integral part of her healing practice.

In the dream of my mother line I am shown where the break from the indigenous origins of our lineage occurred. I saw and felt the vitality that was lost to the women in the generations that were born after we were severed from the fiery female figure in the tree. For generations the women in my lineage have been separated from their indigenous roots. It was not only the women in my line who were haunted by this legacy. Roger, also a descendant of this lineage of our mothers, also struggled with this part of our legacy. He encountered it again in the people indigenous to America and looked for a Key into the language of America that might "open a *Box*, where lies a bunch of *Keyes*."[23] Three-hundred years later, the time was now ripe to restore the connection with my indigenous origins. Following psyche's lead through dream and synchronicity and actively participating in imaginal dialogues with the ancestors, this connection has been restored intrapsychically and intergenerationally. My daughters' worldview, ways of knowing and being are rooted through the heart of our mother line to its deepest origins.

Beyond the Biographical Origins of Trauma

In my work with people, a commonly shared belief is that their troubles are a direct result of their childhood experiences. Without a perspective that includes the ancestors as influential in each individual's life, we assign the sole responsibility for our well-being, psychological symptoms, and disease to our parents or primary caregivers. Finding the points where our wounds, inclinations, personal dreams, unfulfilled desires, and burning questions touch different levels of our collective experience through the lives of our ancestors provides a broad and deep context of understanding which extends beyond one's immediate family. This expanded landscape adds to our understanding of what calls and what ails us. There are abundant examples of this dynamic in our stories.

I saw this very clearly with my own daughters. I wanted to be the best possible mother I could be, to provide a solid foundation for them, and avoid doing any serious psychological or physical harm. Given my personal history, it's not surprising that I would attempt to relieve my personal pain by creating a happy family and by attempting to shield them from pain and suffering. I remember that first moment, and the many that followed, of feeling completely helpless when I realized that there was nothing I could do to keep them from their fate. Their individual gifts and the things they would struggle with emerged in spite of and because of their experiences as children but had deeper and more complex origins. The seeds of their particular wounds and gifts were present at birth, a kind of soul imprint, and their experiences with their father and me and in the world provided the elements which brought them into the light of consciousness. What was theirs to answer, redeem or, resolve could be traced in part to their ancestors. I can now see how the work that I've done provides the foundation for who they are and what they are called to do. One of them, as of the writing of this book, has picked up the thread of patriarchal oppression, the other, the thread of racism.[24]

As Kathryn got to know her ancestors through the contents contained in the archival boxes that had been passed down to her, she discerned certain themes and tendencies woven into and through the histories of her ancestors that were intergenerational. Reconnecting with individuals in previous generations photo by photo, and letter by letter, Kathryn's understanding of her ancestors' stories deepened. Learning things she hadn't known, dispelling some of the personal and familial myths that had shaped her life, she became aware of the victim mentality that had been at the core of her personal story. Sitting in our council circle, "talking story," Kathryn experienced a sudden flash of insight. For the first time she wondered if the bitterness she felt so deeply in her bones might have its and origins in her lineage. She found evidence for and traces of bitterness in her lineage. This simple awareness seemed to be accompanied by a sense of relief for Kathryn. The weight of these archetypal energies that Kathryn had identified as personal and attributed to her experience with her parents was now carried by a considerably extended family. With this deeper and broader understanding she felt more compassion for her father and grandmother, and, for herself.

Janis had been treated for breast cancer twice in the last three years. Although she was aware of the anger and grief that she knew was present, she couldn't feel or give expression to it. These feelings were inaccessible emotionally. She worked with her dreams, meditated, talked with astrologers and shamans, all in an effort to access, feel, and express these feelings. Within the first week of engaging in ancestor dialogues and talking with her mother about the people in the abundance of pictures she had found, this anger and grief surfaced with emotional force and intensity. Being in a dialogue with the ancestors seemed to reach into and touch those places where previously shrouded and emotionally inaccessible feelings resided.

She felt and expressed the anger she felt towards her family for leaving her on her own as a child and now, as an adult. As she reached out for her ancestors, her anger increased. They did not reach back. They had never reached out to her or offered her their wisdom. She called this resistance. She did not know whether the "resistance" she felt to engaging in dialogues with the ancestors originated in her or the ancestors. Janis found it difficult to make the kind of connection with her ancestors that she wanted to. However, her anger and grief seemed to be evidence that a connection, as difficult as it was, had been made.

A healer by profession, Janis entered into this work enthusiastically hoping to bring healing to her ancestors. Her intention to heal her ancestors was challenged by the reality of her experience. Her resistance to reaching out during our group and her choice to not have any dialogues with the ancestors mirrored her experience of her ancestors and her family's unwillingness to reach out to her. As difficult as this was, she continued to participate in the group council process. Making the connection between the shroudedness that was characteristic in her ancestors and the shroudedness an astrologer used to describe the Sun in her chart sent shivers through her body.

Do these feelings originate in the lives of our ancestors or are they only a result of our personal experience? Janis asked that question about the resistance she felt—was it hers or did it come from the ancestors? Given Jung's way of describing the psyche and the relationship between the individual and the collective unconscious, the origins are multi-located, threaded through the dynamic web from the personal level to the "central fire." And, in fact, they co-exist and co-originate throughout the web. Whatever is true about where the origination of feelings like Janis's anger and grief and Kathryn's bitterness, what seems to be so is that the place to begin is in one's personal biography. The power and intensity of these feelings are often an indication that their origins extend into the collective dimension of consciousness.

The intensity of feelings a person has, like Kathryn's bitterness, often seem exaggerated given one's actual childhood experiences. People I work with frequently can't find a place of origination in their life that adequately explains how they feel. Following the psyche's guidance through dreams and synchronicities along with genealogical research the affective thread can be traced through the generations and often to a particular ancestor or event. When a discovery like this happens the person usually experiences a sense of relief, as if a weight has been lifted. The work of healing then occurs in the present within an expanded family system that includes the ancestors.

Ancestral Patterns in a Family Lineage

While I was writing Janis's story, after decades of having no contact, her father reached out to her. He called her twice. Not recognizing the phone number, Janis did not answer. He left her a message each time. The third time he called she answered. She was deeply moved when she heard her father's voice on the line. His call to her does not imply a causal relationship between Janis's work with the ancestors and his reaching out to her after years of no contact. However, the timing and nature of this connection suggest that there is a meaningful link.

Janis visited her father a few months after talking with him on the phone. She asked him about the grandmother she had a photograph of but had not been introduced to the only time they had both been at a family reunion. In the photograph, her grandmother is sitting alone at a table against the wall, apart, and seemingly isolated from the rest of her family. Her father told Janis that this woman, his mother, was a mean Cheyenne. Janis hadn't known this during the time our group was meeting. When Janis shared this with me in our final interview, I wondered if the well of rage and grief she had connected with at the beginning of this process might have origins in this part of her lineage. As is evident in Linda Hogan's, Kat Duff's and my stories, this painful history of genocide is not only our cultural but our personal "illness." As the Wampanoag woman told me, many of her people have been in resistance for over 300 years.

And, as Gustafson believes, part of healing this trauma is to feel the grief for the unimaginable losses.

Separation after birth and secret pregnancies were themes Tracy identified as recurring patterns in her lineage. She described her feelings of abandonment; more than understandable given her prolonged separation from her mother after birth and the death of her father when she was 16 years old. Situating her personal story in the context of her ancestors helped her identify and begin to heal these patterns. Her experiences with nature, described in detail in her story, and her experiences in the dialogues all seemed like the responsiveness of generous, loving parents who were and had always been there. She was given reassurance again and again that things would be all right and that they, the ancestors, were listening, had not abandoned her and were still and would always be present in her life. Nature and the ancestors as present in her dialogues with them provided the perfect therapeutic container. Gradually her trust was restored. The legacy of abandonment ends with her.

Alcoholism could be traced through the generations in Tracy's family. During the month our group met her grandmother "lost her taste" for alcohol and stopped drinking. The synchronistic occurrence of the dream that came to me at the time, as described in her story in the previous chapter, suggests that there is a connection between the work Tracy was doing in relationship with the ancestors and this change. In Native Science a dream like this one serves as validation for what is "true."[25] Jerome Bernstein, after reading Tracy's story and this analysis, said the answer to the man's question in the dream is, "yes." He affirmed that doing ancestor work, along with the 12-step Alcoholics Anonymous program and ritual does, in fact cure alcoholism.[26]

As I continue to work with people individually and in groups, the question asked in the dream—does this work, coming into a more conscious relationship with the ancestors through dialogue and ritual, cure alcoholism?—has been answered with a yes many times. There is usually someone in each group, often more than one person, who has a family member who is suffering with an addiction. As the person in the group sees the larger context in which the addiction is situated and engages in active dialogues with the ancestors seeking insight, guidance, and help, the patterns that have anchored the addiction in place begin to shift. It is common for the person in the family who is the addict to experience losing the craving for the substance that had them in its grip. Framing addiction in this larger context and participating in ongoing dialogues with the ancestors personally and in a group can be part of the therapeutic container created to address addiction. The individuals I have worked with gain insight, support, and guidance from their dialogues that facilitates change in the underlying dynamics and patterns of the addiction. The mirroring that takes place in the group is also an integral part of the "cure."

Dealing with addiction in one's family and its effects is often overwhelming. Needless to say, there isn't one right way of approaching addiction that works for every individual or family. Placing addiction in a transgenerational context opens the framework for understanding both the pattern of addiction and how to address it. The co-dependent dynamic of victim, perpetrator, and rescuer, which is characteristic of addiction, can be seen in new ways when one is engaged in dialogues with the ancestors. The deeper and more complex origins of the addiction are often discovered and witnessed. Additionally, the ancestors are there to offer their wisdom, guidance and support. When even one person in a family opens to this, something different begins to happen within the entire family. While feeling free of the craving that drives the addiction appears to be a sudden transformation, it takes time for the patterns that had been contributing to the continuation of this legacy to transform. Like any transformation, it takes consciousness and a willingness to look into the shadows. It is not easy work.[27] I want to emphasize again the necessity of 12-step programs and participating in ritual and ceremony in addition to engaging in ancestral dialogues as an integral part of transforming the pattern of addiction so that it no longer haunts the generations that follow.

Resolving Inherited Intergenerational Trauma

Silences surrounded Linda Hogan's mother and father, and her daughters. Her daughter often "woke struggling and fighting, as if we might hurt her."[28] Linda's granddaughter, like her mother, sometimes woke fighting, "as if such a thing is learned, and remembered by the body, even if unspoken in words. It is as if the stories of the mothers are written into the child's beginnings. I thought so, also, with my own mother."[29] Emotional memory is deeply embodied and transmitted through the generations and re-experienced in the present, especially if it is traumatic or in some way has a high libidinal charge. Through affect, image, and physical symptoms, the ancestral threads within these complexes can be picked up and traced to their multiple points of reference and origins. Although one may not feel possessed by a particular ancestor, one may experience unconscious "possession" by an inherited complex, such as the oppressive patriarchal foundation of Koerner's Mennonite heritage, or the black-robed priest who visited me repeatedly in dreams. When parts of our collective story are excluded from the family and cultural narrative as they are in Duff's story, they are very difficult to access and may be expressed in the physical symptoms of the body.

In her encounter with CFIDS and her attempts to heal herself, Kat Duff discovered that she was a living sacrifice for the sins of her fathers. Duff reminds us that the idea that our individual illnesses are part of a larger tapestry has deep roots in Western traditions. Renaissance physicians saw what happened in the body as a reflection of what was happening in the greater cosmos.[30] Ancient Greeks, Egyptians, early Christians and Jews understood that the welfare of an individual is shaped by forces that extend throughout space and time and our sufferings are "shared by all."[31]

While this larger context can result in greater insight, the potency of the collective nature of the shadow, due to its specific resonance with one's personal psychology, story, and complexes, can be very difficult, if not overwhelming. When one is dealing with a legacy like alcoholism, shroudedness, dark magic, Puritanical Christianity, or uprootedness accompanied by a longing for home, one needs a strong ego and a healing container that is substantial enough to support the amplified field. The complex has characteristics familiar to us from our personal story, but that is only a single thread in a complex web. Picking this thread up and following it brings us into relationship with the psychic energy that is carried in the stories and the lives of our ancestors, to the broader and deeper web of the collective unconscious across and through time, space, the psyche, and matter.

Engaging in dialogues with the ancestors using the ancestor altar as a ritual container can evoke the emotional wounds that we carry from our family of origin. In my personal experience, and as appears to be true in Janis's and Kathryn's story, our experiences of our parents and for me, grandparents, can be so difficult that a protective barrier of anger exists. These feelings need to be experienced and worked with consciously through the levels within the complex in order for the feelings of love and support from the ancestors to flow more freely. Diane's experiences were an example of the pure flow of support, guidance, and love that is available from the ancestors. Before doing this work she spent years after the death of her parents working through the hurt and anger she felt. It appears from our stories that as one picks up the thread and follows it from one's individual life through the lives of one's ancestors and back again, the collectively inherited patterns may be transformed and healing may occur not only for the individual, but for one's living relatives, the ancestors and one's descendants.

JoEllen needed to see the pattern of patriarchal oppression in her lineage, to see and experience it in all of its manifestations and offer forgiveness through all the levels from personal to familial, to cultural, finally reaching to the deepest collective level for her daughter Kristi's healing to be complete. After doing this in her vision quest, the pattern of motherless children that had plagued the women in her lineage finally came to an end. Linda Hogan and her father, returning to what was left of her grandmother's home, found expression for the anger and hurt that had remained unspoken for generations. Recognizing that her suffering was the suffering of an entire people was the beginning step in transforming the silences, the unspoken pain that wove itself through Linda's life—her own inability to speak as a child, her wordlessness—into a life filled with expression and a story about love.

Kat felt a weight lift from her as she participated in ceremonies and rituals for the Sioux who had died as a result of her ancestors' actions. Tracy's grandmother stopped drinking. I experienced spontaneous forgiveness for my grandfather and felt love flowing freely between us. Step by step, the legacy of failed *coniunctiones* that threaded through Roger's and my life began to mend. From a perspective that separates mind and body, spirit and matter, individual from collective, and human from the land, that sees healing in mechanistic terms of cause and effect, it is difficult to understand this kind of healing.

Jaffe finds that in "the great majority of legends the deliverance or redemption of the spirits comes from a relationship between them and a human being."[32] The following passage from Jaffe's chapter on "Ghosts" beautifully conveys what is at the heart of being in a more conscious dialogue with the ancestors.

> What the legends and the letters seem to convey is the need to make peace with these powers, to listen to them, to admit them to our lives and our consciousness. . . . Then—and only then—can the process of integration become a work of salvation for ghosts, gods and men.[33]

Whatever one believes about the existence of the soul after death, these "ghosts" of memory have archetypal weight. I would suggest that when these "ghosts," the ancestors, are engaged with consciously, the result is similar to what one experiences when one comes into relationship with any complex—an "easing of psychic tension," and "an undreamed-of expansion and enrichment of life."[34]

Connections with the Cosmos—and Beyond

Each individual enfolds and is enfolded in the cosmos. Not only do traumas, patterns, complexes, shadow, unanswered questions, and dreams thread their way through this interconnected web of relations, but from an Indigenous Science perspective, as each of us continues to engage in a process of coming-to-knowing and responds to what is being asked for in the present—witnessing, taking reparative action, forgiving—we affect the entire cosmos.[35]

Janis asked an interesting question in our group: If the ancestors are in Spirit, why can't they just fix things?! This question was at the core of Janis's experience of the ancestors—why should she take care of and heal them when they were not there for her? Her feelings of what she called "resistance" toward the ancestors and her question are not uncommon in the people I've worked with. This is especially true, and very understandable, for those of us who have suffered a lot at the hands of our parents and grandparents.

Is there a responsibility the living have in relationship to the dead? Jung believed that the dead are dependent on the living for the answers to their questions, for learning and evolving. Accordingly, he proposes that change only happens through embodied existence in this physical world of clashing opposites. The Dagara believe that the ancestors depend on the living to address any wrongs, imbalances, and disharmony that were a result of their actions, to heal the unearthed abuses and maintain harmony within and between the worlds.[36] They see the relationship between the ancestors and the living in this way:

> Ancestors are at a disadvantage because they know how to improve things and yet they do not have the body required to act on what they know. We are at a disadvantage because, although we have bodies, we often lack the knowledge required to carry things out properly.[37]

Taking Some's and Jung's ideas into account, it seems that there is something particular to the experience of being embodied that is necessary to the psyche, to addressing and healing what is out of harmony as well as to the development of consciousness. If we accept this, the question then becomes how does one listen and respond when the ancestors "speak?"

In her chapter on "Unredeemed Ghosts," Jaffe offers many accounts of people being "haunted" by ghosts who seek reparation for their actions in life. Adhering to Jung's theoretical framework, she does not answer the question whether or not these ghosts are real. According to Jaffe, it is important that these ghosts are seen as personifications of psychic contents of an individual's soul, "as an image of memory, and equally as an apparition independent of" the individual.[38] A meaningful interpretation can only come from "the interplay of both aspects."[39] From the stories people shared with her she concludes that "the act of forgiving a deed or transgression brings peace" to both deceased and the person who forgives.[40] She also found stories in which, rather than forgiveness, a "redeeming punishment" was needed. It appears, from her research, that "the dead" are dependent on

the living for resolution and redemption. Conversely, the living are dependent on "the dead" who carry the memory and burden of personal, familial
and collective shadows for direction and guidance.

The Importance of Ritual and Practice

According to Some, ritual has the potential to uproot dysfunctions. Ritual
like dream, serves as a bridge between consciousness and the unconscious.
It provides a container, a sacred space, within which the invisible world is
connected with the physical world. Within this connection what is intended
and worked on in this world has an effect within the unconscious, the realm
of the dead, the world of the ancestors. In our work as a group, and as
described in Kat's, Linda's and JoEllen's stories, ceremony and ritual provided containers and practices that facilitated connection, awareness, healing, and transformation. The importance of indigenous healing practices
and the role of community was apparent in Kat's, Linda's, and JoEllen's
stories. The group process of council and personal use of the ancestor altar
were essential components in the process of healing for each of the women
in the group. The efficacy of these practices is evident in our stories.

My initiation into the ancestral, cultural, and historical aspects of
trauma occurred in ritual space. My personal story serves as an example of
the healing effects of a consistent practice of dialogue with the ancestors
over time. While the part of my story that is shared in Chapter 10 is rich
with experiences of forgiveness, acceptance, love, support, and guidance,
these experiences are the result of many years of intense work. Like Kathryn, I began doing ancestor dialogues with archetypal figures whom I had
"met" in dreams and in the natural world. The natural and archetypal world,
in my experience, was trustworthy. Human beings, some of who were now
ancestors, were not always. The last person I wanted on my ancestor altar
was my grandfather. It took years of conscious work with a therapist, personal and communal rituals, tending dreams, and listening to the voices of
nature to open myself to the love and support that were available from the
ancestors.

One of the keys that allowed me to consider the possibility that this
trauma could be healed was what I learned from Malidoma Some. My
psychological understanding of trauma didn't include the recognition that
my grandfather had a different perspective as an ancestor than he did when
he was alive, that he could see the effects of his actions, and that he wanted
to do what he could to promote healing and restore balance. After participating in a weekend ritual process in community with Some, I understood
the experience of my grandfather reaching out to me and returning on a

wave of love from a new perspective. Combining this new understanding with what I knew psychologically about the experience of trauma allowed me to address this deeply rooted wound in ways that transformed the suffering at many levels beyond the personal.

I created a personal ancestor altar and added my grandfather's and grandmother's picture. I placed a dream catcher over it. My experience of support from the other ancestor figures—Hawk, Grandfather, Roger, Buffalo, Grandmother (the fiery figure in the tree from the dream described earlier), my personal father—provided the safe ritual container where my rage and grief and the painful history it reflected could be held and healed. The experience of spontaneous forgiveness described in my story seemed to completely and finally clear the physical, emotional, and mental ties that continued a legacy of abuse and bound this pattern to me in the world.

It is critical for people in modern western culture to do the psychological work along with the imaginal, ritual and ceremonial work. What is not in Diane's story as written is the work she did related to her family wounds prior to participating in this group. She told me that through her shamanic training with Alberto Villodo, she had released and healed enough of this wounding personally that she could open to the love and support of her father as an ancestor. Diane's and my experiences of love, support, and guidance from our ancestors were the result of years of conscious work, a clear intention, trust in the psyche and a consistent practice using dialogue and ritual. As one participates consciously in a dialogue with the ancestors, the capacity for love and support to flow between and through the generations is gradually restored.

A Labyrinthine Labor

Based on my experience I would describe the process of healing between the ancestors and each individual as labyrinthine. Walking the labyrinth of personal and ancestral trauma and suffering, one approaches the center and moves away again in a path which is always moving toward the center. Walking this path, one experiences deeper levels of forgiveness, acceptance, and healing. Coming closer to the center opens a natural flow of support and love from and towards the ancestors. Rather than a shortcut directly to the center, this work is a direct way into and potentially through what Jung's describes as complexes.

From the experiences shared, the healing that takes place as a result of coming into a more conscious relationship with the ancestors occurs through and within personal, familial, and collective levels. It is a process that is not causal, but involves a complex of patterns interwoven through,

across and within the generations and through the levels of the unconscious. Working in this way has an effect on the individual and their family,
ancestors and descendants. The patterns described above appear within an
individual in relationship with one's personal family and ancestral lineage.
The next section offers two examples of the way this occurs between individuals from different families of origin.

Interpersonal Ancestral Patterns

Through genealogical research, Tracy was able to follow the journey of her
ancestors back through time, across the North American continent and an
ocean to her European roots. As she discovered each new ancestor, learning pieces of their history, she added them to her altar. Tracing the path
of her husband's ancestors she found that both of their ancestral lineages
originated in the Alsace Lorraine region of Europe. Forced to leave their
home in Europe, their ancestors had been moving continuously from place
to place since they left that region seeking a place to call home.

Her husband felt a need to keep moving. First, Tracy wondered if, and
then began to feel that, they were re-enacting an old pattern. As her research
unfolded, she realized that she and her husband were part of a continuing
journey that began centuries ago when their ancestors left Europe in search
of a new place to put down roots. She recognized that her need for a home
and a sense of rootedness, counter-posed by her need to keep moving was
something that remained unresolved in her lineage. Having identified this
pattern, Tracy decided she wanted to find a place for her family that they
could settle into and call home. Three months after making this discovery,
she and her husband bought a home. Did finding the ancestral origins of
this pattern allow her to feel less compelled by its unconscious nature and
enable her to make a different choice?

The story of John Cotton and Roger Williams, like Tracy's and her
husband's ancestors, continued in the present. What remained unresolved
between our ancestors continued to be unconsciously reenacted in the relationships of their descendants. Our stories bring a dynamic to light that
leads to some interesting questions about interpersonal ancestral patterns
and the way those patterns may be embodied in the present.

Having access to genealogical records and historical documents
helped us place our personal stories in the context of our ancestors' stories.
I have found that even when genealogical information isn't available,
information about this dynamic is often presented in dreams and can be
discovered in dialogues with the ancestors. Even without specific genealogical information, imagining the patterns and complexes in one's

relationships within this larger context may contribute to a deeper under-standing of the origins and nature of the dynamics in one's interpersonal relationships.

The Land, Collective Trauma, and Grief

Jung recognized that a relationship exists between the ancestors and the land— "the past has sunk into the earth." One cannot separate oneself from place. According to Cajete, for Native Americans, America—this place, this land, this continent—holds our collective memory. All of us who are born to this land called America are connected, whether unconsciously or consciously, physically and psychically to the memories of this land. Gus-tafson believes that the violence and destruction done to this land and its peoples, still inadequately recognized, witnessed and grieved, "soaks the American soil" and affects all who live here, waiting to be resolved.[41]

Our individual and collective grief are inseparably and intimately intertwined. For the Dagara, unfelt and unexpressed grief grows stronger reaching hurricane force which can sweep one away.[42] Reconnecting with the collective levels of trauma and grief takes time, a strong ego, an ade-quate *temenos*, a perspective that does not limit the experience of emotions and complexes to the personal level and the willingness to personally experience the suffering and the wound in the heart of the collective and ancestral shadow.

Moving with and through one's personal complexes and family his-tory is challenging work. Experiencing the grief and anger within collec-tive trauma as evidenced in these stories, is almost unbearable. Trauma in the collective psyche is a force as powerful as a hurricane. It is challenging to stay present to and conscious of this kind of experience. Christopher Bache encountered this level of collective suffering through holotropic breath work. He found it nearly unbearable and difficult to describe

the places I was in, the destruction I was part of, the searing pain and torment of thousands of beings tortured to their breaking point and then beyond. Not individuals but waves of people.[43]

The question of how each individual experiences and is in relationship with the deeper collective levels of ancestral trauma and grief, the levels below the personal unconscious as delineated by Jung, is most clearly evi-dent in Kat's, JoEllen's, Linda's, and my stories. Each of our stories dem-onstrates the link between personal ancestral and collective trauma in a different way. Our personal suffering, symptoms, and illness connected us to specific people, places and times within a multileveled collective story.

Kat's, Linda's, and JoEllen's and her daughter Kristi's experiences are clear examples of the nature and process of healing of this dynamic. Linda's story shows the direct connection between collective and personal trauma. Kat's story illustrates the way the body "remembers" what has been hidden from consciousness. The painful truth of the actions of her ancestors, which had been left out of her family narrative, was written in the language of psyche on her body. She and I share a history of sexual abuse. There seems to be a direct psychic and physical connection between our personal experience and the abuse suffered by the land and the people native to it. JoEllen's and Kristi's story is an example of the way the oppression in her Mennonite heritage affected the lives of the women in her lineage, resulting in a pattern of motherless children. The archetypal figure of the black-robed priest who appeared in many of my dreams for years haunted the lineage of women from whom I am descended. This particular archetypal energy, and, I would surmise, the actions of actual priests, created a severing from the origins of my maternal lineage as they experienced the same kind of oppression as the women in JoEllen's lineage had.

Diane's, Janis's, Tracy's, and Kathryn's ancestors came to this land from Europe in the 1800s. Three of the women had German ancestors. Two had ancestors who came from the Alsace Lorraine region of Europe. As Tracy said, they left Europe for America, seeking a better life. I have no German ancestors. I was the only woman in the group who knew of ancestors who were here before and during the colonization of this continent. Janis would only discover her Cheyenne roots after our group ended. It seems that the collective ancestral field of this group was predominantly one of immigrants rather than early settlers and colonists or, like Hogan, American Indian. This may have been why my paternal great-grandparents came forward[44] for the first time in the dialogue that took place on the morning of the day the group began. They also immigrated to this country from Sweden and Denmark in the 1800s. The impulse that inspired this relocation, what drew my great grandparents and the other women's ancestors to this continent, was different than the one that inspired Roger Williams and his contemporaries to come to this land. These immigrants encountered a different America than the one Roger and other seventeenth-century Europeans encountered.

A dream occurred, synchronistically, while I was writing the stories in Chapter 10. The dream began in Santa Barbara. I was there/here, where I live in the present. The dream landscape changed and I found myself standing in a field in France. I was in Europe to meet with people who had found out about me and wanted me to come to their town and interview them during our group. There were three other with me as I started this journey. They were younger, probably in their twenties. They were very interested in the work I was doing. I had a sense that they were there to learn from me. I had a map to guide me. It showed me the route to Germany. To get to the people who wanted to be interviewed, I had to walk through France and into Germany. I was concerned about making it to the appointment in time.

In one part of the dream, still in France I believe, I walked through an old university built from hand-carved stones. I entered through one side of the building and went out through the opposite side. I walked down stone steps onto a dirt road. The dirt road went through an area that was beautiful and forested. I was looking at the map and asking for help with directions as I stood with the university at my back and the road in front of me. A man appeared and told me about a plane that could get me to the town where the people were waiting to be interviewed more quickly. I chose to walk. The "time" I was in seemed to be a time that was better served by walking. To get to the town where these people were waiting, I had to walk through a town which was clearly dangerous. The name of the town was Hassel-dorf.[45]

I found myself at the entrance to the town as soon as I knew its name. There were several people there who had come to meet me. They were expecting me. They were guarded and suspicious. The people in this town were shadowy figures who were not to be dealt with lightly. I didn't feel any sense of personal danger about going into this town. When I met the people who greeted me, I knew the shadow in this town was racism. I won-dered if the people I met in this shadowy town and the people who wanted me to interview them were connected in some way to, or were actually the ancestors, of the women in the group who were from Germany and Alsace Lorraine. Perhaps the ancestral field that was opened within the group was offering some of the ancestral and collective stories and complexes within this particular group to me through this dream. As with any dream, its meaning has continued to unfold with time.

There were only hints of connection to the deeper collective memory of the trauma and grief Some, Gustafson, and Cajete describe, in the stories of the other women in the group. However, there were indications that this collective grief might be present in Janis's and Kathryn's stories. Janis talked about an almost overwhelming rage and grief the origins of which she could not find. Kathryn wrote about how her "body grieves from the pain" of loneliness, of not belonging. Perhaps the grief that Janis accessed through this work and the depth and intensity of grief Kathryn experienced had origins not only in their personal history, but also in the stories of their German ancestors and the story of this land and its indigenous people.

Although the experience of suffering is felt as, and *is* very personal, it is likely that it has multiple origins. Reconnecting with the origins of this suffering at the ancestral, clan, national, and deeper collective levels of the unconscious through affect, dreams, nature, story, dialogue, images (photographs, dream images, visions), and other iconic pieces of memory and memorabilia, contributes to a more complete understanding of our personal experiences and suffering. Addressing family patterns within this larger collective context allows for healing—redemption and resolution—in which balance can be restored within the individual and their lineage. This restoration of balance, coming into Tao, within an individual, as in the story of the Rainmaker, brings greater balance to the collective.

Longing to Belong

Longing to belong was a theme that was immediately present in our group. In our first group session Kathryn described herself as "a dropped pearl from a long strand of pearls." Tracy shared her longing to feel a sense of rootedness to a place, to live in a home that belonged to her where she could establish a connection with the earth. Janis shared her story of going to a family reunion, not feeling connected, and not knowing who the strange woman was at the table. As we shared our stories, telling, listening, and mirroring what we heard, we felt a deepening sense of connection. The group's desire to meet more frequently reflected our need for community and our need to have places of belonging.

Janis and her mother longed for the stories that had been lost and the wisdom of elders. Tracy longed for a home, a nest, a place where she could put down roots in the land and grow things. My experience of and relationship with the world as a Borderlander had not been mirrored, nor could I express it, in my family, school, church, or among my friends. I was different and didn't feel as if I really belonged anywhere except in nature. Resigned, but not without hope, I looked for "my people," and a place where I felt like I belonged. Kathryn found no sustenance or nourishment in her family. She did not experience a sense of belonging in her family of origin. In fact, she felt that her very existence had been compromised by her parents. Janis and Kathryn asked again and again, "Who is my family?" One of the most poignant questions was asked by Kathryn: "After I am dead, who will remember me?" Her longing to belong seemed to be connected to a continuity within which she was known and would be remembered.

What seemed to be true to different degrees for each of us was a lack of this sense of belonging within our families of origin. Janis and Kathryn felt and expressed this in a way that brought the archetype of *orphan* into our group. Kathryn did not experience her family or her body as a hospitable home. She was not the first in her line to experience this deep sense of not belonging. Her Irish paternal grandmother was never considered to be a part of the family she married into. Her parents were also described as the black sheep in their families. Kathryn did not explore the connection between her longing to belong and the experiences of her ancestors in any direct way.

Sometimes lacking a sense of belonging to one's family creates a longing that leads into the larger world. Kathryn found a family of the heart with her friends and in the archetypal figures she placed on her altar. Her ancestor altar was her attempt to fashion a home, "a place where [her] heart can be seen and held in love." She welcomed her ancestors into her home through this altar. Rather than feeling that her relationship with them compromised her existence, creating this altar and feeding them nourished her. While photographs of her ancestors and other memorabilia sat in unopened boxes in the garage, her ancestor altar, through her graciousness, became a place for her ancestors to reside.

Even after doing this work, the ancestors are not a source of sustenance for Kathryn. Everything she grasps for in this world dissolves. Her longing for a sense of belonging and meaning here always seems to slip through her grasp. She has been a spiritual seeker for as long as she can remember. Her choice to put archetypal figures on her altar rather than her personal family could be seen as an indication that her life was a journey oriented toward a home in spirit—"the land of the dead." After completing this work with the ancestors, she felt it was time for her conversation with the divine to begin. The ancestral soul work was a step in her process of returning home.

As Janis looked at the pictures of her ancestors and tried to establish a connection, her experience of disconnection with her family and ancestors increased. Her anger and grief intensified. She and Kathryn recognized each other as kindred spirits. It is interesting to note that Janis came to the first group with a bag of photographs. By the last group she came with only a few. Kathryn arrived at our first group with one photograph of her parents. Having unearthed her ancestors from the boxes in which they had been stored, she came to the last group with a bag full of photographs filled with stories that were new to her about her ancestors. While both of these women turned to nature, spirit, and their "family of the heart" seeking a sense of belonging, their longing to belong remained.

Where does a sense of belonging come from, and why was it something that was missing in different ways and degrees for each of the women in this group? Could the longing to belong, to put down roots, to experience the wisdom of elders be related to being on soil that is not the soil of our indigenous ancestors? Thinking about the way our distant ancestors lived, the Dagara, and the people indigenous to this land, it seems that a deep sense of belonging comes from understanding one's origins and one's place in the world and within the larger story of creation.[46]

Although we have made progress technologically, differentiated our egos, and developed critically thinking left brains, at the deeper levels of the psyche the archaic, indigenous aspect of consciousness is still a part of our inheritance. I am reminded of the story of my friend who recognized something in the Native American woman who talked about her people. She recognized that she did not have the same sense of belonging that her classmate had been born into. Her personal story and history had origins that were unknown to her, scattered across continents. My friend felt and feels loved and seen by her parents. She is happily married, and has two children, good friends, and a strong sense of community. Even with this foundation, she recognized and longed for the experience of connection and belonging she heard in her classmate's story.

Many Americans live far from the geographic and psychic origins of their ancestors' world with its particular, indigenous stories, customs, and rituals. I remember my paternal grandparents, first-generation Americans born to Swedish and Danish immigrants, telling me how lucky I was to be an American. They had done everything they could to erase traces of their Scandinavian heritage and assimilate themselves into this culture to insure that their children and grandchildren could live the American dream. When I researched my mother's father's ancestors through census records, I discovered the country of origin changed every ten years with each new census. First the records showed they were Irish, then French, and finally of American descent. The word "American" was crossed out. Over it the word "English" was written. Their identity as Irish and French seemed to be changed to match the country of origin of their neighbors. After 30 years, they identified themselves as being of "American" descent. This was then translated into "English." My great grandparents and the ancestors of the other women in the group, as immigrants to this continent, were anxious to become and be identified as Americans rather than Danish or French or German. The collective levels of the American psyche have diverse origins.

Barbara Hannah uses the word "belong" to describe Jung's relationship with Switzerland. Like the mountains, he was rooted in its soil.[47] Bollingen, a place of timeless existence in which Jung felt a sense of timelessness, as if he was connected to and simultaneously in many centuries, was built on the land of his ancestors. Jung's encounters with the unconscious, his use of art, and analysis, and his time at Bollingen reconnected him more consciously with the ancestors. The connections Jung made between his life and the unanswered questions of his ancestors, his experiences of the imperishable world that is our psychic heritage, and his intimate connection with the land all contributed to his feeling that his life was a "historical fragment" within a much larger text.[48] His sense of continuity within a larger con- "text" came from a vision in which he knew he "would meet those people to whom [he] *belong[ed]* in reality.[49] His sense of belonging, in part, came from his relationship with the ancestors who he encountered in the land and in psyche.

Living on the land one was born from and into—where the bones of one's ancestors rest, where the stories of one's ancestors and their wisdom sits in the landscape—grounds, nourishes, and sustains a deep sense of belonging, one in which body is connected to earth *and* spirit through and within time and space. A cosmology with creation stories and wisdom stories, ceremonies and rituals, that come from the land and have been passed down through countless generations, provides a context which connects each individual life *through* time and space and *in* time and place to herself, her family, her clan, her nation, and to that which is eternal. As the Navajo elder said, there is no distance between the creating and this moment or any other moment in time. A vital cosmology born out of being in relationship with the land connects each individual with the ancestors, the unconscious, the land, nature, and the "great mysterious." This connection is continuously renewed for each individual and for the community through story, ceremony and ritual. One belongs to the people, to the land and to all of creation.

Gustafson told me that the Sioux and most Native Americans believe that it takes seven generations living in a place before a person experiences that sense of belonging.[50] Given this understanding and what we learn from Jung, it is no wonder that the women in this group longed for a sense of belonging.

The Cosmologically Orphaned Child

Hillman believes that we lost our relationship with our "cosmological parents" and along with that, our connection to the ancestors. In his words, "[t]he parents have swallowed them up."[51] I would say it differently. Without a connection to the ancestors and to the archetypal mother and father, our cosmological parents, we look to our biological parents to fill this archetypal vacuum. Speaking as both daughter and mother, this is an impossible expectation to meet. My younger daughter expressed this as only a four-year-old can when she told me she wanted to find her "real" mother. The orphan or step-child archetype naturally constellates in the absence of cosmological parents, and, I would suggest, in the absence of a true connection with the ancestors. I want to make a clear distinction between the actual experience and the archetypal experience of being orphaned. The stories shared in this book contain both.

The archetype of "orphan" came into our first circle. Feeling like an orphan seems to be the result of the inadequacy of the personal family to provide an satisfactory sense of mirroring and belonging. In the absence of a coherent cosmology and community that is connected to *and* connects one with the ancestors, the land, one's origins, and with spirit, it seems that the burden and emotional weight of longing to belong, the need for elders and stories of wisdom, is placed on the immediate family each of us is born into. One's sense of belonging is intimately connected with one's relationship with the ancestors and the land, and, with a reconnection with the "archaic" part of the collective unconscious.

The orphan archetype has always appeared in the first group of every ancestor group I've facilitated. It is usually the experience of one of the people whose family came here as immigrants sometime in or after the mid 1800's. If Gustafson is correct, that it takes seven generations of living on this land to feel one's roots connected to this soil, then I would suggest that the orphan archetype is an indication of feeling uprooted from one's homeland and orphaned from the bones and land of one's ancestors.

I remember as a child wanting to "go home." I knew there was a place that I had come from where I belonged. I imagined and felt it was not in my family or this world. Learning the story of my ancestor Roger, returning to Providence, visiting the places my ancestors lived for generations and are buried, feeling known and welcomed by that land, gave me a profound sense of belonging to a place and a people. Seeking and finding a "family of the heart," for Kathryn and Janis seems to partially fill this longing. Janis's longing for the wisdom of the elders is sought, but not found. Seeking a sense of real family and of belonging can become literalized. Kathryn sought substantive belonging through the acquisition of beautiful objects. Tracy's need for a sense of rootedness is concretized into owning a home.

Through her participation in this group, Tracy would recover a deep sense of belonging. She would also buy a new home and put down roots. In one moment of experiencing her deep longing for a sense of rootedness and her feelings of anxiety about not having a home, Tracy looked down and found a perfect bird's nest at her feet. As she picked up the nest she heard the words, "Mother cry to me, hear my words softly spoken, lost but not forgotten." It is as if the cosmological mother, the Earth herself, was speaking to Tracy in that moment in response to her need. She heard this as the voice of her ancestors. With this reassurance came a sense of belonging to and being held within a larger cosmological home. Her anxiety eased.

Through genealogical research, Tracy followed the journey of her and her husband's ancestors. Her excitement and enthusiasm grew with each revelation, each new face and new story. She shared these discoveries with with her family. Piece by piece, Tracy was able to create a more complete and substantial picture of her family tree with ever widening branches than she had at the beginning of this process. As this tree grew, so did her sense of belonging to something larger.

During one of her dialogues Tracy had an experience of a profound connection with nature and the ancestors. Lying on the dirt, listening to the sounds of hummingbird, hawk, beetle, dove, and the wind, knowing that her ancestors also heard these sounds, she felt the deep connection between generations past, present, and future in that moment through the presence of nature. Feeling this continuity between her life and that of her ancestors and her descendants in nature, she is at home on this earth and at peace in that moment. Her genealogical discoveries, her stories about hawk, and her experiences with nature and in her dialogues with the ancestors are becoming a personal cosmology. As she trusts the validity of her experiences, these stories take root in her being and her longing for home transforms into a sense of peace and connection with the Earth, her ancestors, and herself.

In our first group Kathryn described herself as an orphan. She felt nurtured and sustained as she "fed" the ancestors on her altar. Meeting her ancestors and her parents through the contents in the archival boxes, she began to see the way she fit into a more complex story. When Kathryn discovered that her breast cancer had metastasized she turned to the divine and took meditative walks on the beach. In response to her offering of one feather in prayer, the ocean returned hundreds of feathers the next day. Through these experiences she experienced the generosity of love and connection that she longed for.

JoEllen Koerner's story provides an interesting counterpoint to the experience of longing to belong that was shared by the women in our group. She grew up in the Mennonite tradition which served as the foundation for generations of her family. It is a culture that is connected as vitally to the land as it is to Spirit. This heritage survived a move from Germany to Russia and finally to the Dakotas, where she was born. The tradition of her family and their history as Mennonites was preserved in the stories, photographs, ceremonies, and rituals passed down through the generations. Her deep appreciation for her family and her ancestors and her sense of belonging is apparent throughout her story.

She was born into a tradition that had stories, rituals, and ceremonies that were connected to the land and that connected her to generations of her ancestors. Even with the history of orphaning in her lineage, she never questioned her sense of belonging. Instead of longing to belong, she found herself pushing against the edges of the traditions of her Mennonite ancestors and the tradition of allopathic medicine. While staying connected with her roots, she wanted to move forward into new territory. Through her professional work and the healing crisis with her daughter, the traditions that were part of her foundation, evolved.

In contrast, Linda Hogan's story is one born out of the physical displacement, genocide, and loss of the traditions of her people. Her story is one of recovering the lost pieces of her ancestors' lives and in the process, restoring her sense of herself and belonging. The difficult work of gathering the pieces and reconnecting with one's ancestral and collective roots after dislocation from the land of one's ancestors is poignantly and painfully described in her story and the stories of her adopted daughters. Her story began in silence and pain and emerged as one of healing, history, survival, reconnection, belonging, and love. Dislocated from the land of her ancestors and their traditions, Linda's story shows the way reconnecting with the land, history, rituals, and ceremonies of her ancestors were a restoration of her connection with herself with the earth and cosmos. In her words: "When the sun falls on the arm, it is touched. Then she, you and I, may travel beyond human construction and invention. Even knowing that the horrible and beautiful are together in the world, we pass the threshold into something finer."[52]

Building a Place of Belonging: A Personal Reflection

This book began with my personal story. As part of this process of coming into a more conscious relationship with my ancestors, I returned to the land where they had lived, built homes, had children, died, and were buried, I listened for their stories, feeling their presence, in order to create a pathway and connection from the soles of my feet into and through my body, psyche and the land. Doing genealogical research, searching historical records, and reading what had been written by and about my ancestors was also part of this work.

I looked for ways to answer, redeem and resolve what my ancestors, specifically Roger, had left unfinished. While I was working on this section I had the following dream:

> I am in a town that has the feeling of an intentionally created community. It's rustic, earthy. The buildings are made from wood. We grow our own vegetables and make our own clothes. We live in harmony with nature in a sustainable and conscious way. "Back to the earth" is the phrase that comes to mind as descriptive of the essence of this community. Although our way of living is "back to the earth," the community has a sense of the future, rather

than being sometime in the past or a return to some nostalgic idea of what living in harmony with the earth means.

I am standing on a balcony or deck that is part of one of the buildings with a man, older I think. The balcony faces and looks out onto the main street, which is a wide dirt road. I have the sense that he and I are leaders in this community. This dream figure/man who I'm with on the balcony is the kind of dream figure whose presence brings one's awareness to something that would otherwise not have been seen. We're on the balcony talking. I look down and see a chapel that has just been built. People are putting the finishing touches on it and setting up chairs inside. He and I talk about the chapel. Feeling the reality of this church/chapel as I look at it, I have a flash of awareness and recognition. I say to him "all I've ever wanted is a church that I could put my symbols in."

I realize this is that kind of church, a place where anyone's and every-one's way of connecting with and expressing their personal relationship with Spirit is welcome. I am moved as I realize this is actually possible, a reality. (I am aware now that I have longed for this but thought it was an idealistic, impossible dream.) I realize and tell him that at the deepest level I am Christian, that Christ comes to me in dreams and that I know and have experienced the Holy Spirit. (This is actually somewhat of a surprise to my conscious self. It does make sense ancestrally, as I come from a long line of Christian ministers. I have had an experience of being filled with and healed by the Holy Spirit and Christ has come to me in other dreams. However, identifying myself as Christian at a soul level and feeling the truth of that in my dream body was a surprise when I woke up with and in the memory of the dream.) In the dream, I experience a deep, complete happiness and sense of peace. I have the deepest sense of belonging I have ever felt.

However . . . in the next part of the dream I am walking on the main street. It's a main thoroughfare that runs through the center of this town. There are many other people on this street and in the buildings on this street. They are all going about their business. I am still feeling very happy, at home, at peace, and excited. I am carrying a cradle with a baby in it. A woman is walking toward me. I see she is angry. Propelled by anger, she confronts me by coming forcefully towards me and pushing herself into me. I wake up.

As a Puritan and separatist, my ancestor, Roger, was not welcome in England. After coming to this North American continent, he was exiled from Massachusetts for heresy. He created a community, an experiment in which church was separated from state, and where decisions would be arrived at by mutual consent not dictatorial, theocratic authority.[53] Founded on his concept of soul liberty, all in this community worshipped as they so chose. Quakers, Jews, and individuals who were considered heretics found a home here. The first synagogue on this continent was built there. Providence, according to the Colonial Women's History Project, is also the place where "the first legal decision in the seventeenth-century New England colonies to uphold a woman's right to "freedom of conscience," that in matters of thought and belief, a woman could be seen as independent of her husband's control," was made[54]

I discovered the following piece of information only after having this dream. From his reading of the Bible, Williams believed that baptism should only be administered to those who had voluntarily and consciously confessed their personal faith.[55] He, along with others, founded the first Baptist church in 1638. The church was, however not a physical structure, but consisted of the congregation of people. Ever restless spiritually, even after establishing this new church, Williams continued to search in the Bible for evidence of the "true church." I believe there was something in this land and its indigenous people that called to and informed his thinking and his spirit with regard to his search. He came to the conclusion that only when Christ returned could a genuine "New Testament church" be created.[56] While Williams, like many of his contemporaries, thought we were on the verge of a new millennium, unlike many of his contemporaries, he did not think Christ's return would involve political rule. Rather than resulting in a national church and theocratic state, his return would restore the true, apostolic church.

He was passionate about and spent much of his life advocating "soul liberty." Addressing England's Parliament in 1643, Williams would state as paraphrased in more modern language by Gaustad, "When persons are forced to conform to a mode of worship that their 'hearts embrace not,' then they have been violated in the very depths of their being."[57] What my ancestor advocated for and created in Providence, Rhode Island—a sanctuary for people of different faiths, a community where all could worship as they so chose—existed now in this dream. The true church my ancestor sought, where every person is free to worship as they so choose, has been created and exists as a reality in the psyche and now, in my consciousness.

This dream echoes Roger's direct experience of Christ and the Holy Spirit and seems to reconcile indigenous spirituality with Christianity. Using his story to amplify mine, my understanding of this dream was expanded and deepened. The story of my ancestor works in a way similar to the way myths, fairy tales and folk tales might be used to amplify a dream. His dream of a social democracy, the separation of church and state, and his concept of "soul liberty" could only be realized to a certain degree in his lifetime. The dream that was burned to the ground on March 29th in 1676, two-hundred and seventy-six years before I was born, is reawakened in me and, as Jung would say dreamed forward.

The angry woman who ran at me in the dream was a dream figure whom I had encountered fourteen years ago in another dream. In that dream, like many other dreams during that time, a war was raging. In the first dream this figure was wearing army fatigues, standing at a kitchen sink doing dishes. She seemed to be an insignificant figure. Rather than interpreting this dream, I tended it using the process of animation.[58] I watched her carefully noticing every detail as she stood at the kitchen sink washing dishes and then asked her if she would talk with me. In response to my invitation, she turned and threw a pot at my head. She was enraged. Each day following this dream, for a total of seven days, I spent time in dialogue with this dream figure. She had been raped and asked nothing less of me than to see the truth about patriarchal oppression and my own collusion with it. A poem about the loss of innocence all too young, of rage, grief, and love was the result of this first encounter.

Working with this more recent dream, I realized the angry woman who threw a pot at my head was the same angry woman who ran at me in the street. In both dreams she was actually an ally. She held what I could not yet feel and could not yet express—all the rage and grief that I had dissociated from out of necessity when I was a child and young woman being molested. Her function was to protect me. In this most recent dream, she carried the anger and fear I have about expressing and bringing my work—the baby in the cradle—into the world fully utilizing head and heart, my Logos-oriented Western consciousness and Borderland consciousness in an integrated way. I believe she also carries the rage that extends through generations of women in my mother line who were severed from their indigenous origins.

This dream figure, now recognized, and engaged with using Dream Tending techniques, has transformed. She is no longer throwing pots at my head or trying to run me down on the street. Now, she sits at a desk wearing glasses, writing. Her anger has transformed into passion. She knows the wound, knows the world, and embodies fierce compassion that is grounded in her experience of suffering in the world. As long as I stay related to her there is no chance of becoming inflated! She has become an ally as I integrate and fully embody my Borderland consciousness and as I write this book. Her passion, critical thinking, and ability with words assist me in my teaching and writing. Her understanding of suffering opens me to greater capacities as a facilitator of healing.

The relationship between my personal wounding, the trauma of this land and its people, the failed *coniunctio* that was also one of the themes of my ancestor Roger's life, the severing within my mother line from the indigenous roots of a sacred tree with its fiery figure, coexist in the present in me. As I reconnect the threads of the ancestral tapestry with its wounds and questions and discover the roots of my being; my body, mind, heart, and soul experience a deeper and more profound sense of belonging to myself, my family, this land, the Earth and the cosmos. In the mystery of the psyche, as my ancestors' questions are addressed and answered in ways that could not be answered in his time, I move more fully into conscious expression and embodiment of my own life.

Recovering and reestablishing the connections with one's ancestors, placing one's stories in this larger context, is one of the ways recovering one's sense of belonging can take place. It is a process that takes time and a willingness to delve into the shadows and depths of one's personal suffering as it exists in relationship with one's ancestral and our collective story. As threads are picked up and the pattern of the tapestry is revealed, a personal cosmology begins to take shape. The connections that were made by some of the women in the group between their story and the stories of their ancestors indicate that this work has the potential to open one to a deeper and greater sense of connection with one's ancestors, to oneself, to the earth, and to the cosmos in ways that begin to reestablish a sense of belonging in personally meaningful ways.

Living the Life One Was Born to Live

Each of us, according to Jung, is a collection of inherited "ancestral spirits."[59] Jung likens the individual psyche to a puzzle which at first is somewhat disjointed. Psychological development or individuation involves putting the pieces of the puzzle together and discerning the secret of one's particular pattern. As defined by Jung, individuation denotes "the process by which a person becomes a psychological 'in-dividual,' that is, a separate, indivisible unity or 'whole.'"[60] Jung uses the concept of squaring the circle to describe this process. As Jung sees it, "this rounding of the personality into a whole" is the goal of any psychotherapy that is more than "a mere cure for symptoms."[61]

The relationship between the conscious and unconscious and the process of individuation are intimately linked. At the heart of the process of individuation is becoming conscious of what has been excluded from consciousness and integrating seemingly irreconcilable opposites in the psyche. In the shadows of consciousness, are repressed and forgotten memories as well as our unique gifts. Becoming conscious of and integrating emotions, beliefs and memories that have been hidden from consciousness because they are too painful or too contradictory to one's image of oneself, of others or of the world, is part of the process of individuation. I would suggest that seeing our lives as a unique expression within the continuity of a larger history and the lives of our ancestors is an integral part of reintegrating disowned parts of our personal, ancestral, and collective shadow and discerning our particular pattern and gifts. With each discovery we are reconnected with the soul of the world. As Linda Hogan discovered "it was knowledge of the depths, and this is what stories try to teach us, even our own; that what's below and beneath and inside is a generative, life-giving power."[62]

Our stories contain many examples of painful personal, ancestral and cultural shadows. They also show the ways in which our wounds are the crucible for our unique gifts. The "patterns" that were particular to each of us had their origins in the lives of our ancestors. Through dialogue, dream work and synchronicities we discovered the way the thread of our individual life was woven into the familial, tribal, national, ancestral, and archetypal levels of the psyche. Seeing how the thread of our life was part of the whole tapestry of being, how each piece of the puzzle fit together into the cosmological puzzle, the "particular pattern" of who we were revealed itself. Each of us became more conscious of what had been hidden from consciousness through our dialogues with the ancestors, genealogical research and our group process, we were doing the challenging work of individuation.

Each one of us as a "historical fragment" within a longer story, comes into this world with a particular "pattern" that is, according to Jung, a response and answer to what is unresolved, unredeemed and unanswered. The pattern of our particular life, our genius and gifts, become evident and are developed as we listen and respond to the "lament of the dead" with love. Every person, every gift, is an important part of the integrity and well-being of the interconnected web of kinship. Engaging in a more conscious dialogue with the ancestors each of us can more consciously and fully live the life that is ours alone to live. Doing so contributes to the well-being of all our kin. I would suggest that in addition to our lives being a response to what is waiting for resolution, redemption or an answer, each of our lives is also in service to our descendants.

For the Dagara, each person's genius and unique gift originates in the "Other World" and is sacred. Every individual born to the Dagara is mentored and supported into maturing into an adult who fulfills their purpose.[63] From the moment a person is born, others within the community have a responsibility to assist that person in delivering their gift to the world. Everyone in the community is responsible for and has an integral role in insuring that each person's genius is awakened, nurtured, and mentored. If this is not done, the person as well as their genius dies.[64] If any individual's gift is not delivered it then falls to that person's descendants to do so.[65]

When this occurs, descendants will then have to deliver their particular gift *and* that of their ancestor(s).

For the Dagara, the ancestors are intimately and vitally connected with the world of the living. When a person dies they continue to be part of the community.[66] "Death is not a separation but a different form of communion, a higher form of connectedness with the community, providing an opportunity for even greater service."[67] Jung's dialogues in *The Red Book* with "the dead" are evidence of the connection and relationship between the world of the living and the ancestors. In Jung's personal story there are many examples of the way his father, mother, and wife continued their connection with him after their deaths through dreams and visions and played important roles in his individuation. The death of each of his parents and his wife were an initiation into a deeper relationship with himself and his work assisting him in contributing to our collective wisdom.

Diane's story is filled with dialogues, dreams and synchronicities in which her ancestors, specifically her father, mother, and grandfather, guide and support her on her path in life. When she talks about them, it is clear that they are still very present in her life. She invites them into dialogues and into her dreams on a regular basis. They also come in dreams at times when she does not consciously invite them. When she has doubts, they affirm her choices. Each next step is supported by them with gifts and affirmations. Her story is rich with examples of the guidance and wisdom they have to offer.

Through dreams and active dialogues, Diane's ancestors provide the kind of mentoring and support that the Dagara believe is available for each of us. Diane's ancestors assist her in discerning the secret of her particular pattern. Their gifts and support are very particular to what she needs, perfectly timed, sometimes literal and often symbolic. The pencils her father gives her in a dream come in a clear package. They hold and reflect the quality of creativity and offer specific tools for her to bring them into expression. She knows and feels that her ancestors want her to be and express who she is authentically, to walk her own path in life and be happy. During one of her first ancestor dialogues, she was told that doing this work with our group would help her receive and embody the gifts from one of her dreams.

In our first group session, Diane said, "What my father took from me in life, he has given back to me in death." Responding to her father's fear of her femininity and creativity, she became one of the boys. Her life path changed when she encountered her father's spirit in a ceremony in Mexico. As an ancestor, he tells her, "Live your own life." It appears that her father served her in life by inflicting the perfect wound, and, in his process of dying, and as an ancestor, by providing the resources, experiences, and gifts that support her in living *her* life. The seed for Diane's life was present at birth, activated through her suffering at her father's hands and consciously embraced and expressed in the second half of her life.

After reading her story for the first time as I had written it, she turned to me and said, as she pointed to the first paragraph in her story, "You know, this *is* where my story begins." The experience of her father's presence with the medicine man opened her perception to a new way of seeing reality and changed the course of her life. At another turning point in her life, right after leaving her job as an accountant to devote more time to her creative expression and healing practice, her grandfather appeared to her in a dream. He walked across a plank, joyfully and fearlessly doing acrobatics. This demonstration by her grandfather of walking this plank in his own way affirmed Diane's choice to step into her work as a healer.

Tracy's story has many examples of the way an ancestor can be present in one's life in a different form after death. Tracy experienced her father's reassuring presence in a variety of ways in nature, especially her experiences of hawk. In several dialogues she heard the reassuring words, "be gentle." Through her experiences of the ancestors' presence and her deepening connection to them over the months our group met, Tracy feels she is "coming home to herself." This is an apt metaphor for the process of individuation. She knows and understands who she is "tucked in, part of a family quilt that's been handed down to which she is adding her individual piece." She sees herself reflected in her ancestors' stories, longings and suffering. As she consciously connects the threads of her life with her ancestors, she becomes more conscious about her sense of direction and purpose. Her choice of a field of study for graduate work makes more sense to her now in light of what she has learned.

My experience with my father is similar to Diane's. In one dream he tells me he can only take me so far, that I need to walk the rest of the way on my own. He gives me the gift of a walking stick. In a dream that follows, years later, I die in his arms. The symbolism of death and rebirth is common in dreams associated with the transformational process of individuation; the rebirth into another being, "that larger and greater personality maturing within us."[68] Following these dreams, I had experiences which enabled me to gradually, slowly and carefully remove the bullet lodged in my heart, and open to the love and support available to me from my grandfather, father, mother and other ancestors. I would never have imagined being open to my grandfather's love. I would also come to understand that the ways I was wounded by my parents and grandparents were perfect initiations in which the seeds of my soul would be activated. Similar to Diane's experiences, what my parents and my grandfather took from me in life, they gave back to me in perfect ways at perfect times after death.

In our first interview Kathryn told me that she wanted to have time to devote to her art, but she didn't see how that was going to be possible. She wished that her father had supported her artistic expression. She has been carrying around photographs and other memorabilia that were saved and passed on from her ancestors' lives. She had not had the energy or heart to go through these boxes. She began this work feeling no connection to her ancestors and did not feel supported, sustained, or nurtured by them. In fact, she felt her very existence had been compromised by her parents. The word she used to describe how she felt was bitterness.

Between our first and second group session, she opened the boxes and began going through the archives. She came to our last group session carrying a bag of photographs and other ancestral relics. She was very excited. She carefully took each item from the bag, shared with us who the people were and what she had learned about them, and then placed each one on the ancestor altar in the center of our circle. It would take time to go through all of the boxes and create the albums. When the boxes were finally empty, and everything had been placed into albums and into the world again, the room that had been used for storage would be clear, open, and empty. Finally putting this "burden" down, she could use this newly opened space for an art studio. Having the space for and creating an art studio occurred as a result of her process of integrating the new "truths" she discovered about her parents, grandparents and more distant ancestors in the archival boxes. Withdrawing each object from its box was like going into the unconscious and encountering what lived in the shadows. As objects were withdrawn, so were many of her projections. Her perception of herself and her personal story changed with each new discovery.

Kathryn's story depicts the process of individuation in a very literal way. She had been carrying around boxes filled with objects from her ancestors that she'd never seen. She experienced this as a burden. The weight of the boxes was a literal burden. Their contents were a psychological weight. Going through her family's archives is a concrete portrayal of the process of coming into a more conscious relationship with the ancestors—gathering and sorting through the bits and pieces of her ancestors' lives as they could be discerned in photographs, dreams, imaginal dialogues, census records, notes, and stories that had been passed on. As each new piece of her legacy was found, she questioned its place in her personal story and wondered if there was a place for her in theirs. The myth of her life became more visible and she began to see her parents and ancestors more as complex human beings than as characters in a story. The image of the singular stone supported by an arch of stones that was on the front of Kathryn's journal seems to be a fitting image for the way each of us in the group recognized our place in relationship with those who had come before. The keystone's place was defined by the supporting stones on either side. Without the keystone, the other stones would fall. It seems like a particularly fitting image for Kathryn. She is the last in her line and her life is directed toward spirit.

When One's Parents Are Still Living

Janis came into the group with high expectations about what was possible. Her experience was far from what she hoped for and quite different than Diane's, Tracy's, Kathryn's, and mine. She did not experience her ancestors as supportive and loving presences. Janis did have an experience of synchronicity in the coincidence of her grandmother's birth date and the building she was considering renting office space in. This is the only ancestor Janis had whom she had known and felt close to in life. Other than that one experience, it seemed that her experience of being in a more conscious relationship with the ancestors evoked more painful feelings than guidance or support. In fact, her story centered on her feelings of the lack of support she received in life and the ancestors' unwillingness to reach out to her.

Janis is the only woman in the group whose parents were both still living at the time. It seemed that her more conscious relationship with the ancestors released libidinal energy that had been frozen, inaccessible, and blocked. In her first dialogue anger and grief came to the surface full force. Reflecting on her experience a few months after our group ended, she said that her relationship with her family and the ancestors is more realistic now. It appears that the work she did allowed her to see, feel, and accept things about her family that had been too painful to experience. Based on Janis's experience, I began to wonder how engaging in a more conscious dialogue with the ancestors when one or both parents are still living affects the experience of personal family complexes and one's experience of the ancestors' support.

If we look at the ancestors from the Dagara perspective, once a parent has become an ancestor his or her perspective on life and relationship with living descendants changes. According to Jung, when a person dies the emotional ties that bind her to her relatives, sink into the unconscious where "they activate a collective content."[69] This would suggest that when one's parents are living the emotional ties that bind are experienced very personally within the immediacy of the relationship. Janis's experiences of grief and rage were still tied to and being reenacted in her personal relationship with her parents as well as being part of an ancestral, collective content in the unconscious. Very few of the people I've worked with have parents who are still living. Similar to Janis, for those whose parents, one or both, are living, the reparative work, and the work of individuation needs to include working with the dynamics in one's relationship with living relatives as well as the ancestors.

When parents are living, we continue to have experiences with them that seeded and continue to affirm the original family and personal complexes. Our interactions tend to reinforce these patterns. From a psychological point of view, those complexes have not yet fallen away from the world into the collective contents of the unconscious. From the Dagara point of view, one's parents while living do not have the "higher" perspective that is available to them after death. Doing the necessary psychological work as part of the work of addressing ancestral and cultural complexes is important for anyone in modern western culture. It is especially critical for individuals whose parents are still living. In my experience, when a parent or both parents are still living, including a deceased grandparent or another ancestor from one's family as an ally is extremely helpful in assisting individuals in unraveling the ties that bind them to those parental and familial complexes.

When there is still an unintegrated aspect of a complex, when a complex still carries a powerful affective charge, after someone dies, especially if it's one's mother or father, it seems that there are two figures or aspects of that ancestor that are present in the dialogue. One, like my initial experience of my grandfather, is purely loving. The other, is like a caricature of the person, a personification of the complex. Working with the personified complex is supported by feeling and seeing the loving ancestor who is behind it as one works with the more problematic personification of the complex.

Working with personal family complexes after the deaths of my grandfather and my parents, was different than when they were still living. I worked with these complexes in dialogues with the personified negative aspects of the complex supported by the loving presence of the ancestor who had, as Malidoma suggests, a "higher" perspective. As a result of this conscious engagement the two figures who had been split, the caricature of the complex and the loving ancestor, integrated into one figure who contained it all—the good, the bad and the ugly. I was then able to open more completely to the love and support that was available from them. The clearest example of this is in the story of my grandfather. My first experience of him as an ancestor was one of pure love. I could not accept it. It would take years of doing the hard, very necessary, psychological work and many ancestor dialogues and rituals before I would be able to authentically forgive him and open to his love.

In Service to Well-Being

Biographies begin in relationship with a time, a place, and a family. As we followed the symptomatic, emotional, and synchronistic threads and placed them in the context of the stories of our ancestors we began to see that our individual lives were part of a greater web of relationships that transcends the boundaries of time and space. The healing that took place reached beyond the boundaries of our circle. This is most evident in Tracy's story of her grandmother losing her taste for alcohol and Janis's father reaching out to her for the first time in 20 years.

Immediately following our last group session Diane attended a family wedding. She spent three weeks with her sister, nephews, and their families. She attributes her ability to see family dynamics more clearly to her experiences in our group. She saw the ways the patterns that she is aware of now that are common to her lineage were lived out and through her nephews. She and her sister talked more openly about their relationship with their father. Emotions and feelings that had not been felt or expressed before were.

For most of the individuals I work with, their dialogues with the ancestors usually bring them face to face with intergenerational trauma, illness, addiction, abuse, and other intergenerational family patterns. This is where the work usually begins. In light of what we now know from Jung, the Dagara, and American Indian understanding of the "unearthed abuses" that haunt us, this is not surprising. Generations of ancestors, untended, are waiting for their lament to be heard and for us to respond with love. As patterns are transformed and healing occurs, we can open more easily to the support and guidance that is available to us from the ancestors. What is apparent for the women whose stories are shared in this book and for the many other individuals I've worked with is that tending our relationship with the ancestors is always in service to restoring balance and harmony, to the well being that, as the spirit of the depths tells Jung, decides how we live. Following the path backward we create a new pathway for love to flow between the generations through each of us in the present moment.

Every Step We Take is Supported by a Thousand Ancestors

A scene from the movie *Amistad*, based on actual events in this country's history, John Adams and Cinque talk in Adams' greenhouse the night before their case is to be heard in front of the Supreme Court, seems apropos. Cinque, along with other men, have been seized from their homeland of Sierra Leone and sold into slavery.[70] They free themselves from their shackles and successfully take over the slave ship, only to be captured by the US Navy, brought to Connecticut, and put on trial. Although the case is won, it is appealed and eventually goes to the Supreme Court. This part of their dialogue (which I recorded from the DVD) seemed particularly poignant. It occurs the night before Adams presents this case to the Supreme Court of the United States. Adams tells Cinque that it is going to be an exceptionally difficult test. In response, Cinque tells Adams they are not going into this alone. Adams says, of course, they have right on their side. Cinque meant his ancestors would be with them. Calling into the past, "far into the beginning of time," Cinque begs his ancestors to help him. He finishes with these words: "And they must come . . . for at this moment I am the whole reason they have existed at all. In his speech to the Supreme Court Adams also calls on the ancestors—Washington, Jefferson, Franklin Adams and others—the ancestors of the guiding principles on which this government is founded, in a very moving and eloquent speech.

Each individual life matters. From the perspective of the ancestors, each descendent is the whole reason they have existed at all. We are each individual "historic fragments" whose lives are interwoven into the lives of our ancestors reaching back to the beginning of creation. Knowing where one comes from in the broadest and deepest sense informs who one is and the direction of one's life. Within these connections, as one finds oneself in the crowd of ancestral spirits, the meaning of our suffering is revealed in ways that assist us in embracing our fate and embodying and fulfilling our destiny. Simply said—the ancestors, as part of our larger community, support and guide us in living the life we were born to live. This work reconnects us in ever widening circles to our origins, has the potential to reconnect us with the soul of the world and ultimately leads us back to ourselves and our individual, unique and necessary life.

CHAPTER 12

Implications for Jungian Psychology and Healing

Everything is deeply connected intergenerationally; what happens to one generation affects generations that follow. We must therefore be good stewards with the life we are given.

—JoEllen Koerner[1]

While the archetypal level of the collective unconsciousness is sometimes taken into account therapeutically, looking at one's personal story and individual history within the context of one's ancestors as it is woven into the various levels of the collective unconscious is not. Current clinical models and approaches to healing, for the most part, do not include the concept that each individual life exists in the broader and deeper interrelated context that is the foundation of Indigenous Science and a necessary and integral aspect of ancestral soul work. Nor do most models and practices reflect the changing paradigm Tarnas, Bernstein, and others identify as part of the evolutionary movement of consciousness at this particular time in our collective story. Bernstein believes that it is only in the last few years that the Western psyche can even approach these ideas in all of their complexity.[2]

In *Living in the Borderland*, Bernstein describes the limitations of most current Western models of psychology for working with transrational experiences. He discusses the differences between and importance of using both Western and Navajo concepts of healing when working with patients. Jungian psychology, according to Bernstein, and I would concur, is the only psychology "that unqualifiedly embraces transpersonal experience and spirituality as an integral part of normal human experience and an essential consideration in clinical practice."[3] Creating a bridge between Jungian psychology and Indigenous Science, two different but complementary ways of seeing and knowing ourselves and our world, establishes the necessary theoretical foundation for understanding and therapeutically applying what is now visible through our stories as they exist in the broader and deeper context of ancestral, historical, and cultural stories.

The stories offered in this book are a small but significant initial exploration into the nature and dynamics of the relationship between the ancestors and individuals in modern Western culture through the experiences of a few women. As we opened to the possibility that our suffering and our gifts found places of origination beyond our experiences within our immediate families, we discovered the voices of our ancestors speaking to us in our physical symptoms and traumas, our longing to belong, in dreams, nature and synchronicities, our grief and rage, and even in our interpersonal relationships. This exploration was not only transformative for each of us personally; it was also transformative for our families and for the ancestors themselves.

Recognizing that we were being addressed by the ancestors was a turning point in identifying and healing inherited patterns that had previously been attributed only to our immediate family history. Our experiences suggest that family patterns like addictions and abuse may have ancestral origins. The deeper origins of our gifts and of what calls us into life also have origins within these levels. While our experiences are unique and not necessarily generalizable or predictive, they are representative of the kinds of experiences and underlying dynamics that are characteristic of the relationship between the ancestors and those of us who are living in this world.[4] Our encounters and the effects of engaging in an active dialogical process with the ancestors have implications for the way we understand and address our physical, emotional, mental, spiritual and collective well-being. The dynamics that can be observed in our stories, I would suggest, are pertinent for those who are living on the same soil where their ancestors' bones are buried, as they were for Jung, as well as for those of us who, in this ever increasingly globally connected world, have ancestors from different lands than the land where we are currently living. Whatever lands our ancestors came from and wherever we are currently living, discerning where the origins of one's symptoms and gifts are located within the levels of the unconscious is an important aspect of this work.

Personal and Cultural Complexes—The Sins of the Fathers

As Jung stated, and as is evident in our stories, our inheritance includes the sins and debts of our forebears. The memories of these sins and debts, if no longer conscious, reside in "the land of the dead," the unconscious, and in the land itself. Over time, these "sins," like a snowball rolling down a hill, gain momentum and weight across generations and within the collective. When untended, harmony and balance are lost not just personally, but in our families, communities, nations, the planet, and the psyche. If it has

been generations since one has tended one's relationship with the ancestors, there could be many inherited sins waiting to be addressed, resolved,
and redeemed.

Our personal biographies recall very specific times, places, and events
in the lives of our ancestors. Resituating our personal stories in the context
of our ancestors' stories opens the possibility for new ways of understanding and healing personal and transgenerational patterns. Strong emotions,
somatic symptoms and the iconic images of the psyche can provide the
thread of connection between consciousness and what is hidden in the
shadows of the unconscious waiting to be remembered. Picking up a thread
from the present and following it through the labyrinth of the levels of the
unconscious, we may discover the complex nature of the origins of our
wounds, gifts and individual purpose.

Through our stories we can see that the composition of our complexes
are multi-levelled. Differentiating the levels of the collective unconscious
provides a context for listening, understanding and addressing the ways
particular patterns from an often complex ancestry with a diversity of lineages are remembered and expressed. Although the same archetypal spark
is threaded through each level, its iteration in one's ancestry through family, clan, nation, and the ever more inclusive levels, has specificity unique
to each of our individual, familial, ancestral, and cultural heritages.

Jung's theory of complexes provides a theoretical framework for
understanding the nature of the phenomenon of intergenerational trauma as
it is expressed and experienced in the present. Each complex has an archetypal nucleus. According to Jolande Jacobi, the "face" and nature of the
complex is comprised of a variety of associations "stemming in part from
innate personal disposition and in part from individual experiences condi-
tioned by the environment."[5] For example, mother is a collectively shared
archetypal core complex. Each culture, time, and place has its own representation and experience of the mother archetype. Each individual's experience of this archetype, while culturally influenced, is unique based on
their personal experience of mother and, I would suggest, their ancestry.[6]

Complexes, which are autonomous by nature, "seem—like all manifestations of the unconscious—not to belong to the ego . . . to be qualities
of outside objects or persons, in other words, *projections*."[7] Jacobi defines
projection as the "automatic extrapolation of a psychic content into an
object."[8] A projection is a manifestation of unconscious contents that are
"foreign" to the ego, to one's self-identity, one's image of oneself or the
world, into objects outside of oneself. This could be another person, family, ethnic group, nation, or any part of the natural world. Jacobi writes;
"Everything that is unconscious in man is projected by him into an object
situated outside his ego."[9] The concepts of alien and "other" hold the

essential nature of the experience of a projection. Recognizing the face and nature of one's complexes and the way they affect our perception of and reactions to others and the world is at the heart of Jungian psychology.

Having an intellectual understanding of any particular complex is important. However, for transformation to take place, connecting with the feeling tone and the emotional power that characterizes the complex is necessary. According to Jung, the excess, unconscious emotional energy that is stored in the complex has to be discharged and assimilated. Only when it is fully experienced and known can the projection be withdrawn from the world and integrated into consciousness.[10] According to Jacobi, in her explanation of Jung's theory, this occurs through a dialectical process with the personified complex.[11]

Someone asked me if this work was necessary for everyone to do. I've found that there is often one person in a family who seems to be the one who is called to work with the intergenerational traumas and patterns of addiction, suicide or motherless children. I have come to imagine those individuals as the crows in their family—the ones who are the "shit eaters," the ones who pick the bones clean until they are white.[12] However, coming into a more conscious relationship with one's ancestors is valuable whether or not there is significant trauma in one's family.

Diane's story is one example of someone who did not have significant personal or intergenerational trauma to address. She experienced her ancestors as supportive presences who provided ongoing guidance that helped her with the changes and choices she faced in her life. Her life, as she saw it, "began" with her first experience of an ancestor's, her father's, presence. Her life clearly began before that moment. What "began" that day in Mexico was a conscious awareness of her gifts. Her career path unfolded in a new and very unexpected way as a result of this encounter. For all of us, coming into a more conscious relationship with the ancestors informs our understanding of our fate and destiny, opens us to the ancestors' support and guidance, and to a deepened sense of belonging. This experience is poignantly expressed in every episode of the television show "Who Do You Think You Are?"[13]

Ancestors and Complexes—A Multi-levelled Approach

My experiences with clients and the experiences of the women whose stories are shared in this book, suggest that the levels Jung's identifies within the unconscious also exist in our complexes in a way that is unique to each individual. Whatever one believes about the soul after death, Jung's theory of complexes provides a way to understand and work with the dynamic of intergenerational complexes and ancestral influences psychologically. For the purposes of considering the implications of this work from a purely psychological framework, I'd like to put aside for the moment questions about whether or not any aspect of consciousness continues after the death of the body, whether or not the soul has a continuing existence after death, and whether or not the ancestors are "really real" and have an actual existence just on the other side of this reality.

The stories shared in this book contain many examples of the way engaging in a dialogue with an ancestor—which can be understood psychologically as a dialectical process with a personified complex—fits Jung's conceptualization of the autonomous nature of complexes as well as his ideas about the process that is necessary for the integration of these complexes into consciousness. The entry point and thread of connection to any complex is always through affect and image. In our stories, connecting to the ancestral origins of our personal wounds was often the result of following a powerful emotion, bodily sensation or image. Abandonment at birth was a theme in Tracy's personal experience of being born and giving birth. Tracy re-experienced this sense of abandonment and control at the hands of patriarchal medical practices during childbirth as an ancestral memory. There are many other examples of this in our stories. Through the dialogues each of us "came-to-know" that our personal experience was the tip of the iceberg of a complex that also had ancestral and cultural elements.

A purely psychological way of understanding the presence of an ancestor or a spirit would be as an autonomous complex.[14] However, from a close reading of Jung, we see that this is a partial understanding. Jung differentiates between the figures of the unconscious and the "spirits of the departed," as he experienced them in dreams. In his account of his experience of his wife in a dream about a year after her death he writes, "I knew that I had been with her in the south of France, in Provence and had spent an entire day with her."[15] Years after his dream of the "bewigged gentleman," one of "an assemblage of distinguished spirits of earlier centuries," he would come to understand that this figure was "an ancestral spirit, or spirit of the dead."[16] In one instance the figure is an individual; in the other, the figure embodies an ancestral spirit from another time. In yet another encounter Jung comes face-to-face with a figure who "lives the history of the world."[17] Each of these figures is particular to a different level of the collective unconscious.

Acknowledging an ancestor as a "really real," presence, as Jung does explicitly in his dream of Emma, is not incompatible with recognizing the archetypal nature of the complex he or she may also personify. The reality of a dream figure, a ghost, or an ancestor who one encounters in a dialogue as "really real" does not mean that one isn't also working with a personified complex. Both ways of imagining the presence and reality of an ancestor are valid. The perspective that an ancestor is, in some form, the person we knew in life, *and*, that there may be a complex that is related to and activated by their presence sheds light on the shadows of these shadows. Considering and engaging with the ancestors from both perspectives has therapeutic value.

As you might imagine, my relationship with my mother was complex. For years after she died I experienced her in my dialogues as two figures—one was the loving, joyful soul who danced with the glass of champagne off into the world behind the world, the other was a personification of the complex I was so familiar with. I engaged in dialogues with both. Each informed the other. The affective charge embodied in the figure of the "terrible mother" finally, after five years of intense work, transformed. The two figures of mother—terrible and loving—were no longer split in two in the imaginal figure and in my experience and memory of my personal mother.

Near the end of this process, in addition to the traumatic memories of my mother, I began to remember experiences with her that were loving, supportive and joyful. My mother's last question to me, her last words, were, "do you know I love you!?" It was more a desperate, demanding plea than a question. I couldn't answer her then. There was a vacuum between us. In that vacuum was the complex. Gradually, I opened to the love that had always been there and could answer her last question to me with a "yes." The imaginal work, as is always the case, was mirrored in my relationships in the world.

When I work with clients I always hold a place for both figures—the personified complex and the loving ancestor. As I stated previously, for individuals in modern Western culture, it is critical to provide a psychological container when engaging in any ancestral work, especially when there is significant trauma or a pattern of addiction in the lineage. As is evident in the stories shared in this book, coming into a more conscious dialogue with the ancestors in a way that does redeem, resolve and bring "salvation" to them does not happen in one ritual or one dialogue, or even in a month of group work.

When an individual participates in rituals or other types of work designed to facilitate a relationship with the ancestors it can open the door to very difficult material. When that door is opened by anyone in a family, the entire family feels the effects. It is not uncommon when a person participates in an ancestral soul work group for the "problem" to surface in the family in a very compelling way by the second week. What is available in this work is the loving support and guidance that is always available from the ancestors and the support of the group. That, in my experience, is the difference that makes the difference between recovering and being cured, between a partial withdrawal of a projection from the world and a more complete transformation of the complex. This complete transformation is most apparent in JoEllen's experience of patriarchal oppression in her vision quest.

Cultural and Ancestral Complexes

Each of us is related to the collective human story in very specific ways through our ancestors. Our experience of collectively shared cultural and historical traumas, like racism or patriarchal oppression, is informed by specific events, times and places in our lives, in the lives of our ancestors and the history of the land on which we live. Listening to how the ancestors are "speaking" to us through synchronistic dates, family stories and photos, dreams and imaginal dialogues can reveal the connection between their past and our present. As a result, each complex at the collective levels is shaded, colored and experienced in a unique way by each individual. Including the possibility that our ancestors are implicated in our personal as well as our cultural complexes opens us to understanding these complexes in new ways.

The stories shared in this book expand our understanding of the relationship between individual, familial, ancestral, and cultural complexes. Like pieces of a hologram, each person and each lineage experiences and expresses cultural complexes in a unique and personal way. Identifying where our personal story and the stories of our ancestors are connected to our collective history informs the way cultural complexes are constellated within our psyche. Engaging in a more conscious dialogue with the ancestors brings to light the particular contours of these very individually configured multi-layered complexes. Transformation of the complex, from the personal through the levels of the collective, happens as we feel the emotional resonance between the personal, ancestral, and cultural aspects of a complex. As these connections are made and one listens and responds, the unconscious emotional energy that has been held in the shadows is felt and experienced in a way that has the potential to reach into and be transformative within the many levels of the complex for each of us personally, and, I would suggest, also for our ancestors and descendants.

Our stories suggest that in addition to cultural complexes there are ancestral complexes. The bitterness in Kathryn's lineage, the shroudedness in Janis's, addiction in Tracy's, and a loss of faith in God in mine are some examples. Ancestral complexes are specific to one's family lineage, situated at the family and clan levels of the collective unconscious. Our stories suggest that ancestral complexes are, like cultural complexes as described by Singer and Kimbles, a result of "trauma, discrimination, feelings of oppression, and inferiority at the hands of another."[18] Recognizing and experiencing the relationship between individual trauma in the present and ancestral and collective trauma as it exists in one's lineage through dialogue and ritual, brings one face to face in personally meaningful ways with cultural complexes. Addressing and working with the cultural complex in this multi-levelled way contributes to bringing consciousness to and transforming the complex at the cultural level within each individual.

This dynamic can be seen in the particular way Tracy, JoEllen and I experienced the patriarchal complex. While sharing an archetypal core, the face and experience of patriarchal oppression at the familial, clan and national levels, was unique for each of us. For Tracy, this face was personified in the doctor present at birth. For JoEllen, it was in the faces of the women, men and the God of her Mennonite heritage and the Western medical tradition. I experienced the reality of this oppression in many forms: at the hands of my grandfather, in my relationship with my personal mother, in the dream of the women in my mother line, and in the rape and colonization of the land. At the clan level, this complex appeared to me as the black-robed Christian priest and as the men and women in JoEllen's Mennonite tradition. The black-robed priest was both oppressor and oppressed. At the ancestral level, the story of this patriarchal complex lived in the women in my mother line who had been severed from their indigenous roots and the source of their feminine power.

Each level within a complex has its story. Following the thread of affective resonance through the levels of the collective unconscious, hearing the laments, questions, pleas, demands, and stories in each iteration, results in a more complete understanding and experience of what lives in the shadows of "the land of the dead" waiting to be remembered, redeemed and resolved. My connection to that moment in our collective story when Providence was burned is a clear example of the relationship between an individual complex and ancestral, cultural and historical complexes. The cultural historical complex that Gustafson identifies is personified in the Native American figure I encountered in the imaginal dialogue described in Chapter 1. At first I was the Indian, identified with him through my personal experience of trauma psychically and somatically. As I stayed with the powerful emotional and physical experience, the personal and cultural aspect of the complex began to differentiate. The cultural level of this complex became distinct and personified in the figure of the Indian. Standing on the hill, no longer identified but in relationship with the Indian, I experienced the connection and relationship between the personal and cultural levels of this complex.

Following the differentiation between the Indian and myself, my ancestor Roger appeared. His presence revealed the ancestral aspect of the cultural complex. In the present, I connected in a very personal way with the story of this land and its people and with the story of my ancestor through the intense somatic and affective re-experiencing of the PTSD that was part of the legacy and a result of the trauma I experienced growing up. The way this collectively shared cultural complex was constellated in my psyche was specific to my lineage and personal experience of childhood trauma.

Integration of the shadowed pieces of any complex requires knowing and experiencing it fully. As is evident in Linda's, Kat's, JoEllen's and my stories, to be complete, healing the personal experience of trauma had to include and address the complex through its ever more collectively inclusive levels. Although our stories are different, the process, experience and outcome of healing in this comprehensive way is similar. My experiences of the complex at each level informed the other levels in ever deepening and widening circles of understanding. The pattern of motherless children finally ended when JoEllen witnessed and experienced the reality of the patriarchal complex in all of its forms and was able to find forgiveness in her heart that reached into and transformed this complex as it existed within the many levels of the unconscious.

Understanding our complexes in this way changes the way we see, interpret and understand our personal and cultural complexes. Even though we may be unconscious or unaware of the specific nature and origins of a particular cultural complex within our personal lineage, the way it is constellated affects us in the present and colors the personal experiences we have in very particular ways. I've witnessed many people in the moment when they open to the possibility that their personal experience of addiction or a hauntingly powerful emotion like bitterness may have origins that extend into their ancestry. In these moments it appears that the emotional resonance within the field of the psyche expands beyond the boundaries of one's self. In these moments of expanded awareness, righteousness, resentment, anger, fear and hurt are often replaced by feelings of profound empathy and compassion when the person's story reaches beyond the boundaries of their personal history.

The connections can be as complex and comprehensive as JoEllen's or as simple as Kathryn's realization that the bitterness she felt might have be echoed in the experience of her ancestors. Being connected to the cultural complex in a very personal way, the cultural complex is fully experienced and worked with as one would work with any complex. These moments are transformative. Kathryn felt deeper empathy and compassion for herself and her parents as she discovered evidence of feelings of bitterness in the stories of the women in her lineage. Forgiving my grandfather, something that had seemed impossible, occurred spontaneously only after my understanding and therapeutic work with my personal trauma expanded to include the ancestral and cultural levels.

The political, the historical, the cultural *is* personal. And, the personal is political, historical, and cultural. This is at the heart of Linda's story. Linda, Kat, and I experienced the tragic cultural legacy of colonization and oppression that Gustafson believes has yet to be fully addressed, in very individual ways. Each of us has ancestors who were personally involved at different times in history with the collective history of genocide, dislocation and trauma suffered by the people native to this land, to America. Each of us responded to the particular history we carried in our bones through ritual and ceremony in ways that were reparative for each of us personally, and, I would suggest, for those who had come before and those who will follow. Recognizing, acknowledging, witnessing, experiencing, and grieving this history as it was remembered in the present through our individual stories was an important part of our personal healing journey. Although Janis did not have an experience of directly connecting the rage and grief she felt to this collective story, I would suggest that it was part of her inheritance from her Cheyenne grandmother whose picture fascinated her from the moment she saw it. I believe with more time she would have made this connection herself.

In their essay on the relationship between personal and collective trauma, Weisstub and Gallili-Weisstub observe that "cultural traumas and complexes which develop in response to the traumas are linked to a group's inability to mourn."[19] Gustafson describes the grief that saturates this land and the psyches of all those who live on in America.[20] I experienced this grief during the transferential dialogue that brought me back to that moment in King Philip's War when my ancestor stood on the hillside overlooking Providence as it burned. The experience of this collective grief was almost unbearable. Mourning and grieving the losses that were and *are* a result of these historical, collective traumas is at the heart of healing this trauma personally, ancestrally and collectively.[21]

As Ezechiel tells Jung in *The Red Book*, it is the responsibility of the living to redeem "those roaming dead" and restore what was "created and later subjugated and lost."[22] Following the threads of one's personal story through the interconnected levels of the unconscious, "seeing, admitting, and weeping," as Gustafson suggests, contributes to transforming the cultural complex.[23] Taking reparative action is an integral part of healing collective trauma. Individual and collective action is a natural and necessary response for anyone who is psychologically grounded in a cultural complex transformed by grief, rather than one that is split by blame and guilt.

It appears to me that there are those, like Kat and myself, who have a direct responsibility to redeem and restore balance and harmony as it exists in and relates to specific incidents in the lives of our ancestors that is part of our collective story. Some do not. Although Diane had a direct link through John Bozeman to a time when Indians in Montana were being displaced and slaughtered, she didn't experience or become aware of any way this part of her family legacy needed to be addressed by her during our group. This aspect of her ancestry did not seem to call for her attention or any specific action in response to her ancestor's legacy or the cultural complex Gustafson identifies. I have two sisters and a brother. We share the same ancestry. My sisters and I were all molested by our grandfather. However, their personal stories are not informed by the same collective stories as mine. They do not feel a connection with Roger and do not experience their childhood trauma in relationship with the ancestral, cultural or ecological trauma as I do.

Identifying the origins of the cultural complexes as they are constellated in and experienced by an individual informs one's response-ability personally, ancestrally and culturally. The experiences shared in this book open many questions about each individual's relationship with cultural complexes.[24] The dream of Hasseldorf and my experience of intense sadness while writing Kathryn's story, suggests that, for people living on in America, particularly those descended from more recent immigrants, there may be traumas that are waiting to be addressed from the land of one's ancestors that are still alive and potent in the psyches of their descendants. The experience of collective trauma that infuses this land and the cultural complexes that result from that trauma may be experienced differently by more recent immigrants than by the descendants of earlier colonizers and settlers. And, the cultural complexes that are the most potent and influential in an individual's life may arise from the culture and land of their ancestors.

Following the natural and organic process of the unconscious, guided by dreams, synchronicities, and what comes to light though imaginal dialogues, each of us can become aware of how our personal and ancestral complexes are implicated in and specifically connected to cultural complexes. Whether or not and how particular cultural complexes are experienced is something that each person has to personally explore. Looking at the ancestral dimension of cultural complexes can add to one's understanding of personal illness and trauma and inform what is being asked for in the present in response to cultural complexes like racism in a way that is transformative and healing personally and collectively. Reconnecting with the origins of collective trauma as it exists within the stories and experiences of our ancestors contributes to healing and transformation, personally, within one's family, and through one's lineage and the various levels within the collective unconscious. In this way, our personal and cultural complexes are also transformed one person, one story at a time. One step at a time, sometimes running, sometimes standing in the same place unable to move, we are always moving within and through the levels toward the center of the self, and opening the channel for love to flow between the generations.

Racism and the National Unconscious

The dream I had of European ancestors while writing the stories of the women in the group brought to light the shadow of racism related to a very particular place in Germany—Hasseldorf—a place that in actuality borders on Denmark. The people's clothes, the landscape and the buildings in the dream indicated a specific historical time, a time when roads were not paved, probably some time before the Industrial Revolution. The ancestors in the dream from that part of the world and that time lived in the shadow of racism and sought redemption. They asked to be interviewed, to have their stories heard. The dream indicated that listening to their stories, witnessing this shadow, was the key to their redemption. These shadowed cultural complexes exist in each of us.

Every woman in the group had German ancestors except for me. My father's grandparents immigrated from Denmark and Sweden. My guess is that although I don't have German ancestors, it is likely that this shadow may also be present and have origins in my Scandinavian ancestry. Racism, like any emotionally charged psychic content, has psychic vitality and energic power which, if unacknowledged and unwitnessed has transgenerational consequences. I would suggest that this shadowed memory was constellated as a result of this particular group of women coming together.[25] This dream indicated that the shadow of racism as it exists in the psyche of individuals born on American soil with German ancestry, might have origins in the homeland of their ancestors. This racism originated not at the personal or familial levels of the unconscious, but at the ancestral level. It pointed to racism as it existed in the culture and land of our German ancestors, not the racism that is so deeply rooted in the history of American culture. This is one specific example of the complexity of the shadow in the American psyche that Jung advised his analysts to approach carefully.

It is interesting to consider our understanding of and responses to racism in light of this dream. If this dream is listened to from the perspective presented in this book, for some of us, addressing racism in the present requires witnessing racism as it exists at the ancestral level of the collective unconscious in the stories of our European ancestors. Picking up this thread and responding to the need expressed by the ancestors in the dream brings consciousness to the origins of racism on this continent in a very personal way. Recognizing how we are related to these shadows through our ancestors is the beginning of transforming the story in the present. To address the effects of racism, action in the world is critical and necessary. Finding the threads of connection as they are woven into the ancestral level of cultural complexes like racism within one's lineage informs how each of us responds personally to its effects in both the inner and outer worlds.

Individual and Collective Individuation

As Jung describes it, the "land of the dead," the unconscious, reaches back into "a preconscious and prehistoric world."[26] These historical antecedents carry a memory that points to and shapes the future. Wherever one enters the story, time and again, one is looking into the mirror. It is not only our grandfather's French nose we see, it is a particular combination of the complex shadows, memories and gifts of our ancestors and all our relations. For the women whose stories have been shared, looking deeply into this mirror brought us face to face with those things in our ancestry that waited in the shadows until redeemed and resolved. Reflected in the depths of our lineage we also saw the qualities, resiliencies and gifts that made us uniquely who we are. For some of us, discovering what questions were ours to answer opened us to a deeper understanding of our vocation. What pursued us became our pursuit.

Our stories suggest that for some of us, coming into a more conscious relationship with the ancestors is an integral part of the process of individuation. Jung describes this process as a differentiation of oneself from the collective and an integration of the fragmentary pieces of soul that reside in the unconscious. Photograph by photograph, memory by memory, story by story, we pick up the pieces of personal, ancestral and cultural shadows and integrate them into a story that is uniquely ours. In this process of individuation as we more consciously engage with the reverberating echoes of the stories of our ancestors, we experience a deep relatedness to all our relations and to the soul of the world. Rather than being at the hands of an unconscious fate, we participate consciously in giving shape to our destiny. Following the path backward, the goal becomes not to change the past, but to embrace and add our small and very particular part to the continuing, ever evolving, collective story.

I began to wonder about the relationship between an individual, his or her family and the greater collective body as it relates to the process of individuation. If complexes are multi-generational and multi-leveled within the collective unconscious, and, if transformation in one affects transformation within the entire interconnected collective web, might individuation also occur within a family, within one's lineage? JoEllen's, Kathryn's, Diane's, and my stories placed in relationship with each other and Jung's experiences and theories provide insight into this question.

JoEllen experienced the effects of the patriarchal shadow in herself, her daughter's suffering, her ancestors and her Mennonite tradition. In her vision quest she saw its many faces and expressions and felt its effects directly and painfully. After experiencing waves of forgiveness that reached into all these levels of male oppression in the universe, a song of authenticity played in her heart. What was being asked of her now? To live authentically. Living authentically is at the heart of individuation. After her experience in the vision quest she returned to the world transformed. It "stripped away the pretense and the veneer that had coated [her] beliefs, dictated [her] choices, and shaped [her] behaviors."[27] At the end of her book she writes, "As we come to know ourselves, we suddenly see the Collective Self. . . . Scarcity is replaced with abundance, judgment is replaced with compassion, and fear is replaced with love."[28]

Wanigi Waci told JoEllen that when she forgave all male oppression in the world the women in her lineage would also be healed. Her story suggests that her personal individuation was intimately connected to the cultural complex in her lineage, from her Mennonite culture into the collective and deepest archetypal layers of consciousness. If complexes are distinguishable but related within the levels of the collective unconscious, then it follows that when one consciously engages with the shadow through the levels as JoEllen did, individuation would also occur within and through each level, always moving towards the center of the Self. This integration of the shadow and process of individuation was also interwoven into the lives of her descendants. Her daughter Kristi's healing was dependent on and connected to JoEllen's confrontation with the patriarchal shadow that haunted the women in their lineage. Released from the shadow of oppression through forgiveness, love, compassion, and joy now flowed freely within her through her ancestral and cultural lineage creating a "new forward" for her daughter and grandchildren.

Death and the End of the Ancestral Line in the World

When I began this exploration I was very curious about individuals who were the last in their line. I have been fortunate to have known two women who were the last in their line, one whose story is shared in this book. The other woman I know personally who is the last in her line has a story that is strikingly similar to Kathryn's. Like Kathryn, all of the family heirlooms, photographs and mementos had been bequeathed to her. She too found a place for these things in the world, honoring each piece and each ancestor as she did so. Both women led lives that were devoted to spiritual seeking and practices. I would describe each of their lives as spiritual pilgrimages. If, as Jung suggests, we are each a historical fragment within a story whose beginning and end reach far across time and space, and, if the dead are dependent on the living who exist in a world of change for resolution, redemption and answers, what, if anything, is signified in the life of the last person to be born in a bloodline. What might it suggest about the relationship between an individual, their bloodline and the collective with regard to individuation?

In her book *An Archetypal Approach to Death, Dreams and Ghosts*, Jaffe concludes:

> death appears as a process during which separate parts of the personality . . . come together to form a unity. This is in keeping with the task imposed upon the dying man, of releasing himself from life, in the course of which he must take back into himself whatever belongs to his nature but is still in the world and projected into the environment. This detachment, or withdrawal of projections, does not, of course, take place only at the hour of death . . . but starts when life is being most intensively lived, when the light of consciousness begins, slowly but irresistibly, to turn away from the zenith and towards the decline. From that moment on, man is faced with the task of directing his gaze inward as well as outward, in order to discover in himself what he has experienced in the world and through others. Only then is he able to become what he is. From the psychological standpoint the union with beloved or related souls at the moment of death connotes a merging of partial souls. It is an image of the soul achieving wholeness—as if death were completing what had already begun decades before.[29]

Jaffe's idea of the psychological significance of death may inform our understanding of someone who is the last person born in a lineage that spans millennia.

The stories of these two women are remarkably alike and significantly different from the stories of other people I've worked with who have descendants. Each woman had the same response to what had been bequeathed to her—it felt like a burden, and, it was hers to carry and take care of. Each item in the boxes that had been bequeathed to them carried a piece of the family's story and held a part of the family's soul. The consideration each woman gave to every inherited object and the thoughtfulness and care she gave to finding the right place in the world for each was compelling. It was not something either woman took lightly or did hastily.

Time was spent with every item in every box. Sorting through each iconic bit of their family's history was an encounter with forgotten family memories, inherited patterns and complexes. Both of these women encountered the "partial souls" of her family in a very literal way.

One by one, Kathryn held each object in her hands, listened to what it had to say about her family, and, after experiencing whatever it evoked in her, decided what she would do with it. She discovered pieces of her parents' stories which expanded her understanding and empathy for them. These keepsakes brought unknown pieces of the people and stories of many generations of her family to light. Kathryn found affirmation for her gifts, interests, and particular aptitudes in her ancestry. She also discovered the deeper origins of her suffering.

Her process with the objects in these archives was very similar to shadow work in the process of individuation—coming into conscious relationship with shadowed aspects of oneself, one's family and the world, experiencing them, accepting their "truth" and releasing oneself from their grip. Projections were withdrawn as she encountered the "truth" that photographs, letters, diaries, and keepsakes told. Some questions were answered with a photograph. Some objects gave rise to more questions, many that would never be answered. Letting go piece by piece, both women returned the physical representations of the "partial souls" of their families to the material world they came from and to which they belonged. Rather than being part of the family "baggage," each photograph, each item that carried some aspect of the projection of the world, was literally returned to it.

As discussed in Chapter 4, Jung describes the process of individuation as finding the secret pattern of oneself by putting together the pieces of the puzzle of "ancestral spirits." Putting the pieces of this puzzle together is likened to an alchemical process in which a chaotic collection of disjointed and disparate elements are, in their original condition, contained within a circle. This task seemed to be accomplished in a very concrete way by each of these women. They literally engaged in the process Jaffe describes that takes place at the moment of death. Kathryn gathered the pieces of the puzzle of her family and organized them into albums that told the story of her family. In our last group Kathryn brought the albums she had created from the things she'd found in the boxes. Her ancestor altar now bridged the archetypal, ancestral, and personal. She planned to bequeath these albums to others for safe-keeping once they were completed. As both women who were the last in their line described it, this process was informative, deeply moving, and liberating.

Their lives as spiritual seekers directed toward knowing God involved coming into a very conscious relationship with their worldly family. From his personal encounter with the unconscious, Jung came to understand that "there is no linear evolution; there is only a circumambulation of the self. Uniform development exists, at most, only at the beginning, later, everything points toward the center."[30] One way to look at the process these two women participated in is as a movement towards the center of the self. Circumambulating the individual self, the family self, the self of their lineage and the ineffable, archetypal Self, brought them back to the center of their own life.

Just as each individual is a historical fragment snipped out of a longer story, each lineage may also carry a unique history and telos with particular questions to be addressed and answered. Imagined in this way, the family serves as a historical fragment within our shared collective story. If we look at one's lineage as a whole unto itself, similar to an individual with regard to the task of individuation, and if we imagine that there comes a time when what is unresolved, unredeemed, and unanswered in each lineage has been adequately addressed, what is the significance of being the last in one's line?

Kathryn's story appears to be a story of completion, not just of her life, but of the life of her family in this world. She did the difficult and demanding psychological work of individuation. While this is something each individual who is psychologically oriented in their life may engage in, there appeared to be something perceptibly different in Kathryn's experience. In its essence, and as she described it, she was tying up the loose ends of the threads of her family.

As I write, Kathryn's words come to mind. They express her experience simply and poignantly. "When lived from a place of bitterness, life becomes a lament instead of an authentic experience of living." Remembering Ezechiel's words to Jung, to listen to the lament of the dead and accept them with love, it seems to me that Kathryn did exactly this as she went through her family's archives. As she finished this task, rather than "lamenting" that life was not what she "hoped it would be," she felt she was living the life that was hers to live. I was deeply moved by the depth of her acceptance of herself, her parents, and her ancestors. Sharing the albums with us during our last group, she seemed to be acknowledging the reality of the story of her entire family, as she knew it, and embracing it all with love. Knowing her at the end of her life I can say that she crossed the threshold of death not lamenting, but with joy. In one of our council circles she asked, "Who will do this work for me when I'm gone?" Her question stayed with me. If I were to answer it now I would say to her, "I believe for you and your family, there is no more work to be done, at least at this worldly level of existence." And, you are remembered now as your story is shared.

Impersonal Karma and Individuation

In his autobiography Jung acknowledges that he has "no answer to the question of whether the karma" he was living was a result of past lives, "or whether it is not rather the achievement of my ancestors, whose heritage comes together in me. Am I a combination of the lives of these ancestors and do I embody these lives again?"[31] He follows this question considering other possibilities that would answer the deeper question about the meaning of our existence. While he didn't come to any definitive answer, he did come to believe that there was an "impersonal karma within a family," which is passed from generation to generation.[32]

In his chapter "The Work" in *Memories, Dreams, Reflections* we can see the way the questions that were Jung's to answer were multi-levelled in their origination. This is also evident in his dialogues in *The Red Book*. There is one aspect of this impersonal karma that I'd like to note that is relevant to the concept of personal individuation and individuation within one's lineage. As described in Chapter 4, Jung's work was directly related to and picked up the threads of "the cure of souls," questions of faith, and the dark side of the image of the divine, to name a few, from his parents. After his dream in which both of his parents "appeared burdened with the problem of the 'cure of souls,'" he realized that this was [not theirs, but was] his task.[33] Jung's understanding of this and other dreams informs our understanding of the impersonal karma that exists in the relationship between oneself and one's parents.

Margaret, my younger daughter, began to experience the presence of her Danish great-great-grandmother, Grandma Schmidt, in dreams and as an imaginal presence. This was coincidental with the ancestor dialogues I was conducting with the dream figures who were in the town shadowed by racism and my Scandinavian ancestors. She has been in college in North Carolina for the past three years, the deep South. She chose to explore racism as a cultural complex as the topic for her senior thesis. She was unaware of the dream I had about the shadow of racism while writing Kathryn's story. Nor did she have any idea about the possible origins of racism in our lineage. It seems to me that she has picked up this thread and may, in doing her thesis work, help bring more consciousness to the shadow of racism that is part of our ancestral legacy and part of the legacy of America, especially associated with the South, where she has been living for the past three years. While this is only one story, it leads to questions about the way "karma" is worked through in families and the way it may be integral to the process of individuation.

When she was eleven years old Melissa and I were having a conversation about what, if she could do one thing in her life, she would do. It was a question that was part of a "crossing the threshold" ceremony that was being done with her 5th-grade class. She thought about it and said that it wasn't right that women were treated differently than men. That was what she wanted to change. As she has matured and gained more life experience, this impulse has taken shape. Her feminism is bone deep. It appears that she is living a life that is informed but not bound by the legacy of patriarchal oppression that had been haunting our lineage for centuries. Through these two examples and other experiences, I see some of the threads that run through our lineage. I have done my part, as my parents and grandparents did theirs. My daughters have picked up particular threads and are weaving their stories into the web. Each of us contributes, as Jung stated, an "infinitesimal" amount of variation and differentiation to consciousness.

The questions that were Jung's to answer, the work that was his to complete, was a result of and responsive to the "impersonal karma" he identified that exists in families. His concept of individuation is directly related to responding to the "impersonal karma" in one's family. This "impersonal karma" as it is interwoven into the levels of the unconscious from personal to archetypal is seen very clearly in my story. A failed marriage between head and heart, body and spirit, masculine and feminine, archaic and modern, was at the heart of the "impersonal karma" in my lineage. By consciously engaging with what was being asked of me in the present personal, familial, and ancestral wounds were healed. My personal healing and transformation was visible in the world and experienced by me on all levels from the physical to the spiritual. Roger's transformation and the transformation of the women in my lineage as imaginal figures seem to indicate that the healing reached into the deeper levels of the psyche.

I would suggest that each of us contributes to the individuation of our lineage, each generation contributing an infinitesimal amount to consciousness and that each lineage contributes in a particular way to our collective individuation. Does, and if so, how does this understanding matter? Applying the Jungian concept of individuation to one's lineage adds dimension to our understanding of the process of each person's individuation. It also contributes to our understanding of the dynamics at play in Jung's conceptualization of the development of consciousness over the eons of human existence. Stated psychologically, this work contributes to our collective individuation and the evolution of consciousness in ways that are very particular to each of us and to our families.

Tending one's relationship with the ancestors always brings one back to the center of the labyrinth, to one's individual life. Transformation in the psyche has an effect in the world, and, transformation in the world has an effect on the psyche. They are distinct and integrally

inseparable. To heal the gash in the land and her own body and the ancestral and collective psyche, Kat had to remember and honor the people
who had suffered at her great-grandfather's hands. There are many
examples in out stories of the interconnected nature of psyche and world.
Change occurs as each individual listens and responds to what is unredeemed, unresolved, unanswered, from ages past and to the calling of
future generations.

While our stories indicate that there is much intergenerational reparative work that needs to be done, I have come to understand that this work
is fundamentally, at its heart, in service to opening the pathway for love to
flow more freely between the generations. As our connection with the
ancestors becomes more conscious, we also benefit from their wisdom,
support and guidance. Wherever this journey into the "land of the dead"
takes one, whatever is healed or learned or asked for, it is always directed
toward this life here and now and in service to the well being of all.

The Interconnected Web of Being and the "Great Work"

Each of us and those to whom we belong, our ancestors and our descendants, were represented to me in a dream as a multi-dimensional web with
points of light shining throughout. This dream occurred in 2007 when I
was just beginning my doctoral research. Each soul consciousness was a
point of light within this intricate four-dimensional interconnected web.
Each light was an integral part of the web, always in relationship within it
to the web itself and to all the other points of light. There were parts of the
web that appeared to be broken, some places where the connecting threads
appeared to be thinner, and some where the threads were substantial, puls-
ing and bright. Some lights seemed to be more active and to emanate more
light. This web was timeless space, in which past, present, and future
were simultaneously present. Paradoxically, each light also appeared to be
located in and connected to specific moments and places in time, through
each individual light.

My task in the dream was to find a way to step into and through the
web without breaking or disturbing it. In the dream I felt clueless about
how to do this. My perception and ability to act in the dream time, within
this multi-dimensional web, was limited by my three-dimensional consciousness and my concern about doing harm.[34] I stood on one side of the
web, looking into it. A man stood on the other side looking back at me. In
the dream, at one moment he was located beside me and in the next, he was
visible on the other side of the web. He had somehow navigated his way
through it to the other side. He stood, looking at me through the web,

waiting for me to remember how to be in relationship with this web without disturbing it and to join him on the other side.

This image and the felt sense of this web offered a glimpse into the nature of the reality of the ancestral web of connections that is the foundation for this work. This image depicted individual consciousness as a light within an interconnected, interdependent web that incorporated, but was not limited to three-dimensional space and time. There is always inaccuracy in finding words to describe and represent the perceptions and understanding of the reality of the psyche within a three-dimensional, embodied framework. It is no wonder the figures of the unconscious take on cloaks of personification, or appear in aspects of the natural world in forms that are more congruent with and accessible to our conscious perceptions of reality. Learning how to be in relationship with this web is an ongoing process. The stories shared in this book are examples of how to move in relationship with this web and what happens when one does so more consciously.

When we engage more consciously with this dynamic web of being, where the dialogue will take us in the web at any given moment is unknown. We may find ourselves connected to a specific time and place, related to a historical event, or a foreign and distant landscape. Even if foreign and unfamiliar, these places, people and moments in time are, like repressed or buried memories, parts of our biography that are always present in the psyche but have yet to be consciously integrated into consciousness. What appear first as separate and disconnected pieces of memory are actually pieces of a puzzle that reveal parts of a continuous story. Sometimes a note, photograph, landscape, emotion, a physical sensation, illness, or a dream, can be the key that unlocks a chain of connections. Sometimes we cannot find a thread to hold onto. Some mysteries are solved while others retain their original inscrutability.

As I was working on this chapter I had another dream. It was simple, but deeply moving. In the dream I was in the midst of the cosmos, suspended in the night sky among a canopy of stars. This "land"scape was reminiscent of the web in the dream described above. I felt completely at peace and joy filled. I looked down and saw a beautiful, vivid spring-green cord that extended from the center of my body connecting me to the Earth far below. Running down the center of this cord was a dark red line, a bloodline. Waking into the memory of this dream, I felt an embodied, vibrant, resonant connection with both the Earth and the cosmos through the bloodline that flowed within the natural liquid green, vital, living fluid of nature in the cord that connected me to the Earth.

My experience in this dream expanded my understanding of each individual's relationship with the cosmos and the Earth. I knew then that being in a more conscious relationship with the ancestors is part of the ecological work that is so necessary at this time in the history of our planet. Our modern, western, egoic consciousness separated from its roots in the Earth and in the psyche needs to be greened. Originating in the cosmological matrix of being, our individual bloodlines, centered in the living green fluid of nature, connect us to this Earth. Part of the greening of consciousness involves opening to and tending our relationship with the world of the ancestors, "the land of the dead" as human beings who are connected through our bloodlines to the body of the Earth.

That morning, after waking from the dream, I made my first cup of Earl Grey tea and, as I always do, went to my home office to write. As I walked into the room, the books on the shelves drew my attention. Thomas Berry's book *The Great Work: Our Way into the Future* stood out. Berry dedicates this book to all the children, not just human, but the winged, the four-legged and finned, the floral and arborous. According to Berry, there have been many "Great Works" in human history. He perceives that the Great Work of this time "is to carry out the transition from a period of devastation of the Earth to a period when humans would be present to the planet in a mutually beneficial manner."[35] Berry believes that it's time for us to recognize that we are part of "a single integral community of the Earth" and to find ways to live sustainably and in harmony with all life on this planet.[36] While he attributes the devastating damage done to the planet to humans, he believes that every part of this integral community has its own voice and role in the Great Work of our time. For Berry, "the entire universe" must be "involved in the healing of the damaged Earth."[37]

Berry believes that our future rests not on some scientific insight or socioeconomic arrangement, but on our capacity for relatedness and presence to all beings, and our "participation in a symphony" or a "renewed presence to some numinous presence manifested in the wonderworld about us."[38] He believes what is needed is something "beyond our present cultural traditions" individually and collectively. This fundamental shift requires radical new cultural forms which "place the human within the dynamics of the planet rather than the planet within the dynamics of the human."[39] To accomplish this he suggests that we turn to our "genetic coding" whose "tendencies are derived from the larger community of the Earth and eventually from the universe itself" for our primary source of guidance.[40] The "genetic coding," as Berry imagines it, includes the archetypal forms that are the part of our inheritance and the foundation of consciousness. This concept is fundamental to Jung's psychology.

This underlying archetypal matrix of consciousness connects us through time and space to all of creation.[41] As Jung states in his essay, "The Significance of Constitution and Heredity in Psychology," we are no different than "primitive" humans with regard to the archetypal foundation of consciousness. We are all part of an interrelated whole that transcends the boundaries of time, space, and species. Psychological wellbeing, according to Jung, is dependent on living in harmony with the unconscious.[42] However, our modern, egoic consciousness, fearing that our freedom and autonomy will be compromised, understandably resists the influence of the unconscious and reconnecting with the "archaic" roots of consciousness.[43]

Jung's conceptualizes the unconscious as "intelligent and purposive" and compensatory to consciousness "in an intelligent way, as if it were trying to restore the lost balance."[44] He ends his essay on the significance of constitution and heredity stating unequivocally that neglect and disregard of the collective unconscious results in pathological disturbances. These disturbances are apparent in our psychological and physical symptoms, our interpersonal, cross-cultural and cross-species relationships, and the rapidly increasing extinction of species, climate changes, and the poisoning of our living planet.

Gustafson believes that the human community must either find its way back to our indigenous roots psychologically and in relationship with the Earth or "there will be no earth or soul to pass on to our children seven generations from now."[45] Being in a more conscious dialogue with the ancestors facilitates *and* necessitates a reconnection with our "archaic," "primal," "original" mind. According to Gustafson, this "inner indigenous one,"

> this ancient being has been subdued and forgotten by the western way of life—a way of life that has uprooted itself from the earth and the earth we are. It has made harsh demands on the fundamental ways of the soul: how we worship, how we play, how we structure family, how we politic, how we run our economy, or how we imagine the future unto the seventh generation.[46]

Gustafson believes, and I and my ancestors wholeheartedly agree, to "redeem the inner Indigenous One" is a task that is critical "for each of us and for our culture as a whole."[47] As Bernstein has observed, the reconciliation of this separation from the roots of consciousness and, consequently from nature, is "a natural evolutionary dynamic" that is evident in individuals he identifies as Borderlanders.[48]

In May 1958 Jung talked with students at the Institute in Zurich. The questions asked and his responses were recorded. He was asked what humans are to do with his "primitive, chthonic nature."[49] He described analysis as "a long discussion with" the "two-million-year-old man," the "Great Man," in "an attempt to understand him" and yourself in relationship with him.[50] Developing our relationship with the "Great Man" we come-to-know ethics, not morality, but an ethics that is grounded in the interconnected nature of the psyche. Jung told these students the way through things "that look desperate and unanswerable" is to ask yourself how "*you yourself* [are] *going to answer.*"[51] Asked, "Does the cycle of this dialogue [with the unconscious] continue permanently, or has man a special place in it?" Jung responded:

> That is what you learn: what your role is, where you are in the divine economy, in the order of things. You see yourself in a new light because you have added the information of the unconscious. You have added things you didn't dream of—a new aspect of yourself and of the world.[52]

Gathering the pieces of the ancestral puzzle, finding the threads of connection, and discovering the continuity of our bloodline on this planet, brings us into relationship with the unconscious, ourselves, each other and the world in very particular ways. Perhaps being in dialogue with the ancestors, especially with the great-grandmother of us all—the "Great Man"—and living one's life as an ethical response to what one comes to know, is an aspect of what Berry envisions as the foundation for our response as humans to the planetary wide ecological crisis.

Connecting with our ancestral roots and the indigenous roots of consciousness brings us into relationship with the generations who came before and those who will follow in the immediacy of our life in the present. Being in a more conscious, dialogical relationship with the ancestors has the potential to reconnect us with the roots of consciousness, the wisdom of our ancestors, the dreams of our descendants and the heart and soul of the world. As we reconnect with the roots of consciousness we experience ourselves as part of a dynamic, interconnected cosmological web of being connected to the Earth through our bloodline. Linda Hogan expresses this beautifully. "We are in part, the body of the earth. It might be that this place of ours is alive and radiant with the dreams of humankind, as well as the power of, the motion of, air on a feathered wing of the eagles remembered flight when the wind blew."[53]

When we reconnect with the deep roots of consciousness, we experience a natural and intimate connection with the Earth. And, when we feel a deep connection with the Earth, we reconnect with the roots of consciousness. The two go hand in hand. Reconnected, we shift from a human-centered consciousness to one that is cosmologically Earth-centered. Psyche and soma, spirit and matter are experienced as part of the same fabric. Berry describes it in this way:

> When we speak of the natural world we are not speaking simply of the physical world but of the psychic-physical mode of being found in every articulated entity of the phenomenal world.[54]

This shift in consciousness, this reconnection with the two-million-year-old human, naturally results in a different, natural ethic of reciprocity. This is the "spiritual ecology" that is at the heart of Native Science.[55] Gustafson believes that "The earth itself must now be seen as the altar upon which the great transformations and discoveries are made. It is also the one symbol that can unite us all since we are all of it and on it."[56] Looking at ourselves in relationship with the Earth as our "immediate context of existence" situated within a galaxy, situated within "a universe of galactic systems that emerged into being some fifteen billion years ago," according to Berry, "establishes a 'comprehensive context'" for "any consideration of human affairs." I have a card on my altar which says, "Be kind to everything that lives." Everything includes, but is not exclusively human. Everything is the "comprehensive context" Berry describes. Reconnecting with the deep roots of consciousness situated within the greater cosmos, opens the possibility of experiencing ourselves in relationship with all things, in all places at all times. From this understanding we are naturally inclined to act as a servant to "well-being" as the spirit of the depths suggests.

Jung's psychology affirms the basic tenet of Indigenous Science—"spiritual ecology"—in which the interconnected nature of being is the guiding ethical principle. In his essay, "After the Catastrophe," written after the end of the Second World War, Jung observes:

> Since no man lives within his own psychic sphere like a snail in its shell, separated from everyone else, but is connected to his fellow-men by his unconscious humanity, no crime can ever be: an isolated psychic happening. . . . The murder has been suffered by everyone, and everyone has committed it.[57]

While writing this essay Jung became aware of how deeply he was affected by what had happened in Germany during the war. Although he wasn't German, he felt a deep sense of guilt about what had been done. According to Jung, this experience of psychological guilt is felt by everyone who "was anywhere near the place where the terrible thing happened."[58] He identifies his experience of guilt as one of *participation mystique*. This is particularly fascinating in light of Bernstein's work and the natural ethic Jung suggests arises out of a connection with the deepest roots of the psyche.

As some of our stories explicitly depict, traumas like the genocide and atrocities committed in World War II, are remembered in the psyche and our bodies for generations until adequately witnessed and responded to. Viewed from a Jungian perspective, psyche and matter are two different aspects of the same thing. Although fundamentally distinct, they are not separate. Psyche, body and Earth are of the same fabric, intimately connected transcending the boundaries of time and space. A wound to any part of this web of being at any time is experienced by and affects the entire community, both living and dead. Whether conscious of it or not, each of us suffers the pain of the Earth body and all of our relations in the same way Jung suggests each of us suffers a murder.

Held in the shadows of psyche these "murders" gather increasing energetic vitality with each generation's forgetting. Like the shadow of racism in the dream described in the previous chapter, these historical and cultural traumas seem to remain frozen in specific times and places, returning, like the dead from Jerusalem, in the present until their stories are witnessed and their questions are answered,. Tending these ancestral figures, responding to the history that is marrow deep with appropriate reparative action, the dead are redeemed and past traumas are resolved. When we open ourselves to the possibility that the ancestors play a significant part in our lives, we also open ourselves to the support, guidance, wisdom, and love that is available to us through them.

Just as the experience of trauma transcends time and space, affecting psyche and matter in each individual and the collective body, transformation, healing, or an expansion of consciousness within one aspect of this web affects the entire fabric. The story of the Rainmaker exemplifies the dynamic that is at the heart of ancestral soul work. Being in a more conscious relationship with the ancestors—finding the places that are out of harmony, connecting one's personal experience of disharmony and disease with that of the collective through this relationship, and using the variety of techniques which are available for dialogue, healing and reparative action—we participate consciously in a dynamic process that, through each individual, contributes to bringing the family and greater community of being back into harmony with the Tao.

Bringing consciousness to and healing the ancestral trauma is an integral and necessary part of healing our physical and psychic body, the ancestral and collective psychic body and the Earth body. Jung came to know that our relationship with "the hereafter" is ultimately in service to this one life that is ours alone to live. Finding and being in relationship with the ancestors, with our roots, reconnecting with those to whom we belong, matters in the present and informs the legacy we leave for the generations that will inherit this Earth. Following the path backward not only contributes to our personal well being, it is a response to and contributes to the well being of all things in all times and places. Being in a more conscious relationship with the ancestors is part of the ecological reorientation that is part of the emerging cultural narrative of this time.

As Tarnas, Bernstein, and others observe, we are experiencing a paradigm shift and an evolution in collective consciousness. The story is changing. As Cajete sees it,

This new synthesis is coming from very deep within the collective consciousness of human beings. Metaphorically, this is like the process that created our world and landmasses, a result of continual activity deep within the Earth. Such activity eventually reaches the point where it erupts, and new terrain, waterways, plants and animals result.[59]

Karel and Iris Schrijver, a physician and astrophysicist explore "the natural flow that inexorably ties our human experience to the universe" in *Living with the Stars: How the Human Body Is Connected to the Life Cycles of the Earth, the Planets, and the Stars*.[60] Looking at life as "astrophysicians" they affirm that

> we are, indeed, stardust, in a very literal sense. Every object in the wider universe, everything around us, and everything we are, originated from stardust. Thus, we are not merely connected to the universe in some distant sense: stardust from the universe is actually flowing through us on a daily basis, and it rebuilds the stars and planets throughout the universe as much as it does our bodies, over and over again.[61]

The knowledge of modern Western science and the wisdom of the psyche as expressed in the dreams of the stars seem to mirror each other.

This book began with a dialogue between Indigenous Science and Jungian psychology. It seems fitting that as this book comes to its close we would return to the place where it began but in a new place and with new understanding. In *The Red Book* Izdubar, the embodiment of indigenous wisdom, tells Jung that he has been lamed by science. Through active imagination, Jung finds a way to heal Izdubar and restore him to wholeness "again." Years after carefully recording his encounters with the unconscious in *The Red Book*, Jung would state that "psychology is doomed to cancel itself out as a science and therein precisely it reaches its scientific goal."[62] It appears that modern Western science, Indigenous Science and Jung's psychology are different and complimentary ways of seeing into the mystery of life on this planet. As in the story of Izdubar, the split that existed between indigenous knowing and modern science is beginning to find a natural resolution and reconciliation. The imaginal realm of psyche, and Jung's psychology, can serve as a bridge. As old and new stories, indigenous and modern, and the reality of dreams and the discoveries of science meet, the paradigm is shifting and the new "myth" is constellating.

We live in extraordinary times in which we have an increasingly global perspective and identity. Finding our common ancestor Lucy, and now, as of this editorial moment, the *Homo naledi* found in South Africa, seeing the Earth from the perspective of the stars, and being connected through the internet, we are indeed increasingly in a global narrative in which we see ourselves as part of a worldwide web. As I write, I wonder if unearthing the ancestors in our personal stories is, like unearthing the bones of our pre-human ancestors, an aspect of the work that will provide part of the new foundation for our evolving collective story.

Linda Hogan writes, "Walking, I am listening to a deeper way. Suddenly all my ancestors are behind me. Be still, they say. Watch and listen. You are the result of the love of thousands."[63] Take a moment and look at your life from the perspective of being an ancestor. You are with those who came before you and those yet to be born looking back at your descendants as they live their lives moving forward in time. Imagine that you can see your entire lineage from the first born to the last in your line. Imagine yourself as an ancestor, one of the thousands whose love expresses itself and is embodied now in your descendants. Who we are at this moment in time is a result of the countless generations that have come before and a response to the generations that will follow.

Vine Deloria devoted his book *The World We Used to Live In* to understanding "the scope and intensity of the spiritual powers possessed by our ancestors."[64] The stories he shares are based on eyewitness accounts of healing and the effects of sacred rituals and ceremonies as practiced by American Indian tribes from across the North American continent. He offers this:

> The uncritical acceptance of modernism has prevented us from seeing that higher spiritual powers are still active in the world. . . . We need to glimpse the old spiritual world that helped, healed, and honored us with its presence and companionship. We need to see where we have been before we see where we should go, we need to know how to get there and we need to have help on our journey.[65]

It appears to me that the time is ripe to follow the path backward, to listen to the lament of the dead and respond with love.

Notes

Preface

1. Jung, *Memories, Dreams, Reflections,* p. 3.
2. Bond, *Living Myth: Personal Meaning as a Way of Life,* p. 3)
3. Ibid.

Chapter 1: Introduction to the Work

1. Jung, *The Red Book Liber Novus; A Reader's Edition,* p. 347.
2. According to Jung, the shadow consists of all those aspects of ourselves that are contrary to our conscious idea of who we are. All that we wish we were not is exiled from consciousness but continues to exist in this unconscious shadow. It is not only the "dark" side of our nature but certain of our gifts, talents, and unknown capacities that comprise the shadow.
3. Jung, "Psychology and Religion," p. 77 [CW11, para. 133].
4. Jung, "Analytical Psychology and Weltanschauung," p. 376 [CW8, para. 729].
5. Jung, "The Structure of the Psyche," p. 157 [CW8, para. 339].
6. Jung, *Symbols of Transformation,* p. 177 [CW5, para. 258].
7. Jung, "Analytical Psychology and Weltanschauung," p. 376 [CW8, para. 729].
8. Jung, *The Red Book Liber Novus; A Reader's Edition,* p. 202.
9. Some, *The Healing Wisdom of Africa.*
10. I want to acknowledge the great diversity of perspectives within and between different individuals and cultures regarding what happens to us after we die. Although this is a topic that carries much interest and is worthy of exploration, one that has engaged our human imagination since Paleolithic times, it is beyond the scope of this book.
11. Jung, *Memories, Dreams, Reflections,* p. 291.
12. Johnson, *On the Path of the Ancestors,* pp. 33 & 34.
13. Cajete, *Native Science;* Colorado, "Bridging Native and Western Science;" Peat, *Lighting the Seventh Fire.*
14. Deloria Jr., *C. G. Jung and the Sioux Traditions.*
15. Plotkin, *Soulcraft: Crossing into the Mysteries of Nature and Psyche,* p. 204.

16. Peat, *Lighting the Seventh Fire,* pp. 69–70.
17. Author's personal journal, May 2001.
18. Romanyshyn, *The Wounded Researcher.*
19. These words are copied from my journal which I wrote as I experienced this particular transferential dialogue. They express the immediacy of the experience. The figures in this imaginal experience are animated presences as described by Aizenstat (2009). A description of the process of animation is presented in Chapter 10. The feelings described above created an emotional resonance which linked me to this animated presence. The feelings were simultaneously felt by me and existed as essential qualities of the figure. Initially I felt myself as both the figure and myself due to this emotional resonance. As I stayed with this feeling, differentiation occurred and the imaginal presence came into clearer and distinct focus.
20. *Amerindian* is the generalized term my ancestor Roger Williams used when referring to the people native to this land when he wasn't referring to them specifically as Narragansett or Wampanoag or the other tribes he knew.
21. Jung, "The Transcendent Function," [CW8] (See also "On Psychic Energy" in CW8).
22. Jung, "The Psychological Foundations of Belief in Spirits," p. 315. [CW8, para. 598]
23. Jung, "Richard Willhelm: In Memoriam," p. 56, [CW 15, para. 81].
24. Jung, "Synchronicity: An Acausal Connecting Principle," p. 441, [CW8, para. 850].

Chapter 2: The Threads of Fate

1. Meade, *Fate and Destiny*, p. 2.
2. Jung, "Analytical Psychology and Weltanschauung," p. 376 [CW 8, para. 729].
3. Hannah, *Jung, His Life and His Work.*
4. Ibid., p. 18.
5. Jung's conceptualization and differentiation of levels within the psyche corresponds to the below worlds in Navajo cosmology. In Navajo, we humans live in the fifth world. Below this world are four other worlds. These worlds are archetypally hierarchical in both systems (Bernstein, personal communication, December 5, 2010).
6. I refer the reader to Jung's *Man and His Symbols* for a more comprehensive explanation. The last book written by Jung right before his death, this is the only book written especially for the general public.
7. Jung, *Memories, Dreams, Reflections*, pp. 234–235.
8. Bernstein, *Living in the Borderland.*
9. Ibid., p. 126.
10. Taylor, *The Healing Power of Stories,* pp. 235–236.
11. Jung, *Memories, Dreams, Reflections*, pp. 235–236.

12. Ibid., pp. 223–224.
13. Ibid., p. 226.
14. Ibid., p. 237.
15. Ibid.
16. Ibid., p. 233.
17. Jewell & Abate, *The New Oxford English Dictionary,* p. 616.
18. Hillman, *The soul's code,* p. 191.
19. Meade, *Fate and Destiny,* p. 3.
20. Ibid., p. 28.
21. Ibid., p. 4.
22. Ibid., p. 3.
23. Roger's compass is iconic. It is so closely associated with him that they sell replicas in many of the historic museums in Rhode Island.
24. Hannah, *Jung, His Life and His Work,* p. 26.
25. Jung, *Memories, Dreams, Reflections,* p. 90.
26. Ibid., p.90.
27. McGuire & Hull, *C. G. Jung Speaking,* p. 359.

Chapter 3: Beyond Biography

1. According to James Hillman in *The Soul's Code,* one's daimon often conceals itself until the time is right. In high school I paid little attention in history classes, deeming them completely irrelevant and meaningless, focusing instead on current events and imagining a future that was based on peace and love. Imagine my surprise when I got pulled into history through the insistence of my daughter, my dreams and my personal wound. Even more surprising was the realization that in the past that was particularly mine lived the imagination of a future based on peace and love.
2. LaFantasie, *The Correspondence of Roger Williams,* p. 722.
3. J. McNiff, Director of the Roger Williams Memorial, personal communication, March 29, 2005.
4. LaFantasie, *The Correspondence of Roger Williams,* p. 752.
5. Gaustad, *Liberty of Conscience,* p. 127.
6. LaFantasie, *The Correspondence of Roger Williams,* p. 722.
7. Ibid.
8. Ibid.
9. Ibid., p. 719.
10. Ibid., p. 720.
11. Rubertone, *Grave undertakings, p. 16.*
12. Ibid., p. 16.
13. LaFantasie, *The Correspondence of Roger Williams,* p. 723.
14. Ibid.
15. Ibid.
16. Ibid.

17. Drake, *King Philip's War*, p. 2.

18. Ibid., p. 168.

19. Jung, *Memories, Dreams, Reflections*, p. 248.

20. The use of the term "savage" among 17th century English carried a different meaning and connotation than it does in this time. It meant one who is indigenous, who has not been corrupted by civilization. Pure in nature, "savages" embodied man's inherent goodness. (personal communication, John McNiff, March 2005)

21. Teunissen & Hinz, Introduction, *In A Key Into the Language of America*, p. 39

22. Jung, *The Red Book Liber Novus; A Reader's Edition*, p. 345.

23. Ernst, *Roger Williams*.

24. There are historical signs denoting this land, which includes Clark's family's farm as part of it, as My Lady's Manor.

25. I was painfully aware of the history of this land. Before I even knew about the ancestral connection between myself and Clark, I felt compelled to walk the land barefoot, saying prayers, singing and drumming, offering what I could with the intention of honoring the original people of this land and the land itself. This was not out of a sense of guilt, but from a felt sense that things were out of balance and that I might, through my actions and intention, bring some witnessing, acknowledgement, tears of grief, and possibly healing to this land. My daughters, very young at the time, wondered what I was doing and sometimes joined in. I think the way they lived with that land as toddlers and children was blessing in itself. I can only hope that some good came from this.

26. Schutzberger, *The Ancester Syndrome*, p. 66.

27. Ibid., p. 68.

28. Polishook, *Roger Williams, John Cotton and Religious Freedom*, p. 2.

29. Ibid., p. 28.

30. Ibid., p. 27.

31. Gaustad, *Roger Williams*. Providence was referred to by people in the Massachusetts Bay Colony and in England as the "latrina" of New England.

32. State of Rhode Island Commission on Women, 2011.

33. Rhode Island Commission on Women: Verin Colonial Women's History Project, http://www.ricw.ri.gov/committees/comm_verin.php (retrieved July 16, 2015)

34. Williams, *A Key Into the Language of America*, p. 133.

35. Teunissen & Hinz, Introduction, *In A Key Into the Language of America*,

36. Williams, *A Key Into the Language of America*, p. 83.

37. Teunissen & Hinz, Introduction, *In A Key Into the Language of America*, p. 37.

38. Ibid.

39. Gustafson, *Dancing between two worlds*, pp. 9 & 16.

40. Ibid., p. 10.

41. Teunissen & Hinz, Introduction, *In A Key Into the Language of America*, p. 39.

42. Tarnas, *Passion of the Western Mind,* p. 416.
43. Ibid., p. 418.
44. Ibid., p. 12
45. Tarnas, *Cosmos and Psyche,* p. 26, and, Bernstein, *Living in the Borderland.*
46. Bernstein, *Living in the Borderland,* p. 122.
47. Ibid., 2005, p. 124.
48. Ibid., p. 10.
49. Ibid., pp. 122–123.
50. Ibid., p. 9.
51. Gustafson, *Dancing Between two Worlds,* p. 74
52. Peat, *Lighting the Seventh Fire,* p. 4.
53. Ibid., p. 50.
54. Ibid., p. 53.
55. Ibid., p. 53.
56. Cajete, *Native Science,* p. 62.
57. Jung, "The Psychology of the Child Archetype," p. 163 [CW 9i, para. 276].
58. I had many of these experiences prior to having the theoretical understanding Jung's work provides. Wanting to understand what was happening, I sought spiritual teachers, various therapies, and, finally, depth psychology and Jung. I am deeply grateful for Bernstein's work.
59. Some, *The Healing Wisdom of Africa,* p. 61.
60. Jung, *The Red Book Liber Novus: A Reader's Edition,* p. 341.
61. Jung, *The Red Book Liber Novus; A Reader's Edition,* p. 342
62. Aizenstat, *Dream Tending.*
63. Ibid., p. 55.
64. Rubertone, p. 23.
65. Some, Ancestor healing ritual, 2010, November 29.
66. In Latin, the words for 'apple' ("malum") and for 'evil' ("malum") are nearly identical.
67. Rubertone, *Grave Undertakings,* p. 23.
68. Ibid.
69. Ibid., p. 38.
70. Valerie Ogden, in her article in the Huffington Post titled, "The true stories behind classic fairy tales," discovered that many fairy and folk tales, while mythic and archetypal, are often based on historical events. Ogden asserts that "fairy tales, as we know them today, derived from spoken legends which were based on facts."
71. When I told my sister Laurie about my research, she asked, "Why you? Why not me or...?" It's an important question. In no way do I presume to be special or chosen. In fact, this experience has been extremely humbling. The context provided by Jung has been invaluable. We are all part of our commonly shared collective experience and story. Each of us is an integral part of all of creation. Each of us carries and is a response to the legacy that is our inheritance. The way the different levels of the collective unconscious are expressed in each of us is unique. What is ours to answer, redeem, reconcile,

and dream forward is different for each individual within a family. Without my sister, brother, daughters, ex-husband, and grandfather, the web would be incomplete and questions would remain unanswered. Some of us have lives and stories that become more visible and public. It does not mean that I or what I'm experiencing is any more or less significant than any other person or their experiences. I am in service to this story and this legacy. My hope is that this story may open the window of perception for others helping them see the ancestral and collective connections in their own life in whatever ways they exist.

72. White, *A History of the Warfare of Science with Theology in Christendom*, p. 194.
73. Ibid., p. 194.
74. The specifics of Clark's and my differing opinions, disagreements about spirituality, oppression, social and political ideas aren't necessary to make the point that is important and relevant for others. It is out of respect for Clark's and our daughter's privacy that I choose not to share more of the details about this. My wish is that by bringing more consciousness to this that my descendants will have a more solid foundation on which to stand.
75. Gaustad, *Liberty of Conscience*, p. 103.
76. Jung, *The Red Book Liber Novus; A Reader's Edition*, p. 343.
77. Conducting an ancestor dialogue incorporates Aizenstat's work of dream council, Some's use of an ancestor altar and Jung's process of active imagination. For a complete description of this process see Chapter 11.
78. Jung, *The Red Book Liber Novus; A Reader's Edition*, p. 123.
79. Ibid., p. 234.
80. Ibid., p. 340.

Chapter 4: Jung and the Land of the Dead

1. Jung, *The Red Book*, p. 121.
2. Jung, *Memories, Dreams, Reflections*, p. 299.
3. Ibid., p. 320.
4. Jung, "The Soul and Death," p. 414 [CW8, para. 815].
5. Jung, *Memories, Dreams, Reflections*, p. 97.
6. Ibid., p. 96.
7. Ibid., p. 99.
8. Ibid.
9. Jung, "Two Essays on Analytical Psychology," p. 192 [CW7, para. 303].
10. Ibid., p. 191 [CW7, para. 302].
11. Ibid., p. 192 [CW7, para. 303].
12. Ibid., p. 191 [CW7, para. 303].
13. McGuire & Hull, *C. G. Jung Speaking*, p. 380–381.
14. Jung, "The Role of the Unconscious," p. 10 [CW10, para. 14].
15. Jung, *Memories, Dreams, Reflections*, p. 172.

16. Ibid., p. 172.
17. Ibid., p. 173. It is interesting to note that mummification itself and the elaborate rituals related to mummification were conducted to insure resurrection of one's spirit into the afterlife. In Chinese medicine, wood is the first element, the element of new life and rebirth. The composition of the figures seems to carry their nature of being both dead and alive.
18. Ibid.
19. Jung, "Analytical Psychology and Weltanschauung," p. 364 [CW8, para. 702].
20. Jung, *Memories, Dreams, Reflections*, p. 173.
21. Jung, *The Red Book Liber Novus; A Reader's Edition,* pp. 340–342.
22. Smith, *Jung and Shamanism in Dialogue*, p. 103.
23. Jung, "Basic Postulates of Analytical Psychology," pp. 349–350 [CW8, para. 673].
24. Jung, "Archaic Man," p. 63 [CW 10 para. 128].
25. Jung, *Memories, Dreams, Reflections*, p. 291.
26. Ibid., p. 291.
27. Ibid.
28. Ibid., p. 320.
29. Jung, "Two Essays on Analytical Psychology," p. 185 [CW 7, para. 293].
30. Ibid., p. 185 [CW7, para. 293 & 305].
31. McGuire & Hull, *C. G. Jung Speaking*, p. 378.
32. Jung, *C. G. Jung letters, Vol. 1: 1906–1950*, p. 257.
33. Jung, "The Role of the Unconscious," p. 11–12 [CW10, para. 15].
34. Jaffe, *An Archetypal Approach to Death, Dreams, and Ghosts*, p. 58.
35. Jung, "Psychology and Spiritualism," p. 313, [CW18, para. 748].
36. Jung, "The Psychological Foundations of Belief in Spirits," p. 318 [CW8, footnote 15].
37. Jung, *Memories, Dreams, Reflections*, p. 306.
38. Ibid., p. 301.
39. Ibid., p. 190.
40. Ibid., pp. 190–191.
41. Ibid.
42. Ibid.
43. Ibid.
44. Ibid., p. 308.
45. Ibid., p. 191.
46. These experiences occurred within four years of each other. The dream in 1912. The encounter, in 1916.
47. McGuire & Hull, *C. G. Jung Speaking*, p. 80.
48. Jung, *Memories, Dreams, Reflections*, p. 232.
49. Ibid., p. 232.
50. Ibid., p. 10.
51. Ibid., p. 191.
52. Ibid., p. 11.

53. Ibid., p. 236.
54. Jung, *Nietzsche's Zarathustra,* p. 643.
55. Jung, *Nietzsche's Zarathustra,* p. 941.
56. Ibid., p. 1267.
57. Ibid., p. 1401.
58. Ibid.
59. Ibid., p. 1402. Jung's generalizations regarding "primitive" medicine men were derived from his experiences, which were mostly with African peoples. Jung's contact with American Indians was limited. Although the above accurately describes the practice of African or Australian medicine men, it is not an accurate description of Navajo and other American Indian shamanic work. One of the problems with Jung is that his understanding of indigenous people was limited by his personal, cultural, and theoretical framework. He lumped all indigenous people together as representative of "primitive" consciousness and generalized his observations (Bernstein, personal communication, December 6, 2010).
60. Jung, "Introduction to Wickes's Analyse der Kinderseele," p. 41 [CW17, para. 84].
61. Ibid., p. 43 [CW17, para. 43].
62. Ibid., p. 44 [CW17, para. 93] It is interesting to note that Jung refers to the child's soul in what appears to be a more metaphysical use of the word. It begs the question about what Jung believed to be true with regard to the soul.
63. Jung, *Dream analysis: Notes on the seminar given in 1928–1930 by C.G. Jung,* p. 320
64. McGuire & Hull, *C. G. Jung Speaking,* p. 383.
65. Ibid., p. 385.
66. Ibid.
67. Ibid.
68. Jaffe, *An Archetypal Approach to Death, Dreams, and Ghosts,* p. 102.
69. Ibid., p. 104.
70. Ibid.
71. Jung, *Memories, Dreams, Reflections,* p. 233.
72. Ibid., p. 90.
73. Ibid., p. 318.
74. Ibid.
75. Ibid., p. 92.
76. Ibid., p. 215 (emphasis mine).
77. Ibid., p. 48.
78. Ibid., p. 96.
79. Ibid., p. 307.
80. Ibid.
81. Ibid.
82. Ibid., p. 306.
83. Ibid., p. 305.

84. Ibid.
85. Jung, C. G., "The Transcendent Function," p. 69, [CW8, para. 131].
86. Ibid., p. 73, [CW8, para. 143].
87. Ibid.
88. Ibid., p. 89, [CW8, para. 186].
89. Ibid., p. 90, [CW8, para. 189].
90. Jung, *Memories, Dreams, Reflections,* p. 315.
91. Although Jung left the question about whether or not the individual soul had any continued existence after death, he did say that, given his experience, it seemed that individual consciousness did have some continuing existence after death.
92. Jung, *Memories, Dreams, Reflections*, pp. 315–316
93. Ibid, p. 214.
94. Ibid.
95. Ibid., p. 309.
96. Ibid.,
97. Ibid.,
98. Ibid.
99. Jung, *C.G. Jung letters, Vol. 2: 1951–1961,* p. 284.
100. Ibid., p. 225
101. Ibid.

Chapter 5: Between Life and Death

1. In a conversation with Marion Woodman I would refine my understanding of this figure. In Jungian terms she was the negative animus in the mother. This conceptualization has been extremely important in my understanding and healing of the wounding that is both personal and intergenerational, and is rooted in the historical/cultural narrative.
2. It is not uncommon for people who have experienced trauma to have recurring dreams of battles and wars between good and evil. See Kalsched, *The Inner World of Trauma: Archetypal Defenses of the Personal Spirit.*
3. Jung, *Mysterium Coniunctionis*, pp. 464–465 [CW14, para. 662].
4. Ibid, p. 462, [CW14, para. 660].
5. This process is based on the process of Dream Council created by Steve Aizenstat as described in his book on Dream Tending. Aizenstat, *Dream Tending: Awakening to the healing power of dreams).*
6. In 2002 I began seeing a Jungian therapist. Although she wasn't a trained analyst, she had been in Jungian analysis herself. My initial dream presented an image of this transformation. I sat on a cliff overlooking the ocean. A killer whale, jaws agape, leapt from the ocean heading right toward me. As her white-tooth-lined mouth wrapped itself around my head, holding it gently, I heard, "this is what it's like to be mothered." This dream heralded the ancestral work that followed.

7. The animus as described by Jung is the the archetypal "inborn image of men." This concept as imagined and described by Jung has been revised by women analysts. I refer the reader to Susan Rowland's book, *Jung: A Feminist Revision,* and Irene Claremont de Castillejo's *Knowing Woman.* Simply stated the "negative animus" is an internalization of the male aggression against women.

Chapter 6: Reimagining the World—Reimagining Ourselves

1. Jung, *The Red Book Liber Novus; A Reader's Edition,* p. 129.
2. Bernstein, *Living in the Borderland,* p. v.
3. Smith, *Jung and Shamanism in Dialogue.*
4. Some, *The Healing Wisdom of Africa,* p. 9.
5. Ibid., p. 10.
6. Some, *Of Water and the Spirit,* p. 10.
7. Jung, *The Red Book Liber Novus; A Reader's Edition,* p. 491.
8. Ibid., pp. 495–496.
9. Jung, *Nietzsche's Zarathustra,* p. 1541.
10. Some, *Of Water and the Spirit,* p. 9.
11. McGuire & Hull, *C. G. Jung Speaking,* p. 30
12. Some, *The Healing Wisdom of Africa,* p. 129.
13. Ibid., p. 130.
14. Ibid.
15. Metzner, *The Well of Remembrance,* p. 5.
16. Jung, "Two Essays on Analytical Psychology," p. 190 [CW7, para. 300]
17. Some, *The Healing Wisdom of Africa,* p. 133
18. Pert, *Molecules of Emotion,* p. 310.
19. Tarnas, *Passion of the Western Mind,*
20. Ibid., pp. 386–387.
21. Smith, *Jung and Shamanism in Dialogue,* p. 112.
22. Peat, *Synchronicity,* p. 257.
23. Smith, *Jung and Shamanism,* p. 113.
24. Ibid., p. 114.
25. Ibid.
26. Some, *The Healing Wisdom of Africa,* p. 149.
27. Deloria, Jr., *Jung and the Sioux Traditions,* p. 84
28. Deloria Jr., *God is Red,* pp. 152–153.
29. Kremer, "Perspectives on Indigenous Healing," p. para. 11.
30. King, "A critique of Western psychology from an American Indian Psychologist," p. 47.
31. Ibid., p. 50.
32. McGuire & Hull, *C. G. Jung Speaking: Interviews and encounters,* p. 30.
33. Jung, "The Role of the Unconscious," p. 13 [CW10, para. 18].
34. Jung, *Memories, Dreams, Reflections,* p. 225.

35. Hannah, *Jung, His Life and His Work*, p. 11.
36. McGuire & Hull, *C. G. Jung Speaking*, p. 81.
37. Jung, "The Role of the Unconscious," p. 13 [CW10. para. 19].
38. Jung, "Mind and Earth," p. 31 [CW 10, para. 53]
39. Jung, *Nietzsche's Zarathustra*, p. 1542
40. Ibid., pp. 1542–1543
41. Grof, *When the Impossible Happens*; Bache, *Dark Night, Early Dawn*.
42. Jung, *Memories, Dreams, Reflections*, p. 229.
43. Ibid., p. 230.
44. Ibid.
45. Ibid., p. 231.
46. Ibid.
47. Ibid.
48. Jung, "Synchronicity: An Acausal Connecting Principle," p. 452 [CW 8, para. 865].
49. According to many Native American traditions, it is seven generations before one can really say they are native to this land. Fred Gustafson, personal communication September 20, 2015.
50. Cajete, *Native Science*, p. 187.
51. Ibid.
52. Ibid., p. 205.
53. Deloria Jr., *God is Red*, p. 172.
54. Ibid., p. 171.
55. Ibid.
56. Ibid.
57. Cajete, *Look to the Mountain*, p. 85.
58. Lacourt, "Coming Home: Knowing Land, Knowing Self," p. 71.
59. Hannah, *Jung, His Life and His Work*, p. 18.
60. McGuire & Hull, *C. G. Jung Speaking*, p. 20.
61. Hannah, *Jung, His Life and His Work*, p. 162.
62. Jung, "The Complications of American Psychology," p. 510 [CW10, para. 969].
63. McGuire & Hull, *C. G. Jung Speaking*, p. 335.
64. Ibid.
65. Ibid.
66. Ibid.
67. Jung, "The Complications of American Psychology," p. 511 [CW 10, para. 972].
68. Jung, "Mind and Earth," p. 47 [CW 10, para. 99].
69. Hannah, *Jung, His Life and His Work*, p. 162.
70. Personal communication, May 27, 2015.
71. McGuire & Hull, *C. G. Jung Speaking*, p. 196.
72. Deloria, *Playing Indian*, p. 2.
73. Ibid., p. 3.
74. Ibid., p. 7.

75. Jung, "The Psychological Aspects of the Kore," p. 188 [CW9i, para. 316].
76. Ibid.
77. My mother told me that her father was Indian, originally from Canada. I have tried to trace the genealogy of that part of my family but have been unsuccessful. In the census records I could find, the family's nationality changed every 10 years depending on the nation of origin of the people who were their neighbors. In the last record I found, when asked what nationality they were, they identified themselves as American. That word was crossed out by someone. Over American "English" was written. Every marriage prior to my grandmother's and grandfather's had been between two descendants from the original English colonists. My grandfather, even after their engagement, was not allowed to sit at the dinner table with my grandmother's family. I wondered if the dream spoke to these two aspects of my bloodline—English and Indian.
78. Tarnas, *Cosmos and Psyche*, p. 26.
79. Tarnas, *Passion of the Western Mind*, p. 422.
80. The term *participation mystique* is a troubling yet useful construct. Although it is descriptive of a way of perceiving and being in relationship with the world that has been sacrificed and lost to differentiated, modern consciousness, it can be taken and has been used to imply and describe primitive consciousness as lacking ego awareness. Although different than the ego consciousness with which we are familiar, indigenous peoples on this continent prior to the advent of Europeans had ego consciousness and ego awareness. (personal communication, Bernstein, March 29, 2010)
81. Tarnas, *Cosmos and Psyche*, p. 26.
82. Tarnas, *Passion of the Western Mind*, p. 443.
83. Jung, "Archaic Man."
84. Jung, *Modern Man in Search of a Soul.*
85. For an excellent discussion of this I refer the reader to Deloria Jr., *C. G. Jung and the Sioux traditions: Dreams, Visions, Nature and the Primitive.*
86. Jung, *Modern Man in Search of a Soul*, p. 144.
87. Jung, "Archaic Man."
88. Jung, *Modern Man in Search of a Soul*, p. 140.
89. Ibid., p. 130.
90. McGuire & Hull, *C. G. Jung Speaking*, p. 397. The words *primitive* and *indigenous* are historically, politically, and emotionally laden. The problems faced by Indigenous peoples around the world have been and are of such serious concern that the United Nations established an advisory committee to the Economic and Social Council, a permanent forum to review issues faced by indigenous people around the world. In this work I use the term *indigenous* in its generic sense, being native or of original origin, as well as the way in which it is commonly used by the United Nations to refer to a people who inhabit a specific geographic region with which they have the earliest known historical connection. When possible and appropriate I specifically name the Indigenous people to whom I am making reference.

91. Jung, "Mind and Earth."
92. Jung, *The Red Book Liber Novus; A Reader's Edition*, p. 278
93. Ibid.
94. Ibid., p. 279.
95. Ibid. p. 281.
96. Jung, *Memories, Dreams, Reflections*, pp. 245–246.
97. Some, *The Healing Wisdom of Africa*, pp. 16–17.
98. Jung, *The Red Book Liber Novus; A Reader's Edition*, p. 284.
99. Some, *The Healing Wisdom of Africa*, p. 8.
100. Ibid., p. 9.
101. Ibid.
102. Ibid., p. 8.
103. Ibis., p. 9.
104. Ibid., p. 84.
105. Ibid., p. 9.
106. Ibid.
107. Ibid., p. 8
108. Hillman & Shamdasani, *Lament of the Dead*, p. 8.
109. Jung, *The Red Book Liber Novus; A Reader's Edition*, p. 187.
110. Ibid.
111. Hillman & Shamdasani, *Lament of the Dead*, p. 2.
112. Ibid., p. 164
113. Ibid., p. 83.
114. Jung, *The Red Book Liber Novus; A Reader's Edition*, p. 119.
115. Ibid., p. 119.
116. Ibid., p. 129.
117. Cajete, *Native Science;* Deloria Jr., *The world we used to live in*; Deloria, Jr., *C. G. Jung and the Sioux Traditions*; Some, *The Healing Wisdom of Africa*; Some, *Of water and the spirit.*
118. Jung, *The Red Book Liber Novus; A Reader's Edition*, pp. 344–345.

Chapter 7: Following the Path Backward to Create a New Forward

1. Hillman & Shamdasani, *Lament of the Dead*, 2013, p. 38.
2. Peat, *Synchronicity.*
3. Cajete, *Native Science,* p. 81.
4. Jaenke, *Personal Dreamscape as Ancestral Landscape,* p. 6.
5. Jung, *Modern Man in Search of a Soul,* p. 130
6. Tarnas, *Cosmos and Psyche*; Tarnas, "Is the Modern Psyche undergoing a rite of passage?"; Tarnas, *Passion of the Western Mind.*
7. Deloria, *God is Red,* p. 68.
8. Ibid.
9. Jung, *Memories, Dreams, Reflections*, p. 305

10. Jung, "The Soul and Death," p. 414 [CW 8, para. 814].
11. Cajete, *Native Science*; Colorado, "Bridging Native and Western Science;" Peat, *Synchronicity.*
12. Peat, *Synchronicity*, p. 26.
13. Deloria Jr., *Spirit and Reason*, p. 39.
14. Some, *The Healing Wisdom of Africa*, p. 61.
15. Jung, *Aion.*
16. Ibid.
17. Some, The Healing Wisdom of Africa, p. 63
18. Peat, *Synchronicity*, p. 257.
19. Deloria Jr., *Spirit and Reason*, p. 37.
20. Jung, *Memories, Dreams, Reflections*, p. 237
21. Some, *The Healing Wisdom of Africa*, p. 32.
22. Colorado, "Bridging Native and Western science," p. 54.
23. Peat, *Synchronicity*, p. 200.
24. Deloria Jr., *C.G. Jung and the Sioux traditions*, p. 89
25. Ibid., p. 92
26. Stephen Karcher, personal communication, May 19, 2007.
27. Colorado, "Bridging Native and Western Science."
28. Jung, "The Symbolic Life," p. 287 [CW18, para. 684].
29. Jung, "Synchronicity: An Acausal Connecting Principle," p. 414 [CW8, para. 815].
30. Deloria, *C. G. Jung and the Sioux Traditions,* p. 81.
31. Ibid.
32. Ibid., p. 88.
33. Ibid.
34. Deloria Jr., *Spirit and Reason.*
35. Ibid., p. 362.
36. Some, *The Healing Wisdom of Africa.*
37. Ibid., p. 54.
38. Some, "Calling on our ancestors: The healing connection."
39. Andrews, *Animal Speak*, p. 131.
40. Deloria Jr., *God is Red*, p. 171.
41. Personal communication November 2014.
42. Cajete, *Native Science,* p. 210.
43. Jung, "Flying saucers: A Modern Myth of Things Seen in the Skies," p. 411 [CW10, para. 780].
44. Peat, *Synchronicity*, p. 32.
45. Deloria, *C.G. Jung and the Sioux Traditions*, p. 80.
46. Hillman & Shamdasani, *Lament of the Dead*, p. 17.
47. Ibid., p. 67.
48. Jung, *The Red Book Liber Novus; A Reader's Edition,* p. 133.
49. Ibid., p. 134.
50. Ibid.
51. Cajete, *Native Science,*

52. Tarnas, "Is the Modern Psyche Undergoing a Rite of Passage?"
53. Colorado, "Bridging Native and Western Science."

Chapter 8: A Shared Collective Legacy

1. Hogan, *The Woman Who Watches Over the World*, p. 203.
2. Duff, *The Alchemy of Illness*; Hogan, *The Woman Who Watches Over the World.*
3. Felman, "Education and Crisis, or the Vicissitudes of Teaching."
4. Duff, *The Alchemy of Illness,* p. 5.
5. Ibid.
6. Ibid., p. 6.
7. van der Kolk & van der Hart, "The Intrusive Past: The Flexibilitly of Memory and the Engraving of Trauma," p. 172.
8. Duff, *The Alchemy of Illness*, p. 118.
9. Ibid., p. 23.
10. Lorenz, "Amnesia/countermemory."
11. Caruth, "Introduction," p. 5.
12. Homans, *Symbolic Loss*, p. 23.
13. Duff, *The Alchemy of Illness*, pp. 122–123.
14. Hogan, *The Woman Who Watches Over the World*, p. 59.
15. Ibid., p. 56.
16. Ibid., p. 43.
17. Ibid., p. 35.
18. Ibid., p. 56.
19. Ibid., p. 54.
20. Ibid., p. 53.
21. Ibid., p. 59.
22. Ibid.
23. Buck, *Killing Beauty in North America,* p. 6.
24. Erikson, "Notes on Trauma and Community," p. 187.
25. Hogan, *The Woman Who Watches Over the World,* p. 115.
26. Ibid., p. 16.
27. Ibid., p. 128.
28. Ibid., p. 115.
29. Ibid., p. 77.
30. Ibid.
31. I believe Hogan (2001) is referring to Coercive Restraint Therapy, a highly controversial method of treating children with attachment disorders. The method was first introduced in the 1970s by Robert Zaslow.
32. Ibid., p. 29.
33. Ibid., pp. 127–128.
34. Ibid., p. 16.
35. Ibid., pp. 49–50.

Chapter 9: Unearthing Abuse—Collective Grief

1.   Hillman & Shamdasani, *Lament of the Dead*, p. 24.
2.   Some, *The Healing Wisdom of Africa*, p. 91.
3.   Jung, *The Red Book Liber Novus; A Reader's Edition.*
4.   Deloria Jr., *C.G. Jung and the Sioux traditions,* p. 149.
5.   Meade, *Fate and Destiny,* pp. 316–317.
6.   Hogan, *The Woman Who Watches Over the World,* p. 59.
7.   Singer & Kimbles, "Introduction."
8.   Ibid.
9.   Jung, "A Review of the Complex Theory," [CW8]
10. Ibid., p. 96 [CW 8, para. 201].
11. Ibid., p. 100, [CW8, para 208].
12. Ibid., p. 103, [CW8, para. 215].
13. Singer & Kimbles, *The Cultural Complex.*
14. Ibid., p. 4.
15. Ibid., p. 6.
16. Ibid., p. 7.
17. In his essays, "Wotan" and "After the Catastrophe" in *The Collected Works,* Vol. 10, Jung's writes about the effect of powerful archetypal energies on nations.
18. Jewell & Abate, *The New Oxford American Dictionary.*
19. Hurley, "Grandma's Experiences Leave a Mark on Your Genes."
20. Gustafson, *Dancing Between Two Worlds,* p. 24.
21. Ibid., p. 20.
22. Reconnecting with this aspect of consciousness through dream, synchronicity, symptom and place is described by Taryria Ward, Kimme Karen Johnson and Karen Jaenke in their doctoral dissertations. Ward, *Reawakening Indigenous Sensibilities in the Western Psyche* Jaenke, Personal *Dreamscape as Ancestral Landscape*; Johnson, *On the Path of the Ancestors: Kinship with Place as a Path of Recovery.*
23. Hogan, *The Woman Who Watches Over the World,* p. 116.
24. Gustafson, *Dancing Between two Worlds,* p. 26.
25. Ibid., p. 20
26. Weisstub & Galili-Weisstub, "Collective Trauma and Cultural Complexes, p. 166.
27. Gustafson, *Dancing Between two Worlds,* p. 20.
28. Ibid., p. 21
29. Jung, *The Red Book Liber Novus; A Reader's Edition,* pp. 344–345
30. See Chapter 6 for a comprehensive exploration of this concept.
31. Drake, *King Philip's War,* p. 119.
32. Ibid., p. 119.
33. When rain comes in a dream it often signifies grief.
34. Lepore, *The Name of War,* p. xi.
35. The name of this war, as it was called by the English, has led to impas-

sioned contention. "Each word in its title . . . has been disputed." Whether Metacom, Philip's Algonquian name or Philip is the name this man called himself and went by is disputed. It is referred to as Metacom's Rebellion by those who celebrate Indian resistance. The word King is viewed as being a title the English assigned that was intentionally derisive. According to Lepore, this reflects "what the fighting was about in the first place; it was a contest for meaning—and the colonists won." Lepore, *The Name of War*, xv-xvi.

36. I refer those who are interested in learning more about the name of this man and the name of the war to Lepore's chapter, What's in a Name in her book *The Name of War*. Lepore, *The Name of War: King Philip's War and the Origins of American Identity.*

37. Hogan, *The Woman Who Watches Over the World*, p. 59.

38. As I work with more people I have come to wonder if the sexual abuse of people on this continent is a symptomatic acting out of the unconscious legacy of abuse to the native peoples, animals, water, mountains, plains . . . in an effort to remember and redeem a very bloody and devastating history. In no way do I want to minimize the personal experience and effects of trauma. I am all too familiar with this myself. I am interested in exploring the origins and nature of trauma as it informs our understanding of trauma the healing process—personal, familial, ancestral, cultural and ecological.

39. Colorado, "Bridging Native and Western Science," p. 52

40. Ibid., p. 52

41. Peat, *Lighting the Seventh Fire*, p. 286.

42. Jung, *The Red Book Liber Novus; A Reader's Edition,* p. 116.

43. Sabini & Jung, *The Earth has a Soul,* p. 211.

44. Ibid.

45. Ibid., p. 213.

46. Silko, *Ceremony,* p. 69.

47. Jung, *The Red Book Liber Novus; A Reader's Edition*, p. 340.

48. Gustafson, *Dancing Between two Worlds*, p. 15.

Chapter 10: Five Intergenerational Stories

1. Estes, *Women Who Run with the Wolves*, pp. 14 & 19

2. Zimmerman & Coyle, *The Way of Council.*

3. Plotkin, *Soulcraft.*

4. I've found that each group I've worked with appears to be comprised of individuals whose stories are connected in significantly non-random and meaningful ways. There are often themes and experiences within a group like homelessness, bitterness, breast cancer, immigration to this land at the same time, and shared countries of ancestral origins. There is a synergistic dynamic within each group that facilitates each individual's healing. An awareness in one person will spark a new awareness in another.

5. Schutzberger, *The Ancestor Syndrome.*
6. Ibid., p. 73
7. Ibid., p. 84
8. Some, *The Healing Wisdom of Africa.*
9. Aizenstat, *Dream Tending.*
10. All quotations in these stories are the words of the woman whose story is being told. All quotations come from the original sources listed above— journals, notes from interviews, personal communications, emails. Which particular source a quote comes from will *not* be noted in the story. Every quote comes from one of the original sources which are in a file under that woman's name.
11. JoEllen Koerner's story is based on her published story, which includes her reflections on, understanding, and interpretation of her personal experience. Unlike the presentation of the other women's stories, some theoretical understanding and meaning will be woven into my retelling of her story. Some of the interpretations are from the written texts and are so noted. Other interpretations are mine. The interpretive aspects of this retelling are included to provide insight into and a context for the collective aspects and ancestral foundation implicit in all of the individual stories presented in this chapter.
12. Deloria, *C. G. Jung and the Sioux Traditions*, p. 116.
13. Bernstein, *Living in the Borderland*, p. v.
14. Deloria, *C. G. Jung and the Sioux Traditions.*
15. Ibid., p. 130.
16. I believe this fence also references the Borderland which Bernstein has identified as the "place" into which our modern collective consciousness is evolving.
17. "Black German" is an American slang phrase that refers to ethnic and cultural roots of people of Dutch and German ancestry. The term "Black Dutch" first appeared in colonial history. It was used to identify individuals who were from the Netherlands who had darker skin than other Europeans. Their darker skin was thought to be a result of children of Spanish soldiers and Dutch women during the occupation of the Netherlands by Spain in the 16th century. It has been used since colonial times as a derogatory slang term for any American of European descent who had dark skin.
18. Shaman and shamanism are popular terms in American culture today. A common synonym is medicine man or woman. As defined by Harner in *The way of the shaman*, "Shamanism represents the most widespread and ancient methodological system of mind-body healing known to humanity" (p. 40)
19. The phrase "came present" describes my experience of the way in which an ancestor or figure appears in the process of the dialogue. It is as if someone who hadn't been there suddenly appears as if she walked into the room, or in this case, into conscious awareness through the field created in the imaginal dialogue.

20. Koerner, *Mother Heal MySelf.*
21. Ibid., p. 22.
22. Ibid., p. 25.
23. Ibid., p. 50.
24. For a full description of this experience and others with the Sioux, I refer the reader to JoEllen's book. I highly recommend reading her entire story.
25. Ibid., p. 127.
26. Ibid., p. 132.
27. Ibid., pp. 134–135.
28. Ibid., p. 135.
29. Ibid., p. 149.
30. Ibid., p. 154.
31. Ibid., p. 171.
32. Koerner, *Mother Heal MySelf,* pp. 171–174 These pages are the pages in Koerner's book that describe the experience of her vision quest in her words. I haven't put footnotes in the text for each quote in these last few paragraphs between when I introduce this part of her story and this endnote.

Chapter 11: Varieties of Ancestral Experience

1. James, William (2012-05-16). *Meaning of Truth*, Kindle Locations 9–11.
2. Jung, *The Undiscovered Self,* p. 249, [CW10, para. 493].
3. Ibid., p. 250, [CW10, para. 495].
4. I find this to be true of all of the ancestral soul work groups I conduct. It seems that the group that forms has certain themes in common. Doing this work individually is powerful. Doing it in a group seems to facilitate the process of each individual.
5. Hogan, *The Woman Who Watches Over the World,* p. 15.
6. This was everyone's experience. In the next round of council, each woman shared that she felt someone had come into the circle as Diane rang the bell. Thinking and describing came after the direct experience.
7. Koerner, *Mother Heal MySelf,* p. 171.
8. Some, Calling on our ancestors: The healing connection, 2008.
9. McGuire & Hull, *C. G. Jung Speaking,* p. 385.
10. Jung, "Synchronicity: An Acausal Connecting Principle."
11. von Franz, *Number and Time,* p. 292.
12. Jung C. G., *Mysterium Coniunctionis*, pp. 464–465, [CW14, para. 662]
13. Deloria Jr., *C. G. Jung and the Sioux Traditions;* Some, *The Healing Wisdom of Africa.*
14. Deloria, *God is red,* p. 152.
15. Jung, "Synchronicity: An Acausal Connecting Principle," p. 518, [CW8, para. 967].
16. Ibid.
17. Some, Calling on our ancestors: The healing connection, 2008.

18. Some, *The Healing Wisdom of Africa.*
19. See story in Chapter 7.
20. A ropes course is a challenging outdoor personal development and team building activity which usually consists of high and low elements such as rappelling down a cliff, walking across a beam suspended high between two trees, negotiating a tight rope, and scaling a wall. Low elements take place on the ground or only a few feet above the ground. High elements are usually constructed in trees and require a belay for safety.
21. Andrews, *Animal Speak*, p. 152.
22. Ibid., p. 154.
23. Williams, *A Key Into the Language of America*, p. 83.
24. See Chapter 12, Impersonal Karma and Individuation
25. Peat, *Synchronicity*, p. 265.
26. J. Bernstein, personal communication, December 3, 2010.
27. Although this work done individually has an effect on addictive patterns within a family, I have found that participating in a group seems to facilitate more substantial change more immediately.
28. Hogan, *Woman Who Watches Over the World*, p. 91.
29. Ibid.
30. Duff, *The Alchemy of Illness.*
31. Ibid., p. 105.
32. Jaffe, *An Archetypal Approach to Death, Dreams, and Ghosts*, p. 102.
33. Ibid., 104
34. Ibid., p. 103.
35. Peat, *Lighting the Seventh Fire*; Cajete, *Native Science.*
36. Some, Calling on our ancestors: The healing connection.
37. Some, *The Healing Wisdom of Africa.* p. 196.
38. Jaffe, *An Archetypal Approach to Death, Dreams, and Ghosts*, p. 130.
39. Ibid., p. 131.
40. Ibid.
41. Gustafson, *Dancing Between Two Worlds.*
42. Some, *The Healing Wisdom of Africa.*
43. Bache, *Dark Night, Early Dawn*, p. 64.
44. When I conduct ancestor dialogues I go to my ancestor altar, light a candle, and extend an invitation. When I use the phrases "came present," or "showed up," it is exactly that. It is as if someone came into the room, only instead of a physical person, it is an imaginal, autonomous presence.
45. Hasseldorf is an actual town in Germany. It is in the northern part near the Baltic Sea and Scandinavia. This was a surprising discovery. I don't know what the town's history is or whether any of the women's ancestors have any connection to this town. Years later I would discover that there was a strong possibility that this shadow of racism did have origins in my Scandinavian ancestors.
46. Cajete, *Native Science*; Some, *The Healing Wisdom of Africa.*

47. Hannah, *Jung, His Life and His Work*, p. 11.
48. Jung, *Memories, Dreams, Reflections*, p. 291.
49. Ibid.
50. Gustafson, personal communication, October, 12, 2014.
51. Hillman, *The Soul's Code*, p. 88.
52. Hogan, *Woman Who Watches Over the World*, p. 205.
53. Gaustad, *Roger Williams*.
54. State of Rhode Island Commission on Women, 2011.
55. Gaustad, *Roger Williams*, p. 52.
56. Ibid., p. 53.
57. Ibid., p. 92.
58. Aizenstat, *Dream Tending*.
59. Jung, *Nietzsche's Zarathustra*, p. 1401.
60. Jung, "Conscious, Unconscious, and Individuation," p. 275 [CW9i, para. 490].
61. Ibid., p. 289 [CW9i, para. 524].
62. Hogan, *The Woman Who Watches Over the World*, pp. 49–50.
63. Some, *The Healing Wisdom of Africa*, p. 102.
64. Ibid., p. 103.
65. Some, Calling on our ancestors: The healing connection, 2008.
66. Some, *Of Water and the Spirit*.
67. Some, *The Healing Wisdom of Africa*, p. 53.
68. Jung, "Conscious, Unconscious, and Individuation," p. 131, [CW9i, para. 235].
69. Jung, "The Psychological Foundations of Belief in Spirits," p. 315 [CW8, para. 598].
70. Spielberg, Amistad.

Chapter 12: Implications for Jungian Psychology and Healing

1. Koerner, *Mother Heal MySelf*, p. 184.
2. Bernstein, personal communication, December 6, 2010.
3. Bernstein, *Living in the Borderland*, p. 123.
4. Since this group met, I have worked with many individuals and several other groups. I continue to find the same dynamics and patterns that were discovered in this group in others. I refer the reader to the following sources for information on intergenerational trauma specific to African American, Native American and other peoples. Duran, 2006; Mullan-Gonzalex, 2012; Bennet & Kennedy, 2003.
5. Jacobi, *Complex, Archetype, Symbol in the Psychology of C.G. Jung*, pp. 8–9.
6. I refer the reader to the description of the dream of my mother line as recounted in Chapter 5. This dream depicted the wound, the nature of the

wound, the origins of the wound and the archetypal origins of "Mother" as it exists in my lineage through my mother. Although I have Scandinavian ancestors through my father, "Mother," as it exists through the levels of the collective unconscious, is particular to my English ancestry. While there may be things waiting to be resolved, redeemed and answered with regard to "Mother" in other parts of my lineage, what is calling for attention is clearly presented in this dream. Following psyche's lead is critical to understanding what is being asked of us in the present with regard to the past and future.

7. Jacobi, *Complex, Archetype, Symbol in the of C.G. Jung*, p. 13.
8. Ibid., footnote, p. 48.
9. Ibid.
10. Jung, "A Review of the Complex Theory."
11. Jacobi, *Complex/Archetype/Symbol in the Psychology of C. G. Jung*, p. 11.
12. The dream of the hawks flying into the bone white trees written about in the previous chapter and this image that came when I was working with another group seem to indicate that white bones are nature's representation of the intention and result of doing this work.
13. http://www.tlc.com/tv-shows/who-do-you-think-you-are/
14. Jung, "The Psychological Foundations of Belief in Spirits."
15. Ibid., p. 309.
16. Jung, *Memories, Dreams, Reflections*, p. 307.
17. Jung, *The Red Book*, p. 234.
18. Singer & Kimbles, "Introduction," p. 7.
19. Weisstub & Galili-Weisstub, "Collective Trauma and Cultural Complexes," p. 164.
20. Gustafson, *Dancing Between Two Worlds.*
21. From my imaginal experience of the grieving women described above I would suggest that this is also true for the patriarchal complex in this culture. The dynamics Gustafson describes seem applicable.
22. Jung, *The Red Book Liber Novus; A Reader's Edition*, p. 340.
23. Gustafson, *Dancing Between Two Worlds,* p. 26.
24. In doing this work, in addition to following psyche's lead with regard to ethnicity and culture, within an individual's lineage, I am also curious about how the person self-identifies consciously.
25. I felt a responsibility in the years following this dream and have worked with the figures using Aizenstat's technique of Dream Tending. I believe that these shadowed cultural complexes exist in each of us. Recognizing how we are related to these shadows through our ancestors is the beginning of transforming the story.
26. Jung, "Conscious, Unconscious, and Individuation," p. 279 [CW9i, para. 279]
27. Koerner, *Mother Heal MySelf,* p. 205.
28. Ibid., p. 206.
29. Jaffe, *An Archetypal Approach to Death, Dreams, and Ghosts,* p. 55.

30. Jung, *Memories, Dreams, Reflections*, p. 196.
31. Ibid., p. 317.
32. Ibid., p. 255.
33. Ibid, p. 214.
34. As a personal aside, "Doing harm" is one of the complexes I've been dealing with for as long as I can remember. Like any other complex this particular one comes to me through my ancestors. Years after having this dream, on my birthday, I worked with a shaman to clear what could be cleared that was between me and bringing my work more fully into the world. The field opened to my father and our Scandinavian ancestors. It was a lineage of shamans. At some time they had practiced dark magic and had done serious harm. It fell to me to "clear" this.
35. Berry, *The Great Work,* p. 3.
36. Ibid., p. 4.
37. Ibid., p. 20. The movie Avatar tells this story beautifully.
38. Ibid.
39. Ibid., p. 160.
40. Ibid.
41. Le Grice explores this concept of the underlying archetypal matrix of consciousness through myth, science and astrology in *The Archetypal Cosmos.*
42. Jung, "The Significance of Constitution and Heredity in Psychology," p. 113 [CW8, para. 231].
43. The ego, according to Bernstein, emerged from the collective unconscious. Differentiated, rational and "highly functioning," a consciousness centered in ego initially perceives the collective unconscious as "irrational and threatening." Bernstein, *Living in the Borderland,* p. 35.
44. Jung, "Conscious, Unconscious, and Individuation," p. 282 [CW9i, para. 505].
45. Gustafson, *Dancing Between two Worlds,* p. 78.
46. Ibid.
47. Ibid.
48. Bernstein, *Living in the Borderland,* p. 17.
49. McGuire & Hull, *C. G. Jung Speaking,* p. 361.
50. Ibid.
51. Ibid.
52. Ibid.
53. Hogan, *Woman Who Watches Over the World*, p. 206.
54. Berry, *The Great Work,* p. 57.
55. Cajete, *Native Science,*
56. Gustafson, *Dancing Between two Worlds,* p. 77.
57. Jung, "After the Catastrophe," p. 198 [CW10, para. 408].
58. Ibid., p. 197, [CW10, para. 405].
59. Cajete, Native Science, p. 208
60. Schrijver, K. & Schrijver, I. *Living with the Stars: How the Human Body is Connected to the Life Cycles of the Earth, the Planets, and the Stars, p. viii.*

298 NOTES

61. Ibid. pp. 8–9.
62. Jung, C. G. (1981). "On the Nature of the Psyche," p. 223, [CW 8, para. 429].
63. Hogan, *Woman Who Watches Over the World,* p. 145.
64. Deloria, *The World We Used to Live In,* p. 428.
65. Ibid., p. xix.

Bibliography

Aizenstat, S. (2011). *Dream Tending: Awakening to the Healing Power of Dreams*. New Orleans, LA: Spring Journal.

Andrews, T. (1997). *Animal-Speak: The Spiritual & Magical Powers of Creatures Great & Small*. St. Paul, MN: Llewellyn Publications.

Bache, C. (2000). *Dark Night, Early Dawn*. Albany, NY: State University of New York Press.

Bennet, J., & Kennedy, R. (Eds.). (2003). *World Memory: Personal Trajectories in Global Time*. NY: Palgrave Macmillan.

Bernstein, J. (2005). *Living in the Borderland: The Evolution of Consciousness and the Challenge of Healing Trauma*. NY, NY: Routledge.

Berry, T. (1999). *The Great Work: Our Way into the Future*. NY: Three Rivers Press.

Bond, J. S. (1993). *Living Myth: Personal Meaning as a Way of Life*. Boston, MA: Shambala

Braud, W. (1998). "An expanded view of validity." In W. Braud, & R. Anderson (Eds.), *Transpersonal ResearchMmethods for the Social Sciences: Honoring Human Experience* (pp. 114–127). Thousand Oaks, CA: Sage Publications.

Buck, C. (2001). *Killing Beauty in North America (Unpublished doctoral dissertation)*. Pacifica Graduate Institute, Santa Barbara, CA.

Cajete, G. (1994). *Look to the Mountain: An Ecology of Indigenous Education*. Durango, CO: Kivaki Press.

Cajete, G. (2000). *Native science: Natural Laws of Interdependence*. Santa Fe, NM: Clear Light Publications.

Caruth, C. (1995a). "Introduction." In C. Caruth (Ed.), *Trauma: Explorations in Memory* (pp. 3–12). Baltimore, MD, The Johns Hopkins University Press.

Caruth, C. (1995b). "Recapturing the past." In C. Caruth (Ed.), *Trauma: Explorations in Memory* (pp. 151–158). Baltimore, MD: Johns Hopkins University Press.

Chief, S. (2005). *How Can One Sell the Air?* Summerton, TN: Native Voices.

Colorado, P. (1988). "Bridging native and western science." *Convergence*, XXI (2/3), 44–67.

Claremont de Castillejo, I. C. (1973). *Knowing Woman: A Feminine Psychology*. Boston, MA: Shambala

Deloria Jr., V. (2009). *C. G. Jung and the Sioux Traditions: Dreams, Visions, Nature and the Primitive*. (P. J. Deloria, & J. Bernstein, Eds.) New Orleans, LA: Spring Publications.

Deloria Jr., V. (1994). *God is Red: A Native View of Religion*. Golden, CO: Fulcrum Publishing.

Deloria Jr., V. (1999). *Spirit and Reason*. Golden, CO: Fulcrum Publishing.

Deloria Jr., V. (2006). *The World we Used to Live in: Remembering the Powers of the Medicine Man*. Golden, SO: Fulcrum Publishing.

Deloria, P. J. (1998). *Playing Indian.* New Haven, CT: Yale University Press.

Deloria, P. J. & Bernstein, J. S. (2009). "Carl G. Jung and the Sioux Traditions: Jung's 'primitive'" revisted. *Lecture presented for the New Mexico Society of Jungian Analysts.* Santa Fe, NM.

Drake, J. D. (1999). *King Phillip's War: Civil War in New England, 1675–1676.* Amherst, MA: University of Massachusetts Press.

Duff, K. (1993). *The Alchemy of Illness.* NY, NY: Bell Tower.

Duran, E. (2006). *Healing the Soul Wound: Counseling with American Indian and Other Native Peoples.* NY: Teachers College Press.

Erikson, K. (1995). "Notes on trauma and community." In C. Caruth (Ed.), *Trauma: Explorations in Memory* (pp. 183–199). Baltimore, MD: The Johns Hopkins University Press.

Ernst, J. (1932). *Roger Williams.* NY, NY: The MacMillan Company.

Estes, C. (1995). *Women Who Run with the Wolves.* NY, NY: Ballantine Books.

Felman, S. (1995). "Education and crisis, or the vicissitudes of teaching." In C. Caruth (Ed.), *Trauma: Explorations in Memory* (pp. 13–60). Baltimore, MD: The Johns Hopkins University Press.

Gaustad, E. (2005). *Roger Williams.* NY, NY: Oxford University Press.

Gaustad, E. S. (1999). *Liberty of Conscience: Roger Williams in America.* Valley Forge, PA: Judson Press.

Grof, S. (2006). *When the Impossible Happens.* Boulder, CO: Sounds True, Inc.

Gustafson, F. R. (1994). *Dancing Between Two Worlds: Jung and the Native American Soul.* Mahwah, NJ: Paulist Press.

Hannah, B. (1997). *Jung, His Life and His Work: A Biographical Memoir.* Wilmette, IL: Chiron Publications.

Harner, M. (1990). *The Way of the Shaman.* NY, NY: Harper & Row.

Hillman, J. (1996). *The Soul's Code: In Search of Character and Calling.* NY, NY: Warner Books.

Hillman, J., & Shamdasani, S. (2013). *Lament of the Dead: Psychology after Jung's Red Book.* NY, NY: W. W. Norton & Co.

Hogan, L. (1996). *Dwellings: A Spiritual History of the Living World.* NY: Touchstone.

Hogan, L. (2001). *The Woman Who Watches over the World.* NY, NY: W. W. Norton & Company, Inc.

Homans, P. (2000). *Symbolic Loss.* Charlottesville, VA: University Press of Virginia.

Hurley, D. (2013, June 11). "Grandma's experiences leave a mark on your genes." *Discover*, Retrieved from http://discovermagazine.com/2013/may/13-grandmas-experiences-leave-epigenetic-mark-on-your-genes

Jacobi, J. (1959). *Complex/Archetype/Symbol in the Psychology of C. G. Jung.* (R. Manheim, Trans.) NY: Bollingen Foundation.

Jaenke, K. A. (2000). *Personal Dreamscape as Ancestral Landscape.* Unpublished doctoral dissertationa. California Institute of Integral Studies.

Jaffe, A. (1999). *An Archetypal Approach to Death, Dreams and Ghosts.* Canada: Daimon.

Jewell, E. J., & Abate, F. (Eds.). (2001). *The New Oxford American Dictionary.* NY, NY: Oxford University Press.

Johnson, K. K. (2001). *On the Path of the Ancestors: Kinship with Place as a Path of Recovery.* Unpublished doctoral dissertation. California Institute of Integral Studies.

Jung, C. G. (1981). "A review of the complex theory." In H. Read, et al., (Eds.), *The Collected Works of C.G. Jung (Vol. 8)* (R. Hull, Trans., pp. 92–106). Princeton, NJ: Princeton University Press. (Original work published 1948).

Jung, C. G. (1990b). "A study in the process of individuation." In H. Read, et al., (Eds.), *The Collected Works of C.G. Jung (Vol. 9i)* (R. Hull, Trans., pp. 290–354). Princeton, NJ: Princeton University Press. (Original work published 1950).

Jung, C. G. (1970). "After the catastrophe." In H. Read, et al., (Eds.), *The Collected Works of C. G. Jung (Vol. 10)* (R. F. Hull, Trans., 2nd ed., Vol. 10, pp. 194–217). Princeton, NJ: Princeton University Press (Original work published 1945).

Jung, C. G. (1970). *Aion.* In H. Read, et al., (Ed.), *The Collected Works of C.G. Jung (Vol. 9.ii.),* (R. F. Hull, Trans.) Princeton, NJ: Princeton University Press. (Original work published 1951).

Jung, C. G. (1981). "Analytical psychology and Weltanschauung." In H. Read, et al., (Eds.), *The Collected Works of C.G. Jung, (Vol. 8)* (R. F. Hull, Trans., pp. 358–381). Princeton, NJ: Princeton University Press. (Original work published 1931).

Jung, C. G. (1978). "Archaic man." In H. Read, et al., (Eds.), *The Collected Works of C.G. Jung (Vol. 10)* (R. F. Hull, Trans., pp. 50–73). Princeton, NJ: Princeton University Press. (Original work published 1931).

Jung, C. G. (1981). "Basic postulates of analytical psychology." In H. Read, et al., (Eds.), *The Collected Works of C.G. Jung (Vol. 8)* (R. F. Hull, Trans., pp. 338–357). Princeton, NJ: Princeton University Press. (Original work published 1934).

Jung, C. G. (1973). *C. G. Jung Letters, Vol. 1: 1906–1950.* (G. Adler, Ed., & R. Hull, Trans.) Princeton, NJ: Princeton University Press.

Jung, C. G. (1975). *C. G. Jung Letters, Vol. 2: 1951–1961.* (G. Adler, Ed., & R. Hull, Trans.) Princeton, NJ: Princeton University Press.

Jung, C. G. (1990). "Conscious, unconscious, and individuation." In H. Read, et al., (Eds.), *The Collected Works of C.G. Jung (Vol. 9.1)* (R. Hull, Trans., 2nd ed., pp. 275–289). Princeton, NJ: Princteon University Press (Original work published 1939).

Jung, C. G. (1984). *Dream Analysis: Notes on the Seminar Given in 1928–1930 by C. G. Jung.* (W. McGuire, Ed.) Princeton, NJ: Princeton University Press.

Jung, C. G. (1978). "Flying saucers: A modern myth of things seen in the skies." In H. Read, et al., (Eds.), *The Collected Works of C.G. Jung (Vol. 10)* (R. F. Hull, Trans., pp. 307–412). Princeton, NJ: Princeton University Press. (Original work published 1931).

Jung, C. G. (1974). "Introduction to Wickes's Analyse der Kinderseele." In H. Read, et al., (Eds), *The Collected Works of C. G. Jung (Vol 17)* (R. F. Hull, Trans., pp. 37–46). Princeton, NJ: Princeton University Press. (Original work published 1931).

Jung, C. G. (1989). *Memories, Dreams, Reflections.* (A. Jaffe, Ed.) NY, NY: Vintage Books (Original work published 1963).

Jung, C. G. (1978). "Mind and earth." In H. Read, et al., (Eds.) *The Collected Works of C.G. Jung (Vol.10)* (R. F. Hull, Trans., pp. 29–49). Princeton, NJ: Princeton University Press. (Original work published in 1931).

Jung, C. G. (1955). *Modern Man in Search of a Soul.* (W. Dell, & C. Baynes, Trans.) NY, NY: Harcourt, Inc.(Original work published 1933).

Jung, C. G. (1974). *Mysterium Coniunctionis,* In H. Read, et al., (Eds.), *The Collected Works of C. G. Jung,* (R. F. C.Hull, Trans.) *(Vol. 14).* Princeton, NJ: Princeton University Press. (Original work published 1955).

Jung, C. G. (1988). *Nietzsche's Zarathustra: Notes of the Seminar Given in 1934–1939* (Vol. 1). (J. Jarrett, Ed.) Princeton, NJ: Prindeton University Press.

Jung, C. G. (1988). *Nietzsche's Zarathustra: Notes on the Seminar Given in 1934–1939* (Vol. 2). (J. Jarrett, Ed.) Princeton, NJ: Princeton University Press.

Jung, C. G. (1981). "On psychic energy." In H. Read, et al., (Eds.), *The Collected Works of C. G. Jung (Vol. 8)* (R. F. Hull, Trans., pp. 3–66). Princeton, NJ: Princeton University Press. (Original work published 1948).

Jung, C. G. (1981). "On the nature of the psyche." In H. Read, et al., (Eds.), *The Collected Works of C.G. Jung (Vol. 8)* (R. F. Hull, Trans., pp. 159–236). Princeton, NJ: Princeton University Press. (Original work published 1954).

Jung, C. G. (1970). "Psychology and alchemy." In H. Read, et al., (Eds.), *The Collected Works of C.G. Jung (Vol.12)* (R. F. Hull, Trans.) Princeton, NJ: Princeton University Press. (Original work published 1953).

Jung, C. G. (1989). *Psychology and Religion: West and East.* In H. Read, et al., (Eds.) *The Collected Works of C. G. Jung* (R. F. C. Hull, Trans.) *(Vol. 11).* (R. F. Hull, Trans.) Princeton, NJ: Princeton University Press. (Original work published 1940).

Jung, C. G. (1989). "Psychology and spiritualism." In H. Read, et al., (Eds), *The Collected Works of Jung (Vol. 18)* (R. F. Hull, Trans., pp. 312–316). Princeton, NJ: Princeton University Press. (Original work published 1948).

Jung, C. G. (1978). "Richard Willhelm: In memoriam." In H. Read, et al., (Eds.), *The Collected Works of C. G. Jung (Vol. 15),* (R. F. Hull, Trans.) Princeton, NJ: Princeton University Press. (Original work published 1930).

Jung, C. G. (1956). *Symbols of Transformation.* In H. Read, et al., (Eds.), *The Collected Works of C. G. Jung (Vol. 5).* (R. F. Hull, Trans.) NY, NY: Pantheon Books.

Jung, C. G. (1981). "Synchronicity: An acausal connecting principle." In H. Read, et al., (Eds.), *The Collected Works of C. G. Jung (Vol. 8)* (R. F. Hull, Trans., pp. 417–519). Princeton, NJ: Princeton University Press. (Original work published 1952).

Jung, C. G. (1978). "The complications of American psychology." In H. Read, et al., (Eds.), *The Collected Works of C. G. Jung (Vol. 10)* (R. F. Hull, Trans., pp. 502–514). Princeton, NJ: Princeton University Press. (Original work published in 1930).

Jung, C. G. (1990). "The psychological aspects of the Kore." In H. Read, et al., (Eds.), *The Collected Works of C. G. Jung (Vol. 9i)* (R. F. Hull, Trans., 2nd ed., pp. 182–203). Princeton, NJ: Princeton University Press (Original work published 1951).

Jung, C. G. (1981). "The Psychological Foundations of Belief in Spirits." In H. Read, et al., (Eds.), *The Collected Works of C. G. Jung (Vol. 8)* (R. F. Hull, Trans., pp. 301–318). Princeton, NJ: Princeton University Press (Original work published 1948).

Jung, C. G. (1990). "The psychology of the child archetype." In H. Read, et al., (Eds.), *The Collected Works of C. G. Jung (Vol. 9i)* (R. F. Hull, Trans., pp. 151–181). Princeton, NJ: Princeton University Press (Original Work Published 1951.

Jung, C. G. (2009). *The Red Book Liber Novus; A Reader's Edition.* (S. Shamdasani, Ed.) NY, NY: W.W. Norton & Co.

Jung, C. G. (1978). "The role of the unconscious." In H. Read, et al., (Eds.),*The Collected Works of C. G. Jung (Vol. 10)* (R. F. Hull, Trans., pp. 3–28). Princeton, NJ: Princeton University Press. (Original work published 1918).

Jung, C. G. (1981). "The significance of constitution and heredity in psychology." In H. Read, et al., (Eds.), The *Collected Works of C.G. Jung (Vol. 8)* (R. Hull, Trans., pp. 107–113). Princeton, NJ: Princeton University Press (Original work published 1929).

Jung, C. G. (1981). "The soul and death." In H. Read, et al., (Eds.), *The Collected Works of C. G. Jung (Vol. 8)* (R. F. Hull, Trans., pp. 404–416). Princeton, NJ: Princeton University Press. (Original work published 1934).

Jung, C. G. (1981). "The structure of the psyche." In H. Read, et al., (Eds.), *The Collected Works of C. G. Jung (Vol. 8)* (R. F. Hull, Trans., pp. 139–158). Princeton, NJ: Princeton University Press. (Original work published 1931).

Jung, C. G. "The symbolic life." In H. Read, et al., (Eds.), *The Collected Works of C.G. Jung (Vol. 18)* (R. Hull, Trans., pp. 267–290). Princeton, NJ: Princeton University Press (Original work published 1939).

Jung, C. G. (1969). "The Transcendent Function." In H. Read, et al., (Eds.), *The Collected Works of C. G. Jung (Vol. 8)* (R. F. Hull, Trans., pp. 67–91). Princeton, NJ: Princeton University Press. (Original work published 1916).

Jung, C. G. (1978). "The undiscovered self." In H. Read, et al., (Eds.), *The Collected Works of C.G. Jung (Vol. 10)* (R. Hull, Trans., pp. 245–306). Princeton, NJ: Princeton University Press. (Original work published 1957).

Jung, C. G. (1977). *Two Essays on Analytical Psychology,* In H. Read, et al., (Eds.), *The Collected Works of C. G. Jung (Vol. 7)* (R. F. Hull, Trans.) Princeton, NJ: Princeton Univeristy Press. (Original work published 1917).

Jung, C. (1978). "Wotan." In H. Read, et al., (Eds.), *The Collected Works of C.G. Jung (Vol. 10)* (R. Hull, Trans., pp. 179–193). Princeton, NJ: Princeton University Press. (Original work published 1936).

Kalshed, D. (2014). *The Inner World of Trauma: Archetypal Defenses of the Personal Spirit.* NY, NY: Routledge.

Kimbles, S. L. (2004). "A cultural complex operating in the overlap of clinical and cultural space." In T. Singer, & S. Kimbles, *The Cultural Complex: Contemporary Jungian Perspectives on Psyche and Society* (pp. 199–211). NY: Routledge.

King, J. (2012, Summer). "A critique of Western psychology from an American Indian psychologist." (N. Cater, & J. Bernstein, Eds.) *Native American Cultures and the Western psyche: A Bridge Between, Spring, 87,* pp. 37–59.

Koerner, J. (2003). *Mother, Heal MySelf: An Intergenerational Healing Journey Between Two Worlds.* Santa Rosa, CA: Crestport Press.

Kremer, J. (1995, Spring). "Perspectives on indigenous healing." *Noetic Sciences Review, 33, Spring 1995* . Retrieved September 10, 2007, from Noetic Sciences Review: http://www.noetic.org

Lacourt, J. A. (2012). "Coming home: Knowing land, knowing self." (N. Cater, & J. Bernstein, Eds.), *Native American Cultures and the Western psyche: A Bridge Between, Spring: 87,* pp. 61–76.

LaFantasie, G. W. (1988). *The Correspondence of Roger Williams (Volume II: 1654–1682).* Providence, RI: Brown University Press/University Press of New England.

Le Grice, K. (2012). *The Archetypal Cosmos.* Edinburgh, UK: Floris Books.

Lepore, J. (1999). *The Name of War: King Phillip's War and the Origins of American Identity.* NY, NY: Vintage Books.

Lorenz, H. (2004, October 15). "Amnesia/countermemory." *Lecture presented as part of When history wakes: Cultural and Ecological Memory Lectures.* Santa Barbara, CA: Pacifica Graduate Institute.

McGuire, W., & Hull, R. (1977). *C. G.Jung Speaking: Interviews and Encounters.* Princeton, NJ: Princeton University Press.

Meade, M. *Fate and Destiny: The Two Agreements of the Soul* (2nd ed.). Seattle, WA: Green Fire Press.

Metzner, R. (1994). *The Well of Remembrance.* Boston, MA: Shambala Publications, Inc.

Mullan-Gonzalez, J. (2012). *Slavery and the Intergenerational Transmission of Trauma in Inner City African American Male Youth: A Model Program - From the Cotton Fields to the Concrete Jungle.* Unpublished Doctoral dissertation. California Institute of Integral Studies.

Ogden, V. (2015, January 5). The true stories behind classic fairy tales. *Huffington Post.* Retrieved from http://www.huffingtonpost.com/valerie-ogden/fairy-tale-true-story_b_6102602.html

Peat, F. D. (1987). *Synchronicity: The Bridge Between Matter and Mind.* NY, NY: Bantam Books.

Peat, F. (1994). *Lighting the Seventh Fire: The Spiritual Ways, Healing and Science of the Native American.* NY, NY: Birch Lane Press.

Pert, C. (1999). *Molecules of Emotion: Why You Feel the Way you Feel.* NY, NY: Simon & Schuster.

Plotkin, B. (2003). *Soulcraft: Crossing into the Mysteries of Nature and Psyche.* Novato, CA: New World Library.

Polishook, I. H. (1967). *Roger Williams, John Cotton and Religious Freedom: A Controversy in New and Old England.* Englewood Cliffs, NJ: Prentice-Hall.

Romanyshyn, R. (2007). *The Wounded Researcher: Research with Soul in Mind.* New Orleans, LA: Spring Journal.

Rowland, S. (2002). *Jung: A Feminist Revision.* Malden, MA: Blackwell Publishers, Inc.

Rubertone, P. E. (2001). *Grave Undertakings: An Archaeology of Roger Williams and the Narragansett Indians.* Washington, DC: Smithsonian Institution Press.

Sabini, M., & Jung, C. G. (2002). *The Earth has a Soul: The Nature Writings of C. G. Jung.* (M. Sabini, Ed.) Berkeley, CA: North Atlantic Books.

Schrijver, K. & Schrijver, I. (2015). *Living with the Stars: How the Human Body is Connected to the Life Cycles of the Earth, the Planets, and the Stars.* Oxford, UK: Oxford University Press.

Schutzberger, A. A. (1998). *The Ancestor Syndrome: Transgenerational Psychotherapy and the Hidden Links in the Family Tree.* (A. Trager, Trans.) NY, NY: Routledge.

Silko, L. (1977). *Ceremony.* NY, NY: Penguin Books.

Singer, T., & Kimbles, S. (2004). "Introduction." In T. Singer, & S. Kimbles (Eds.), *The Cultural Complex* (pp. 1–9). NY: Routledge.

Smith, M. (1997). *Jung and Shamanism in Dialogue.* Mahwah, NJ: Paulist Press.

Some, M. (2010, November 29). "Ancestor healing ritual." *Lecture presented as part of weekend ritual process.* Ojai, CA.

Some, M. (2008). "Calling on our ancestors: The healing connection." *Lecture presented for Mind and Supermind continuing education lectures.* Santa Barbara City College, Santa Barbara, CA.

Some, M. (1994). *Of Water and the Spirit.* NY, NY: Jeremy P. Tarcher, Putnam.

Some, M. (1993). *Ritual: Power, Healing and Community.* NY, NY: Penguin Compass.

Some, M. (1999). *The Healing Wisdom of Africa: Finding Life Purpose through Nature, Ritual, and Community.* NY, NY: Jeremy P. Tarcher/Putnam.

Tarnas, R. (2006). *Cosmos and Psyche: Intimations of a New World View.* NY: Routledge.

Tarnas, R. (2000). "Is the modern psyche undergoing a rite of passage?" In T. Singer (Ed.), *The Vision Thing: Myth, Politics and Psyche in the World* (pp. 251–267). NY, NY: Routledge.

Tarnas, R. (1991). *Passion of the Western Mind: Understanding the Ideas that have Shaped Our Worldview.* NY: Random House.

Taylor, D. (1996). *The Healing Power of Stories.* NY: Doubleday.

Teunissen, J., & Hinz, E. (1973). "Introduction." In R. Williams, J. Teunissen, & E. Hinz (Eds.), *A Key into the Language of America* (pp. 13–69). Detroit, MI: Wayne State University Press.

van der Kolk, B., & van der Hart, O. (1995). "The intrusive past: the flexibility of memory and the engraving of trauma." In C. Caruth (Ed.), *Trauma: Explorations in Memory* (pp. 158–182). Baltimore, MD: The Johns Hopkins University Press.

von Franz, M. L. (1974). *Number and Time.* Evanston, IL: Northwestern University Press.

Ward, T. (2004). *Reawakening Indigenous Sensibilities in the Western Psyche* (Unpublished doctoral dissertation). Pacifica Graduate Institute, Santa Barbara, CA.

Weisstub, E., & Galili-Weisstub, E. (2004). "Collective trauma and cultural complexes." In T. Singer, & S. Kimbles (Eds.), *The Cultural Complex: Contemporary Jungian Perspectives on Psyche and Society* (pp. 147–170). NY, NY: Routledge.

White, A. D. (1896). *A History of the Warfare of Science with Theology in Christendom (Vol. 1).* London: Macmillan & Co., Ltd.

Williams, R. (1973). *A Key Into the Language of America.* (J. Teunissen, & E. Hinz, Eds.) Detroit, MI: Wayne State University Press.

Zimmerman, J., & Coyle, V. (1996). *The Way of Council.* Las Vegas, NV: Bramble Books.

Index